CANADA AMONG NATIONS 1998

CANADA AMONG NATIONS 1998

Leadership and Dialogue

Edited by
Fen Osler Hampson and Maureen Appel Molot

Toronto Oxford New York
Oxford University Press
1998

Oxford University Press
70 Wynford Drive, Don Mills, Ontario M3C 1J9
http://www.oupcan.com

Oxford New York
Athens Auckland Bangkok Bogotá Buenos Aires Calcutta
Cape Town Chennai Dar es Salaam Delhi Florence
Hong Kong Istanbul Karachi Kuala Lumpur Madrid
Melbourne Mexico City Mumbai Nairobi
Paris São Paulo Singapore Taipei
Tokyo Toronto Warsaw

and associated companies in
Berlin Ibadan

Oxford is a trade mark of Oxford University Press

Canadian Cataloguing in Publication Data
The National Library of Canada has catalogued this publication as follows:
Canada among nations

Annual.
1984–
Produced by the Norman Paterson School of International Affairs at
    Carleton University.
Each vol. has also a distinctive title.
Published: Ottawa : Carleton University Press, 1990–1997; Toronto :
Oxford University Press, 1998– .
ISSN 0832-0683
ISBN 0-19-541406-3 (1998)

1. Canada—Foreign relations—1945– —Periodicals. 2. Canada—
Politics and government—1984– —Periodicals. 3. Canada—Politics and
government — 1980–1984
Periodicals. I. Norman Paterson School of International Affairs.

FC242.C345   327.71   C86–031285–2
F1029.C3

This book is printed on permanent (acid-free) paper ∞.

Printed in Canada

CONTENTS

CONTRIBUTORS

John M. Curtis is the Senior Policy Adviser and Co-ordinator of the Economic Policy Bureau, Department of Foreign Affairs and International Affairs.

Jean Daudelin is a Senior Project Officer with the Canadian Foundation for the Americas.

Edgar J. Dosman is a professor in the Department of Political Science, York University.

Tim Draimin is the Senior Policy Adviser with the Canadian Council for International Co-operation.

John English is a professor in the Department of History, University of Waterloo.

Paul Halucha is a doctoral candidate in the Department of Political Studies, Carleton University.

Fen Osler Hampson is a professor in The Norman Paterson School of International Affairs, Carleton University.

Robert Lawson is a Political Desk Officer in the Non-Proliferation, Arms Control and Disarmament Division, Department of Foreign Affairs and International Trade.

Steven Lee is the National Director of the Canadian Centre for Foreign Policy Development, Department of Foreign Affairs and International Trade.

David Long is an associate professor in The Norman Paterson School of International Affairs, Carleton University.

Maureen Appel Molot is a professor in the Department of Political Science and professor and Director of The Norman Paterson School of International Affairs, Carleton University.

Dean F. Oliver is a post-doctoral fellow at The Norman Paterson School of International Affairs, Carleton University.

Colonel Alain Pellerin (retired) is the Director of the Speakers Program, Canadian Council of International Peace and Security.

Linda C. Reif is a professor in the Faculty of Law, University of Alberta.

Elizabeth Smythe is an assistant professor at Concordia College, University of Alberta.

Denis Stairs is the McCulloch Professor in the Department of Political Science, Dalhousie University.

Brian Tomlinson is a Development Analyst with the Canadian Council for International Co-operation.

Robert Wolfe is an assistant professor in The School of Policy Studies, Queen's University.

ABBREVIATIONS

ADM	Assistant Deputy Minister
AEEI	autonomous energy efficient improvement
AES	Atmospheric Environment Service
AGBM	Ad Hoc Group on the Berlin Mandate
AP	anti-personnel (mines)
APEC	Asia Pacific Economic Co-operation
ARF	Asian Regional Forum
BHN	basic human needs
BIAC	Business and Industry Advisory Committee
BITs	bilateral investment agreements
CANADEM	Canadian Research Bank for Democracy and Human Rights
CARICOM	Caribbean Economic Market
CCAEC	Canada-Chile Agreement on Environment Co-operation
CCF	Co-operative Commonwealth Federation
CCFPD	Canadian Centre for Foreign Policy Development
CCIC	Canadian Council for International Co-operation
CCME	Canadian Council of the Ministers of the Environment
CCS	Canada Country Study
CCW	Convention on Certain Conventional Weapons
CDM	clean development mechanism
CDS	Chief of Defence Staff
CEE	Central and Eastern Europe
CF	Canadian Forces
CFE	Conventional Forces in Europe
CG-18	Consultative Group of 18
CIDA	Canadian International Development Agency
CIDA INC	Canadian International Development Agency Industrial Co-operation Program
CIIPS	Canadian Institute for International Peace and Security
CIME	Committee on Investment and Multinational Enterprises
CLC	Canadian Labour Congress
CMIT	Committee on Capital Movements and Invisible Transactions
CPD	Policy Planning (DFAIT)
CSCE	Conference on Security and Co-operation in Europe
CSD	Commission on Sustainable Development
CWC	Chemical Weapons Convention

DAC	Development Assistance Committee
DAFFE	Directorate on Financial, Fiscal, and Enterprise Affairs
DFAIT	Department of Foreign Affairs and International Trade
DFID	Department for International Development (UK)
DND	Department of National Defence
EAPC	Euro-Atlantic Co-operation Council
EC	European Community
ECE	Economic Commission for Europe
EEZ	exclusive economic zone
EFTA	European Free Trade Association
EIF	entry-into-force
EMU	Economic and Monetary Union
EU	European Union
FCCC	Framework Convention on Climate Change
FDI	foreign direct investment
FMLN	Frente Farabundo Marti des Liberacion Nacional
FTA	Free Trade Agreement (Canada-US)
FTAA	Free Trade Area of the Americas
G-8	Group of Eight
GATT	General Agreement on Tariffs and Trade
GATS	General Agreement on Trade in Services
GDP	gross domestic product
GNP	gross national product
GMOs	genetically modified organisms
HIPC	highly indebted poor country
IAE	International Assistance Envelope
ICBL	International Committee to Ban Landmines
ICDI	Inter-American Council on Integral Development
ICHRDD	International Centre for Human Rights and Democratic Development
ICRC	International Committee of the Red Cross
IFCS	Intergovernmental Forum on Chemical Safety
IFF	Intergovernmental Forum on Forests
IFI	international financial institutions
IFOR	Implementation Force (NATO)
ILO	International Labour Organization
IMF	International Monetary Fund
INC	Intergovernmental Negotiating Committee
IPCC	International Panel on Climate Change
IPF	Intergovernmental Panel on Forests

ITACs	International Trade Advisory Committees
ITO	International Trade Organization
JI	joint implementation
JMM	Joint Energy and Environment Ministers Meeting
KPMG	Kleinveld, Peat, Marwick, Goederler
LRTAP	Convention on Long-Range Transboundary Air Pollution
LDCs	least developed countries
MAI	Multilateral Agreement on Investment
MBIS	Mackenzie Basin Impact Study
MERCOSUR	Mercado Comun del Sur
MFN	most favoured nation
MOU	Memorandum of Understanding
MP	Member of Parliament
NAAEC	North American Agreement on Environmental Co-operation
NAFO	Northwest Atlantic Fisheries Organization
NAFTA	North American Free Trade Agreement
NAPCC	National Action Plan Program on Climate Change
NASA	National Aeronautics and Space Agency
NATO	North Atlantic Treaty Organization
NGO	non-governmental organization
NGI	non-governmental institution
NORAD	North American Aerospace Defence Command
OAS	Organization of American States
OAU	Organization of African Unity
ODA	official development assistance
OECD	Organization for Economic Co-operation and Development
OSCE	Organization of Security and Co-operation in Europe
PCBs	polychlorinated biphenyls
PfP	Partnership for Peace
PJC	Permanent Joint Council (NATO-Russia)
PM	Prime Minister
POPs	persistent organic pollutants
REIO	Regional Economic Integration Organization
SAGITs	Sectoral Advisory Groups on International Trade
SAR	search and rescue
SFOR	Stabilization Force (NATO)
SHD	sustainable human development

START-2	Strategic Arms Reduction Treaty
TMD	theatre missile defence
TRIMs	trade-related investment measures
TRIPs	trade-related intellectual property rights
TUAC	Trade Union Advisory Committee
UN	United Nations
UNCED	United Nations Conference on the Environment and Sustainable Development
UNCTAD	United Nations Committee on Trade and Development
UNDP	United Nations Development Program
UNEP	United Nations Environment Program
UNFPA	United Nations Fund for Population Activities
UNICEF	United Nations Children's Fund
UNPROFOR	United Nations Protection Force (Bosnia)
UPD	Unit for the Promotion of Democracy
USAID	United States Agency for International Development
USTR	United States Trade Representative
VCR	Voluntary Challenge and Registry
WHO	World Health Organization
WMD	weapons of mass destruction
WMO	World Meteorological Organization
WRI	World Resources Institute
WTO	World Trade Organization

Preface

Leadership and Dialogue is the fourteenth volume in the *Canada Among Nations* series produced annually by The Norman Paterson School of International Affairs.

The signing of the Anti-Personnel Landmines Treaty in Ottawa in December 1997 allowed Canadians to end the year on a foreign policy high. Led by Foreign Minister Lloyd Axworthy, Canada was in the forefront of the effort to bring more than 100 states together to sign a treaty banning the production, sale, and use of a weapon that has maimed huge numbers of people and rendered vast acreage unusable for agriculture. The presence in Ottawa of many foreign dignitaries and the large press corps that accompanied them meant that, for a short time at least, Canadians could believe their country was a significant player on the world stage.

What became known as 'the Ottawa Process' was but one of a number of important foreign policy issues in 1997 that constitute the subject matter of this book. Others include the expansion of NATO, the negotiations over the Multilateral Agreement on Investment, the Canadian military in the aftermath of the Somalia affairs, and Canada's indecisive stance at the Kyoto Conference on Climate Change. Whatever their specific issue focus, all of the chapters in the book address the theme of leadership and dialogue as factors in the formulation and implementation of Canadian foreign policy.

We gratefully acknowledge the generous support from the Centre for Foreign Policy Development for the conference at which papers in this volume were first presented. We also appreciate support from the Security and Defence Forum grant of the Department of National Defence and from The Norman Paterson School of International Affairs.

This annual effort involves a number of people whose assistance we are pleased to note. Brenda Sutherland has developed expertise in the production of *Canada Among Nations* as a result of her continuing supervision of the initial editing of the manuscript. Janet Doherty organized the authors' workshop and encouraged the contributors to submit their chapters on time. Georgette Elston provided research assistance to the editors, prepared the list of abbreviations, and assisted with the editing. We are grateful for the editorial support provided by Richard Kitowski and his staff at Oxford University Press.

Leadership and Dialogue went to press shortly after we received the sad news about the death of our colleague and friend, John G. Halstead. Born in Vancouver on 27 January 1922, John joined the Department of External Affairs (as it was then called) in 1946. He served with distinction in a series of diplomatic postings, including London, Tokyo, New York, the United Nations, and Paris. He was named assistant undersecretary of state for European affairs and, after a period of acting as undersecretary, served as deputy undersecretary until his posting as ambassador to the Federal Republic of Germany in 1975. He founded the German Association for Canadian Studies in 1980 and was awarded an honorary doctorate by the University of Augsburg in 1994 and a peace prize from the Association of German Veterans in 1989. He retired from the foreign service in 1982 after serving as Canada's permanent representative to NATO in Brussels. He taught international affairs at The Norman Paterson School of International Affairs, where he was an adjunct professor from 1990 until his death, and also taught at Georgetown University, Windsor, and Queen's. In 1996 John was invested as a member of the Order of Canada. He was a popular teacher, a respected and valuable colleague, and a regular contributor to the *Canada Among Nations* series. John epitomized the very best in Canadian diplomacy and will be greatly missed by his colleagues, friends, and former students. We dedicate this volume to his memory.

Fen Osler Hampson
Maureen Appel Molot
Ottawa, March 1998

1

The New 'Can-do' Foreign Policy

FEN OSLER HAMPSON AND MAUREEN APPEL MOLOT

Major transitions in international politics have historically allowed middle powers to exercise a disproportionate influence in world affairs. In the seventeenth century Sweden was a great power though its status did not last long. Following the Napoleonic wars, Europe's middle powers, Spain, Portugal, and Sweden, were members of the Committee of Eight at the Congress of Vienna and for a while enjoyed considerable influence in maintaining Europe's new balance of power. Likewise, after both world wars, middle powers flexed their new-found muscle, though perhaps more successfully after World War II. Not only was Canada the world's third largest economic power at the end of World War II, but its diplomats were key architects in the construction of the new political and economic orders. Now, with the end of the Cold War and the dawn of a new millennium, Canada once again finds itself to be a significant player on the world stage.

Whether, as in earlier eras, this prominence will prove ephemeral remains to be seen. But there can be little doubt that not since the halcyon days of the 1940s and the so-called golden era of Canadian diplomacy under Lester Pearson in the 1950s has Canada basked under the spotlight of world attention. Much of this attention, of course, has been of our own making. Unlike his phlegmatic predecessor, Foreign Minister Lloyd Axworthy has seized the initiative on a number of important issues: the campaign to ban anti-personnel land-mines, peacebuilding, child soldiers, and human security. In doing so, he has placed Canada at the forefront of coalitions of the 'high-minded' whose aim is to create a better and more just world order that will improve the lot of humankind. That being said, Canada's overall foreign policy track record has been uneven. The complexities of many issues, coupled with divisions at home, make it difficult to chart a new course and to exercise effective leadership on every issue. Four images flash to mind that capture the changing context, complexity, and constraints on Canada's foreign policy.

The first was the signing of the Anti-Personnel Landmines Treaty in Ottawa in December 1997. Canada as a country and Foreign Minister Axworthy as an individual were at the forefront of the global effort to bring more than 100 states together to initial the treaty banning the production, sale, and use of a weapon that has maimed huge numbers of people and rendered countless acreage unusable for agriculture. The presence in Ottawa of many foreign dignitaries and the large press corps that accompanied them meant that, for a short time at least, Canadians could believe their country was a significant player on the world stage.

The second image is less generous. It is that of the Kyoto Conference on Climate Change, also held in December 1997, at which Canada was not a leader in the negotiations but a follower, and a confused one at that. The government experienced serious domestic difficulties in developing a Canadian position for the Kyoto meeting, largely because some provinces and significant domestic industries held divergent views on the level of greenhouse gas reductions to which Canada should commit.

The third snapshot is the early February 1998 debate within the government and in Parliament over whether Canada would participate in the military coalition against Iraq. Given Canada's dependence on its bilateral trade relationship with the United States, we perhaps had little choice but to agree to support the US effort.

Canada dispatched to the Gulf region one patrol frigate, one Sea King helicopter, and two Hercules tankers (for aircraft refuelling), by any count a modest contribution. But the decision sat uneasily with many Canadians, who felt that the use of force against Saddam Hussein would accomplish little and would jeopardize Canada's relations with various Middle Eastern countries. Secretary-General Kofi Annan's mission to persuade Saddam Hussein to accept UN inspectors averted a major international crisis and took Canada off the horns of a dilemma at least for the time being.

The final picture comes in an Industry Canada study entitled 'Keeping Up with the Joneses' (1997). The study vividly illustrates Canada's economic conundrum. Although Canada may continue to rank highest on the UN's Human Development Index, the data assembled in 'Keeping Up' demonstrate graphically that the economy performed poorly in the 1990s. The result is that the income gap between Canada and the US is growing, on average workers in the US are paid more than their Canadian counterparts, unemployment in the US continues to be significantly lower than in Canada, and disposable incomes in Canada lag behind those in the United States.

What these contradictory images reveal is a country anxious to play a global leadership role, but one constrained by the realities of global power politics, the challenges of domestic consensus-building, and the limitations of economic capacity in spite of the fact that the federal government, for the first time in 20 years, balanced its books. Much of Canada's 'current power' to forge and lead coalitions, to set agendas, and to make its voice heard comes from its membership in a range of privileged economic and military clubs, such as the G-7 and NATO, and in a large number of multilateral organizations. Although some critics advocate a reduction of Canadian global institutional commitments in the direction of niche diplomacy (Potter, 1996; Cooper, 1997), in reality our ability to exercise leadership depends on these memberships. That being said, membership has its price in financial and policy terms. Furthermore, we may not be able to count on the support of our friends when we aspire to leadership positions, as we are now discovering in our bid to secure a seat on the UN Security Council for 1999–2000. This is because other states, which are rising in income and influence, seek leadership roles of their own.

None of the above suggests that Canada is not a significant actor on the world stage, but that there may be few opportunities to exercise the sort of 'can-do' leadership demonstrated in the success of the land-mines process. As we will discuss below, a particular constellation of forces facilitated the quick development of a consensus around a treaty to ban these weapons. This happens only rarely in international affairs. As many of the chapters in this volume illustrate, the more common pattern is long negotiations over issues with uncertain success at the end. In such circumstances, leadership may have a different face: it is more likely to lie in quiet diplomacy and behind-the-scenes coalition-building, which are traditional strengths of Canadian diplomacy. The subtitle of the 1998 volume of *Canada Among Nations, Leadership and Dialogue*, has been chosen to capture twin themes that have been prominent in the Canadian foreign policy process under the Chrétien government. The chapters in this book address these themes in their analyses of specific issues of importance to Canada over the last year and a half. This introduction sets the context for the chapters that follow.

UNTANGLING THE CONCEPT OF LEADERSHIP

What does leadership mean in the current global context? Is there one definition or are there many? How dependent is the answer on who is being led, on the economic and military capacity of the state? Does the character of the issue on which a state takes an initiative matter in the projection of leadership? In other words, is it easier to lead on some issues than on others? Does leadership include a projection of national values abroad?

It is not unusual for states and their populations to want to make a difference in the world. Prior to World War II, foreign policy was a low priority for Canadians and their government. Participation in the war changed that dramatically: Canada made a significant contribution to the allied war effort and its bureaucrats in particular played an important role in the construction of the postwar order. We emerged from that conflict a country with a strong economy and a perception that we were a player of consequence in the postwar world (Hampson and Hart, 1995). This sense of Canada's place in the world was captured by the functional concept of representation, conceived in Ottawa during the war, which asserted that size alone was insufficient to determine participation in the councils of the war and postwar period. Capacity for contribution, interest, and expertise should constitute considerations in determining representation (Molot, 1990: 79)

During the early years of the Cold War, the appropriate role for Canada on many issues was that of a 'helpful fixer' (Holmes, 1970; Holmes, 1976). Canada did its best to ensure that the critical relationship between its two major allies, the United States and the United Kingdom, remained strong and trouble-free. Perhaps the apogee of this bridging role came when Prime Minister Pearson suggested the now accepted, but then exceptional, concept of peacekeepers to bring a resolution to the 1956 crisis over Suez. On non-security matters, for example, international trade, as Robert Wolfe and John M. Curtis note in Chapter 7, Canada was an active proponent of the ill-fated International Trade Organization and the General Agreement on Tariffs and Trade. Canada placed a high priority on strong multilateral institutions and on using them to achieve foreign policy goals.

Canada's perception of leadership has changed from that traditional bridging role, appropriate perhaps only in an environment where co-operation within the so-called Western camp was critical (though certainly harder to maintain with the passage of time), to a more individualistic—some might say opportunistic—one, at least as defined by Foreign Minister Axworthy and Prime Minister Chrétien. What the land-mines campaign illustrates is the exercise of Canadian initiative, together with others, to build a coalition of small states to push an issue that may or may not have been on the agenda of the major powers and with which they may or may not have been in agreement. What the short-term and longer-term impact of such a strategy might be on Canada's relations with the most significant of these major powers, the United States, is an issue that will be raised below.

The land-mines process also occurred outside traditional institutions. Although the Secretary-General of the United Nations supported the initiative, the states active in the campaign purposely eschewed working through the UN to achieve the treaty. This may reflect a more flexible use of international institutions and the recognition that the creation of new fora, when needed, may facilitate a positive outcome and avoid the politics attendant upon established institutions, in this instance the opposition to the land-mines effort by some of the permanent members of the UN Security Council.

An important component of leadership is credibility. Paul Halucha, in Chapter 14 on Canada's role at the Kyoto Conference on Climate Change, makes the perhaps obvious, but critical, connection between the capacity to manage the policy formulation process domestically and the capacity to exercise leadership internationally. Leadership is difficult to exercise in the absence of domestic consensus. The leadership role Canada assumed at the 1992 UN Conference on the Environment and Development held in Rio de Janeiro, Brazil (see Chapter 13 by Linda Reif), dissipated in the years following that meeting because Canada was unable to meet the targets set at that gathering for stabilizing and reducing greenhouse gas emissions. Profound differences among Canadian domestic interests—the energy producers and users, the provinces, and environmental groups—about what constituted an acceptable Canadian commitment to stabilize greenhouse gas emissions meant that Canada came to Kyoto without domestic agreement on a target. Prime Minister Chrétien talked of a Canadian position that would be tougher than that of the US, but that would not be too controversial at home. Canada left Kyoto with a higher undertaking to cut gas emissions than had been anticipated, but it was lower than the one agreed to by the United States (McIloy, 1997: A12). Whether the government will lose face at home or abroad because it did not commit to larger cuts than the US, or will be able to sell the agreement to diverse domestic constituencies, remains to be seen. Another possible causality of Canada's difficulties at Kyoto may be the erosion of domestic support for international regimes, which may be seen as forcing the country to take unpopular and costly decisions.

There may be a paradox to the success that Canada achieved with the land-mines treaty, an expectation that we have to follow up that accomplishment with others of equal moral relevance and drama. Will this mean the search for new issues, for example, child soldiers or small arms, both of which were suggested immediately after the December signing of the land-mines treaty, on which Canada can lead? Are there other comparable issues around which an international coalition of the high-minded could be built? Any next step must be carefully evaluated lest Canada quickly dissipate the political capital it garnered as a result of the land-mines success. The pursuit of issues that would allow Canada to attempt to replicate the land-mines case might be to draw the wrong lessons from the experience in terms of both the mobilization of an international coalition on a security issue that excluded the United States and the heavy reliance for legitimacy on the emotional appeal of the subject and the active participation of NGOs in the generation of popular support for the ban.

The lesson might more appropriately be that the land-mines issue was unique precisely because of the constellation of factors that promoted its achievement.

At the same time, strong Canadian support for multilateral institutions continues. At the World Trade Organization (WTO), as Wolfe and Curtis note, Canada has taken a number of initiatives to ensure that this new institution has the capacity to play a role in the governance of the international trading system. This country is working with like-minded nations on the construction of an agenda for the next round of multilateral trade talks and the promotion of support among WTO members for movement to the next stage of regime-building in international trade. Foremost on this agenda are new negotiations mandated for services and agriculture. However, if the WTO is to be an effective institution, the secretariat of the organization should have greater autonomy and should be allowed to provide its own input and analysis of the international trading system and undertake policy initiatives of its own. There is also a need for a ministerial group with limited membership based on a constituency system that would provide political and strategic leadership for the organization. As matters now stand, in the intervals between the biennial meetings of the Ministerial Conference, decision-making functions are carried out by the General Council, whose membership consists of the ambassadors resident in Geneva. The problems of effective management are by no means unique to this body; it has also been acute for the World Bank and the IMF (International Monetary Fund). But if the WTO is to be an effective international body, structural reform is essential. Leadership can only come from the ministers and this requires the establishment of a ministerial body with stronger oversight powers.

There are many ways to exercise leadership in the international system. By forging transnational alliances with non-governmental organizations and other actors in civil society, countries like Canada can reach into the domestic constituencies of other states and mobilize interests supportive of Canadian policies and positions, as illustrated by the success of the anti-personnel land-mines treaty. These new kinds of state-civil society coalitions are obviously a source of empowerment for both states and the non-governmental organizations that form part of these coalitions. In important ways, the multilateral system has clearly extended beyond the formal institutions of multilateral governance represented by the United Nations, its affiliated agencies, and the Bretton Woods system. At the same time, however, we should not forget that the current system of formal multilateral institutions has served Canadian interests well and that major Canadian interests in areas such as trade and the environment will only be advanced through these institutions and structures. Canada thus has a strong interest in the reform of these institutions, particularly in initiatives that will create new possibilities for strategic leadership and sustained collective and concerted action.

DIALOGUE

One of the hallmarks of the Chrétien government has been its commitment to what it described in the 1993 election campaign as the democratization of the foreign policy process. The origins of the Liberal Party commitment to consultation lie in Lloyd Axworthy's efforts during the 1988 election campaign to draw to the Liberals those NGOs who opposed free trade. The ideas on consultation grew between 1988 and the writing of Liberal Party Red Book prior to the 1993 election that brought the Liberals to power.

Contributors to recent volumes of *Canada Among Nations* have assessed whether this undertaking constitutes a significant departure from the stance of previous governments or is hyperbole for public consumption (Nossal, 1995: 37). An irony of this resolve to consult is the continuing lack of general public interest in foreign policy and no political predisposition to stimulate any. This absence of public attention to foreign policy was epitomized by the virtual absence of any serious discussion of foreign policy issues during the 1997 election campaign. If the citizenry exhibits little interest in foreign policy questions, do those seeking office have some responsibility to provoke at least some debate over Canada's international role and responsibilities, questions such as the level of our international aid, our commitment to and capacity for peacekeeping, human rights, etc.? Or is the more savvy political strategy to address questions closer to the concerns of citizens such as jobs, health care, and taxes? To be sure, the Liberal Party campaign statement, *Securing Our Future Together*, contained one chapter on foreign policy. Entitled 'Canada: Looking Outward', it was the last chapter in the Liberals' Red Book and repeated most of the verities we have come to expect about the complexities of Canada's position in an increasingly interdependent world and our resolve to play an active role in 'influencing the international conditions that affect us' (Liberal Party of Canada, 1997: 96).

What the Liberal government did undertake with regularity during its first mandate, and has continued in its second, is the consultation with segments of what can be termed the attentive foreign policy public. The major venues for this consultation, as Steven Lee describes in Chapter 3, have been the national fora held on different issues and in different locations. During 1997, in keeping with the designation of that year as Canada's Year of Asia-Pacific, four such fora examined aspects of Canada's relationships with the countries of that region. In 1998, there will be a major national forum on the circumpolar North. Another government initiative designed to generate the opportunity for input into the foreign policy process was the creation, in 1996, of the Canadian Centre for Foreign Policy Development. The Centre, located as an adjunct to the Foreign Minister's office, replaces the disbanded Canadian Institute for International Peace and Security, which operated at arm's length from DFAIT. In addition to organizing the national fora, the Centre provides funding to organizations and individuals working on foreign policy issues. The establishment of the Centre means that, once again, there are some limited funds available to stimulate research and debate on foreign policy. What perhaps should be assessed are the implications of its close connection to Foreign Minister Axworthy: on the positive side are the opportunities to focus research more directly on the minister's foreign policy priorities and to connect him easily to a set of actors outside the department bureaucracy; on the negative side is the privileging of certain voices over others in the debate over Canadian foreign policy directions.

One of the unique features of the effort to secure wide international support for the land-mines treaty was the very active public participation and advocacy of NGOs, such as the International Committee of the Red Cross and the International Coalition to Ban Landmines. In Canada, Mines Action Canada played a prominent role in publicizing the campaign. Robert Lawson, in Chapter 5, devotes some attention to their activities. The signature of the treaty by so many states was, to some degree, a testament to the capacity of these NGOs to mobilize public sentiment and to influence governments. The experience empowered these groups, who now are among those pressing the Canadian government to find another issue on which to wage an international campaign. But as Denis Stairs notes in Chapter

2, while the issues upon which these NGOs seize may have great popular appeal, they are not necessarily at the centre of Canadian interests. Some of these NGOs may find it difficult to revert to their more traditional advocacy role in which they have to compete for ministerial attention as opposed to being courted and counted on for support. And the government may discover that the mobilization of NGO support generates stakeholder expectations that will be difficult if not impossible to meet.

Although the opening up of the foreign policy process to various groups and interests through dialogue and greater levels of public discussion is obviously a welcome departure from the past and what some disparagingly referred to as a 'Fortress Pearson' mentality among senior bureaucrats in the Department of Foreign Affairs, it would be facile to equate greater levels of dialogue between foreign policy decision-makers and various elements of civil society with the 'democratization' of foreign policy. Ultimately, in a democracy like ours, decision-making authority lies with our elected officials in Parliament and not with the bureaucrats. Parliamentarians, as John English argues in Chapter 4, are unhappy if they are relegated to the back of the room in foreign policy consultations with the public. Furthermore, in any consultation exercise, those elements of the public or interest groups who see themselves as having a stake in particular issues are more likely to mobilize and press their demands and interests in the fora that have been created. This is especially true in foreign policy, where interest in foreign affairs among the general public is limited. Thus, greater levels of dialogue and discussion may simply privilege special interest groups that can capture the fora that have been created rather than developing a genuine public discourse about what Canada's national interests are or should be.

Greater levels of dialogue may not necessarily lead to a more informed discussion about Canada's foreign policy choices for other reasons. As Jean Daudelin and Ed Dosman argue in Chapter 11, on some issues Canada lacks real expertise and there is simply not the kind of strategic depth in our foreign policy think-tanks and universities to allow Canadians to make informed choices on certain issues. The lack of properly funded research institutes and think-tanks in the foreign policy arena in Canada continues to impede informed dialogue between the government and the Canadian public on foreign affairs. Notwithstanding the above, those who embrace the new democratization should not lose sight of the fact that, as Stairs argues, the ministerial game plan has been to build alliances with like-minded NGOs that will further the minister's goals, particularly when faced with a recalcitrant bureaucracy.

NATIONAL UNITY AND FOREIGN POLICY

Although the land-mines treaty process captured headlines at the end of 1997 and generated the questions of leadership and dialogue that are the uniting themes of this volume, other issues of consequence remain on the Canadian foreign policy agenda.

The link between the national unity question and the formulation and implementation of foreign policy continues to be a close one. In an earlier volume we indicated that foreign policy was one of the issues that united Canadians and where opinions polls showed few differences of opinion between Quebecers and the rest of Canada (Hampson and Molot, 1996). This continues to be true at a general level. However, popular support for Canadian initiatives such as peacekeeping or the ban on land-mines does not constrain the Quebec government from taking advantage of opportunities to highlight the particular interests of Quebec and, in doing so, to push the agenda of separation. In 1997, Quebec's search for international legitimacy on the world stage was in evidence when Premier Bouchard visited France at the end of September. At a conference of parliamentarians from Latin American countries held in Quebec City but largely funded by Ottawa, the Canadian flag did not appear and the Quebec government used the opportunity take Quebec's case for sovereignty and independence to the hemisphere. However, at the Francophone summit in Hanoi in November, Premier Bouchard and Prime Minister Chrétien kept their differences to a minimum. The new Quebec Premier, unlike his predecessor, also decided to participate in the January 1997 Team Canada trip to Asia. He then led a 'Team Quebec' visit to China later in the year, though on these occasions the nature of the international travel made him more cautious about the open articulation of sovereignty. Bouchard would have also participated in the Team Canada expedition to Latin America in early 1998 had not the emergency caused by the January ice storm kept him at home. Bouchard's more co-operative stance towards Ottawa in promoting Canadian trade interests sat well with most of his own constituents, suggesting that when it came to international trade Quebec and the rest of Canada had more to gain by working together than separately.

CANADA-US RELATIONS

Premier Bouchard's somewhat more pragmatic approach to Ottawa in the area of trade was also marked by various efforts by the Quebec government to soothe US concerns about the possible breakup of Canada and what this might mean for US investors in Quebec. Although the US President, Bill Clinton, made no secret about his desire to see Canada stay united, what did come as a surprise to most Canadians was US sensitivity to the national unity issue and how closely over the years the US government had tracked Quebec politicians and the sovereignty issue (Bronskill, 1998: A1).

On Canada-US relations more generally, it became increasingly apparent in the second tenure of the Liberal government that, although Prime Minister Chrétien and President Clinton had a close personal relationship, there was political hay to be made in 'Canada bashing' in Washington and 'US bashing' in Ottawa and the provinces. The Prime Minister admitted as much in his ill-publicized remarks at the July 1997 Madrid NATO summit to the effect that tweaking the nose of the Americans played well at home. Of course, when it comes to Senator Jesse Helms—the man Canadians love to hate— Foreign Minister Lloyd Axworthy's trip to Cuba in an effort to engage Premier Fidel Castro on human rights prompted ridicule from Helms and other conservative Washington pundits. When senior staffers on the US Senate Foreign Relations Committee, chaired by Helms, accused Canadian tourists of cavorting with Cuban prostitutes and Canadian businesses of using Cuban 'slave labour', Axworthy delivered a swift and strong rebuke (Koring, 1998: A1). Canada has also held no punches in its criticisms of the failure of the United States to pay its arrears to the UN. Although proponents of the 'quiet diplomacy' school of Canada-US relations shuddered at these verbal repartees, the Axworthy-Helms Punch-and-Judy show was more for political entertainment than anything else.

US bashing by the provinces, in particular by BC Premier Glen Clark in the salmon war, is potentially more serious. As discussed by Linda Reif in Chapter 13, the ongoing struggle to agree on bilateral quotas for the annual catch of Pacific salmon has engaged a wide range of state and civil society actors on both sides of the border.

The 1985 Pacific Salmon Treaty and its ambiguous formula for allocating salmon lies at the heart of the dispute. Canadians argue that US fishers have caught more salmon than Canadians and rapidly declining stocks of salmon on the Pacific coast have aggravated the difficulties of finding an equitable formula. Tensions escalated in 1997 when Premier Clark announced that he would cancel a US lease of a weapons testing facility in BC, and BC fishers, emboldened by the Premier's rhetoric and stance, blockaded a US ferry in Prince Rupert harbour. As a result of grandstanding by local politicians, the polarization and hardening of attitudes have made it more difficult to arrive at a diplomatic solution. Because local interests now effectively control the issue, as noted by Reif, a compromise will be difficult to achieve. In early March 1998, each government named a new negotiator in an attempt to resolve bilateral differences over salmon.

On the trade side, Canada-US relations in the past year and a half have not been as divisive as at some points in time, though differences over the protection of Canadian cultural industries and the treatment of agriculture continue and could well erupt again. Although Canada continues to enjoy a substantial trade surplus with the United States, the buoyant US economy coupled with the lowest unemployment rates in any OECD country have muted protectionist voices in the US Congress and elsewhere. A rising tide does not necessarily lift all boats, but it has made the trade surplus less of an issue in Canada-US relations than it was during the recession of the early 1990s. Where the dependent nature of Canada's trade policy is most apparent is in the US debate about fast-track legislation. President Clinton's withdrawal of fast-track legislation in mid-October 1997 has slowed efforts to remove trade barriers throughout the Western hemisphere. For Canada, a strong advocate of hemispheric free trade and fast-track, these developments came as a blow, further underscoring Canada's inability to control hemispheric integration processes and the hostage position of some aspects of our trade policies to the vagaries of US domestic politics. Because of the uncertainty about the president's capacity to secure fast-track approval, Canada negotiated its own free trade agreement with Chile, which came into effect in July 1997. Canada also pursued free trade talks with MERCOSUR (the trade bloc of the Southern Cone comprising Brazil, Argentina, Paraguay, and Uruguay) during 1997, but was unable to bring the discussions to a successful conclusion in time for Prime Minister Chrétien's January 1998 visit to Latin America. As noted by David

Long in Chapter 10, Canada also moved last year to consolidate its relations with the European Union by signing agreements on customs co-operation and on humane trapping standards.

THE CANADIAN ECONOMY DURING 1997

The Canadian economy has shown steady domestic growth over the last year and Canada is predicted to outperform the rest of the G-7 countries in 1998 (Thomas, 1998: 7). The fundamentals of the Canadian economy are improving markedly: inflation is not now a serious threat, interest rates remain relatively low, business confidence has risen steadily since 1990, and business investment, particularly in machinery and equipment, is growing. Canada's economy during 1997, as for much of this decade, was driven by the external demand for our goods and services. Exports account for slightly more than 40 per cent of Canada's gross domestic product (GDP). The dollar value of Canada's merchandise exports has doubled since the beginning of the 1990s, as has the value of what we ship to our largest export market, the United States. The US purchased 81 per cent of Canada's merchandise exports in 1997 and more than $1 billion of goods a day moves between the two countries. Imports have increased at a similar pace, most notably from the US but from other economies as well.

This picture, although positive, leaves considerable room for improvement. Far too little of the demand for the goods and services Canadians produce is being generated domestically. As a result of several years of recession and slow growth, internal trade has expanded far less rapidly than exports. Moreover, unemployment, at over 9 per cent in 1997, though down to 8.6 per cent by the beginning of 1998, remains stubbornly high. While comparisons are always difficult, they are none the less important to make. Canada's productivity performance in the 1990s—the capacity of the economy to produce more value through greater efficiency—has been poor when compared to that of the US. The Canadian manufacturing sector is only about 70 per cent as productive as that in the US and the gap is widening. US companies invest more heavily in research and development than do Canadian firms, US workers are more flexible in the participation in the knowledge-based economy, and US corporate balance sheets are healthier (Industry Canada, 1997). Although our export performance has been impressive we have to be concerned about how much of the demand for what we produce is a function of quality and competitiveness and how much the result of a lower Canadian dollar. For an economy as dependent on international trade as the Canadian one, these comparisons (and others noted earlier in this chapter) should be sobering. Leadership at the global level, beyond the capacity to undertake new diplomatic initiatives, requires a robust economy. One of the results of fiscal constraint induced by the imperative to lower the deficit has been, as Draimin and Tomlinson note in Chapter 8, the continuing reduction in recent years in Canada's official development assistance (ODA) budget and the preference for tied aid. Although Finance Minister Paul Martin's February 1998 budget restored some money to the aid line that was intended to be cut, Canada's current foreign aid for the 1998–9 fiscal year will fall below 0.3 per cent of its gross domestic product. This figure is a far cry from the official development assistance target of 0.7 per cent of GDP, a long-stated Canadian foreign aid commitment.

Of the range of economic issues on the agenda during 1997, one, the Multilateral Agreement on Investment (MAI) under negotiation at the Organization for Economic Co-operation and Development (OECD) in Paris, generated increasing public controversy in the fall as efforts were made to mobilize public opinion against it. As Elizabeth Smythe outlines in Chapter 12, the MAI is a much more complex and much less publicly engaging cause than land-mines. The negotiations over the MAI have galvanized at least three kinds of domestic interests—those who support the MAI as another step along the road to international governance (though some may have qualms about whether the OECD is the appropriate venue rather than the WTO); those who oppose the concept of the MAI as a serious infringement on Canadian sovereignty; and those who may be supportive of the agreement, but only if it contains an exemption for Canadian culture. The first group is composed primarily of corporations that see the adoption by a larger number of states of the kind of national treatment for investment available under NAFTA as conducive to their interests. The second is a domestic coalition of groups unhappy with the Canada-US Free Trade Agreement and NAFTA and who view the proposed MAI as a charter of rights for multinational enterprises. The last group, composed of cultural industry stakeholders, finds itself with support from the government, which has indicated its refusal to sign a multilateral agreement that does not exclude cultural industries (DFAIT,

1998). This group has also found itself with allies in France, Belgium, and Australia, among other countries, where Canadian cultural industry advocates are viewed as leaders in defending national culture against the onslaught of US entertainment interests. As this volume goes to press it appears as if MAI negotiations will be stalled for some time, at least until some of the outstanding issues can be resolved.

CANADA'S YEAR OF ASIA-PACIFIC

As 1997 began, there were high expectations that it would be Canada's year of Asia-Pacific and the beginning of a new partnership among equals signified by Canada's hosting of both the November Vancouver summit of Asian-Pacific leaders and a range of ministerials leading up to the summit. Canada has the fourth largest GNP in the APEC community and seeks to diversify its trade, investment, and human ties with the region. Although 1997 was almost certainly the year of Asia-Pacific, it was not for the reasons the summiteers wanted. The summit was supposed to focus on trade expansion and promotion; instead, it was hijacked by Asia's financial crisis as international capital took flight from economies mired in debt and cronyism and seemingly impervious to structural and political reform. What was supposed to be a smoothly orchestrated trade promotion show turned into an embarrassing spectacle as human rights protesters chanted outside the summit halls and were attacked with pepper spray by zealous security forces, while inside Asian leaders were lectured by their US counterparts about the urgency of financial and political reforms. There was more than a touch of irony in the official summit photograph of APEC leaders sporting their newly acquired blue shirts and leather bomber jackets (to fend off impending troubles!) that were gifts of the Canadian Prime Minister.

The Asian financial crisis did more than sandbag the Vancouver summit. Its effects continue to reverberate in global markets and financial institutions. For Canada, the consequences will be lasting and possibly quite serious. In the short term, the flight of investors to safe havens like the US had the effect of driving down the Canadian dollar below the psychologically important 70 cent level for a short period in early 1998. A depressed dollar, of course, is a mixed blessing. On the one hand, it increases foreign demand for our exports as they become more competitive; on the other hand, it drives up the price of imports, puts upward pressure on interest rates, and could be inflationary if the dollar stays depressed for too long. The long-term effect of continuing economic difficulties in Asia is reduced demand for Canadian goods, particularly natural resources, and services, which will bite into economic growth in provinces such as British Columbia, which are highly dependent on the Asian market.

As we noted in the introduction to last year's volume of *Canada Among Nations*, 'Canada has placed a great deal of emphasis on improving trade and strengthening its economic relations with the region.' Recent events should not detract from this goal even though the road ahead is a rocky one and we will experience reduced demand for our exports in Asian markets. As we have now seen, Asia's economic and financial health is ultimately linked to market reforms and the openness, transparency, and accountability of the region's political systems. Asian leaders' utterances about 'Asian values' sound increasingly hollow. Thus, we stand by our statement in last year's volume that 'in a region where political stability is by no means assured and local human rights and democracy are growing it will be increasingly important for Canada to strike the right balance in our foreign policy between trade and investment on the one hand and democracy and human rights on the other' (Molot and Hampson, 1997: 17).

CHANGING SECURITY AGENDAS

Canadian security policy has been buffeted not only by the Department of National Defence's troubles in the Somalia Inquiry, but also by continuing debates about exactly where Canada should direct its defence efforts—into traditional security roles and defence methods, into peacekeeping, or into peacebuilding and the new human security agenda. These debates tend to be thrown into sharp relief when procurement decisions have to be made, as in the recent case of naval helicopters. The government's *1994 Defence White Paper* argued for the status quo in terms of Canada's military roles and missions and did not favour drastic cuts to the defence budget. However, as Dean Oliver argues in Chapter 6, the government's implementation of its own policies and recommendations has been lacklustre and driven more by its fiscal priorities than by any overarching sense of what Canada's defence priorities and direction should be. According to Oliver, to the extent there is a sense of vision about Canadian security priorities, it has come more from

DFAIT and Foreign Minister Axworthy's peacebuilding and 'soft security' agenda than from the Department of National Defence itself.

In terms of the future, there is widespread consensus that a key
priority for Canada's armed forces will be to pursue reform initiatives
in the areas of education and training. This was one of the major
recommendations to come out of the commissioned reports that
emerged from the deliberations of the Somalia Inquiry.

Like it or not, as Alain Pellerin notes in Chapter 9, Canadians will
also have to re-examine their role in and commitments to NATO. The
process of NATO enlargement, which began at NATO's July summit in
Madrid when NATO invited the Czech Republic, Hungary, and Poland
to join, has led to accession talks. But there is no assurance that ratification of the new members by legislatures of NATO's current 16
members will occur. Dissident voices in the US Senate, for example,
argue that NATO expansion is not in the US interest, and such opposition is likely to grow. Canada, for its part, is a strong supporter of
NATO expansion. Even so, the subject has not been a matter of active
debate in Canada and the costs of NATO expansion for existing members of the alliance, including Canada, are not widely considered or
even properly understood.

Public opinion polls continue to show that Canadians believe that
peacekeeping is one of the areas where their country can make a
unique contribution to international peace and security. In the last
year and a half, the government has tried to carve out a unique role
for Canada in the area of peacebuilding so as to engage more fully
the various elements of Canadian civil society in the prevention of
conflict and the reconstruction of war-torn societies. This initiative
was announced on 30 October 1996 in a speech given by Foreign
Minister Axworthy to the UN General Assembly. The institutional
focal points for this initiative are a new Peacebuilding Unit within the
International Humanitarian Assistance Unit in CIDA—a working level
committee between DFAIT and CIDA to co-ordinate peacebuilding initiatives—as well as a committee of senior officials in both departments to provide policy direction. Two new funding mechanisms
were created to support the initiative: a peacebuilding fund of $10
million in fiscal years 1997–8 and 1998–9 managed by CIDA and
drawn from the ODA envelope and a $1 million fund managed by
DFAIT and drawn from the department's budget. Various consultative
and partnership mechanisms with the NGO community have also
been created through these initiatives.

In spite of these new initiatives, peacebuilding has gotten off to a slow start. CIDA's component of the fund—which is aimed at quickly providing Canadian expertise to defuse conflicts in troubled countries—had only earmarked about half of its $10 million budget for fiscal year 1997–8, which ended 31 March 1998. What has angered many critics is that nearly $6 million remained in limbo with no concrete plans for its distribution other than for it to be given back to Treasury Board at the end of the fiscal year.

Because recent international efforts to solve conflict in troubled countries such as Bosnia, Somalia, and Haiti have been plagued with problems, traditional peacekeeping efforts, which involve sending in military forces under United Nations command, have fallen out of favour. However, a combination of bureaucratic inertia, lack of proper follow-through, and a seeming inability on the part of Canadian NGOs and civil society interests to move quickly in the direction contemplated by the Foreign Minister has meant that Canada's peacebuilding effort remains a work-in-progress.

'YES MINISTER' AND THE POLICY PROCESS

As the problems of implementing the minister's peacebuilding agenda illustrate, the devil of any new policy is in the details. When Lloyd Axworthy became Foreign Minister, there were a number of efforts to streamline and strengthen program delivery across the bureaucracy and in those departments with a foreign policy mandate. As Denis Stairs notes in Chapter 2, this plan had a number of elements. In June 1996, DFAIT announced a restructuring plan, which reduced the number of assistant deputy ministers from 11 to seven and sought to create a more consultative cabinet-like arrangement at the apex of the ministry. At the ministerial level there was an effort to co-ordinate policy among the five ministers—Axworthy in Foreign Affairs, Sergio Marchi in International Trade, Diane Marleau, Minister for International Co-operation and Minister Responsible for la Francophonie, Secretary of State for Latin America and Africa David Kilgour, and Minister of State for Asia Pacific Raymond Chan—through weekly luncheon meetings. These were easier to plan than to implement. To the extent that there is interministerial co-ordination now, it occurs in a largely ad hoc and unstructured way.

More disturbing is the fact that there is no longer an interdepartmental committee of deputy ministers on foreign policy issues, nor is there at the moment a cabinet committee on foreign policy. In a milieu where the boundaries between domestic and foreign policy are permeable, effective leadership requires co-ordination and central control across departments. Strong ministers like Axworthy can lead their own departments on issues like land-mines, which fall almost solely within their departmental purview. On the other hand, when issues cut across departments, as in the environment, the lack of co-ordination is readily apparent and the result is policy paralysis. In today's world, more issues cut across departments and lines of responsibility than fall neatly within a single domain. In the absence of leadership marked by strong central co-ordination, the propensity for bureaucrats to run circles around their political masters and to undermine policy implementation abounds. The 'Yes Minister' proclivities are all too evident, as noted above, in peacebuilding and the growing battle between DFAIT and CIDA bureaucrats about how to implement Canada's commitments on de-mining.

Like Janus, leadership has a double face. Canada can certainly lead internationally, as it has done recently, but on those issues where there is little consensus at home about what should be done, leadership also requires the capacity to co-ordinate and mobilize political support domestically. It is in the latter area that political leadership will face its real tests.

REFERENCES

Bronskill, Jim. 1998. 'U.S. tracks every move Bouchard makes', *Ottawa Citizen*, 26 Jan.

Cooper, Andrew F. 1997. *Niche Diplomacy: Middle Powers After the Cold War.* New York: St Martin's Press.

Department of Foreign Affairs and International Trade (DFAIT). 1998. An Address by the Hon. Sergio Marchio, Minister for International Trade, to the Centre for Trade Policy and Law, Ottawa, 13 Feb.

Hampson, Fen Osler (with Michael Hart). 1995. *Multilateral Negotiations: Lessons From Arms Control, Trade, and the Environment.* Baltimore: Johns Hopkins University Press.

Hampson, Fen Osler, and Maureen Appel Molot. 1996. 'Being Heard and the Role of Leadership', in Fen Osler Hampson and Maureen Appel Molot, eds, *Canada Among Nations 1996: Big Enough to be Heard.* Ottawa: Carleton University Press, 3–20.

Holmes, John W. 1970. *The Better Part of Valour: Essays on Canadian Diplomacy.* Toronto: McClelland & Stewart.

Holmes, John W. 1979. *Canada: A Middle Aged Power.* Toronto: McClelland & Stewart.

Industry Canada. 1997. 'Keeping Up with the Joneses: How Is Canada Performing Relative to the US?' Special Report. *Micro-Economic Monitor* (June).

Koring, Paul. 1998. 'Axworthy, Helms aide slug it out on Cuba', *Globe and Mail*, 7 Mar.

Liberal Party of Canada. 1997. *Securing Our Future Together*. Ottawa: Liberal Party of Canada.

McIlroy, Anne. 1997. 'Canada to cut emissions by 6%', *Globe and Mail*, 11 Dec.

Molot, Maureen. 1990. 'Where Do We, Should We, or Can We Sit? A Review of Canadian Foreign Policy Literature', *International Journal of Canadian Studies* 1–2 (Spring-Fall): 77–96.

Molot, Maureen Appel, and Fen Osler Hampson. 1997. 'Asia Pacific Face-Off', in Hampson, Molot, and Martin Rudner, eds, *Canada Among Nations 1997: Asia Pacific Face-Off*. Ottawa: Carleton University Press, 1–20.

Nossal, Kim Richard. 1995. 'The Democratization of Canadian Foreign Policy: The Elusive Ideal', in Maxwell W. Cameron and Maureen Appel Molot, eds, *Canada Among Nations 1995: Democracy and Canadian Foreign Policy*. Ottawa: Carleton University Press, 29–43.

Potter, Evan H. 1996. 'Redesigning Canadian Diplomacy in an Age of Fiscal Austerity', in Fen Osler Hampson and Maureen Appel Molot, eds, *Canada Among Nations 1996: Big Enough to be Heard*. Ottawa: Carleton University Press, 23–55.

Thomas, David. 1998. 'Canadian economy expected to top G7 in 1998,' *Financial Post*, 11 Mar.

2

The Policy Process and Dialogues with Demos: Liberal Pluralism with a Transnational Twist

DENIS STAIRS

In old-fashioned but still sometimes useful language, the term 'policy process' refers to the means and mechanisms by which all the 'inputs' that affect public policy—inputs of politics and circumstance alike—are brought together to produce 'outputs'—the decisions and behaviours of government. Since the inputs are so many and varied, however, and since they interact with one another in such kaleidoscopic combinations, it is hard to pin them down 'whole'. They can only be pinned down in parts. In any particular context, therefore, isolating a specific combination of inputs as the real cause of what we are trying to explain is to some extent an arbitrary undertaking—an existential act.

The force of this observation is compounded by the fact that the outputs are as variegated as the inputs. The specific list of potential causal factors to which we are likely to direct our attention in the search for explanatory illumination thus varies with the particular characteristics we are attempting to explain. For these reasons, among others, the post-modernists are partly right—in matters of this kind, all our accounts of 'reality' are artificial constructs.[1]

In attempting, therefore, to identify and dissect the factors in the Canadian foreign policy process that we think are the most significant (or the most interesting), it is possible to give plausible emphasis to any of a wide variety of alternatives. In *Canada Among Nations 1997: Asia Pacific Face-Off,* John Kirton insisted on the 'centrality of the Prime Minister in both the design and the delivery of Canadian foreign policy initiatives which had an importance for the international system as a whole' (Kirton, 1997: 45). It would have been equally possible, however, for him to have focused, not on the Prime Minister *per se,* but on the political and other forces to which he was responding, thereby assigning the greatest causal weight to *them,* rather than to the PM himself. In such a model, the Prime Minister is not so much the architect of foreign policy as its executor, working to adapt it to changing realities whose true origins lie elsewhere.

Somewhat more broadly, useful explanatory revelation might be thought to lie with the conditions that make the pertinent ministers of the Crown the willing (or unwilling) instruments of their public service advisers; or with the political bargaining that prevails among the defenders (and aggrandizers) of competing domains in the bureaucratic environment; or with the class structure, and within it the dominant class to which those in government appear, on some accounts, to be especially attentive; or (more pluralistically) with the interplay of accommodations reached by mutually supportive sectoral élites; or with one or more of a multitude of forces—some dark, some not—in the outside world; or with systemic transformations of the human condition wrought by changes in applied science; or with any of a host of other possibilities. Every such account 'works' (at least in part) for the very good reason that every such account, assuming there is evidence to sustain it, is 'true' (at least in part).[2]

Any of the foregoing themes, and others like them, could easily be pursued in what follows, and a few of them will in fact be given attention at the beginning, if only to chase down one or two of the hares that have been released in the most recent of the volumes in this series. Following these preliminaries, however, the principal focus of the second half of the discussion will be on the character and significance of the government's attempts to open up the policy process to the influence of private constituencies as part of its commitment to the 'democratization' of Canada's foreign policy. How new is this phenomenon? Whence did it come? Why did it come? Is it a passing thing, or a permanent one? Either way, what significance does it have? In particular, what, if anything, does it say about the respective roles of the state and 'civil society' in the conduct of Canada's foreign affairs, and in the contemporary international environment more generally?[3]

PRELIMINARIES FIRST: THE MINISTERS, THEIR ADVISERS, AND THEIR BUDGETS

At the time last year's volume went to press, Lloyd Axworthy was the Minister of Foreign Affairs. He still is, and his continuance in office has apparently brought a new measure of sincerity and determination to the government's commitment to consult with its domestic constituencies—many of them transnationally linked to counterparts in other countries—in both the development and conduct of certain foreign policies. Axworthy's predecessor, André Ouellet, had honoured the form of this commitment, but for the most part had been careful throughout his tenure to remain personally aloof from the consultative process in order to preserve his own freedom of manoeuvre.[4] Axworthy, by contrast, has honoured not only the form but also, in considerable measure, the substance. His reasons for doing so, and the implications of his position, are at the centre of the discussion that will follow below. We will return to him then.

The other minister of senior rank at last year's time of writing was Art Eggleton in International Trade. Eggleton, however, now serves elsewhere, as Minister of National Defence in succession to David Collenette and Doug Young. Collenette had earlier resigned from the Defence portfolio in response (at least on the surface) to a minor impropriety at the hands of one of his personal aides. More probably, he had been displaced by fallout from the Somalia affair. Young, on the other hand, was displaced by his New Brunswick electors—the latter apparently disgruntled by unpalatable changes in the eligibility requirements for recipients of unemployment insurance. In June 1997, following the spring general election, the Prime Minister appointed Sergio Marchi in Eggleton's place. Marchi, like Axworthy, has normally been identified with the left-of-centre wing of the Liberal Party, and had previously served in the Chrétien government as Minister of Citizenship and Immigration and later as Minister of the Environment. To the extent that the 'International Trade' side of the Department of Foreign Affairs and International Trade (DFAIT) represents the hard-headed commercial strain in the department's operations, a certain awkwardness might have been expected to ensue (even if trade promotion was also the most persistently evident international interest of the Prime Minister). None, however, has so far become publicly visible.[5]

Earlier, in January 1996, the Prime Minister had appointed Pierre Pettigrew to the cognate portfolio of International Co-operation and la Francophonie. This arrangement ostensibly gave the Canadian International Development Agency (CIDA) a greater measure of independence from DFAIT at the ministerial level, but at the same time produced an obvious overlap in matters bearing on relations with French-speaking countries overseas. Pettigrew's recruitment and primary political mission, however, were both driven by the national unity question, and he was not to remain in the CIDA job for long. His purpose in being there appears to have been to acquire some practical seasoning in a context that had particular relevance for Francophone constituencies, while pursuing a seat in the House. He was reassigned in October 1996 to Human Resources Development.

The tenure of Don Boudria, who replaced him, was to be of comparably limited duration. In June 1997, after the general election, Boudria became government leader in the House of Commons and was succeeded in the International Co-operation/la Francophonie portfolio by Diane Marleau, a Franco-Ontarian with a bachelor's degree in economics and previous ministerial experience in the Department of Health and in Public Works and Government Services.

At the more junior level, Raymond Chan remained in the position of Secretary of State (Asia-Pacific) when the government was reconstructed in the spring, but the former Secretary of State (Latin America and Africa), Christine Stewart, was moved to the Department of the Environment. She was succeeded by David Kilgour, a Winnipeg-born lawyer with wide experience of government legal work in the western provinces of Manitoba, Alberta, and British Columbia, as well as in Ottawa. Representing Edmonton Southeast, he had previously served as deputy speaker of the House of Commons.

On the face of it, all this would appear to constitute a hopeless and unwieldy arrangement. Two ministers at the head of one department would be awkward enough. But *five or six?* The potential in

Figure 2.1

Department of Foreign Affairs and International Trade, Senior Echelons

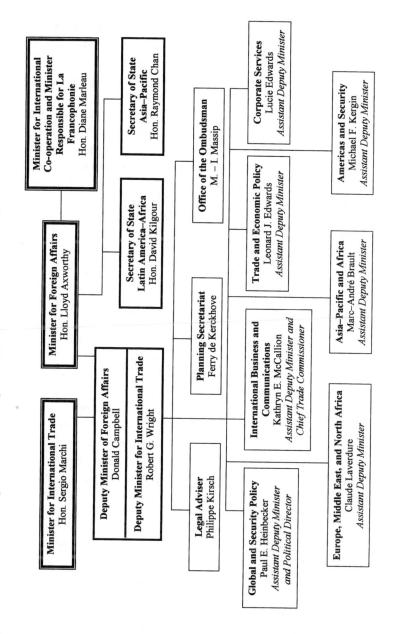

such circumstances for a blurring of the boundaries between competing areas of ministerial responsibility, ambiguity in the bureaucratic chain of command, and a consequent proliferation of turf warfare throughout the system is exponentially increased. Even where the players are co-operatively inclined, the communications overburden that results at all levels from the need to keep everyone securely 'in the loop' is a daunting source of organizational stress in itself.

As John Kirton suggested, one of the proposed solutions to this problem at the ministerial level was to have Lloyd Axworthy convene weekly luncheon meetings of the five to co-ordinate their respective endeavours and ensure a compatibility of policies and behaviours across their respective domains. As might have been expected, however, this process, largely because of scheduling difficulties, had 'atrophied by the autumn' (Kirton, 1997: 35). The meetings are still held on the relatively rare occasions that circumstances allow, but the scheduling problems (given particularly the globe-trotting engagements of all three of the cabinet-level ministers) have been hard to remedy. Most ministerial-level co-ordination, therefore, seems to take place through shifting combinations of ad hoc bilaterals, or through staff, rather than by way of a fixed routine for collective consultation.

The co-ordination problem is leavened to some extent by the fact that not all of the ministers are operating at the same level, so that the requirements are not equally demanding in every case. In particular, the two Secretaries of State, both of whom report to Axworthy, are largely free of the responsibilities for ministerial leadership and administration that accrue to the three senior ministers, and hence they are available to cover such representational and other duties in relation to their respective geographical areas as cannot be met by the ministers themselves. With experience and exposure, moreover, they can develop a capacity to make constructive use of their own contacts in support of government initiatives, as the case of Raymond Chan—well connected with the Pacific in the first place, and now something of an old hand in office—seems to demonstrate. But except in relation to the specific matters with which they have been charged, there is obviously less need than in the other cases for them to be kept fully informed on everything the three ministers are doing.

Axworthy and Marchi, representing respectively the 'primarily political' and the 'primarily economic' wings of the department, clearly need to consult more often, and at the bureaucratic level the competing preoccupations of political and commercial officers are an important and persistent ingredient of the incessant discussions of such policy trade-offs as have to be made and of the various considerations that need to be weighed and weighted in the decision-making that results. This is not, however, a new phenomenon, and there is little evidence to suggest that either the department or the two ministers are finding a *modus vivendi* unusually difficult to maintain. On the basis of the Prime Minister's personal interest in trade promotion and in light of the department's own documentary outpourings going back to the mid-1980s, it could certainly be argued that commercial objectives are ascendant. But this has not prevented Axworthy from pursuing high-profile initiatives in other areas. Since most of these undertakings can be activated without causing complications for commercial policy, serious conflicts seem to have been avoided.[6]

Axworthy's international activism, on the other hand, seems to have complicated somewhat the relationship between his own department and that of Diane Marleau, even if it has not visibly affected the relations of the ministers themselves. This is not because of 'personality politics', or even because the Francophonie portion of Marleau's brief intrudes in a direct organizational way on DFAIT's domain. It comes instead from the fact that DFAIT, with one or two exceptions, is not a 'program-delivery' department but one devoted for the most part to representational, consular, and policy-making functions. It thus lives only by its own operating budget. CIDA, by contrast, is predominantly a program agency, responsible for the annual dissemination to others of substantial, although shrinking, stores of public resources.[7] Within its general mandate, moreover, its expenditures are determined not so much by precise statutory commitments as by the decisions it makes for itself, albeit in varying degrees of consultation with others and with the approval of the minister. Crudely put, CIDA's budget represents one of the few potential opportunities for significant discretionary expenditures that the federal government has to offer. Marleau, at once junior to Axworthy and organizationally obliged to work with him, thus confronts an awkward reality: she has money, but he does not. Given Axworthy's desire to make a substantive mark on the course of world affairs, the temptations that result for him, and the vulnerability that results for her, are clear enough. We will return briefly to one of their practical manifestations below.

The professional DFAIT bureaucracy is headed by the Deputy Minister of Foreign Affairs and the Deputy Minister for International Trade. Notwithstanding what their titles would lead the innocent to expect, however, both deputies report to both ministers. The assistant deputies similarly report to both deputies in an organizational arrangement that greatly multiplies paper flows as the various senior players seek to keep themselves reasonably informed of the conduct of business in everyone else's loop. Partly in response to this sort of problem, but more because of the insistent pressure to economize on spending and the need to convince a darkly suspicious Privy Council Office that DFAIT was seriously trying to contribute in constructive fashion to the new world of lean and mean government, the department in June 1996 had announced a restructuring plan that was to reduce the number of assistant deputy ministers (ADMs) from 14 to seven and excise the position of Associate Deputy Minister altogether. More interestingly, however, the Deputy Minister of Foreign Affairs at that time, Gordon Smith, had also attempted to change the way in which the ADMs operated. More specifically, he had envisaged that they would function as a kind of collective decision-making think-tank, focusing their attention in consultative, cabinet-like fashion on the more general and long-range of foreign policy questions. This adjustment was supposed to be accompanied by a devolution of responsibilities for day-to-day management and decision-making down the organizational ladder to the directors-general, and through them to the directors. The directors-general were to have considerable decision-making authority within their own budget allocations and in relation to the general issues bearing on the international relationships for which they were responsible. These changes were accompanied by a significant reduction in the department's personnel, although the resulting decimation was not nearly so severe as in many other ministries (Kirton, 1997: 36–40).

In assessing the new arrangement after its first six or seven months in operation, John Kirton was able to come to a relatively positive view of its practical effects. There were complaints on the one hand that the ADMs were 'overworked and unavailable to provide the desired leadership on critical issues which erupted.' In particularly urgent cases, on the other hand, individuals among them tended to be drawn into the detailed development of immediately operational decisions in a way that the Under-Secretary had presumably not intended. But the ADM group as a whole seemed none the less to be functioning more or less in the way that Smith had planned, and among other things was having some success in find-ing ways to allocate resources more effectively in line with policy pri-orities (Kirton, 1997: 39–40).

A year later, however, the prevailing judgement in the department seems to be less sanguine. Over the longer haul, many of the ADMs appear to have been reluctant to give up their 'hands on' approach to the management of the problems arising within their respective areas of responsibility, and it may be this, as much as the reduction in their numbers, that has led them to feel overworked (if that is how they truly feel). Some of the directors-general similarly sense that their workloads have increased, and without the compensation they had originally expected in the form of diminished supervision on day-to-day matters by their immediate superiors.

There are several possible explanations for this phenomenon. Most professional students of administrative organizations would probably have anticipated a reluctance on the part of senior person-nel to give up their day-to-day contact with operations. This is largely because officers in circumstances of this kind will tend to think of such contact as crucial to the preservation of their power and to the maintenance of their 'feel' for the texture of what is going on in the domains over which they preside. Many of them are likely to sense (by instinct if not by calculation) that this kind of knowledge is pre-cisely the foundation upon which their influence, together with their capacity to control the decisions and behaviours for which they will ultimately be held accountable, most heavily depends. Such a reac-tion is particularly easy to predict in cases in which a significant rearrangement of functions and decision-making practices is intro-duced in the absence of a fairly extensive turnover of affected per-sonnel. In the current example, virtually all of the seven ADMs deployed at the time the structure was actually put in place (September 1996) were effectively continuing in their previous roles, albeit with new responsibilities added and under a revised concep-tion of the kinds of roles they were expected to perform. They could accommodate fairly smoothly to the straightforward enlargement of their domains, but with one or two exceptions they appear to have found the new definition of their function in the hierarchy signifi-cantly harder to absorb.

It is conceivable that a different result might have been obtained if the original seven had been dispatched to embassies abroad, to be replaced by successors brought in from elsewhere. But even if this had been thought feasible and appropriate, the magnetic attraction of day-to-day operations, relative to collegial deliberations on the broader issues and their longer-term implications, would probably have been difficult to overcome. In any case, the current assessment seems to be that the think-tank feature of the restructuring experiment is not really working. Gordon Smith's recently appointed successor, Donald W. Campbell, may not have a great interest, moreover, in reviving it. If that is the case, it may well be allowed to die a gradual and unheralded death, there being no obvious need either to proclaim its passing or to provide it with a decent burial.

In the meantime, the government as a whole has continued to operate under tight financial constraints resulting from the deficit-cutting measures instigated by Paul Martin's system-wide program review. More than one commentator (previous contributors to this series among them) has observed that DFAIT has not been hit quite so hard in this process as some of the other ministries (Molot and Hampson, 1997: 3; Kirton, 1997: 37). That this is so, however, may be a reflection less of its capacity to mobilize political assets in its own defence than of the kinds of expenditures that it has to undertake. It has already been observed that Foreign Affairs is not primarily a 'program' department. Its functions are geared to policy-making and representation. By federal government standards, its budget is relatively small, and significant cuts are difficult to make without gutting the organization itself or damaging Canada's international visibility in ways that Ottawa has not thus far been prepared to accept. The Main Estimates for 1997–8 project the department's total expenditures (net of revenues) at $1.3 billion, down just over $77 million (or about 5.6 per cent) from the previous year. A further cut of about $33.5 million (2.6 per cent) is planned for 1998–9, at which point the budget is expected to level out.

These are not Draconian numbers, even if interpreted against a backdrop of reductions in earlier rounds, but they have to be understood in the context of how the department spends its money. In 1997–8, for example, approximately 35.8 per cent of its expenditures (including revenue transfers) were devoted to personnel, 33.8 per cent to goods and services (transportation, communications, professional services, rentals, utilities, and the like), and 5.7 per cent to items classified as capital (land, buildings, machinery, and equipment). Once the saving on 'nickels and dimes' has been done, most of these items approximate fixed costs—unless downsizing decisions of a very dramatic sort (the closing of a substantial array of missions abroad, together with the desks to which they report in the department's offices at home) are seriously initiated. Such decisions, however, would have the effect of weakening the organizational instruments of government itself, while having relatively little overall impact on the public purse. Presumably, this calculation has protected the department from more trenchant assaults than the ones it has experienced to date.

The department's remaining expenditures, 25 per cent of the total, are its 'transfer payments'. Composed of 'grants' and 'contributions', and coming in some cases as close as the department gets to program delivery, these are potentially more vulnerable to financial crackings-of-the-whip, and there is no question that discretionary expenditures in this area have been hit hard. In the three years since 1994–5, they have dropped by more than 37 per cent (as compared with a 3 per cent decline over the same period in expenditures on goods and services, a 16 per cent decline in expenditures on capital, and a 4.6 per cent *increase* in expenditures on personnel).[8] On the other hand, the biggest outlays in this category are largely allocated to major multilateral institutions—the United Nations and its various specialized agencies, NATO, the Commonwealth, and so on—and here, too, there are obvious constraints on the government's freedom of manoeuvre. The result is that the greatest damage has been done to activities that may be broadly described as promotional, including grants and contributions under the so-called public diplomacy 'business line'.[9]

It follows from what has just been said that the most substantial contributions of the Canadian foreign policy community to the government's deficit reduction mission have really come, not from DFAIT, but from CIDA and the Department of National Defence, where the budgets are much more substantial and where expensive programs can be more easily subjected to discretionary cuts. From the financial and administrative points of view, this is perfectly understandable, and no student of complex organizations under financial duress will have difficulty identifying the pattern. The immediate and obvious result is a significant erosion of the tangible assets available to the government for buttressing Canada's representational presence in the international community at large. This has led to suggestions that Canada should focus its international attentions more narrowly on areas in which it can practise a constructive form of 'niche' diplomacy, an argument that was briefly reviewed last year in the introductory chapter to *Canada Among Nations 1997: Asia Pacific Face-Off* (Molot and Hampson, 1997: 2–4).[10]

Given the momentum that supports the continued maintenance of Canada's global diplomatic establishment, the pursuit of niche diplomacy may be hard to bring off, however. That momentum is rooted not merely in bureaucratic inertia, but more substantially in the demands and expectations of a multitude of constituencies at home and abroad, as well as in the fear that the edifice itself may be difficult to reconstruct once it has been demolished. In such a context, the setting of operational priorities by means of reasoned deliberation often turns out to be less rational in practice than it seems to be in principle. This is particularly so when a long-term capacity for responding to the unexpected—that is, to politically, economically, or morally intrusive international developments wherever and whenever they occur—is also assumed to be essential. What may thus have to be avoided is not so much the *breadth* of the geographical, institutional, and functional focus that an ability to react to the eclecticism of contemporary international relations requires (eclecticism and 'ad hocery' in foreign affairs are inevitable), but rather the rhetorical commitment to ambitiously specific aspirations that are beyond the government's real willingness or capacity to pursue.

But this is to pontificate, evidence in itself that the time has come to turn away from the ministers, their advisers, and their budgets, and to address the democratization theme to which reference was made at the beginning.

DIALOGUES WITH DEMOS: NGOS AND OTHER INTERESTS

In an August 1997 *Globe and Mail* article, 'How interest groups are shaping foreign policy', Barbara McDougall, Secretary of State for External Affairs in the government of Brian Mulroney from 1991 to 1993, observed that the 'inputs' (her term) to foreign policy are changing. 'The influence of pin-striped diplomats', she wrote, 'is being displaced by high-profile pressure from a variety of disconnected interests.' Drawing in particular on an analysis by Jessica Matthews of the role played by 'coalitions of the willing' in advancing so rapidly the cause of a treaty to ban land-mines, she noted that the 'rise of ad hoc non-governmental organizations as influences on foreign policy is gaining momentum as technology revolutionizes the ability of individuals to attach themselves to others for very specific purposes.' Not all the causes pursued in this way, however, were equally benign. 'Canada's terms of trade, for example, have been negatively affected at various times by special interests in three of our historic and most economically vital activities: fish, furs and forests.' For McDougall, this development raised a number of questions:

> Most important for governments, who is accountable—and to whom? Foreign policy defined as defending the national interest is not high on the agenda of most members of the public today in virtually any country. The components of national interest, on the other hand—trade, the environment, labour-force standards—are of vital concern to separate and increasingly narrow but highly vocal sectors of the public. How governments will respond to this fragmentation of interest has yet to be determined, but foreign policy will never be the same. (McDougall, 1997: A23)

'Never' is a long time, and it depends in any case on what we call 'the same' and what we treat as 'different'. But the phenomenon to which McDougall was referring is certainly very real. In Canada it may have a particular relevance because in recent years it has been given such enthusiastic government encouragement and support. In May 1993 Lloyd Axworthy and Christine Stewart, then the chair and vice-chair respectively of the Liberal Caucus Committee on External Affairs and National Defence, introduced the *Liberal Foreign Policy Handbook*, in which the party committed itself to what it called the 'democratization of foreign policy' (Liberal Party of Canada, 1993a). The commitment to an 'open process for foreign policy-making' was repeated in the party's election platform (the so-called 'Red Book') the following September. Among other things, a Liberal government would establish a National Forum on Canada's International Relations, and parliamentary committees would 'be given a wider role in developing foreign policy initiatives' (Liberal Party of Canada, 1993b: 109).

So it did, and so they were. A National Forum was convened in Ottawa in March 1994 to initiate two major parliamentary reviews, one of foreign policy and one of defence policy. The Forum's invitation list included approximately 130 names, carefully selected to respond to the familiar panoply of Canadian representational criteria—region, language, ethnic identification, sex, vocation, interest group affiliation, and professional expertise. More than 100 observers from inside the political and bureaucratic apparatus also attended the proceedings, albeit in some cases sporadically. So diverse an assemblage could not agree on much. But in an age in which government-by-consultation is both demanded and expected, it could certainly agree that the experiment ought to be repeated again in subsequent years, as it has been, with gatherings at the regional level being added to the mix. Most recently, in 1997, National Forum meetings were held in Victoria, Waterloo, Halifax, and Quebec City, and were attended, as usual, by a combination of representatives from non-governmental organizations (NGOs), academe, government, labour, and business.[11]

In the meantime, during 1994 the two parliamentary reviews proceeded apace. As it turned out, the committees in each case were to hear more than 800 witnesses, many of them representing organized groups. The latter emanated from a wide array of positions on the spectrum of policy preferences (Stairs, 1995). At the end of these consultative processes, both committees produced lengthy reports. Elaborate statements of government policy were then issued in reply.

Such consultative processes were not entirely new. As long ago as the late 1960s, the Trudeau government had launched a foreign policy review during the course of which the Department of External Affairs, in formal obeisance to the requirements of what was then called 'participatory democracy', had organized a series of meetings with academics for the ostensible purpose of reviewing major areas of Canada's foreign policy. The premise (to which the Prime Minister's Office presumably subscribed with considerably more enthusiasm than did the professionals in the department itself) was that the bureaucracy was too deeply entrenched in its established policy positions and too immobilized by ingrained habits of mind to respond effectively to ongoing changes in the international political environment. Intellectual stimulus was required if innovation was to ensue. Perhaps it could come from diversifying the range of ideas in play. Exposing foreign service officials to the ruminations of academics, some of whom had been visibly critical of various aspects of Canadian foreign policy, might be a part of the remedy.

Even before the Trudeau government's review, however, standing committees of Parliament had begun to examine not merely the financial estimates of the pertinent departments but also the substance of foreign and defence policy issues, and to do so increasingly with the help of witnesses recruited from outside the immediate circles of government. Initially, in the early 1960s, the emphasis was on 'experts' of one kind or another, but as the practice intensified in the late 1970s and into the 1980s, it became more common to attract inputs from interest and advocacy groups as well. As time went on, this development seems to have been reinforced by an increasingly populist array of expectations with regard to the conduct of government more generally. Such pressure doubtless came in part from changes in the Canadian political culture, encouraged among other things by the entrenchment of a Charter of Rights in the written portion of Canada's eclectically composed constitution. It may also have been aggravated by a growing public distrust of conventional political processes at a time of economic and constitutional malaise. In the particular case of foreign policy, the effect of these forces appears to have been compounded further by technologically driven improvements in global communications. The latter helped not only to generate a greater awareness of the process of globalization itself, and of the extent to which problems abroad can have repercussions at home, but also to bring other peoples' miseries vividly into Canadian view, and thereby arouse Canadian moral concern. This had the effect of making the miseries themselves a matter of Canadian political import, and hence of Canadian public business.

These same developments in communications technology also facilitated the mobilization of representational interests across national boundaries, that is, on a transnational basis. In an increasingly interactive world, multinational NGOs became (in political terms) the 'social policy' counterparts of multinational corporations, and they were not very favourably disposed to the notion that the state ought to be left to manage its foreign affairs largely on its own.[12]

The desire to participate in the process by which foreign policy decisions are made was increasingly accompanied by an interest in being directly embroiled in the conduct of diplomacy itself, and in some cases even in the practical implementation of such results as ensued. The most recent and spectacular example is provided by the land-mines case, which is considered in detail by Bob Lawson in Chapter 5 in this volume. The political and diplomatic process that led to the land-mines treaty was largely triggered by NGOs. Certainly it was facilitated by them. And now the results, on the ground, will have to be implemented with their help.[13]

Again, however, this is not so much a new departure as a further extension of patterns that have been in train for some time. As long ago as 1972, the Canadian delegation to the Stockholm Conference on the International Environment was accompanied by advisers from the Canadian Labour Congress, the National Indian Brotherhood, the National Youth Conference, the Canadian Federation of Agriculture, and the Mining Association of Canada. NGOs were everywhere in evidence, partly to lobby, partly to confer among themselves in parallel with government representatives. By the time of the Rio Conference on the same subject 20 years later, NGO personnel were being included in the membership of the Canadian delegation itself, and according to David Runnalls, this was true of the official representation from a total of more than 30 countries (Runnalls, 1993: 139). And once more, NGO encounters were organized in parallel with the official conference—although this time even more elaborately so, as groups with similar interests exchanged information, ideas, and intelligence, and plotted their lobbying efforts on site. In many cases, they also maintained continuous contact with their respective home offices, sometimes with a view to orchestrating the application of pressure on politicians and government officials in their respective capitals (Ottawa included), both directly and through the media. These patterns have become increasingly routine at almost all major multilateral conferences, and parallel meetings are now a regular feature even of G-7 summits.[14]

The use of non-governmental advisers has become quite common in the context of bilateral negotiations as well, particularly when the issues at stake are of the economic or functional variety. In the Canadian case, this has been particularly true with trade negotiations, but the precedents go back a long way and are not confined to discussions of trading arrangements alone. In the 1970s, for example, the Canadian team negotiating the boundary between the Canadian and American Exclusive Economic Zones in the vicinity of Georges Bank included among its advisers the head of the Nova Scotia Fishermen's Association, a fleet captain with National Sea Products, a union representative, the skipper of a fishing boat, and an official of the Atlantic Fishing Vessel Owners' Association.

While we recognize the continuities reflected in the NGO phenomenon, however, there is no question that new elements are also at work. Among them, first of all, is a dramatic increase in the size of the NGO population, both at home and internationally. As the foregoing discussion suggests, moreover, NGO activities are intruding far more pervasively than ever before into the policy-making process itself. In addition, more NGOs are now concerned with what might be described as 'international public goods' rather than with 'possessive' or acquisitive interests of a sort that could be interpreted as reflecting no more than the self-serving appetites of their own members.[15] These public goods are sometimes genuinely transnational in character (*everyone*, presumably, will benefit from the preservation of the ozone layer), but they are often aimed, too, at the relief of miseries—political, economic, social, and so on—located in sovereign jurisdictions far away that have no discernible link to any immediate Canadian interest.[16]

   This combination of characteristics has led some NGOs, as well as a few independent analysts, to claim (implicitly if not explicitly) that we are witnessing the beginning of a transition to a new kind of international order in which the system of sovereign states will be succeeded by a considerably more diverse array of international regimes. The erosion of state power was first associated with the rise of multinational corporations and subsequently with the more general processes of globalization. To this erosion at the hands of the 'liberal right', therefore, there is now added a further erosion from the 'liberal left'. NGOs are increasingly pervasive forces in international politics. They pursue remedies to problems that are either indifferent to state boundaries (because they are transnational) or complicated by them (because they are housed in sovereign jurisdictions that lack the resources or the will to deal with them). And their objectives are guided above all by a desire to respond not to the appetites of the self but to the needs of the common. 'The common' is here identified not with the citizenry of any given state, but with humanity at large. Since the miseries at issue are so dire—related, as they are, to poverty, disease, environmental decay, the depletion of resources, famine, torture, the heartless exploitation of women and children, and sundry predations of prejudice, superstition, and autocratic rule—their urgency is hard to deny. To dispose of them is a compelling mission. But in responding to them, states, and the state system, seem often to get in the way and to be a part of the problem, not of the solution. In the interest of humanity, therefore, those who are the custodians of the state must be evaded or brought to heel. Either way, their claim to primacy—their insistence on being 'sovereign', on being the 'last-say' decision-makers—must be attacked, and their supreme position in the hierarchy of legitimacy subjected to challenge. For the independent analyst, it should be noted, the interest in all this may amount to nothing more than a still unsettled matter of empirical observation, a puzzle about what is going on in the real world. Not all observers would agree on what the available evidence is saying about this, but the question itself is simply concerned with whether the Westphalian state system is, or is not, being transformed into something completely different. For some of the NGOs and their advocates, on the other hand, it is a matter also of normative preference: the system is changing, thank Heaven! Or, the system is changing, we hope!

This is, of course, an extreme interpretation, and increasing evidence suggests it will not survive a closer look. Certainly most of the NGOs involved in the 'Ottawa Process' that led to the land-mines treaty knew full well that, while they might pressure the state system to act, they could not actually take its place. And there is an intensifying resistance on the part of many academic students of international relations to the notion that the challenge from either the liberal right (representing the forces of the global economy) or the liberal left (reflecting civil society) will ultimately weaken the state itself or destroy the state system as a whole.[17]

The state, after all, does have powerful assets at its disposal. Among them is the authority to regulate. It is true that this authority can be delegated to international bodies and that new supranational regimes can then ensue. But the delegation must still be arranged by intergovernmental agreement, and the act of delegation is itself conditional. In principle it can be withdrawn, even if the political and other supports that develop around almost any regime, once it has been established, sometimes make this an improbable prospect. Since much of what is required by way of a response to global challenges entails regulatory initiatives, moreover, it can be argued that the growing influence of the NGO community will have the effect of increasing the need for government-instituted action, rather than of decreasing that need.

Much the same can be said of the power to enforce. Enforcement authority, too, is sometimes delegated (albeit for very restricted purposes) to international institutions, but the process is usually accompanied by a plethora of 'ifs', 'ands', and 'buts', and such arrangements are still conditional on interstate agreement.

Even more significantly, NGOs have the power to beg, but only states have the power to tax, and with it the power to accumulate public resources on a substantial scale. That power brings with it not merely the power to spend, but also the obligation to do the spending in accordance with what can reasonably and persuasively be defended as a public interest or, alternatively, as a manifestation of public will. Absent the development of a global system of taxation, this, more than any other factor, is the Achilles' heel of any argument that rests on the dispensability of the modern state. It is particularly so in a context in which most of the problems at issue cannot be addressed in a serious way without the expenditure of substantial stores of public funds. In matters of government, certainly, there is no escaping the import of the old adage: 'S/he who pays the piper, calls the tune.'

Related to this reality is another. Resources, relative to needs and wants, are always scarce. It follows that not every public good can be equally well served. Trade-offs therefore have to be made and balances struck. But NGOs, specialized as they are, cannot make trade-offs. They can only pursue their own agendas. In that sense, they have the *easy* decisions. States, by contrast, have the *hard* ones. And the hard decisions cannot be avoided. Such decisions may be made unilaterally, or they may be made in concert with other states. They may even be made by formal votes in intergovernmental organizations. But there is no escaping their being made, and there is no escaping the fact that only governments can do the job.

And finally, there is the inescapable concern of the liberal constitutionalist, which is that, in the making of *all* these decisions, some process of democratic accountability, however imperfectly embodied it may actually be in our political institutions, must be maintained. In liberally constituted polities, this accountability mechanism is available only through the workings of the apparatus of state. NGOs, by contrast, may sometimes be democratically accountable to their members, but they are no more accountable to the other—and competing—components of the *demos* (people) than are the most Machiavellian and ruthlessly self-serving of multinational enterprises. The hard truth of the matter is that we have not thus far been able to design a better mechanism for the preservation of liberty and the avoidance of oppression than the properly constituted liberal democratic state. That not all states are properly constituted, or liberal, or democratic, goes without saying. But what also goes without saying is that, in the absence of the state, liberty cannot be preserved and oppression cannot be avoided. Those who are concerned above all to serve the world's victims must presumably understand the import of this ancient observation. In the pursuit of justice, however defined, the state may be a poor thing, but it is all we have.

These reflections lead to an alternative, if somewhat old-fashioned, interpretation of what the NGO phenomenon really represents—an interpretation that accords rather better than the radical view with the recent behaviour of the Canadian foreign policy community, among a handful of others. For when all is said and done, the NGOs ultimately amount to public service interest groups, distinguished from their more traditional antecedents only by their transnational structures and connections and by their focus on causes that often lie beyond the sovereign jurisdiction of the countries in which they originate or from which they seek to extract resources. Because the initiatives in which they are interested usually require action from more governments than one, and because they now have at their disposal techniques of electronic communication that are instantaneous, relatively cheap, and almost impossible to intercede, they have both the incentive and the capacity to operate in tandem with others against a multiplicity of governments at once. Like the states in whose behaviour they are interested, they can form coalitions in opposition to their adversaries and thereby amplify their influence in the pursuit of complementary objectives. Like domestic interest groups of the traditional kind, they can sometimes exploit certain tactical advantages over government bureaucracies, in the sense that they can bob, and weave, and shift their targets in response to changes in the locus of decision or the arrival of new opportunities for making their point. The Greenpeace organization is the classic example of an international pressure group that exploits this freedom of manoeuvre in guerrilla-like style, making sophisticated use of media-manipulation techniques in the process. Governments—being more lugubrious in their decision-making because of their inescapable need to cope with competing considerations, and hence to engage in lengthy internal negotiations as they make their decisions—are often left floundering in response.

These are interesting phenomena, and the transnational ingredient, reflective of changes in the character of the international agenda as well as of the opportunities that new communications technologies have helped to create, is more evident than it used to be. But in purely analytical terms, the *process itself* is not very different from the one that traditional pluralist interpretations might have led us to expect. The NGOs do what interest groups have always done, and governments respond to them accordingly. Such influence as the

NGOs display comes partly from the application of conventional pressure techniques, coupled with the fact that they are often the experienced custodians of a knowledge and expertise, and sometimes even a 'delivery' capability, that governments find useful in both the formation and execution of policy. In time-honoured fashion, symbiotic relationships frequently ensue between the NGOs, on the one hand, and the interested agencies of government, on the other. In the Canadian foreign policy community, CIDA's contractual arrangements for program delivery with what it describes as the 'voluntary sector' provide the most obvious and persistent, but by no means the only, examples. Last year's land-mines treaty would appear to be leading to comparable arrangements in the administration of what amounts to an elaborate initiative in disarmament and arms control, a security issue-area traditionally thought to be the business of the state alone (notwithstanding its being the subject from time to time of volatile constituency representations).

It may be suggested in response that there is a commonality of motive among the groups identified with civil society (however divided they might be over their respective priorities) that demands that they not be treated in a simple interest group framework. Among other things, that framework rests on the benignly pluralistic premise that, in a kaleidoscopic world of constantly shifting and perennially competing interests, almost everyone comes out reasonably well in the end. NGOs are predominantly concerned with victims. The agents of the global economy are predominantly concerned with victors. Is this not a fundamental distinction—the distinction between the weak and the strong?

Leaving aside the technical question of how the victims can best be served in the long run, and by whom, there is some truth in this. But such a distinction is not so much analytical as it is a matter of distributive politics. The NGOs do represent a kind of 'classless left'—'classless' not only because their various positions do not depend on a homogenized class-interest interpretation of the foundations of politics, but also because their own agendas are diverse. When it comes, for example, to the pursuit and deployment of resources, whether economic or political, they are frequently in vigorous competition with one another. Traditional interest group analysis, with its emphasis on the dynamics of countervail, might have been expected, in fact, to predict their arrival. They are the political response of pluralists on the left to the globally accelerating power of pluralists on the right. Where either liberty or anarchy prevails, it might be argued, the pattern is ever thus.

CIVIL SOCIETY AND CANADIAN FOREIGN POLICY

In light of this discussion, we now return to the Canadian case. It was earlier observed that Lloyd Axworthy, as Minister of Foreign Affairs, has seemed to be somewhat more assiduous than his predecessor in honouring the substance, as well as the form, of the Liberal commitment to extensive constituency consultation in the development of Canada's foreign policy. It could be argued that this is the consequence, in part, of his having been the principal author of the commitment in the first place, but that merely begs the question of why he was so keen on making it. Part of the answer is obvious, and it relates to his general political orientation, which has been geared to the left of his party's somewhat elastic range of policy preferences. To that extent, there may have been a natural inclination to gravitate in foreign affairs, as in other matters, to a posture that would have the effect of opening up the policy process to the influence of 'classless left' elements. From the purely partisan point of view, the initiative may also have been regarded as a way of making the Liberals appear more congenial to constituents who would otherwise gravitate almost automatically to the New Democrats.

But once in office, Axworthy moved much more vigorously to support open consultation than a mere obeisance to his party's formal commitment would have required. Particularly intensive use has been made of the Canadian Centre for Foreign Policy Development (see Chapter 3 in this volume by Steven Lee) as a vehicle for promoting communications with NGOs, academics, and other interested constituents (not all of them necessarily specialists in foreign affairs *per se*). The purpose is not so much to encourage their direct participation in the making of foreign policy decisions as to kick up ideas and proposals that can facilitate innovative policy development. Among other things, the hope is that this will keep the DFAIT bureaucracy more fully aware of new opportunities for constructive intervention, and of potentially novel ways of pursuing them, that derive from the increasingly 'international' experience of Canadians outside the government apparatus.[18]

The Centre has not, of course, displaced the consultations that already take place through the department's operational offices. In the Global and Human Issues bureau, for example, there are frequent consultations with a wide variety of other players, including not merely NGOs and other elements in the voluntary sector, but also other federal departments, various agencies at the provincial level, and so on. As a case in point, a February meeting each year with NGOs and others who have a particular interest in human rights is part of the preparatory process leading up to Canadian participation in the annual proceedings of the Human Rights Commission of the UN.[19] Contact is also maintained with environmental groups, sometimes on their own and sometimes jointly with other stakeholder groups (e.g., representatives of the business community), and there are consultations with other combinations of constituency organizations, depending on the subject at issue. Similar discussions are ongoing, of course, with business interests and others (e.g., through the Sectoral Advisory Groups on International Trade, or SAGIT) in connection with trade policy and related matters, although officials operating outside the economic area seem to be quite conscious of the fact that the business community has powerful political assets that the NGO community lacks. This gives the department an additional rationale for taking particularly vigorous initiatives in reaching out to the NGO community: they help to level the field.

In addition to these well-entrenched practices, whose origins preceded Axworthy's accession to the Foreign Affairs portfolio, the minister has established at least two vehicles designed to give him at least some capacity for responding quickly and flexibly to what might be described as left-Liberal targets of constructive opportunity. Both are manifestations of his October 1996 'Canadian Peacebuilding Initiative'. The first (and most expensive) of the two, the Canadian Peacebuilding Fund, was established jointly with CIDA in the Pettigrew-Boudria period, with a budget of $10 million extracted from the agency's resources for development assistance for each of two fiscal years, 1997–8 and 1998–9. Founded on a conception of 'peacebuilding' as 'conflict prevention, conflict resolution of post-conflict reconciliation activities', the focus of the fund is 'on the political and socioeconomic context of the conflict rather than on military or humanitarian aspects', and its resources are deployed as 'an adjunct to local peacebuilding efforts', rather than as 'a substitute for them'. In rapid-reaction style, it is designed 'to respond quickly to urgent peacebuilding needs', with the objective of promoting 'local peacebuilding initiatives by acting as a catalyst'. Projects are approved jointly by the two ministers on the recommendations of an interdepartmental committee, and the 'funds are then channelled through implementing partners', with CIDA's Canadian Partnership Branch serving 'as a gateway for interested NGOs' (CIDA Peacebuilding Unit, 1997).

The second vehicle, more modestly endowed because it was established with DFAIT resources alone, is the Canadian Peacebuilding Program. With a budget of $1 million, its objectives are said to be threefold:

A) to build Canadian domestic capacity for peacebuilding through research, policy development, public consultations, and training;
B) to strengthen Canada's ability to influence the agendas of multilateral mechanisms for peacebuilding;
C) to support catalytic peacebuilding projects in countries, or in policy areas, that are not eligible for Canadian official development assistance (ODA) and therefore are not eligible for support from the Peacebuilding Fund.

So far, the program has been used to support the development of CANADEM, the Canadian Research Bank for Democracy and Human Rights; to help the Canadian Peacebuilding Co-ordinating Committee (described as 'a national network of Canadian NGOs/NGIs involved in peacekeeping activities in all their aspects' and as 'the principal interlocutor for the Canadian Government on peacebuilding issues'); to 'coordinate a series of regular government/NGO consultations on thematic and country-specific peacebuilding issues'; to support a seminar in Canada on 'Strengthening Regional Institutions for Conflict Resolution', so that senior representatives of various regional organizations can exchange 'experiences and lessons learned in conflict prevention and to develop more effective instruments to promote peacekeeping'; to fund 'the Canadian Peacebuilding Capacity Survey, aimed at developing a database of peacebuilding activities undertaken or planned by the NGO, research and academic communities in Canada'; and other projects of a similar kind (DFAIT Canadian Peacebuilding Program, n.d.).

These are obviously small-scale enterprises, reflecting the financial limitations of the DFAIT portfolio, as discussed earlier. Even so, the tapping of ODA resources for the Canadian Peacebuilding Fund, an Axworthy initiative, was viewed with a somewhat wary eye by the battle-hardened in CIDA. A diversion of a mere $10 million into a discretionary pot from which expenditures would be led by DFAIT was not a major problem in itself. But other diversions might follow, whetted appetites being what they are.

The interesting feature of these various developments, however, is not so much how they relate to the budgetary politics that sometimes intrude on relations between cognate departments of government but the manner in which they reflect the minister's approach to getting what he wants out of a department whose priorities (he may presume) differ from his own. It seems quite clear, in fact, that Axworthy's active cultivation of relations with the NGO and academic communities, in particular, is designed to provide him with a base of both political and informational supports that will allow him to force the process of innovation and to countervail, in at least some degree, the more conservative of his department's own inclinations. More succinctly, he has been using his natural 'left-agenda' constituency as a vehicle for promoting his purposes in the context of a professional bureaucracy that he suspects has 'right-agenda' preoccupations. And against heavy odds in a context of serious financial constraint, he has tried to develop some discretionary room for expenditures that serve both his constituency and his purposes.[20]

Close students of Axworthy's career should not be surprised by any of this. He used the same sorts of strategies, and for the same sorts of reasons, when he was Minister of Employment and Immigration in the period from 1980 to 1983. Anxious then to shift his ministry's emphasis from 'the prevailing "enforcement mentality to one that has a much higher sense of compassion," a shift that included an increase in the annual flow of immigrants', he 'resorted to outside task forces and reports from special advisers', considerably expanded his roster of personal 'exempt staff' (personnel recruited independently of the Public Service Commission), and routinely bypassed the formal bureaucratic lines of communication where this was convenient for the purpose of advancing his objectives. A similar pattern emerged during his tenure as Minister of Transport from 1983 to 1984 (Bakvis, 1991: 190). It is hardly surprising, in light of these and other earlier displays, that he should now be making so much use of the NGO community as a political buttress for advancing his own priorities. It can still be argued that these priorities are not reflective of the *real* action in Canadian foreign policy, which is ultimately dominated by economic preoccupations and interests. But if that action is essentially an irresistible given, the minister may well feel that he must make his own contribution by filling such other policy vacuums as he can find.

All this leads, however, to a final observation. As noted before, the transnational public interest NGOs, unlike their private interest counterparts, often represent the case for a form of state altruism, presenting themselves as a manifestation of the public conscience. It follows that, while their aspirations may have public *appeal*, they need not always embody the public *interest*. In these circumstances, the voluntary support of the pertinent minister, and preferably of the government as a whole, becomes critical. In its absence, these NGOs must rely for their influence on such pressures as their appeals can generate in the attempt to force the government's hand. But because their objectives are so distant from the preoccupations of other Canadian publics, their roots in domestic politics are correspondingly shallow. They are therefore easily dislodged. Issue-fatigue, the spectacular failure of a well-intentioned mission, the lack of visibly positive returns from expensive overseas initiatives, the diversion of an urgent issue of domestic politics (such as national unity), a serious campaign of opposition from a more securely grounded domestic interest—all these and more can quickly put such causes on the back-burner. Precisely because they *are* transnational, the NGOs can try to compensate for their vulnerability by allying themselves with appropriate interests and governments abroad, so that what Ottawa evades at home (if it is so inclined), it cannot evade in encounters overseas. But this is a much more difficult, and much less reliable, politics upon which to depend.[21] The fact remains, therefore, that the influence of many (not all) NGOs, unlike the influence, say, of the Alliance of Manufacturers and Exporters, is highly vulnerable to decay, and heavily dependent for its survival on a willing government's active sympathy. Thus, it is hardly surprising that many of those who have commented on the success of the land-mines campaign have made so much of the importance of what they have called 'partnership'. In the Canadian context, Axworthy needed the NGOs. But the NGOs needed Axworthy, too.

It is hard, therefore, to escape the obvious conclusion: NGOs are public interest groups with a transnational twist. Far from rivalling the state, and the state system, they must live in it.

NOTES

1. This should not, of course, be taken to mean that 'any construct will do'. The evidence has to fit.
2. The ready availability of so many apparently competing but actually complementary accounts of 'reality' explains why there is such a constant turnover in the 'great debates' that engage the attentions of theoretically inclined academi-

cians. They never run out of possibilities, particularly when their extraordinary capacity for fine-tuning even the most well-seasoned of explanatory instruments is taken into account.

3. Much of what follows is based on interviews with public servants and others in Ottawa who would prefer, for various reasons, not to be identified. I am immensely grateful for their assistance. I am indebted also to the Social Sciences and Humanities Research Council of Canada, as well as to The Norman Paterson School of International Affairs at Carleton University, for the financial assistance that made it possible for me to conduct the interviews in Ottawa. Herman Bakvis and Jennifer Smith of Dalhousie University's Department of Political Science both made helpful suggestions on matters of substance, as did several of the other contributors to this volume. I thank them all. Such nonsense as has survived in spite of their best efforts is, of course, my own.

4. During the 1994–5 foreign policy review, for example, Ouellet, like his colleague Roy MacLaren on the trade side, had made it clear that the findings of the Parliamentary Joint Committee and others who were involved in the consultative process would all be taken into account, but other inputs would be considered, too. The department itself was told to allow the committee to operate on a completely independent basis. An arm's length committee, however impressed by constituency representations, would have no more than arm's length influence (Stairs, 1995: 110).

5. This appears to have been a puzzlement to the editors of the *Globe and Mail*, who in their grading of cabinet ministers at the end of the year awarded Marchi (like the Prime Minister himself) an unflattering 'C'. The Prime Minister, they noted, had put 'a left-winger into a right-wing cabinet job'. Marchi had then started 'sounding like a right-winger, at least on trade matters'. That the editors of the *Globe and Mail*, of all people, should display even a mild disgruntlement at the spectacle of a 'left-winger' displaying right-wing habits of mind is a trifle mystifying. Perhaps they were responding to their other intelligence, which was that Marchi was 'apparently true to his left-Liberal heritage within the confines of Cabinet discussions' (*Globe and Mail*, 1998: A4).

6. There is, however, an ongoing tension between the government's desire to pressure foreign powers into meeting Canadian standards on matters related, say, to human rights, on the one hand, and its interest in promoting trading relationships wherever there is profit to be had, on the other. The problem is compounded by the insistence of so many human rights advocates that canons of fairness, consistency, and integrity all require that the same sauce must be given to every goose—that if the government sanctions one human rights violator, it should be sanctioning the others, too. The tension surfaced awkwardly, if briefly, at the Asia Pacific Economic Co-operation (APEC) meeting in Vancouver, in November 1997, when Axworthy made the case for modifying trade relations in accordance with human rights performance standards but was effectively contradicted in later remarks by the Prime Minister.

7. For a discussion on the amount and character of Canadian aid, see Chapter 8 by Draimin and Tomlinson.

8. The increase in personnel expenditures should not lead to the conclusion that salaries are rising. Given their qualifications, foreign service officers are horribly paid. This, when combined with the flattening of the department's employ-

ment-profile pyramid and the resulting decline in the promotion rate, has apparently contributed to a serious haemorrhaging of its personnel. The business community, among others, has been known to complain that public servants are overpaid and underworked. But in the highly qualified categories, if not in others, that same community shows every sign of being delighted to raid the government of its 'best and brightest'—at junior and senior levels alike—with the help of sometimes massively greater salaries and far more congenial conditions of work. The implications for the quality of Canadian government over the longer term are not encouraging.

9. The foregoing discussion is based on data contained in the department's *1997–8 Estimates*, which are freely available at the department's Internet Web site (<http://www.dfait-maeci.gc.ca/english/infoweb/estimates/menu-e.htm>). Interestingly, most of the financial tables in this material are organized in a way that conforms to the eight 'business lines' to which the department now claims that its activities are devoted:

- International Business Development
- Trade and Economic Policy
- International Security and Co-operation
- Assistance to Canadians Abroad (Consular Services)
- Public Diplomacy
- Corporate Services
- Services to Other Government Departments
- Passport Services.

The allocation of specific activities to these various notional endeavours is largely, however, an arbitrary enterprise. So, also, is the process of linking such activities in each case to a corresponding operational cost. In these circumstances, the room for creative accounting is considerable. Hence it is difficult to determine from the more general expenditure tables what is really going on. The most illuminating of them is probably the last (Figure 45—'Details of Financial Requirements, by Object'). This is because it organizes the data along traditional lines (personnel, goods and services, capital, and so on). Budgeting by objective, and then manipulating the way in which the objectives themselves are conceived and categorized to make them politically more fashionable and appealing, thus does not necessarily lead to transparency (and hence to accountability). Unfortunate political repercussions can sometimes ensue. In the present context, for example, there has been an obvious disconnect between DFAIT's advertised commitment to the 'projection of Canadian values and culture' abroad, on the one hand, and its actual expenditures on overseas academic and cultural operations, on the other. This reflects an awkward reality: the considerations that underlie the department's declaratory accounts of its policy priorities are very different from the ones that govern how it responds to financial constraint. Old hands will know why. But the inevitable result is that changes in the allocations of resources do not necessarily coincide with the priorities to which the department is formally committed. Charges of hypocrisy automatically ensue. Not surprisingly, constant repetition of this sort of display gives government and politics a bad name. MPs should take note!

10. See particularly the literature referred to in their note 2, p. 18.
11. It should be noted, however, that representation from the business community is often sparse and difficult to recruit. This was true in 1994, at the time of the defence and foreign policy reviews. The phenomenon almost certainly reflects the compartmentalization of many of the issues. Provided that it has in place the kinds of trade and investment policies it prefers, the business community is content to concede the conduct of most so-called 'civil society' issues to other players. There are occasional points of overlap (e.g., on the environment, and on human rights questions), but these are awkward matters for many businesses with countervailing preoccupations to address in public. In such cases, therefore, they presumably find it more convenient to register their concerns by routes that are more discreet. Those, incidentally, who wish to obtain a list of those who attended the 1997 National Forum gatherings can choose either to await the release of the *1997 National Forum Report* by the Canadian Centre for Foreign Policy Development or to consult the Internet at <http://www.cfp-pec.ca/english/nlist.htm>.
12. The debate over the degree to which the making and conduct of foreign policy ought to be an open and transparent process has a long history. In this century, it began in earnest with the Wilsonian response to the exposure of the 'secret treaties' that were thought to be among the causes of World War I. The brief experience of 'open diplomacy' at the Paris Peace Conference in 1919 resulted in second thoughts from such close students of the subject as the British diplomat, Harold Nicolson, and the American journalist, Walter Lippmann. In Canada, a comparable discussion ensued in the mid-1960s over the practice of what was called 'quiet diplomacy', particularly in the context of relations with the United States. Changes in the subject-matter of the international agenda and transformations in communications technology, however, are clearly giving the debate a new flavour.
13. It will be interesting to see how this works out in practice. The NGOs were particularly effective in building and sustaining the political foundation upon which the treaty was ultimately constructed, largely because their objective was so simple and so hard to contest and because they refused on principle to accept the notion that it could be compromised. The need to engage in the kinds of trade-offs that compromise normally requires was therefore avoided. The problem now, however, will be to maintain this unity of purpose in a context in which different NGOs have different priorities in their approach to dealing with the practicalities of implementation and in which they will rival one another in the pursuit of supportive funding from government sources.
14. The inclusion of NGO representatives on official government delegations, rather than the consultative process *per se*, gives occasional cause for concern among at least some DFAIT officials. In particularly sensitive cases, the department sometimes prepares two briefing books for its delegation, not one—the first for government personnel, and the second for the delegation's other members. At the same time, however, officials are beginning to rely more and more on NGOs for expertise and information, as well as for assistance in the delivery of their programs, and this is having an impact on how the two sides are coming to view one another. If the level of trust continues to grow over time, the differentiation of roles may weaken further. This, of course, raises other questions.

For example, some NGOs are likely to be trusted more than others—a reality already becoming visible to the various players, and that complicates the task of trying to keep everyone happy.

15. This distinction cannot be drawn too starkly, of course. It is part of the liberal thesis that the free and active pursuit of private interests ultimately maximizes the public interest, too. At the same time, NGOs that profess to be dedicated only to the service of a higher and selfless cause, whether at home or abroad, may none the less have important institutional, professional, employment, and other interests at stake that are deeply pertinent to their own welfare.

16. Great attempts are made, of course, to *establish* such links, even if the cause-and-effect connections are dubious on their face and impossible to verify by empirical means. Trying to do something about poverty in central Africa is an important and worthwhile endeavour, but this is not because the condition of the economy in Chad has much to do with the security of Canada. The reason for stretching the argument in this way is obviously to provide a foundation for legitimizing the expenditure of Canadian taxpayers' money on the welfare of non-Canadians.

17. The literature on this question is becoming voluminous. A useful, and very recent, review of the arguments and the principal titles, with particular reference to the case of environmental politics, can be found in Raustiala (1997).

18. The extent to which this is really happening is unclear. The impact is certainly uneven. Many line officials seem to regard the Centre as somewhat offside, since it does not appear to them to impinge very directly on their day-to-day activities. On the other hand, there is also some concern that the Centre's consultations with outside groups may occasionally have the effect of raising unreasonable or inappropriately directed expectations. In any case, from the point of view of setting priorities, its greatest impact is likely to come by way of the political leadership.

19. For an interesting discussion of the human rights example, see Bush (1996).

20. This is not an entirely new phenomenon, either. Douglas Roche, while Ambassador for Disarmament, tried many years ago to use his Consultative Committee for Disarmament and Arms Control Affairs in much the same way. He had less success. But then, he was not the minister!

21. It is pertinent to observe that relatively few governments, so far, take the NGOs as seriously as do those in Canada, Scandinavia, and the Low Countries. In many cases, moreover, such NGOs as may be in evidence are in fact the 'top-down' artefacts of government itself—acting, for example, as proxies for state authorities in absorbing assistance from overseas.

REFERENCES

Bakvis, Herman. 1991. *Regional Ministers: Power and Influence in the Canadian Cabinet*. Toronto: University of Toronto Press.

Bush, Kenneth D. 1996. 'NGOs and the International System: Building Peace in a World at War', in Fen Osler Hampson and Maureen Appel Molot, eds, *Canada Among Nations 1996: Big Enough to be Heard*. Ottawa: Carleton University Press.

Canadian International Development Agency, Peacebuilding Unit. 1997. *The Peace-building Fund*. Hull: Multilateral Program Branch. Brochure.

Department of Foreign Affairs and International Trade (DFAIT), Canadian Peacebuilding Program. (Web site/ongoing). *The Canadian Peacebuilding Program of the Department of Foreign Affairs and International Trade*. Ottawa: mimeo.

Globe and Mail. 1998. 'Grading the ministers from A to F', 1 Jan.

Kirton, John J. 1997. 'Foreign Policy Under the Liberals: Prime Ministerial Leadership in the Chrétien Government's Foreign Policy-making Process', in Fen Osler Hampson, Maureen Appel Molot, and Martin Rudner, eds, *Canada Among Nations 1997: Asia Pacific Face-Off*. Ottawa: Carleton University Press.

Liberal Party of Canada. 1993a. *Liberal Foreign Policy Handbook*. Ottawa, May.

————. 1993b. *Creating Opportunity: The Liberal Plan for Canada*. Ottawa, Sept.

McDougall, Barbara. 1997. 'How interest groups are shaping foreign policy', *Globe and Mail*, 1 Aug.

Molot, Maureen Appel, and Fen Osler Hampson. 1997. 'Asia Pacific Face-Off', in Fen Osler Hampson, Maureen Appel Molot, and Martin Rudner, eds, *Canada Among Nations 1997: Asia Pacific Face-Off*. Ottawa: Carleton University Press.

Raustiala, Kal. 1997. 'States, NGOs, and International Environmental Institutions', *International Studies Quarterly* 41, 4 (Dec.): 719–40.

Runnalls, David. 1993. 'The Road from Rio', in Fen Osler Hampson and Christopher J. Maule, eds, *Canada Among Nations 1993–94: Global Jeopardy*. Ottawa: Carleton University Press.

Stairs, Denis. 1995. 'The Public Politics of the Canadian Defence and Foreign Policy Reviews', *Canadian Foreign Policy* 3, 1: 91–116.

3

Beyond Consultations: Public Contributions to Making Foreign Policy

In the future our success internationally will hinge on our ability to harness the creative ideas in all sectors of Canadian society through an open policy process.

(DFAIT, 1997d)

Foreign Affairs Minister Lloyd Axworthy presents both the goal and the challenge for policy-makers and for Canadians. The goal is international success, including better foreign policy. The challenge is to open up the policy process to Canadians and their creative ideas. Since spring 1996, the Canadian Centre for Foreign Policy Development (CCFPD) has been a mechanism for engaging Canadians outside government in foreign policy-making and for promoting the value of public contributions inside the formal policy process. It is worth taking note of early experiments, lessons learned, policy-making changes, and the impact of public contributions on Canadian foreign policy.

ORIGINS

The Centre was created in response to the recommendations of the 1994 Special Joint Committee of Parliament review of Canadian foreign policy and the government's commitment to strengthen democracy in foreign policy-making. The committee called for increased dialogue with Canadians and greater public input to foreign policy-making. The government's 1995 Foreign Policy Statement promised that the voice of Canadians would be heard in the foreign policy process. This promise originated when, in opposition, the Liberal Party (and others) criticized the abolition of the Canadian Institute for International Peace and Security (CIIPS) and vowed to re-establish a public role in foreign affairs.

Public recognition that foreign policy-making has been too closed to outside participation and not transparent enough has been apparent for an even longer time. More than a decade ago, the 1986 Special Joint Committee of the Senate and of the House of Commons on Canada's International Relations noted, 'ultimately a foreign policy concocted in isolation in Ottawa poses inherent political risks. . . . Canadians are knocking on the door of this country's foreign policy with more messages to deliver: they want in' (Special Joint Committee, 1986).

In an indirect way the Centre for Foreign Policy Development is a descendant of the late CIIPS, poorer, but with a much more explicit role in policy-making. While CIIPS had a broad mandate that included public education on security and arms control, in-house and contracted research, a database, and library development, it had no formal role in policy-making. CIIPS, with $5 million per year and a staff of 42, was shut down in 1992. Its residual funds became the Co-operative Security Competition Program, $4 million over two years targeted to peace, security, and arms control research projects. A number of these projects were in the $100,000 range, yet they, too, had no formal link to policy-making (or public reporting).

FUNDING AND STRUCTURE

The Centre's budget ($1.5 million in 1997–8) is an accumulation of the last of this funding and some other consolidated Department of Foreign Affairs and International Trade (DFAIT) 'grants and contribution' funds. The Centre is housed at the department for two reasons. Thanks to partnership with the Policy Planning Staff, DFAIT provides considerable support in overhead and staff time contributions (accountant, contract management, policy planning contact officer, Web-site manager). As an autonomous but in-house agency, it has immediate access to policy-makers, providing opportunity for policy development consultations and the input of public views. This arrangement allows the Centre's four (non-public service) staff greater access and greater results than would be the case if the Centre were outside the Pearson Building.

GOALS AND MANDATE

The Centre shares a strategic goal with the Department of Foreign Affairs and International Trade, parliamentarians, and others: better foreign policy for Canada. The Centre's other strategic goal is process change in the development of foreign policy: adding to the menu of policy options and democratic legitimization of foreign policy by integrating a public dimension into foreign policy-making.

The new and important idea is public contributions to 'making' foreign policy. This is a departure from more traditional government consultations with stakeholders. To facilitate public contributions to policy-making the Centre has a specific role to:

- alert citizens to opportunities for public contributions;
- promote a policy development network across the country;
- support policy development capacity in civil society and with indigenous peoples;
- help integrate public contributions to foreign policy-making.

The tools available for these tasks include:

- the Minister's Advisory Board, which identifies issues that would benefit from public contributions to policy development;
- the policy options project fund (named to honour the late diplomat and teacher, John Holmes);
- funding to help strengthen policy capacity;
- the Centre's Web site for policy education, capacity-building, and policy conferences;
- the annual National Forum on Canada's International Relations.

There are both external (public) and internal (department) challenges to creating a window for public contributions to policy-mak-

ing. The public one, to identify people across Canada with an interest, or potential interest, in contributing to foreign policy-making, is
a priority. That priority includes the assessment of the capacity of
individuals and institutions to make policy-relevant contributions to
foreign policy-making now and in the future. These efforts include
cross-Canada discussions with university experts and researchers
to explore how they might add policy options to their academic
research. Round tables with NGO activists at the community level
explore how they might add policy options to their program and
advocacy work. The discussions promote collaboration among
experts and academics as well as between universities and NGOs.
They also have resulted in the creation of a network of policy development contact people and groups across Canada (with the recent
additions of Sherbrooke and Prince George, there are now 21 groups).
These groups generated and hosted over 20 policy development projects during the past year and are scheduled to host up to a dozen
events in the coming months.

Building the Web site has been another start-up task. The Web
site is being designed to provide policy development information,
links to other foreign policy sites, youth education (capacity-building in the next generation), and policy development conferencing
(starting in French with Francophone universities and NGOs in three
provinces). Working with the Media Awareness Network, senior high
school teaching units are available on peacebuilding (including land-
mines) and will soon be available on Canada-US culture and sovereignty issues.

Within the department, a special task has been to establish regular input and feedback with various branches of DFAIT to raise awareness of policy development needs, contribute public views to policy-making, and inform citizens about the results of their work and
continuing policy development. A consultation, comment, and feedback system is now in place and a working partnership has been
established with the policy planning staff. A member of the policy
staff is assigned responsibility for day-to-day contact with the Centre
staff and the Centre's national director works in close contact with
the policy director-general. The Foreign Affairs Minister and previous deputy minister, Gordon Smith, signalled the department's commitment to building this working relationship in a joint letter to all
its employees and embassies in December 1996: 'public generated
views and policy options will inform the Department's policy making and public efforts will add value to the Department's work. In

this way *policy advice from the Department to the Minister should include the results of public consultations.* . . . The creation of the Centre reflects an important commitment to a greater public role in foreign policy making' (Axworthy and Smith, 1996).

Feedback and communications include a regular newsletter with a mailing list of 3,000, Web-site information, brochures, published policy options results in co-operation with *Canadian Foreign Policy* and *Études Internationales,* and reports and occasional papers. Early tasks included an assessment of the strengths, weakness, and capacity of the academic community in international relations (Molot et al., 1996) and an assessment of the NGO community's capacity to engage in policy development by the NGO umbrella group, the Canadian Council for International Co-operation (CCIC) (Draimin, 1997).

PROJECTS

The Centre responds to three sources of policy project ideas: citizens, the minister, and the department. Citizens are encouraged to propose relevant policy development/policy option projects. The criteria for approving public proposals are:

- policy relevance (projects must contribute to and advance debate on Canada's foreign policy and its needs);
- involvement of youth (as researchers, trainees, participants, rapporteurs);
- collaboration among individuals and institutions and across the academic-NGO divide.

Because of time pressures and diminishing resources available to academics and NGOs, every effort is made to be encouraging and user-friendly. There is no formal application form. Project proposals can be short and need only to state clearly the policy relevance, goals, organization, and participants of the project. Efforts are made to discuss improvements to proposals with their authors before they are evaluated by the Project Committee. There is a funding ceiling limit of $20,000 for major projects and $10,000 for smaller studies and round tables. Citizen proposals are reviewed regularly by the Project Committee, which later recommends them to the minister for his approval.

From time to time, the minister calls upon the Centre to undertake projects to solicit public or expert views and to generate new

or reconsidered policy options. Projects responding directly to the minister's requests usually take the form of round tables that bring together department officials (including desk officers responsible for the subject), academics, other experts, NGOs active in the field, and sometimes senior journalists and MPs. The minister's Advisory Board identifies strategic and emerging foreign policy issues for the attention of the minister and, subject to the minister's approval, for public contributions to policy ideas and options. The Centre undertakes projects with the public (policy options papers, round tables, conferences, expert reports) to address those issues.

The Centre's mandate includes working with the department and providing assistance on issues that would benefit from public views or expert studies. From spring 1996 to January 1998, the Centre commissioned or supported 158 policy development projects (policy options papers, seminars, round tables, and conferences).[1]

THE NATIONAL FORUM

Since 1996, the Centre has been responsible for the annual National Forum on Canada's International Relations. The objective of the Forum is the generation of public views and policy ideas on a subject identified by the minister for public attention and discussion. The Forum differs from other policy options projects in that it is a discussion with a view to longer-term policy capacity-building in civil society. The Forum is designed to include a wide range of sectors of civil society: local community leaders, journalists, business, labour, and professional groups, as well as academics, experts, and foreign affairs NGOs. It also promotes broad participation from across Canada by holding the meetings in several cities across Canada. In 1997, the Forum meetings were held in Halifax, Quebec City, Kitchener-Waterloo, and Victoria. The National Forum is also meant to respond to the need for public debate in modern society, as was recently advocated by writer Michael Ignatieff: 'In place of public dialogue, we have celebrity chat shows. In place of a public forum for debate, we have nothing but academic conferences' (Ignatieff, 1997).

WHAT'S NEW?

The invitation to Canadians to contribute their creative ideas in policy-making is a new development in government and public policy.

This certainly goes beyond the more traditional government consultations with stakeholders and interest groups. While this invitation has been used from time to time on an issue basis or to develop a public policy approach or theme (environment, health, federal-provincial relations), the Centre's mandate and work comprise a new experiment in day-to-day process change in policy-making. It is an experiment that is attracting attention across government, as government itself seeks to respond to changes in political culture, reduced internal policy capacity, and a desire to 'do things different'. The Centre was noted in the governing Liberal Party's Red Book II: 'the Centre presents a new opportunity for Canadians to engage in the process that leads to foreign policy decisions' (Liberal Party of Canada, 1997: 102). Activities are also brought to the attention of the House of Commons Foreign Affairs Committee by the minister: 'examples of public diplomacy work to date include the establishment of the Canadian Centre for Foreign Policy Development and the National Forum on Canada's International Relations' (DFAIT, 1997b). Twenty-five senior government officials, from 15 departments, expressed great interest at a cross-government seminar hosted by the Privy Council Office (PCO) on 23 January 1998. 'Although you have only been in existence for a short time, the rapidly growing interest and participation of citizens in the Centre's activities is a testament to the potential future role of citizens in foreign policy making' (Walker, 1998).

Internally, there is a growing and sympathetic recognition that public contributions can add real value to policy-making. In 1998 the department created a new assistant deputy minister (ADM) for both policy and communication. In his first address to the department, ADM Hugh Stephens signalled the importance of the public-department partnership in policy-making:

> We are all involved in one way or another in both communications and policy. CPD (Policy Planning) is a central unit in the Department engaged in strategic planning. They, in cooperation with the Canadian Centre for Foreign Policy Development, with whom they work in close contact, also engage with the academic community, think tanks and the informed public on foreign policy issues. (Stephens, 1998)[2]

The Minister of Foreign Affairs regularly points out the value of public contributions to policy work and the work of the Centre, as he did in his opening speech to the international land-mines treaty-signing conference, 2 December 1997, and in his speech to the annual peacebuilding consultations, 18 February 1998 (DFAIT, 1997a, 1998b).

EARLY LESSONS

Many Canadians have the capacity, will, and even enthusiasm to contribute to foreign policy options and policy-making; they just need to be given opportunities to do so, along with a little support and encouragement. Nearly 400 people participated on their own time (and often own expense) in the seven National Forum workshops and four National Forum meetings in 1997. Others have been willing to assemble, sometimes on very short notice, for urgent policy options discussions or current affairs issues such as Bosnia, NATO enlargement, Nigeria, and Burma. Throughout communities from St John's to Victoria, experts, young academics, NGO activists, and others have organized and participated in policy option round tables, prepared option reports, and presented papers. While gaps exist in the university research and international relations policy capacity, as do limits to the capacity of NGOs to engage in policy work, many Canadians do 'want in' to foreign policy-making and are able to make valuable contributions to policy thinking and options.

Canadians in communities away from Ottawa and those in cities other than the largest ones have been especially active in their interest and participation. This may be because they have been, or felt, out of the loop in the past. Some foreign policy thinkers and activists in the capital and largest cities may feel they already have access to policy-making and policy-makers.

There is a need to continue to widen the circle of participation. Creative ideas from all sectors of Canadian society require special efforts for those sectors and those Canadians who have not had easy access to foreign policy-making in the past. In particular, women, young scholars, youth, indigenous people, northerners, new Canadians, and people in academic disciplines and professional groups not traditionally in the foreign policy loop need invitations and opportunities to participate.

In the past year, the Department of Foreign Affairs has been open and sometimes eager to respond to the added value that public contribution brings to policy thinking and policy-making. This is especially true for the younger officers and the department's policy community. There is a combination of reasons at work: recognition that the open policy process/democratization train has left the station (and those going anywhere should be on by now), recognition that pressures of time and reduced human resources result in severely limited capacity inside the formal policy-making process, and sincere interest in the creative ideas and options that can be generated outside government and the bureaucracy. This recognition of the value of public contribution is evident in the number and range of requests from the department to the Centre for public engagement to address policy issues. For example:

- Framework for human rights policy
- Education in the Americas
- Round table on Nigeria
- Development of international law
- Protection of the seas
- The future role of the ambassador.

Just as the line between foreign and domestic policy is blurred (and, increasingly, what is global is also local and vice versa), the distinction among foreign policy, aid policy, trade policy, defence policy, and a range of other policy areas with international implications (environment, labour, justice, etc.) is also less than distinct. This poses a challenge to policy-making and to public contributions to policy-making. Predictably, many Canadians do not make categorical distinctions among these related policy areas and overlapping departmental territories. Both inside and outside government, the time may be approaching for a comprehensive assessment of the relationships among the various elements of Canadian international/global activities, responsibilities, policies, and policy development, especially the broad overlaps in peacebuilding, human rights, democratic development, good governance, and the role of aid, NGOs, and civil society in international relations. Government-civil society partnerships in future activities may require greater public capacity and, therefore, government support.

A final note on early lessons. Leadership by the Minister of Foreign Affairs is essential in creating the opportunity for public participation in policy-making, in promoting process and culture change inside the department, and in ensuring that public contribution to policy thinking is given attention, value, and potential impact on policy-making. In an assessment of the 1986 foreign policy review, Don Page notes:

> It is through the minister that the most effective bridge lies between the public and the DFAIT and between the public and parliamentarians on the making of Canadian foreign policy. . . . Ultimately, even limited democratisation of foreign policy making cannot be effective without the strong leadership of the minister of Foreign Affairs who is responsible for making it happen. (Page, 1994: 595–7)

The early days and early experiments of the Canadian Centre for Foreign Policy Development support this conclusion absolutely. An open policy process and a public role in policy-making have been established as priorities by the minister and have been promoted by him at every opportunity. This leadership has created the opening for public participation and for department response. The goal is to create a permanent window for public participation and ongoing department response to openness and public diplomacy.

IMPACT

In the end, Canada's foreign policy is made by the Minister of Foreign Affairs, other ministers, and members of the cabinet. The goal of an open policy process and public contribution is to enlarge the menu of ideas, options, and policy choices for officials and ministers. Canadians who have undertaken and contributed to the 150 Centre projects and both National Forum meetings (1996 and 1997) have done that. For example, policy option papers such as *Women and Peacebuilding, Civil Society in Guatemala, NATO Enlargement,* and *Bosnia after the 1996 Elections* have generated policy developments.

Round tables that brought together experts and others from different backgrounds and sectors of society have been especially useful. The Burma round table in Vancouver in the spring of 1997 generated new options for the development of Canada's Burma policy later in the year. The Nigeria round table with Commonwealth NGOs defined specific opportunities for policy and international activity. A day-long discussion circle with indigenous peoples and others made innovative suggestions about the role of indigenous peoples in Asia-Pacific relations and in foreign policy, contributing to the appointment of Blair Favel as a special Foreign Affairs adviser on indigenous peoples, the creation of a Division of Aboriginal and Circumpolar Affairs within the department (February 1998), and the regular inclusion of Aboriginal youth in policy development events. Middle East round tables helped prepare the minister for his 1997 visit to that region as well as focused attention on refugee, water, and other peacebuilding issues. The Ottawa round table with Canada's education community contributed valuable ideas and specific content to Canada's negotiating preparations for the 1998 Santiago Summit of the Americas.

The 1997 National Forum on Asia-Pacific issues made several dozen recommendations. The value and impact of those recommendations were acknowledged by the minister within days of receiving the draft report:

> In about two weeks I will be tabling in Parliament a document that is the result of the National Forum that we have undertaken over the past year on Canada's role in Asia Pacific. And having read the report, I can confirm to you that it has a number of fascinating initiatives to propose. But what is important in that report—is that Canada should use all the tools at its disposal—look at the full array of contacts and exchanges, public and private, and work on a multitude of fronts in order to establish ourselves as a truly major player. (DFAIT, 1997c)

That report was tabled in Parliament on 6 November 1997, provided to the organizers of the People's Summit, and summarized in a full-page op-ed piece by the *Vancouver Sun*, and reportedly it proved useful to ministers in their bilateral talks with their Asian counterparts at the APEC meeting in Vancouver in late 1997.

The impact of particular ideas, options, and events will always be difficult to measure and assess. Policy-making in a democratic society must be pluralist, accommodating, and, in the end, accountable through ministers. What we can measure is the contribution of creative ideas by Canadian society to an open policy process. That contribution and that opening continue to grow. This is why the change is drawing attention at home and abroad.

The new British government, within a framework agreement to improve contacts and exchanges about foreign policy-making and other interests, has consulted the CCFPD extensively about a British national forum and a greater public role in Whitehall foreign policy (DFAIT, 1998a). In London on 2 March 1998, Axworthy noted these discussions 'on our experience and common interest in public participation in foreign policy, including NGO partnerships, public diplomacy and opening up foreign policy to democratic participation. I am pleased that these discussions are to continue in coming months, and wish the British government well in their thinking and planning towards a National Forum of their own' (DFAIT, 1998b). Likewise, the director-general of German foreign policy, Harald Kindermann, reported in January 1998 that 'after consulting our embassies around the world, it is clear you are in the forefront of recognizing the potential of civil society' (Kindermann, 1998).

Canadians have an enviable opportunity to contribute to open foreign policy at home and at the same time to set an example for others. Public engagement in policy-making and in the conduct of Canada's international relations is vital for the future of nation-building at home and influence abroad. Canadians everywhere are invited to take up the challenge of creative ideas and the opportunities of a more open foreign policy process.

NOTES

1. For further information, see the CCFPD Annual Report 1997 and Web-site updates.
2. A record of his full speech is also available on the DFAIT Web site.

REFERENCES

Axworthy, Hon. Lloyd, and Gordon Smith. 1996. Letter to all employees from the Deputy Minister and the Minister of Foreign Affairs, 6 Dec.

Department of Foreign Affairs and International Trade (DFAIT). 1997a. Address by the Hon. Lloyd Axworthy, Minister of Foreign Affairs, to the Opening of the Mine Action Forum, Ottawa, 2 Dec.

———. 1997b. Address by the Hon. Lloyd Axworthy, Minister of Foreign Affairs, to the Standing Committee of Foreign Affairs and International Trade, Ottawa, 27 Nov.

———. 1997c. Address by the Hon. Lloyd Axworthy, Minister of Foreign Affairs, to the Canadian Institute of International Affairs, Regina, 4 Oct.

———. 1997d. Address by the Hon. Lloyd Axworthy, Minister of Foreign Affairs, on Sustainable Development in Canadian Foreign Policy, Vancouver, 17 Apr.

———. 1998a. Address by the Hon. Lloyd Axworthy, Minister of Foreign Affairs, to the Canada Club, London, 2 Mar.

———. 1998b. Address by the Hon. Lloyd Axworthy, Minister of Foreign Affairs, to the opening of the NGOs Peacebuilding consultation, Ottawa, 18 Feb.

———. 1998c. Follow-up note, Cook-Axworthy, to 'Canada and the United Kingdom Towards the Next Millenium: A Joint Declaration', Ottawa, Jan.

Draimin, Tim. 1997. *Canada's International Cooperation: NGOs and Policy.* Occasional Papers no. 2, Ottawa: Canadian Centre for Foreign Policy Development, June.

Kindermann, Harald. 1998. German Foreign Affairs, Bonn. Notes from a meeting, 28 Jan.

Ignatieff, Michael. 1998. *Queen's Quarterly* 104, 3 (Fall 1997). Reprinted *Ottawa Citizen*, 15 Feb. 1998: D9.

Liberal Party of Canada. 1997. *The Liberal Plan-1997, Securing Our Future Together: Preparing Canada for the 21st Century.* Ottawa: Liberal Party of Canada.

Molot, Maureen, et al. 1996. *The State of Canada's Foreign Policy Research Capacity.* Occasional Papers no. 1. Ottawa: Canadian Centre for Foreign Policy Development.

Page, Don. 1994. 'Populism in Canadian Foreign Policy: the 1986 Review Revisited', *Canadian Public Administration* 37, 4 (Winter): 573–97.

Report of the Special Joint Committee Reviewing Canadian Foreign Policy. 1994. *Canada's Foreign Policy: Principles and Priorities for the Future.*Ottawa.

Special Joint Committee of the Senate and of the House of Commons. 1986. Report on Canada's International Relations, *Independence and Internationalism.* Ottawa.

Stephens, Hugh. 1998. Town hall speech to department employees, Ottawa, 16 Jan.

Walker, Jeff. 1998. Record of remarks, PCO Consultation Workshop, Ottawa, 23 Jan.

4

The Member of Parliament
and Foreign Policy

JOHN ENGLISH

For most of Canadian history, Canada's House of Commons had no committee on foreign affairs. When Paul Martin arrived in Ottawa in 1935, fresh from studying international affairs in Geneva and international law at Harvard, he discovered there was little that a government backbencher interested in foreign affairs could do to express that interest. He quickly made friends with some members of the bureaucracy who shared his foreign policy interests. One of them, Norman Robertson, encouraged him to ask a question in the House on Japanese politics. He did so and discovered quickly, in his own words, 'from the expression' on Mackenzie King's face 'that [he] had pulled a boner.' Mackenzie King, Martin later recalled, 'did not encourage private members to speak out on international relations.' The Foreign Affairs portfolio remained within the Prime Minister's Office until 1946; no separate committee on foreign affairs would be established until 1949, when King left office (Martin, 1983: 181).

Things are better now for private members. There is a Committee on Foreign Affairs and International Trade, and the Liberal Party Red Book of 1993 called for a participatory foreign policy in which members of Parliament played a central role. 'A Liberal government', the Red Book declared, 'will also expand the rights of Parliament to debate major Canadian foreign policy initiatives, such as the deployment of peacekeeping forces, and the rights of Canadians to regular and serious consultation on foreign policy issues' (Liberal Party of Canada, 1993: 109). Following another Red Book undertaking, the Liberal government after the 1993 election established a Special Joint Committee of the Senate and the House of Commons to Review Canadian Foreign Policy. The government responded specifically to the recommendations of the report and accepted many of them. The parliamentary committee has also produced significant reports on a range of matters, from circumpolar co-operation to child labour and government assistance to small business exporters, and, in this Parliament, the Multilateral Agreement on Investment. The Red Book commitment to consult Parliament before significant foreign policy decisions are made was initially met through House of Commons debates on each commitment, but, lately, the committee has held the debates and has received expert testimony from Foreign Affairs officials and others. The device has worked well and seems to command non-partisan support.

Until the mid-1980s, committees could study specific questions only when a minister authorized them to do so. This practice sometimes had embarrassing consequences. One committee chair noted for his controversial views waited for over a year for a minister's authorization. One day the phone call from the minister finally came. The minister asked that the committee undertake hearings on a highly significant topic. The chair quickly called together the committee. Just as the committee was assembling, the party whips rushed in and announced: 'The House has been dissolved.' The minister laughed last and no doubt heartily. In 1983 and 1985, however, committees gained the authority to meet year-round and determine their own agenda. Committees now have great freedom to choose topics and to study them with vigour and appropriate assistance. When one considers that Mackenzie King would not even allow a committee on foreign affairs to exist, one realizes that such independence is important for the MP interested in foreign policy questions.

There are other apparent improvements. When Paul Martin reflected on his colleagues in 1935 and those elected in Trudeau's first government in 1968, he claimed that the latter group was far more interested in broader questions and international aspects of Canadian politics than the members in 1935. The concern of the first Trudeau class was no longer the local post office or the appointment of a customs inspector. Today, the class of 1968 seems parochial when compared with members elected in 1993. In 1970, in a Parliament of 263 members, 16 were born outside of Canada, 26 had studied outside of Canada, and 17 had worked outside of Canada. In 1994, in a Parliament of 295 members, 29 were born outside of Canada, 50 studied outside of Canada, and 22 had worked outside of Canada. Canada now enjoys a Parliament with many members with international experience, a committee structure that permits considerable freedom, and assistance far beyond the wildest imaginings of Paul Martin in 1935. Why, then, do so many members of Parliament echo his frustration of those earlier times?

The statistics mask many differences as well as the major limits that face the Canadian member of Parliament, especially when compared with his/her counterparts in the United States and Great Britain. He/she faces such limits because of the character of the Canadian Parliament, the type of background MPs possess, the nature of constituency politics, the diversity of the Canadian population, and the committee system of Parliament.

Canada's Parliament meets approximately 60 per cent of the year, except in election years when the number of days in session drops considerably. The majority of members do not live in Ottawa but rather commute weekly to their homes, often many hours distant. The availability of virtually unlimited air passes makes this vagabond life possible, but it also makes sustained focus on particular issues most difficult. When one member of Parliament read Jack Pickersgill's memoir, *Seeing Canada Whole*, published in 1994, he remarked on how much more interaction there was among members in Pickersgill's day when committees were not interrupted by votes in the House and, most significantly, when members lived too far from home to permit them to fly home on weekends or, more accurately, on Thursday afternoon to return on Tuesday morning.

Members now have passes allowing them to fly anywhere in Canada with or without spouse or children, but they have neither budget nor 'points' that would permit them to travel outside of Canada. In Parliament itself, the multiparty system and, in this Parliament, the narrow majority mean that much time is occupied with voting, procedural matters, and other time-consuming parliamentary tasks. Moreover, party discipline prevents the kind of initiatives available to American congressmen and senators. Bill Richardson's active personal diplomacy as a congressman, which led to his appointment as the American UN ambassador, would not have been possible for a parliamentarian in Canada. One finds Richardson's counterparts in Britain, Germany, and especially Scandinavia, where less stringent rules on legislators' activities make personal diplomacy possible and where legislative tenure has tended to be much longer. Indeed, some Scandinavian legislators are absent for months at a time on international work.

Recent academic research supports this argument. David Docherty's *Mr. Smith Goes To Ottawa* concludes that 'Parliament acts to push members away from the capital and to pull them towards their local ridings.' The result is they spend more time in their constituencies 'at the expense of their more parliamentary-based responsibilities'. This tendency is particularly marked by recently elected members and is less prevalent among senior members, of whom there have been few recently (Docherty, 1997: 203).

Canadian MPs today have considerable interest in foreign policy, but when compared with their counterparts of 25 years ago they have, on the whole, less international background in terms of their education or work experience, limiting their understanding of the contemporary international system. Certainly, more have been born outside the country and in countries not represented in previous Parliaments. In 1970, seven of the 16 non-Canadian births were from Britain and five from the United States. In 1994, six of the 29 were born in Britain but only two in the United States. There were five from Asia and five from Italy alone. Members can speak of the Punjab, Croatia, Hungary, Armenia, and other countries with personal experience lacking in previous decades. The partisan nature of this experience tends to make government and opposition leaders nervous.

In the Parliament elected in 1993, the Official Opposition was a party dedicated to Quebec separation. The practice of earlier times, even in the days of Mackenzie King, of taking opposition members to international conferences became difficult, if not impossible, to follow. In the Parliament of 1949, several private members from the Liberals, the Conservatives, and the CCF attended the UN in the fall for six weeks. The technique was cleverly used by Lester Pearson to create non-partisan support for his foreign policy initiatives, even with John Diefenbaker in the early 1950s (English, 1993: 213–14). That practice rarely occurs now. In part, the explanation lies in the character of recent Parliaments. Bloc Québécois members, it was feared, might use the occasion of international gatherings or activities to promote the cause of separation. In the Parliament elected in 1997, the Official Opposition, the Reform Party, is wary not only of foreign travel by Members of Parliament but also of the cost of Canadian internationalism. The Reform Party refuses to 'pair', a practice whereby a member of the governing party and of the opposition agree to be absent for parliamentary votes, that allowed some independent initiatives by members. In some senses, the Reform Party reflects the isolationist tendencies found among neo-conservatives in the United States, who regard international institutions and commitments with deep suspicion. This mood and attitude have been largely absent from the Canadian House of Commons since the 1930s.

In the case of the Liberal Party, one finds many members with extensive international experience and interests. However, most of those members find their place in the cabinet or as parliamentary secretaries. Although Prime Ministers Mulroney and Chrétien both reduced the size of cabinet, the current cabinet is only slightly smaller than the early Mulroney cabinets. When over 35 members of the Liberal parliamentary group are part of the ministry, it means that nearly all of the Liberals with strong foreign affairs background are part of the government. About 25 of the remainder are parliamentary secretaries, whose workload and other activities prevent them from working in a sustained way on foreign policy issues. Parliamentary secretaries, for example, are forbidden to accept payment for travel to attend conferences outside of Canada and have no independent budgets to carry out such work.

These constraints are worth noting, but they are probably less important than constituency demands. Because of improvements in transportation and communication, the member of Parliament is now closer to his/her constituency than ever before. Indeed, it is astonishing to think that most constituencies had no members' offices until the 1970s. Members shared a secretary in Ottawa, and that secretary apparently could deal with most of their correspondence. The private member now has an office in the constituency, a personal office in Ottawa, and a staff of four or five employees. Free long distance telephone and fax are available, as well as electronic mail. In Parkinsonian fashion, the work has expanded to meet the staff available. Docherty's surveys of recent members revealed that members spend over two-fifths of their working time on constituency affairs (Docherty, 1997: 178). Today, the average MP in an urban constituency in Toronto, Vancouver, Calgary, and many other smaller cities receives approximately 100 calls per day. According to Toronto MP Dennis Mills, over three-quarters of his calls deal with immigration. In this sense, there is involvement with aspects of Canada's relations with other countries, but that involvement is very specific. In many cases, the presence of significant ethnic communities profoundly influences not only the interests but also the origins of MPs. Although Canada has always had members who have spoken for the interests of other nations such as Israel and Ireland, recent Parliaments have seen an explosion of the 'special interest' politician.

At the first meeting of candidates on foreign policy that I attended as a candidate just before the 1988 election, we began to talk about 'issues' when one of the senior members blurted out: 'The only Canadian foreign policy issue which matters in my constituency is an independent Punjab.' The candidates were not so startled as one might expect, for many had fought nomination battles where the support of the Sikh community was a valuable commodity. Indeed, Liberal membership lists before the 1988 and 1993 elections and the 1990 leadership convention bore testimony to the involvement in the party of Canadians from various areas who, unlike most Canadians, did have strong views on foreign policy issues in their area of origin. At my own nomination battle in 1987, the Kitchener Liberal Association had about 3,000 members, of whom about 800 were of Greek or Cypriot origin and about 600 of Sikh background. Their willingness to come out to vote on a cold December night was much more pronounced than was the case for other association members.

The diversity of the Canadian population has had several effects on the member of Parliament's interest in foreign policy. On the one hand, it has created the special interest MPs described above and particular focus on issues such as locating a Canadian consulate in Amritsar. On the other hand, it has provided new resources that draw Canadian attention to areas previously ignored and give Canada a capacity it earlier lacked when members were overwhelmingly French or British in origin. There are now lively debates about Greek and Turkish issues in which members of Greek origin and others with considerable Turkish populations in their ridings take their respective sides. On the whole, these debates probably have little impact on policy, but they are not ignored. Numerous international parliamentary associations now reflect these interests. The Reform Party generally refuses to participate in their activities, and many others regard their activities with a sceptical eye. For many years, overseas trips have been the method for purchasing loyalty for both government and opposition since party whips decide who participates. Whatever their political purpose, these associations are the principal contact that private members have with international fora.

The major associations receive parliamentary funding, although these funds have been much reduced since 1993. No longer can members take spouses and fly business class, and rarely is there a full delegation. Indeed, Canadian delegations to such parliamentary groups as the North Atlantic Assembly or the Parliamentary Assembly of the Organization for Co-operation and Security in Europe are smaller than those from countries of much less international weight. Moreover, there are problems of balance: there is a funded Canada-Israel Parliamentary Association but no Arab counterpart. Even more troubling are other associations, usually termed 'friendship groups', which have neither parliamentary funding nor sanction. The Canada-Taiwan Friendship Group creates obvious problems, if not for the members who take their spouses on first-class flights to first-class hotels in Taipei. The televised sight of Canadian MPs cavorting in the streets at a presidential rally during the last election in Taiwan no doubt horrified the Asia-Pacific desk at Foreign Affairs.

Some members devote much of their time to parliamentary association work and find it extremely rewarding. Senior members, often with earlier ministerial experience and less concern about re-election, tend to become chairs of these groups. Charles Caccia, for example, has given strong leadership to the Canada-Europe group. His extensive network of connections with European parliamentarians provided valuable assistance to the government during the 'Turbot War' with Spain. Similarly, another former minister, Sheila Finestone, prodded the Inter-Parliamentary Union to consider the land-mine ban in 1997. Members of Parliament, however, share places with senators who have more freedom and, in recent times, more funds to participate in these associations. Although senators and MPs tend to work well together, the tendency of non-Canadians to treat the senators as the 'senior' delegate members irks those from the Commons. Other difficulties arise from the time constraints on Canadian members, especially when parliamentary majorities are narrow or non-existent.

The Council of Europe, at which Canada gained observer status, has 60 days of meetings each year. One Danish parliamentarian told me that she spent about 80 days per year on parliamentary association business. Such a commitment would be unacceptable in Canada to one's caucus, one's colleagues, and, almost certainly, one's constituency. For Canadians, the substance of parliamentary association business does not merit the time of such commitments even though Europeans believe that in their case it does.

It could be argued that Canada does have a direct interest, similar to that of European parliamentarians, in creating links with the United States Congress. The Canada-United States parliamentary group was established, surprisingly enough, by John Diefenbaker and meets regularly for approximately three days to discuss bilateral issues. Discussions have been lively, but the group is less active than it was in the 1980s and certainly cannot be said to be an important component of the bilateral relationship. In the 1980s Peter Dobell, the founder of the Parliamentary Centre, which provides assistance to many groups, called for more exchanges and closer contact because of the growing importance of Congress. Legislators, he argued, have an 'instinctive' respect for each other, which could be useful in Washington where legislators traditionally have distrusted diplomats (Dobell, 1992: 131). His argument was cogent but had little effect. Canadian and American legislators meet rarely and accomplish little of substance together. North American integration may parallel Europe in some respects but not at the legislative level.

For most MPs, foreign policy in the sense one encounters in academic circles is of little concern or interest. There have been major debates on foreign policy issues in the 1990s. One thinks immediately of the Gulf War debate, when many members gave eloquent speeches and revealed serious study of the issue. There have also been good debates on peacekeeping commitments since the Liberals were elected in 1993, and many private members have spoken passionately and well on human rights issues. Reform MP Keith Martin's focus on land-mines has been rightly lauded, and Liberal MP Paddy Torsney's interest in women's issues on the international level is well known. But in the hundreds of pages of *Hansard*, these moments are relatively rare.

The most significant focus on foreign policy occurs in the Committee on Foreign Affairs and International Trade. That committee, chaired by Bill Graham, a distinguished international lawyer, has

had two subcommittees in recent times. One deals with trade matters, the other with human rights concerns. According to the Liberal
whip, more Liberal members ask to be members of the Foreign
Affairs Committee than any other committee. Since 1994, after the
Special Joint Review Committee reported, the Foreign Affairs
Committee has carried out numerous special studies, most of which
have been well received by the media. Some have enjoyed unanimous support, a rare quality for committee reports in recent years
and an indication that normal partisan spirits abate in foreign affairs
discussions. According to Peter Dobell, the Foreign Affairs Committee
has been highly innovative and, in many ways, has created new possibilities for parliamentary committees (Dobell, 1997).

Nevertheless, there are many difficulties with the committee's
operation. Some are specific to it; others are common to the Canadian
committee system. Specifically, the Foreign Affairs and International
Trade Committee has a vast territory to survey but little time to contemplate the details. Three ministers—Foreign Affairs, International
Trade, and International Co-operation—report before the committee,
as do two secretaries of state (Asia-Pacific and Africa and Latin
America). Ministerial appearances are brief and offer little time for
detailed questioning. Moreover, departmental business plans and
estimates are complex and vague. The most determined parliamentary efforts to find out what, for example, Canada is doing in and
about southern Africa are exercises in fact-finding futility. Because of
the range of issues, the committee is often required to 'fight fires' and
respond to immediate demands. Although the committee under
Graham's able leadership has carried out some important and valuable studies, long-range thinking and analysis about Canada's foreign
policy priorities have given way to the urgent though not necessarily most prescient issues. A high turnover of committee membership
means that final consideration of studies occurs after many of the
committee members who heard witness testimony have left.

Graham's frustrations are expressed in a broader sense in a report
of the Liaison Committee of Committee Chairs of the 35th Parliament,
which he chaired. In this report, the chairs of committees reviewed
the current effectiveness of committees in carrying out their functions. The review made several interesting observations. Reports, it
claimed, had little impact on policy. Indeed, the situation may have
been better before 1985 when committees could not set their own
agendas. In those days, 'Ministers who had proposed orders of ref-

erence, usually paid close attention to the committee's report because they and their advisers had selected areas of policy where the government was undecided on how best to proceed and was looking for advice.' Moreover, committee members of all parties proceeded on the assumption that their work would be taken seriously by the government since the government commissioned it (Liaison Committee, 1997: 9).

Even more troubling is the claim that the new power to select subjects of inquiry has meant that the committees pay less attention to the estimates than they did before 1985. A separate report by the Standing Committee on Procedure and House Affairs came to the same conclusion and issued an even more strongly worded recommendation that departmental estimates be given more than perfunctory attention. In the 35th Parliament, several members of the Foreign Affairs Committee tried to discover a way to examine CIDA estimates effectively. After taking advice from independent experts on development assistance, they considered focusing on one country and examining CIDA assistance in detail, but the task was beyond the capacity of a committee whose budget is meagre and whose members' time is limited. In assessing the reasons for the lack of 'conscientious scrutiny of proposed expenditures', the subcommittee on procedure and house affairs pointed to problems with 'rules and structures' (House of Commons, 1996: 81).

The Liaison Committee report, however, suggested the problems are not merely technical. Here some comparisons were made. According to the report:

> Compared to many other legislatures, where committee members have greater security of tenure, this practice of substantial change in committee membership mid-way through a Parliament inevitably means that Canadian members lack the acquired background and the institutional memory that contribute greatly to the quality of committee work. (Liaison Committee, 11)

The Canadian House has other unique problems. There are only 12 committee rooms to serve 19 committees, and the need for interpretation (translation) is absent in other parliaments. Although the multiparty system was not mentioned, the need to deal with five parties rather than two or three, as is the case in the United States and Britain, obviously complicates committee work. There are not only more parties but also more interest groups, and the demand to hear witnesses exceeds the time available to members. Those who appear before committees often find audiences that are a fraction of the full committee. There is, very simply, neither world enough nor time for adequate committee work (Liaison Committee, 11).

The private member in Canada has a shorter political life expectancy than his/her British counterparts and therefore less ability to undertake separate initiatives. In comparison with American congressmen, the Canadian MP lacks the staff, budget, and independence to carry out foreign policy initiatives or even sustained study of a foreign policy issue. Rewards in the constituency for foreign policy interest, with the notable exception of highly ethnic ridings, are rare. Moreover, in the view of the private member, the Canadian bureaucracy is unsympathetic to such initiatives and considerably stronger than its American counterpart. Whether true or not, the comment of a first-term Liberal member—'If the bureaucrats don't buy it, it's dead'—is a widely held opinion among private members on both sides of the House (Docherty, 1997: 234).

The rise of non-governmental organizations allows the bureaucracy to argue that there is an alternative to Parliament in gauging and understanding popular opinion. At the first National Forum on Canadian Foreign Policy, MPs were initially not invited despite the clear statement in the Red Book that the Forum would include 'representation from Parliament and non-governmental organizations, and members of the general public who have an interest or involvement in world affairs' (Liberal Party of Canada, 1993: 109). The chair of the Foreign Policy Review, Jean Robert Gauthier, complained loudly. Nevertheless, at some sessions at the 1994 forum, members of Parliament were not permitted to speak. At one session, the MPs took seats at the back of the room while others gathered around the central table. Someone asked the chair: 'Who are those people at the back?' She replied rather sternly: 'They are members of Parliament. They may stay but cannot speak.' Although NGO representatives and academics were vocal, Canada's elected representatives were stifled. The ambiguity of public representation was clear.

In summary, the Canadian MP is tied tightly to his/her constituency, and most have few incentives to pursue an interest in foreign policy issues unless there is a distinct constituency connection. Nevertheless, foreign affairs debates bring out the best in parliamentarians, and the Foreign Affairs Committee is prestigious for members. This contradiction probably signals that the present does not predict the future, just as it does not reflect the past. The upheavals of the Canadian party system in the past decade are mirrored in Parliament, a Parliament that is clearly in transition. For now, the fragmented Parliament brings a fragmented focus when Canadian parliamentarians look beyond their boundaries.

REFERENCES

Canadian Parliamentary Guide. 1970, 1993, 1994.
Dobell, Peter. 1992. 'Negotiating with the United States', in J.L. Granatstein, ed., *Towards a New World: Readings in the History of Canadian Foreign Policy.* Toronto.
———. with Lynda Chapin. 1997. 'Renewal at the House of Commons', *Parliamentary Government* (Nov.).
Docherty, David. 1997. *Mr. Smith Goes to Ottawa: Life in the House of Commons.* Vancouver.
English, John. 1993. *The Worldly Years: The Life of Lester Pearson 1949–1972.* Toronto.
Liaison Committee of Committee Chairs. 1997. 'Report of the Liaison Committee on Committee Effectiveness'. *Parliamentary Government* (Sept.).
Liberal Party of Canada. 1993. *Creating Opportunities: The Liberal Plan for Canada.* Ottawa.
———. 1996. *A Record of Achievement: A Report on the Liberal Government's 36 Months in Office.* Ottawa.
Martin, Paul. 1983. *A Very Public Life: Volume 1. Far From Home.* Ottawa.
Pickersgill, J.W. 1994. *Seeing Canada Whole: A Memoir.* Markham, Ont.
Standing Committee on Procedure and House Affairs. 1996. 'The Business of Supply: Completing the Circle of Control', Ottawa.

5

The Ottawa Process: Fast-Track Diplomacy and the International Movement to Ban Anti-Personnel Mines

ROBERT LAWSON

The signature of the convention to ban anti-personnel (AP) mines by 122 countries in Ottawa, 2–5 December 1997, brought to a close the first phase of an extraordinary exploration of the potential for new forms of multilateral diplomacy in the post-Cold War era. This was the Ottawa Process, a fast-track diplomatic initiative with the ambitious mandate to deliver what the vast majority of informed observers thought would be impossible—the negotiation and signature of a convention banning AP mines in less than 14 months. There were good reasons to be sceptical about this bold venture. The idea of a treaty banning AP mines had only begun to enjoy the support of a small number of states when, in his concluding speech to the first Ottawa Landmines Conference of 4–5 October 1996, Canada's Minister of Foreign Affairs, Lloyd Axworthy, invited the entire international community to join Canada in negotiating a convention to ban anti-personnel mines by the end of 1997. Fourteen months later Axworthy would welcome 122 signatory and 35 observer governments and over 400 representatives of international and non-governmental organizations (NGOs) back to Ottawa to sign the convention and to develop a global 'Agenda for Mine Action' to ensure the convention is fully implemented, mines are cleared, and mine victims are cared for.

Canada's leadership on the land-mine issue clearly demonstrated the veracity of Andrew Cooper's claim that, 'no longer hemmed in by the rigid contours of the Cold War, many of the fundamental aspects of Canada's foreign policy have opened up' (1997: 281). Axworthy's bold gamble and the successful diplomatic campaign it launched were an indication that the end of the Cold War has indeed witnessed the erosion of many of the traditional boundaries of Canadian foreign policy praxis. While the Ottawa Process deployed many of the traditional skills and practices of Canadian multilateralism it also brought to bear a unique combination of diplomatic strategies and tactics well suited to the opportunities offered by the new geopolitical landscape of the post-Cold War era. This chapter explores the 'nuts and bolts' of the Ottawa Process—the strategies, the tactics, the coalition-building, and the information-based diplomatic tools of this fast-track diplomatic initiative.

A WEAPON OF MASS DESTRUCTION
MOVING IN SLOW MOTION

While AP mines have been used extensively by military forces for decades, it was not until the late 1980s that Red Cross war surgeons and NGO field staffs began alerting the world to the fact that this relatively obscure tactical weapon had mutated into a weapon of mass destruction. However, this was a weapon of mass destruction moving in slow motion—taking one victim at a time in thousands of separate locations in almost every region of the world. Costing as little as US $3 to produce, AP mines were remarkably inexpensive and could be easily deployed in large numbers. United Nations experts estimated that there could be as many as 100 million land-mines deployed throughout 70 countries—most of them in the developing world.[1] By the time the first comprehensive reports on AP mines were published in the early 1990s it was clear that as many as 25,000 people, the majority of whom were innocent women and children, were being killed or injured by AP mines every year. The world had just begun to reap the bitter harvest of millions of AP mines sown during conflicts that had already become synonymous with human suffering—Afghanistan, Somalia, Croatia, Angola, Cambodia, Mozambique, and Bosnia.

Beyond these already grim statistics an even darker picture began to emerge. Land contaminated by AP mines can only be cleared in one of two very costly ways. Manual or mechanical mine clearance is a slow, dangerous, and expensive business, costing as much as US $800 to clear a single mine. The alternative is even more costly, clearing mines one leg or arm at a time. Until mines are cleared, massive tracts of land remain useless for farming, settlement, or economic development, thereby adding starvation, refugee flows, and poverty to the list of difficulties affecting countries struggling to recover from war. The true cost of AP mines to the international community will be billions of dollars in mine clearance costs, victim assistance, and lost socio-economic development opportunities.

THE GROWTH OF THE MOVEMENT TO BAN ANTI-PERSONNEL MINES

AP mines do not distinguish between soldiers or civilians. Nor do they cease to be a hazard to civilians once wars have ended. In short, AP mines are, by design and effect, indiscriminate; over 70 per cent of AP mine casualties over the past decade were civilians. A United Nations Diplomatic Conference convened in 1977 to negotiate an additional protocol (known as the CCW—Convention on Certain Conventional Weapons) to the 1949 Geneva Convention had clearly recognized that the use of AP mines should be restricted under international humanitarian law.[2] While the 1977 CCW Land-mines Protocol placed restrictions on the use of AP mines, by the early 1990s it was clear that these restrictions were not reducing their impact on civilians. The first to call for a total ban on AP mines were members of the NGO community. In the fall of 1991 the Vietnam Veterans of America Foundation and Medico International launched an advocacy campaign to co-ordinate the efforts of NGOs pressing for an AP mine ban. By the fall of 1992 these organizations were joined by Handicap International, Human Rights Watch, the Mine Advisory Group, and Physicians for Human Rights to form the International Campaign to Ban Land-mines (ICBL).

The political terrain of the issue had begun to shift by the time the 54 signatory states of the 1977 CCW Landmines Protocol began a formal review of its provisions in the fall of 1995. Under the leadership of Senator Patrick Leahy (D-V), the United States had started the trend towards unilateral measures to restrict the trade in AP mines, enacting a moratorium on the export of AP mines in October 1992 (Williams, 1994). The International Committee of the Red Cross (ICRC) had launched an unprecedented worldwide media advocacy campaign in favour of a total AP mine ban. The ICBL, by then representing over 350 NGOs from 23 countries, used the Vienna meeting to launch a sophisticated range of pro-ban public advocacy activities. UN Secretary-General Boutros Boutros-Ghali supported a comprehensive ban in his address to the CCW conference. However, despite the growing pressure for a total ban, what emerged from the CCW review conference were incremental improvements to a protocol that continued to legitimize the use of AP mines. Under pressure from Canada's own pro-ban NGO, Mines Action Canada, on 17 January 1996, DFAIT officials announced Canada's support for a total ban on AP mines. Until such a ban could be achieved Canada would observe a unilateral comprehensive moratorium on the production, transfer, and use of AP mines. Canadian officials also began to attend discrete meetings on the margins of the CCW review conference with NGO representatives and other pro-ban states to explore the potential for a new track of diplomatic action on the AP mine issue.[3] At the conclusion of the review conference in Geneva on 3 May 1996, Canada announced that it would host an international meeting to develop a strategy for achieving a comprehensive ban on AP mines.

THE FIRST OTTAWA LANDMINES CONFERENCE

Canadian officials would spend the summer and early fall of 1996 engaged in an intensive series of consultations on the form and content of the Ottawa conference with representatives of the NGO community as well as like-minded and not-so-like-minded states. Caught between a need to clearly identify pro-ban states and the equally important objective of maintaining a degree of political engagement with more sceptical members of the international community, it was decided that states would be invited to participate in the Ottawa conference on the basis of 'self-selection'. A draft Final Declaration of the Ottawa conference was widely circulated prior to the conference and states willing to publicly associate themselves with its content were invited to attend the conference as participants. Those who could not support the Declaration would be welcomed as observers. Ultimately, 50 states, including the United States, France, and the United Kingdom, publicly supported the Ottawa Declaration, which included 'a commitment to work together to ensure the earliest possible conclusion of a legally binding international agreement to ban anti-personnel mines' (Canada, 1996).

The Ottawa conference of 4–5 October 1996, 'Towards a Global Ban on Anti-personnel Mines', brought together 50 participants and 24 observer states as well as a wide range of international and non-governmental organizations. Described as an 'exercise in unconventional diplomacy', the conference featured ministers and officials sharing plenary and workshop platforms with mine victims, parliamentarians, and representatives from international and non-governmental organizations active in advocacy for the ban, mine clearance, and victim assistance. All participants were invited to contribute to an 'Agenda for Action on AP Mines', which listed a number of activities to be undertaken by conference participants to build political will for an AP mine ban. The real news of the conference was made during Axworthy's dramatic closing speech, when he established a deadline for action on the ban, inviting states to work with Canada in negotiating a treaty banning AP mines to be signed in Canada by December 1997.

Axworthy's challenge received the immediate endorsement of the ICRC, the UN Secretary-General, and the ICBL in the form of a standing ovation, an honour not often bestowed upon foreign ministers by members of the NGO community. However, there was no shortage of critics within the diplomatic corps who questioned the wisdom of rapid movement towards a ban as well as the unilateralist nature of Canada's gambit. Even many of those who were supportive of a ban were sceptical, arguing that it would be simply impossible to negotiate a convention banning a weapon in widespread use by dozens of states in less than 14 months. Prominent critics of the Ottawa Process included all five of the permanent members of the UN Security Council. Russia and China rejected the very notion of an AP mine ban. While the US, the UK, and France, in principle, were supportive of a ban they were all openly critical of the Ottawa Process, arguing that this 'coalition of the angels' would have little practical effect on the global AP mine crisis. Informed observers noted that these states shared more than a distaste for the Ottawa Process and its strategic alliance with the NGO community. Each of these states continued to reserve the right to use AP mines. Each also favoured the negotiation of an AP mine ban treaty within the Conference on Disarmament in Geneva, a consensus-based forum that effectively gives each of them a veto over the pace of progress towards a ban.

While Canadian officials fully expected criticism from several quarters, they were, in some respects, more concerned about practical issues raised by sceptical potential allies. The Declaration and Agenda for Action on AP Mines that emerged from the Ottawa conference indicated a relatively high degree of political support for the concept of the ban in almost every region of the world. Canada's growing partnership with the ICBL and ICRC held out the possibility of an even broader mobilization of public will for a ban convention. The ban campaign had also begun to penetrate popular culture—DC Comics had enlisted Superman as well as Batman in the fight against AP mines.[4] However, what was missing was a vision of how all of this political will could best be focused on the complex task of preparing for, and bringing to conclusion, a multilateral negotiation to ban land-mines within a very tight time frame.

Part of the solution was provided by the government of Austria. One of the earliest supporters of the ban, Austria had actually arrived at the Ottawa conference with a rough draft of an AP mine ban convention. In the wake of the Ottawa conference, Austria agreed to become the official 'pen' for the draft ban convention and to host an international experts' meeting in late February to begin broad consultations on the draft convention. The Ottawa Declaration had already named Belgium as the host of the next international meeting on AP mines, to be held in June 1997, providing another potential opportunity for consultations on the draft ban convention. The final piece of the negotiation puzzle was provided by Norway, which offered to host the formal negotiation of the ban convention in the fall of 1997.

In parallel with efforts to solidify the diplomatic negotiation track of the Ottawa Process, Canadian officials were also engaged in a series of consultations with coalition partners on how best to convert a general level of political will for a ban into concrete support for the Ottawa Process from key governments and regions. Research conducted by DFAIT officials on the AP mine policies of the world's governments indicated that, given the right conditions, potential support for the AP mine ban treaty could peak at somewhere over 100 states. In theory at least, this level of support was possible. A total of 156 states voted on 10 December 1996 to support United Nations General Assembly Resolution 51/45s, which called on states 'to pursue vigorously an effective, legally-binding international agreement to ban the use, stockpiling, production and transfers of anti-personnel landmines with a view to completing the negotiation as soon as possible' (UN, 1996). In practice, however, few were willing to commit to a deadline and a treaty that was not even on the table. On a regional basis the greatest potential for growth in support appeared to be in Europe, Africa, and the Americas.

GLOBAL OBJECTIVES, REGIONAL STRATEGIES

What was clearly needed and what was soon developed by Canada was a comprehensive 'critical path' to break down the blizzard of global diplomatic activities into a coherent road-map of bilateral and multilateral opportunities for Canada and its coalition partners to highlight the AP mine problem and emphasize the Ottawa Process solution. While the Ottawa Process would remain global in its scope and objectives, it was clear that support for the process could most easily be generated through an integrated series of regional strategies. In this respect it also became clear that one of the most important objectives of the Ottawa Process should be to engage mine-affected regions in the march towards the ban. Getting mine-affected states to support the ban would be the most direct way to prevent a worsening of the AP mine crisis; states that had already deployed mines would halt any further deployments. The active participation of southern mine-affected states would also be critical to the coalition's efforts to prevent the emergence of a North-South split on key issues related to the ban.

The ICBL and ICRC had already planned major conferences in Africa for February and April of 1997. Canadian consultations with the Organization of African Unity (OAU) in November 1996 yielded an agreement that it should work with Canada, South Africa, and the ICBL and ICRC to host an Africa-wide Land-mines Conference in Kempton Park, South Africa, in late May 1997, just a few weeks before the OAU summit scheduled for Harare in early June. As with other regions, Canadian officials worked to take advantage of the sequence of government/NGO-sponsored African meetings to progressively increase the familiarity with and support for the Ottawa Process. The draft Austrian ban convention was circulated at each of the three meetings prior to Harare. The final declarations of the Maputo (see below) and Kempton Park conferences would express support for the Ottawa Process and urge participants to become active in the other multilateral meetings leading to the negotiations in Oslo and the signature of the ban treaty in Ottawa.

An early and critical victory for the African strategy was South Africa's move to a unilateral ban on AP mines, announced on the eve of the ICBL's 4th International NGO Conference on Landmines, held in Maputo, Mozambique, 25–8 February 1997. Mozambique announced its support for the ban during the conference itself. Attended by 450 NGO representatives from 60 countries, the Maputo conference was a critical juncture in the rapidly evolving partnership between Canada and the NGO community. The final declaration of the Maputo conference would commit the full support of the ICBL and its over 800-member organizations to the Ottawa Process. It would also reinforce the campaign's African strategy, calling on the South African Development Community (SADC) to 'take all measures to make the region a mine free zone' and urged the member states of the OAU to use the upcoming 'OAU Landmine Conference in South Africa in May and the OAU summit in Zimbabwe in June' to implement the OAU resolutions urging a continent-wide ban on anti-personnel land-mines (Final Declaration of the 4th International NGO Conference on Landmines, 1997: 3). With the active support and engagement of South Africa and the OAU, the African strategy was clearly on track. By the end of the Kempton Park conference on 19–22 May 1997, a total of 43 of the 53 members of the OAU would pledge their active support for the Ottawa Process.

Regional strategies for the Americas, Europe, and Asia had also begun to yield results. Building on previous resolutions by the Organization of American States, the foreign ministers of Central America and the Caribbean Community and Common Market (including several mine-affected states) declared their full support for the Ottawa Process, the first regional grouping to do so. Regional and subregional government/NGO conferences to build political will for the Ottawa Process were organized for Stockholm, Sydney, Manila, Ashgabat, and New Delhi.

In total, some 10 global, regional, and subregional multilateral meetings would be held in the 11 months prior to the fall 1997 Oslo negotiations, each designed to pressure national decision-making on the AP mine ban issue.[5] These meetings would also seek to combine state-led diplomatic activism with NGO-led advocacy through the media and a growing number of prominent supporters of the ban movement, including Princess Diana, Archbishop Desmond Tutu, Gracia Machel (wife of the late president of Mozambique, now residing in South Africa), former US President Jimmy Carter, and the new Secretary-General of the UN, Kofi Annan.

Canadian diplomats, who take pride in their skills at quiet diplomacy, provided dozens of backgrounder and on-record briefings to key journalists in the US, the UK, France, Australia, and Japan. An AP mine ban newsletter was developed and widely circulated to all missions and multilateral meetings. Editions of the newsletter were loaded onto a Web site linked to dozens of pro-ban sites maintained by NGOs. A dramatic five-minute Ottawa Process advocacy video was produced and hundreds of copies circulated in multiple-language formats. Behind the scenes, Canadian representatives abroad made countless formal representations to their host governments on the AP mine issue, tracking the development of their policies and urging them to attend Ottawa Process meetings.

By May 1997, the diplomatic negotiation track of the Ottawa Process was well launched and being co-operatively managed by a core group of states, including Austria, Belgium, Canada, Ireland, Germany, Mexico, the Netherlands, Norway, the Philippines, South Africa, and Switzerland. A surprising 111 states attended the first formal consultations on the ban convention held in Vienna on 12–14 February 1997, to 'start the speedy elaboration of a draft text that can serve as a basis for negotiations' (DFAIT, 1997a: 2). The second meeting on the draft text, hosted by Germany in Bonn on 24–5 April 1997, focused on its compliance provisions and attracted 120 states.

Momentum behind the Ottawa Process was clearly growing as governments considered their participation in the next global meeting in the Ottawa Process, the Brussels conference scheduled for 24–7 June 1997. Since mid-March the number of governments pledging their support for the Ottawa Process had grown from 30 to 70. The NGO communities in the UK and France had succeeded in making an AP mine ban an election issue—with both countries becoming Ottawa Process supporters under their new governments. United States officials had promised that they would be reviewing their AP mine policy in July. The diplomatic centrepiece of the Brussels conference was a political declaration that locked in the commitment of states to the final stages of the Ottawa Process—the Oslo negotiations and the signature of the ban treaty in Ottawa in December. Featuring extensive exchanges of views on the draft Austrian text, which would now be forwarded to Oslo as the basis for negotiations, the Brussels conference attracted a total 155 states, 97 of which would sign the Brussels Declaration. Still, many doubted how many of these states would be prepared to sign a legally binding international convention as opposed to a political declaration.

THE OSLO NEGOTIATIONS

The Brussels Declaration would also become the price of admission for the Oslo negotiations. Once again states would be invited to self-select their participation in the next stage of the Ottawa Process, in this case on the basis of a Declaration that made it quite clear the objective of the Oslo negotiations was to achieve a 'comprehensive ban on the use, stockpiling, production and transfer of anti-personnel mines' (Brussels, 1997: 1). The Brussels conference also provided an opportunity for Norway and its core group allies to begin the delicate process of putting in place the diplomatic framework for the actual negotiations due to take place 1–21 September. The name of a highly skilled and internationally respected South African diplomat and senior African National Congress official, Ambassador Jacob Selebi, was circulated as the candidate of choice of the Ottawa Process core group for the presidency of the Oslo conference. Draft rules of procedure for the conference were circulated, based on standard rules of procedures for UN committees, which would enable decisions to be taken by two-thirds vote if consensus could not be achieved.

The ICBL and ICRC used the Brussels conference to launch an aggressive communications campaign focused on the media and state representatives preparing for the Oslo negotiations. Fearing that the rapid growth in the number of Ottawa Process participants would erode the core consensus on the need for a clear and unambiguous ban treaty, the central message of the ban campaign in the final months before Oslo would emphasize the need for a treaty with no exceptions, no reservations, and no loopholes. The concerns of the NGO community appeared to be justified in late August when the US announced its intention to attend the Oslo negotiations as a full participant. In a widely circulated letter to other governments, US *enticism resistance and or reluctance* Secretary of State Madeleine Albright made it clear that the US would be seeking at least five substantive changes to the draft Austrian text. Specifically, US negotiators would be instructed to seek an exception for potential US AP mine use in Korea, a fundamental change in the definition of an AP mine, a delay in the entry-into-force (EIF) of the convention, a strengthened verification regime, and a supreme national interest clause that would enable parties to the convention to withdraw rapidly from their obligations when their national interests were threatened (Albright, 1997: 18–20). Media reaction to the US announcement that it would join the Ottawa Process was generally characterized by cautious optimism, with *The Economist* noting that the 'new convert' should be welcomed as long as 'its real intent is not to sabotage' (1997: 14).

The drama surrounding the beginning of the Oslo negotiations was heightened by the tragic death of one of the ban campaign's most prominent supporters, Princess Diana, on the day before the opening ceremony on 1 September 1997. With 87 full participants and 33 observer states at the table, members of the core group were relieved as the conference formally elected Ambassador Selebi to the conference presidency and adopted the agenda and rules of procedure. With the formal diplomatic framework for the negotiations finally in place, including, if necessary, the option of voting to break deadlocks, Ambassador Selebi moved quickly to establish what would prove to become a diplomatically and administratively efficient plan for the conference. Areas of difficulty would be clearly identified within the first 24–48 hours of the conference and divided for further consultation and problem-solving drafting between Selebi and five 'Friends of the Chair'—Austria, Brazil, Canada, Ireland, and Mexico (Report of the Diplomatic Conference, 1997).

The central fault-line of the Oslo conference quickly formed around the three most problematic US proposals—the Korean exception, the deferral of EIF, and changes in the AP mine definition, the *resistance* core of what US negotiators described as an 'all or nothing package'. The potential for a compromise with the US appeared to be greatest on the issue of a deferral period, which could, in theory, provide time for US forces in Korea and elsewhere to make the transition to an AP mine-free doctrine and force structure. Here the United States enjoyed the public support of Australia, Japan, Poland, and Ecuador, as well as the private sympathy of an unknown, but probably quite large, number of states that saw the political and military-security value of having the last superpower sign the ban convention. Precedent had been established by the 1997 CCW Landmines Protocol, which provided signatories with the option to defer compliance with key provisions for up to nine years. However, the deferral compromise had at least two important strikes against it. Firstly, from a political perspective, a Korea-specific deferral period that would provide the US with special treatment was a non-starter. Yet a more broadly defined deferral article could potentially undermine the practical effect and political credibility of the entire ban convention. Secondly, but perhaps of more importance, the exploration of potential compromises remained virtually impossible as long as US negotiators were unable to break their package, allowing the deferral issue to be discussed in isolation from the vastly more problematic issue of the definition of an AP mine.[6]

The US delegation was quite transparent about its desire for a fundamental change in the definition of an AP mine, noting that the current definition would prevent the future use of US mixed-mine systems such as 'Gator' and 'Volcano', which were pre-packaged and designed to deploy a mix of 'short-lived' AP mines and anti-tank mines (Report of the Diplomatic Conference, 1997). US negotiators argued that AP mines within these mixed systems should be defined as 'anti-handling devices' since they performed essentially the same function as the anti-handling devices that other states attached to their anti-tank mines to protect them against enemy mine-clearance personnel. However, the US systems were not actually attached to the anti-tank mines they were designed to protect and thus would function exactly like AP mines, irrespective of their proximity to the anti-tank mines. Moreover, a ban treaty that legalized the use of AP mines to protect anti-tank mines would be legalizing a practice widely cited by military authorities around the world as the real reason for deploying AP mines in the first place. The short-lived, high-tech nature of the US mines did not make a difference. As one prominent US ban supporter, Senator Patrick Leahy, noted, 'an effective international agreement that is based on stigmatizing a weapon cannot have different standards for different nations' (Leahy, 1997: 1). A number of scheduled and 'special' consultations devoted to the definition problem failed to reveal any real support for the US position.

By the second week of Oslo it appeared that the inability of the US team to break open their package was a reflection of a policy stalemate in Washington. Significant proportions of the media and public, along with a bipartisan congressional team led by Senator Leahy, were calling on President Clinton to 'seize the moment' to provide 'moral leadership' in the drive for the AP mine ban (Leahy, 1997: 1). At the same time, Clinton received an unprecedented 'Open Letter' from 10 retired four-star American generals urging Clinton to reject the emerging ban convention (Barrows et al., 1997). Senator Jesse Helms (R-NC) also weighed in with a letter calling on Clinton to recall the US delegation if the other delegations failed to 'recognize that the US negotiation position in Olso is our *bottom line . . . not a starting point* for debate.' Helms would also argue that the negotiations had become a 'soap box forum for anti-American rhetoric', while the press release attached to the 'Open Letter' to Clinton complained about the 'contempt being expressed by those running the Oslo negotiations for the United States' (Helms, 1997). In the absence of any significant movement by the US during the second week, negotiators moved on to resolve a number of other outstanding issues. After a three-day weekend the US package remained intact. Finally, despite a 24-hour delay in movement towards closure of the conference to provide Washington time to reconsider its bottom line, the package remained unbroken and the US end-game was never reached.

Notwithstanding the views of Jesse Helms, there was little that was anti-American or contemptuous about the diplomatic or NGO activities within and surrounding the Oslo negotiations. On the diplomatic side, the US was simply unable to divert or reverse the political momentum of a multilateral 'ban-wagon' effect that had been gaining strength for several months. Highly mobilized mine-affected regions such as Africa and Central America had, given their relative numbers, become powerful advocates for a clear and unambiguous ban convention. For their part, the ICBL and ICRC had waged a sophisticated communications campaign that delivered a blizzard of pro-ban newsletters, leaflets, posters, fact sheets, press releases, and press conferences, as well phone, radio, and television interviews to a highly attentive and well-informed international media. Foreign Affairs Minister Axworthy had argued in his address to the Oslo NGO Forum that the government-civil society coalition behind the Ottawa Process had indeed developed the 'power to change the dynamics and direction of the international agenda' on the AP mine issue (DFAIT, 1997b: 1). On 17 September, the US team announced that it had no further proposals to make to the Oslo conference. The following day Ambassador Selebi brought formal closure to the Oslo conference against the backdrop of a prolonged standing ovation. A long and difficult journey begun by a few visionary NGOs in the early 1990s had produced what no one had expected—a clear and unambiguous convention totally banning AP mines, the first treaty in history to ban a weapon that has been in widespread use by military forces throughout the world for decades.

THE JOURNEY BACK TO OTTAWA

While there was much to celebrate in the wake of the Oslo conference, there was little time for rest as the Ottawa Process coalition geared up for the final stretch back to Ottawa. Joint initiatives with regional core partners were launched to sell the Oslo text to the reluctant and previously indifferent. A Canadian resolution calling on states to sign the ban convention would form the centrepiece of an intensive lobbying effort within the United Nations fall assembly. The final stage of the Ottawa Process public diplomacy campaign was launched through a range of government- and NGO-sponsored media activities and letter, fax, and poster campaigns. A highly effective series of ICRC black-and-white public service announcements that tracked the journey of a young female mine victim from her hut in Cambodia to the site of the convention signing conference in Ottawa declared that 'the people of the world want a ban on AP mines—now it's the government's turn.' The public diplomacy campaign received a dramatic boost on 10 October 1997 when the Nobel Committee announced that Jody Williams and the ICBL were the winners of the 1997 Nobel Peace Prize. A few weeks later, on 3 November, Williams and Valerie Warmington and Celinia Tuttle of Mines Action Canada joined Prime Minister Chrétien, Foreign Affairs Minister Axworthy, and Defence Minister Art Eggleton outside of Ottawa to participate in the destruction of the last of Canada's stockpiles of AP mines. Finally, there was the task of preparing for the largest multilateral ministerial conference ever held in Canada.

While the primary objective of the second Ottawa Landmines Conference was to open the new AP mine ban convention for signature, Canadian officials also planned to use the meeting to launch what would soon become known as Ottawa Process II. Thus, 'A Global Ban on Landmines: Treaty Signing Conference and Mine

Action Forum' would feature 20 mine action round tables that would
attract one of the best-ever collections of the world's AP mine experts
for consultations on the future of global mine action efforts. Expert
representatives from governments, the UN system, and NGOs would
examine almost every aspect of the international response to the AP
mine crisis, including the mobilization and co-ordination resources
for mine action as well as the ratification, universalization, and implementation of the ban convention in all of its aspects. The results of
these consultations, as well as a listing of mine action initiatives that
states and international and non-governmental organizations would
be undertaking to ensure progress on the AP mine issue, were
included in a 114-page final report of the conference—*An Agenda
for Mine Action*—which was provided to participants immediately
following the close of the conference.[7]

The Ottawa conference attracted a total of 2,400 participants,
including more than 500 members of the international media. Over
a half-billion dollars would be pledged for mine action during the
conference. Canada would announce its immediate ratification of the
new ban convention as well as its intention to devote $100 million
to mine action over the next five years. Canadian officials also used
the Ottawa conference to launch a 'lesson learned' exercise that col-
lected the views of key players within the Ottawa Process as well the
members of the broader AP mine expert community using a range of
survey and focus group-based instruments. Key members of the
Ottawa Process coalition were also asked to attend a one-day Ottawa
Process Forum immediately following the formal Ottawa conference
to examine the lessons learned from the process in more detail. An
additional two days of consultations and planning for Ottawa Process
II were hosted by Mines Action Canada for members of the NGO community on 6–7 December.

Taken together, the activities within and surrounding the second
Ottawa Landmines Conference had succeeded in producing a comprehensive and widely consulted new road-map for the second
phase of the Ottawa Process. The success of the first Ottawa Process
was underscored by the presentation of the Nobel Peace Prize to
Jody Williams and the ICBL in Oslo on 10 December 1997. In the 424
days between the two Ottawa conferences, the Ottawa Process coalition had navigated a complex and very public diplomatic initiative
to a successful conclusion that now enjoyed the support of 122 governments, an achievement described by Prime Minister Chrétien as

'without precedent or parallel in either international disarmament or international humanitarian law' (Chrétien, 1997: 2).

FAST-TRACK DIPLOMACY

There is little doubt that much of the success of the Ottawa Process can be traced to the uniqueness of the AP mine issue itself. Once the true destructiveness of AP mines was made clear to publics, politicians, and policy-makers, the drive towards a ban was almost inevitable. However, there was nothing inevitable about the speed or concrete results of the Ottawa Process itself. There is no shortage of worthwhile issues that have rocketed to the top of the international agenda only to have their momentum blunted and potential solutions buried under the dysfunction of multilateral 'business as usual'. The Ottawa Process clearly pushed the boundaries of multilateralism, building on Axworthy's bold gamble and drawing its strength from new sources of diplomatic influence in the post-Cold War era. International public opinion, transnational NGOs, and revolutions in telecommunications and the mass media have all begun to erode the traditional boundaries and prerogatives of diplomatic praxis. The middle-power/civil society coalition forged by Canada around the AP mine issue was successful in harnessing a number of these new sources of influence, providing a dramatically expanded diplomatic tool-kit for officials developing strategies to influence key decision-makers at state, regional and global levels. Public diplomacy efforts by key foreign ministers and senior officials were effectively combined with NGO-led civil society advocacy campaigns. Videos, posters, fax campaigns, e-mail, conference calls, and the Internet all facilitated the rapid co-ordination and transmission of the key messages of the constantly evolving Ottawa Process.

Multilateral diplomacy remains a contested terrain where middle powers such as Canada often have a home-field advantage. Canada's extensive experience with multilateralism provided a solid foundation upon which the framework of an issue-specific diplomatic initiative could quickly be constructed. But while the Ottawa Process may have emerged as an ad hoc response to the need for immediate multilateral action, it will produce more than a much needed international convention banning AP mines. In a world in desperate need of rapidly organized multilateral responses to complex and large-scale threats to human health, security, and development, the

Ottawa Process holds open the hope that multilateral diplomacy will continue to evolve as a flexible and effective instrument of global governance. With its clear objectives, deadlines for collective action, coalition-building across traditional political boundaries, and full use of the new tools of the information age, fast-track diplomacy in the style of the Ottawa Process is a welcome addition to Canada's multilateral tool-kit.

NOTES

1. While the number of AP mines actually deployed throughout the world could actually be anywhere between 50 million and 130 million, the data on number of mine victims are much more accurate and based on extensive Red Cross and United Nations field research. See, for example, International Committee of the Red Cross (1996).

2. The full title of this convention is the 'Convention on Prohibitions or Restrictions on the Use of Certain Conventional Weapons Which May be Deemed to Be Excessively Injurious or to Have Indiscriminate Effects'.

3. This first meeting of this government/NGO pro-AP mine ban group was held on 19 January 1996 and included representatives from 13 NGOs, the ICRC, and eight governments (Austria, Belgium, Canada, Denmark, Ireland, Mexico, Norway, and Switzerland).

4. Batman's *Death of Innocents: The Horror of Landmines*, 1996, was more advocacy-oriented than Superman's *Deadly Legacy*, 1996, was produced in co-operation with UNICEF as a mine awareness project, and was translated for use in mine-affected countries such as Bosnia.

5. Details on these conferences can be found in issues 1–5 of DFAIT's land-mine newsletter, *AP Mine Ban: Progress Report*.

6. The best 'open' sources of information on the details of the Oslo negotiations are the newsletters and the releases of the ICBL, representatives of which were present in all formal and informal sessions of the Oslo negotiations.

7. Those wishing to keep track of developments related to the Ottawa conference could also plug in to a 'real-time' audio feed of the various speeches and conference events via DFAIT's land-mines Web site.

REFERENCES

Albright, Madeleine. 1997. Letter to Foreign Ministers, 20 Aug. 1997, in International Campaign to Ban Landmines, 1997, *Report on Activities: Diplomatic Conference on an International Total Ban on Anti-Personnel Landmines*, Oslo, Norway, 1–18 Sept.: 18–20.

Barrows, R., et al. 1997. 'An Open Letter to US President Clinton from Robert Barrows et al.', 11 Sept.

Brussels. 1997. Declaration of the Brussels Conference on Anti-Personnel Landmines.

Canada. 1996. *Towards a Global Ban on Anti-Personnel Mines: Declaration of the Ottawa Conference.*

Cooper, Andrew. 1997. *Canadian Foreign Policy: Old Habits and New Directions.* Scarbourgh, Ont.: Prentice-Hall.

Chrétien, Jean. 1997. Message from the Right Honourable Jean Chrétien, Prime Minister—Canada, in United Nations, *Landmines: Demining News from the United Nations.* New York: UN, Dec.: 2.

Delegation of the United States. 1997. *Summary of U.S. Anti-Armour Landmine Systems,* in International Campaign to Ban Landmines, 4 Sept., *Report on Activities: Diplomatic Conference on an International Total Ban on Anti-Personnel Landmines,* Oslo, Norway, 1–18 Sept.: 31.

Department of Foreign Affairs and International Trade (DFAIT). 1997a. AP Mine Ban: Progress Report, 1: 2.

———. 1997b. 'Notes for an Address by the Honourable Lloyd Axworthy, Minister of Foreign Affairs, to the Oslo NGO Forum on Banning Anti-Personnel Landmines, 10 September 1997', 1.

Final Declaration of the 4th International NGO Conference on Landmines. 1997. Toward a Mine Free Southern Africa. Maputo, Mozambique, 25–8 Feb.

Helms, J. 1997. 'Letter to US President Clinton from Jessie Helms, Chair, Senate Committee on Foreign Relations', 8.

International Committee of the Red Cross (ICRC). 1996. 'Anti-personnel Landmines: Friend or Foe?', Geneva: International Committee of the Red Cross.

Leahy, Senator Patrick. 1997. 'Seize the Moment', *ICBL Ban Treaty News,* 9 Sept.: 1.

Report of the Diplomatic Conference on an International Total Ban on Anti-Personnel Land Mines. 1997. Oslo, 1–18 Sept., APL/CRP.5, 18 Sept.

The Economist. 1997. 'The New Convert', 23–9 Aug.: 14.

United Nations General Assembly. 1996. Resolution 51/45 s, 'An International Agreement to Ban Anti-Personnel Landmines', adopted 10 Dec.

Williams, Jody. 1994. 'National Initiatives and Legislation to Limit and Restrict the Production, Use and Transfer of Land Mines', *UNIDIR Newsletter,* Geneva, United Nations Institute for Disarmament Research Newsletter 28/29: 11.

6

The Canadian Military after Somalia

DEAN F. OLIVER

'One of the tools our military needs is peace of mind.'
—*General Maurice Baril, Chief of Defence Staff,*
to the Standing Committee on National Defence and Veterans Affairs,
30 October 1997

The Somalia scandal, and the official inquiries that followed it, rocked the Canadian military to its foundations. Although journalists and some academics continue to berate the defence department for failing to address adequately the problems highlighted by Canada's east African deployment in 1992–3, it is clear that the institution's response to the crisis represented one of the most thorough and painful reassessments of military organization, training, law, and doctrine that this country has ever witnessed. No other internal debate, save perhaps that over unification in the 1960s, comes close in magnitude or potential impact. The Canadian military that enters the next millennium will have been shaped in important ways by the legacy of Shidane Arone, the Somali teen tortured and murdered by members of Canada's élite Airborne Regiment in the spring of 1993. It will also have been coloured by the domestic and international currents swirling around the Canadian Forces (CF) long before the ill-fated Airborne deployed into Belet Huen, developments that helped determine the nature and timing of the mission itself and that were then, in their turn, affected by the fallout from the crisis.

In the wake of the sound and fury generated by Somalia and its inquisitorial denouement, it is still too early to make firm predictions about the future of the post-Somalia Canadian military. The department's official response to the Commission of Inquiry's final report is just a few months old; the more voluminous *Report to the Prime Minister on the Leadership and Management of the Canadian Forces* is of less than one year's vintage, with many of its recommendations still being interpreted by an overwhelmed and overworked bureaucracy. Predictions about the CF's future must be informed by the uncertainty attending such widespread renovation, as well as that occasioned by those same convoluted, interrelated factors that led to the current reformist spasm in the first place: domestic fiscal crisis, rapid international change, bureaucratic and institutional paralysis, public pressure, and private immorality.[1] This chapter cannot offer prophecy where even informed speculation is a dangerous game. Nevertheless, by highlighting several important developments in Canadian military affairs this past year, especially the two major reports completed by successive defence ministers, it seeks to offer tentative guidance on a *likely* post-Somalia future for the Canadian Forces.

DEFENDING THE STATUS QUO

Granatstein and Bothwell have described the Trudeau years, not inaccurately, as 'a long, dark night of the spirit' for the Canadian Forces (1990: 234). The Chrétien years might well be remembered the same way, if for markedly different reasons. While the Trudeau years witnessed a frontal assault on the military by an unsympathetic and reformist political leadership in areas ranging from alliance commitments to equipment purchases, the Chrétien government's first foray into defence policy-making, the *1994 Defence White Paper* (which remains the *modus operandi* of the Defence Department), was a remarkably conservative document. It proved far less damaging to the status quo than many analysts had feared (and therefore far less promising than many others had hoped) and acknowledged the need to retain residual but robust capabilities across the broad spectrum of military categories. Given the far more radical reforms proposed during the fall election campaign by the federal New Democratic Party and during the subsequent defence review by the powerful and well-financed Canada 21 Council, this outcome seemed a welcome reprieve for the beleaguered military and an acknowledgment, however qualified, that the post-Cold War era had not yet overturned entirely either traditional definitions of security or the utility of military force as an instrument of statecraft.

To be sure, it was obvious from the various party platforms during the 1993 federal election that all would not be business as usual for defence policy in the aftermath of victory by the Liberals, New Democrats, or Reformers. The Liberal Party, which according to pre-election polls stood by far the best chance of unseating the reigning Progressive Conservatives, had pledged in its much-discussed Red Book of campaign promises to democratize the decision-making process and to launch full reviews of both foreign and defence policy in light of the demise of the Cold War. Moreover, while in opposition, Lloyd Axworthy, the party's vocal external affairs critic, had supported vigorously a move away from traditional alliance obligations in a manner reminiscent of Trudeau's dissatisfaction with NORAD and NATO in the late 1960s and early 1970s. In Europe, for example, Axworthy supported making the Conference on Security and Co-operation in Europe (CSCE)[2] the cornerstone of European security, a stance that contradicted Canada's half-century of reliance on NATO for that role and that was certain to be met with firm disapproval by the major alliance partners, including the United States, Britain, and Germany. Multilateral, rapid-reaction peacekeeping forces would replace the Cold War's anachronistic security institutions, Axworthy had also argued. 'Canadian forces with a mission for helping keep the peace would help build a more effective security system' (Axworthy, 1992b), while in general Canada should embrace a 'far more activist, internationalist and independent foreign policy' (Axworthy, 1992a: 14).

While prevailing domestic and international circumstances were far different, the similarities in language between Axworthy's pronouncements and those of Trudeau and some of his key advisers a quarter-century earlier (especially the coupling of 'independent' with 'policy') were striking. In both cases, in effect, the argument was predicated on the assumption that a radical new security order would liberate Canada from many of the more irksome restraints of the Cold War, its entangling alliances, dependence on the United States, and the requirement for a large, expensive, and multifaceted military foremost among them. As *détente* waned in the late 1970s, however, culminating in the Soviet Union's invasion of Afghanistan, Trudeau's foreign and defence policies returned grudgingly to a more familiar universe. Axworthy's pre-election views notwithstanding, the possibility remained that post-election events might prove equally unkind to Trudeau's successors. And yet the Liberals' speedy and dramatic cancellation of the EH-101 helicopter contract, one of the cornerstones of military rejuvenation during the Mulroney years and Kim Campbell's brief interregnum, demonstrated that at least some pre-election promises would be kept. Neither the CF's demonstrable need for new search and rescue (SAR) and naval helicopters nor the hundreds of millions of dollars in contract termination fees that the move entailed prevented the decision. It appeared the harbinger of things to come. More defence cuts on way, noted the Toronto Star on 9 November 1993; Liberals need to wean white elephant off its pork diet, argued the paper's national affairs correspondent, Carol Goar, the same day.

But news of the demise of the Department of National Defence (DND) proved greatly exaggerated. After a year of assessment, study, and public consultations, most notably by a special joint committee of Parliament, the resulting White Paper was a status quo document promising a period of stability for the CF and, if its analysis was to be believed, stays of execution for at least some of the military's most prized acquisition programs. The navy, for example, would look for an affordable replacement for its Sea King helicopters instead of the 'Cadillac' EH-101 option of the previous Tory administration and would also look to replace its aging submarine fleet, perhaps by acquiring Upholder-class conventional vessels from the United Kingdom. The army would get new armoured personnel carriers beginning in 1997 and, eventually, replacements for its Cougar close fire-support vehicles. The air force would get virtually nothing, save for new SAR helicopters, and in fact would lose its entire CF-5 fleet, a sizeable number of its CF-18s, and face a 25 per cent reduction in overall expenditures, but it at least survived with its fast air mission intact and with renewed support for its multi-purpose orientation.

It is a telling commentary on the state of the CF in the early 1990s that such cuts and lukewarm endorsements might be viewed as anything other than disastrous, and yet the paper was generally seen as offering the CF a fiscal and organizational reprieve. Moreover, the White Paper offered a respite from the post-Cold War, post-Somalia storm, an indication that the new government, despite the views of some vocal, left-leaning members, had taken a long, hard look at the country's defence posture and judged it sound in most essential respects. The document's main thrust was summed up by the injunction that Canada would maintain 'multi-purpose, combat-capable armed forces able to meet the challenges to Canada's security both at home and abroad'. It was clear that those forces would operate on a much reduced budget—Defence Minister David Collenette proposed deeper financial cuts than had the Parliamentary joint committee—but the basic structure of the military, its commitments and core functions, and its weapons suite remained more or less unchanged. As the White Paper noted with appropriate finality, the Cold War is over, but with its passing had also gone the geopolitical certainties embedded in the East-West confrontation. Canada faces an unpredictable and fragmented world, one in which conflict, repression, and upheaval exist alongside peace, democracy, and relative prosperity (DND, 1994: 3). While the international environment had changed drastically in recent years, in other words, new challenges continued to place a premium on balanced conventional forces and formal alliance commitments. In post-Cold War uncertainty the CF had, evidently, found succour.

Most defence analysts were quietly pleased by the government's directive, recognizing that it might have been far worse, even if many grumbled that inordinate attention to the country's deficit and debt problems was slowly strangling the CF and institutionalizing the long-discussed commitments-to-capability gap. Some groused publicly. Commenting on the failure to replace the obsolete Leopard I main battle tank or to increase the Army's firepower, respected military historian Desmond Morton (who would, in 1997, pen one of four reports by academic experts for Defence Minister Doug Young on the future of the CF) noted caustically that '"combat capable" is a phrase, not a policy.' Had critics been more attentive, Morton argued, they might have condemned the White Paper for its vague reassurances, its lack of long-term vision, and the moves to make the military a Mexican-style gendarmerie, not a high-tech, high-quality force (Morton, 1994).

Lower budgets and equivocation on critical procurement issues would certainly hurt, but retaining balanced forces across the board was an acceptable compromise, if barely so. As many critics and supporters pointed out, a military that continues to do all the same things but with less money and fewer personnel stretches resources and credibility to the breaking point. Still, the measured but supportive tone of John Marteinson, editor of *Canadian Defence Quarterly*, captured nicely the consensus view among the professional defence watchers. 'While we will disagree with some aspects' of the White Paper, Marteinson noted, 'all in all, the new defence policy would appear to be well-conceived, farsighted and sustainable' (Marteinson, 1994: 5). By early 1995, Marteinson's interpretation of the government's new defence budget left him far less sanguine (Marteinson, 1995: 5), but in glimpsing subsequently the depth of anti-military sentiment within cabinet and the Liberal caucus, much of it Somalia-induced, the 1994 White Paper appeared better all the time.

Indeed, in early 1998, as the department continues to uphold the 1994 document as its operative defence policy, analysts are almost uniformly sentimental about the White Paper's good sense and rational choices, cautioning not that it should be abandoned but that its spirit and letter be vigorously upheld. Upon appointment as Defence Minister in October 1996, Martin Shadwick noted, Doug Young's comment that he was 'a peacekeeper, not a warrior . . . fueled media speculation, and military alarm' that the CF's future would eschew the White Paper in favour of 'something akin to the controversial 1994 report of the Canada 21 Council'. There was 'a palpable sense of relief', said Shadwick, when Young told *Canada AM* that 'we have to be able to intervene anywhere in the world where we are required to do so, and we have to have the capability, the combat capability and all of the other aspects, up and running to the best possible level' (Shadwick, 1996: 31). The implied rejection of radical alternatives in Young's remarks gave a strong indication that the defence consensus of 1994 would continue to hold.

The White Paper's conservative tone and compromise position continue to infuriate many defence policy reformers. Taking their cue from the ever-expanding academic literature on the beneficent possibilities inherent in the end of the Cold War, such commentators deplore the government's defence of tradition and see in the Somalia fiasco (and in the Defence Department's public relations response to it) the tangible result of an 'old world' military operating in a 'new world' order. The document itself, they argue, failed the test of democratization inherent in the Liberals' Red Book, as had the joint committee report,[3] and thereby buttressed a defence organization long outmoded by the transformation of both the international system and the nature of security itself. The White Paper 'ignores entirely the issue of an expanded notion of security', one critic argued. 'Despite the emergence of a relatively clear public and parliamentary voice on this issue, an expanded conception of security has yet to find a concrete existence in public policy' (Lawson, 1995: 110). The argument that the policy represented a prudent, well-calibrated response to complex events and continued global uncertainty is not suffered gladly by such critics; arguments grounded in the lobbying process and the relative influence of selected portions of the 'attentive public' are marginally more palatable, but only in as much as they accept explicitly the defence review's inherent bias against radical alternatives and its determined courtship of what is generally labelled 'the defence establishment'.[4] It was representative of 'old thinking' in 1994, in other words, and remains even more so today.

The current government, therefore, unlike that of Pierre Trudeau nearly three decades before, has enjoyed relative peace in its relationship with the mainstream defence establishment for most of its time in office. The 1994 policy remains problematic in some respects, especially given the budget cuts that have followed with monotonous regularity, but it has attracted even more favourable commentary in recent years than when first announced and is now held by many defence analysts as representing the bare minimum of defence effort Canada can produce and still expect its international standing to remain undiminished. This 'rallying around the flag' indicates, in effect, that the document's supporters have made a virtue of dire necessity. As Tom Dimoff noted in the March 1997 *Report to the Prime Minister*, most members of the defence community 'agreed that the *1994 Defence White Paper's* roles, missions and force posture remains sound, particularly the principle that Canada must maintain multi-purpose, combat-capable forces'. Many authorities criticized the government for not moving faster to implement portions of the policy: the White Paper offered a wonderful and attainable goal, they argued, if only the government would take action on its behalf.

Dimoff also noted, however, that some experts had identified a debilitating philosophical and ideological split within government and the bureaucracy over maintaining a combat-capable military versus 'a more constabulary force posture'.

POST-COLD WAR DEFENCE AND SECURITY: TWO VIEWS

This debate was hardly new in the spring of 1997, having been played out before the standing committees on national defence and foreign affairs, at innumerable academic conferences, and in the pages of a hundred professional journals in the years since 1989, but it was one of the first clear indications that fundamental differences over Canadian international security policy within the various organs of government were, perhaps, beginning to have a debilitating effect on policy. Dimoff's commentators, in fact, were reflecting a critical but accurate reading of the evolving relationship between the departments of National Defence and Foreign Affairs and International Trade (DFAIT), especially as it has evolved under Lloyd Axworthy's tenure at DFAIT since January 1996. In particular, it reflects a growing realization among supporters of the White Paper that the real threat to the current status quo in defence policy, for good or ill, comes not from the effects of the Somalia Inquiry *per se* but from the government's DFAIT-led infatuation with soft security and human security, and with the consequent retooling of the country's Cold War military that this self-proclaimed renaissance of Canadian internationalism will entail.

The problem manifests itself in many ways. The government's failure to announce a replacement for the navy's outdated Sea King helicopters, for example, betrays a regrettable determination to avoid grasping the nettle of military capital equipment shortfalls. But the decision to decouple the purchase of search and rescue helicopters from the purchase of naval helicopters, in fact, epitomizes the government's reluctance to address critical procurement issues that cannot be justified readily on humanitarian or peacekeeping grounds. Cormorant helicopters that fly from airfields to pluck drowning sailors from the North Atlantic are politically and morally acceptable by this calculus, despite their cost; Cormorants that fly from the decks of patrol frigates to do precisely the same thing are not. The on-again, off-again discussions over the acquisition of British Upholder-class conventional submarines evince a similar dearth of intestinal fortitude and fiscal commitment and conjure up the usual charges of Cold War paranoia, needless expense, and intellectual sterility. In both cases, naval helicopters and conventional submarines, the military has repeatedly and correctly made the case that replacements are necessary to carry through on the government's White Paper promises only to be rebuffed or delayed by cabinet.

The government's demonstrable lack of interest in the North Atlantic Treaty Organization (see Chapter 9), the bedrock of Canada's international security obligations for the past half-century, provides yet another instance of 'new' security thinking at loggerheads with the old. The Foreign Minister's antipathy for Canada's formal alliances has already been noted, but while the CF's operational effectiveness continues to be buttressed in significant ways by co-operation among NATO allies (in air training, for instance), a fact well appreciated by the CF's senior officers if not always by its ministers, Ottawa's post-Cold War retreat from Europe, begun foolishly under Mulroney, has continued inexorably under Chrétien. The downward spiral of Canada's interest in and influence over NATO counsels, an insouciance clearly evident during the discussions over NATO enlargement and during the virtual non-event that was NATO Secretary-General Solana's fall 1997 visit to Ottawa, has all but segregated the Canadian military from day-to-day contact with its closest allies and most likely partners in future military operations. Indeed, were it not for the NATO mission in former Yugoslavia and ongoing NATO training in Canada, the CF's isolation would already be all but complete, save for contacts with the United States. A preponderance of those, however, occur under the aegis of NORAD, another relic of the Cold War that defence reformers would just as soon abandon.

Still, despite the Foreign Minister's discomfiture with the Defence Department's continued adherence to the 1994 policy statement,[5] the Chrétien defence regime has been relatively consensual. Consensual, that is, if scandals, crises, intense departmental reviews, and the much altered external security environment would not keep getting in the way. There is great irony in this predicament: a government that entered office bent on reforming defence has spent four years upholding, however tenuously, the status quo, only to be deluged at virtually every opportunity by bad news and bad press, plus subtle but unrelenting pressure for security policy reform from the Department of Foreign Affairs and International Trade and, to an equally significant degree, the Canadian International Development Agency. In that Somalia was an inherited scandal, one that, while in opposition, the Liberals had taken great delight in evoking, the irony runs deeper still.

From the outset of the unwanted Somalia malaise, for example, it was clear that both military and government shared some critical common ground in the desire of both to limit fallout from the crisis, the military by localizing blame to a few bad apples in a handful of sub-units, the government by exposing the misdemeanours of its Tory predecessors. The extent to which both parties shared a common view of the emerging security order was far less evident, but the Defence Department's enthusiasm for international peacekeeping (it was, after all, virtually the only game in town) at least indicated that a harmonious approach to foreign affairs was not beyond the realm of possibility. The department's belated epiphany on the utility of the Pearson Peacekeeping Centre, a facility once considered by many senior officers as a harmless encumbrance at best, a Trojan horse of pseudo-military vacuity at worst, represented a more muted endorsement to be sure, but also reflected the same grudging accommodation with post-Cold War realities, domestic as well as international. As the Somalia Inquiry threatened to spin out of Ottawa's control, there was further evidence of a civil-military co-operative axis: curtailment of the inquiry process and, in effect, a declaration of victory in the investigation that would protect political reputations and restore military stability. If coupled with a slate of military reforms, most of them recommended by government-appointed experts, the Defence Minister of the day reasoned, the outcome of the post-Somalia imbroglio might yet protect the essence of the White Paper and, thus, the military's much-cherished general purpose forces.

THE MANY ROADS FROM HERE

Quite aside from the specific recommendations of the Commission of Inquiry into events in Somalia, important though they are, the critical question in assessing the post-Somalia future for Canada's military remains: how long can the assumptions and consensus reflected in the *1994 Defence White Paper*, with its support for the military's general purpose mission, continue to hold? The government's actions in early 1997 in ending the inquiry and commissioning a series of reports on defence organization from friendly academic experts is an indication of the extent to which the current balance between reform and tradition is valued and how difficult sweeping change is likely to be.

Three of the four academics—Desmond Morton, J.L. Granatstein, and David Bercuson—were military historians who supported strongly and sensibly what can only be described as a traditional interpretation of Canada's security posture. The minister's March 1997 report also asked the Prime Minister to stabilize defence planning by placing a floor on spending not much below that which then existed. Several recent spending announcements, especially a $500 million package in fall 1996 and the purchase of 15 search and rescue helicopters for $790 million in late 1997, along with overall improvement in the government's fiscal situation, also seem to militate against precipitate change.

But the seeds of discord in the current policy environment are everywhere in evidence, and with the Defence Department rendered, to a certain extent, *hors de combat* by the public bloodletting occasioned by Somalia, the military remains in a poor position to protect itself against either budget cutters at the cabinet table or defence reformers inside or outside the government's ranks. Nothing demonstrates this better than the failure to have appointed immediately a new Chief of Defence Staff (CDS) in the aftermath of General Jean Boyle's forced resignation in October 1996. Instead, as no one totally free from Somalia's guilt by association could be found, the CF staggered on through a very difficult period in its history with a highly competent but vulnerable acting CDS, Vice-Admiral Larry Murray, who ultimately became, like Boyle and Admiral John Anderson before him, a victim of the inquiry. Tainted by his role in the alleged cover-up and by his occasional testiness as a witness before the Commission of Inquiry, the government judged it politically impossible to confirm Murray as CDS in the aftermath of the commissioners' final report, which gratuitously slammed DND's entire chain of command. While many senior officials argued that another change of leadership would further damage morale and the government's public image, others maintained that Murray was damaged goods and that the post-Somalia period must start with a clean slate. Domestic politics demanded a sacrifice, so instead of rewarding Murray for his able, if short-lived, stewardship, the vice-admiral was retired and replaced by a new CDS, General Maurice Baril.

Baril, a distinguished soldier highly regarded by the troops, began his job without the millstone of the Commission of Inquiry hanging around his neck, but its scores of recommendations will occupy him, new Defence Minister Art Eggleton, and their successors for months and years to come. Moreover, the apparently endless stream of minor public relations disasters throughout 1997[6] and the execrable state of relations between the military and the civilian press corps indicate that Somalia is scarcely the department's only worry. As the *Ottawa Citizen*'s David Pugliese noted recently of DND's relationship with the press, it has never been worse (Pugliese, 1997: 34). Indeed, as Somalia demonstrated, the department's problems, despite the oft-employed 'few bad apples' analogy, ran far deeper than most military officials cared to admit. Education, training, command philosophy, ethics, military culture, the regimental system, and leadership were all dissected during the gruesome Somalia hearings, and all, in some important respects, were found wanting. In other words, just as Vice-Admiral Murray's Somalia baggage made him a political asset of dubious value, so, too, the department's constantly bleeding public relations wound is making it increasingly difficult for the government to act boldly in DND's defence.

In the case of naval helicopters, the argument for replacing immediately the aged Sea Kings is beyond dispute, yet cabinet in late 1997 again delayed the decision, ostensibly in light of complaints by some potential suppliers that the specific requirements laid down by DND in the bidding process privileged the Cormorant. While few policy decisions, or non-decisions, are easily explained and a lengthy delay in the naval purchase was widely expected, this one demonstrated an abysmal lack of political will by the Liberal cabinet.

The Cormorant is a scaled-down version of the GKN Westland-Agusta consortium's EH-101 (a designation now defunct), whose purchase the Liberals vetoed upon entering office in late 1993 at a cost of $473.5 million in contract cancellation fees. The purchase of a modified naval helicopter from the same company with which the former Tory government had originally contracted would undoubtedly pose a public relations challenge. The selection of the Cormorant for Canada's SAR needs in January 1998, after all, prompted a simple but revealing front-page headline in the *Ottawa Citizen: Déjà vu*. Whether or not a review of the naval helicopter requirement indicates problems in the department's tendering process, the government's handling of the helicopter file demonstrates, from 1993 to the present, an inordinate sensitivity to public criticism of expensive procurement decisions and a distressing propensity to view critical CF acquisition projects through a purely political optic.

It is now clear to all but the most intransigent critics that the EH-101 was the proper choice for the Canadian navy in the first place but, having made political hay from canning that option in 1993, the current government was left with a range of equally unpalatable options, from buying nothing or buying a different (and probably inferior) aircraft to buying a stripped-down (and certainly inferior) EH-101 before the last patched up, cannibalized Sea King falls from the sky. Legitimizing each of these possibilities, of course, is the argument that in a less dangerous post-Cold War world Canada no longer needs a highly capable, submarine-hunting naval helicopter.

The argument that the new global security order has permitted not only a peace dividend but a fundamental restructuring of attitudes and defence capabilities is seldom heard from the Defence Department whose colours remain securely fixed to the White Paper's increasingly shaky mast. It is an argument that has gained great currency, however, in the Department of Foreign Affairs and International Trade. DND's uncomfortable predicament in the post-Cold War, post-Somalia period, in fact, has coincided with a period of highly successful public activism by DFAIT. While foreign affairs under Lloyd Axworthy has been pushing vigorously its vision of a new multilateralism and Canadian involvement in soft security, human security, and sustainable human development, it has been notably quiet in addressing publicly questions of military security, alliance commitments, and the linkages between military capability and broader foreign policy objectives. One looks to the foreign affairs Web site largely in vain, for example, for material pertaining to the CF's role in achieving foreign policy objectives, for documents on NATO or NORAD (the minister speaks rarely on either subject), or for the relationship between the new diplomacy and Canada's long-standing strategic interests.

There is nothing inherently new in this disjuncture between Canadian foreign and defence policy, as a recent book on the history of Canada's European policy makes clear (Rempel, 1996), but markedly different under Axworthy's tutelage has been DFAIT's enthusiastic espousal of a definition of security that is radically at odds with the assumptions underlying the CF's current organization and mandate. Soft security, for example, does not require frigates, fighters, or submarines. Given the CF's struggle to pull through the Somalia scandal and the immense demands on the Defence Department's human resources that the reform process entailed, DND's voice in setting the agenda for renewed debate over national interests and the appropriate forces to meet them has thus been, almost by default, effectively muzzled. Having several chiefs of defence staff cycle through the office in a short period has not helped. The cumulative result has been DFAIT's virtual monopoly of the terms of debate over Canadian international security policy, an ascendance bolstered immeasurably by its stunning success over anti-personnel land-mines (see Chapter 5).

Indeed, in the land-mines case, after initial disgruntlement and the impassioned pleas of a core group of military engineers at National Defence Headquarters that Canada not ban outright the CF's highly useful stock of anti-personnel land-mines, DND surrendered the file with astonishing ease. The safety of Canadian military personnel in future conflicts was hardly considered. A forthcoming monograph (Lenarcic, 1998) argues that although DFAIT proved remarkably adept at monopolizing an issue of inherent importance to the military, it blithely dismissed all arguments in favour of the tactical utility of AP mines. Humanitarian concerns simply outweighed military or security considerations, ban advocates argued, rendering largely superfluous the military's professional input.

Positing a useful, if frequently (and tragically) misused, weapon system as simply a humanitarian problem shorn of military considerations demonstrated the extent to which human security had become firmly entrenched as a distinguishing feature of Canadian security policy. While the evolution of security discourse in recent years can hardly be attributed to DFAIT or its current minister, it is nevertheless clear that Axworthy has played a key role in beginning to translate into practice many of human security's more important dictates, including its focus on co-operative humanitarian action outside the established organs of multilateral diplomacy. DFAIT's progress in this direction has perhaps appeared fitful at times, as some of its critics would no doubt maintain, especially over human rights and trade with the Asia-Pacific, but it has also been commendably steady and, in the end, no less dramatic. The land-mines success has been trumpeted as marking the onset of a new era in Canadian statecraft. DFAIT's revitalized and successful foreign policy presence and DND's lingering, post-Somalia paralysis must lead to at least a partial reordering of Canadian security interests, a process that is unlikely to support for long the defence policy status quo represented by the 1994 White Paper. Indeed, one of the distinguishing features of the new diplomacy—its willingness to engage in public confrontation and pressure group diplomacy to achieve results—threatens to usurp almost entirely the defence department's influence over the security agenda.

The long-term implications of DFAIT's approach to security and international relations are by no means certain. During the Ottawa conference in December 1997 to sign the land-mines treaty even Foreign Affairs officials voiced concern over whether the Ottawa Process could be repeated in other areas, thereby questioning whether the much-touted tactic would ever become the new norm. Moreover, the land-mines campaign is in many ways a manifestation of DFAIT's abiding faith in co-operative security, an approach some have criticized for encouraging a rose-tinted view of the international system. By relying on co-operative security measures and providing mostly economic and humanitarian aid, Nastro and Nossal have argued, the Canadian government runs the risk that such measures may not be regarded as valid diplomatic currency, particularly by other governments engaged in more dangerous tasks in attempting to achieve these same ends. To make a difference internationally, the authors conclude, that is, to maintain our status as an important actor and to make sure Canada's voice is heard, we need truly multi-purpose, combat-capable forces (Nastro and Nossal, 1997: 19, 22).

This assessment is far removed from DFAIT's current wisdom on the proper role for military force in the affairs of state. Many of the department's senior personnel, including the minister,[7] appear surprisingly comfortable with having the CF remade into peace police. In public statements on security policy, for example, including those before NATO audiences, the minister spends very little time on collective defence, military operations, or even peace enforcement, but labours continually on such themes as peacekeeping, humanitarian assistance, and basic human security. To be sure, even NATO since 1991 has moved farther in this direction and away from Article V security guarantees than most observers thought possible, as Pellerin argues in Chapter 9 of this volume, but Axworthy's handling of the NATO question is nevertheless unique in his lukewarm and backhanded endorsements of the alliance's current strategic concept, his frequent pleas for more rapid reform, and his thus far cautious but potentially explosive reassessment of Canada's position with respect to the legality of nuclear weapons under international humanitarian law.

A CF oriented primarily towards peacekeeping and a carefully articulated but undeniable critique of Canada's alliance obligations are not yet part of Canada's official foreign policy, but it is clear that the policy requirements of the current DFAIT approach to international security is nudging the government steadily in both directions.

Both options, it is worth repeating, were rejected by the joint committee of Parliament and the Defence Department in 1993–4 and turned down again by Defence Minister Doug Young in his *Report to the Prime Minister* in March 1997. Both options, however, would likely prove far less costly than maintaining current policies and both would continue the trend that has thus far garnered Canada rave reviews in many quarters for its activism and independence. As the recent land-mines signing conference in Ottawa indicated, humanitarian causes make good press; military curmudgeons do not.

DFAIT's well-intentioned espousal of soft security and the new multilateralism, DND's continued attempts to wrestle with the plethora of reforms and recommendations arising from Somalia (132 of the Commission of Inquiry's 160 recommendations were accepted by the Defence Minister), and the government's sensitivity to both financial cost and interest group politics do not bode well for the indefinite continuance of the *1994 Defence White Paper* as the basis for Canada's defence policy. As a consequence, the mix of forces, missions, and personnel training currently supplied by the CF will likely change substantially in the years to come as well. DFAIT's striking success on the land-mines front coupled with DND's understandable introspection makes such a future for Canada's military all the more likely. It must sound, eventually, the death knell for the CF's cherished multi-purpose combat forces, but that day might still be a long way off.

CONCLUSION

The case against Canada's current force mix is not yet supported by the weight of empirical evidence. In this lies part of the outline of the next round of debate over the post-Somalia Canadian Forces. During the 1993–4 defence review, radical reformers proved unable to back their assertions about the fading utility of a traditional military force posture, even with overwhelming evidence of a rise in intrastate conflict. Most defence policy analysts, military historians, and the military community itself were united in defence of the status quo, pointing to the irrelevance of international moralizing in the absence of military capability and to the continuance of military security threats in the frighteningly unstable post-Cold War order. The international community's experience in Bosnia appears to prove their contention: a peace accord was reached only after NATO's impressive military capabilities had been invoked, and it has only been kept (and precariously) by their continued deployment. Events in Haiti, Cambodia, and central Africa have since reaffirmed the point. It was thus noteworthy that in appointing four experts to study the future of the CF in early 1997, Defence Minister Doug Young selected three historians, professional scholars with a predisposition to assess long-term trends and to judge them against empirical evidence, an approach that (almost by definition) guarded against radical policy departures on the basis of recent theory or isolated events.

As the Liberal government moves through its second mandate, defence reformers will have to back their critiques of existing policy with empirical evidence of the status quo's inherent weaknesses. The recent coup in Cambodia, the successful insurgency in Zaire (now the Republic of Congo), and, of course, Somalia and Bosnia have not been kind to this approach, but several impending procurement decisions, especially over naval helicopters and conventional submarines, will provide critics the first opportunity in a post-Somalia era to outline the high cost of traditional security and defence methods. Further, the government's alliance with defence conservatives is tenuous at best, a function of its reluctance to countenance a reduced role in international affairs through reduced peacekeeping capabilities in the first instance, and a shared interest in squelching the Somalia Inquiry in the second. Somalia left the defence establishment badly split in its views on military organization, leadership, and training. It will be difficult to reconstruct that consensus in the event of another major defence policy debate, not least because the inquiry itself and the media feeding frenzy that accompanied it helped polarize defence intellectuals into two camps: those broadly supportive of the commissioners' sweeping recommendations and those supportive of the government's position that the worst excesses had been cured and the time had arrived to move forward.

Now that the inquiry is dead and expensive spending decisions again loom on the immediate horizon, DFAIT's brand of security on the cheap is extremely attractive. Virtually no one in the current cabinet has a military background or record of defending the department against fiscal or policy predations, while the Prime Minister himself is as uninterested and unknowledgeable about defence affairs as any Prime Minister in the country's history. The new Defence Minister, Art Eggleton, unlike his predecessor, does not bring to the portfolio a reputation as a political fixer or troubleshooter, but is known instead more as a manager or administrator. This might well be what the Defence Department needs at this juncture; on the other hand, as long as Foreign Affairs is convinced of its own righteousness in the security realm, a self-image almost visibly enhanced by the land-mines crusade, the CF will need vision at least as much as managerial acumen. DND's own intermittent incompetence, especially in its handling of the Somalia file, has also left the department with few natural allies in Ottawa, despite the immensely favourable publicity generated by the CF's actions during the Red River flood in Manitoba in the late spring of 1997 and the January 1998 ice storm that ravaged eastern Ontario, Quebec, and parts of New Brunswick.

The government's recent actions and key speeches in late January 1998 by both the Minister Eggleton and Chief of Defence Staff Baril appear to indicate that the broad outlines of the White Paper will remain intact in the short term, if for no other reason than the obvious need to restore order and instil confidence in the Canadian Forces after its latest long, dark night of the spirit. Beyond this there are few guarantees. As in the aftermath of the unification debate, the Canadian Forces at present are singularly incapable of defending themselves against enemies within or outside the government. The current policy is an expensive proposition, as Canadian taxpayers will soon be reminded, and in the current Minister of Foreign Affairs defence has a well-informed and influential adversary. Critics of the 1994 document have never conceded the field, especially the Canada 21 Council, and Somalia offered a heaven-sent opportunity for them to make their point. To take perhaps their most telling criticism, the case for a revamped, scaled down, all-peacekeeping military was immeasurably strengthened by the Somalia fiasco and by several of the commissioned reports it produced. Current reform initiatives within the department, especially in the area of education and training, dovetail nicely with reform proposals that emphasize non-military and non-traditional approaches to security.

If the reformers can muster sufficient unity of purpose to build on this base, in part by politicizing impending procurement decisions, it seems difficult to envisage another successful defence of the status quo, at least in the medium to long term, especially in the context of possible debate over a new White Paper, an eventuality seldom mentioned but a logical corollary to the new security paradigm. What will emerge in its place is far from clear, but a cheaper and more lightly armed force oriented almost exclusively to international peacekeeping, peacebuilding, and humanitarian assistance is not only possible but extremely likely.

In spite of the assessments of numerous media commentators, it is unlikely that the CF's commendable, indeed brilliant, response to the Great Ice Storm of 1998, or to last year's flooding in Manitoba, will enhance appreciably its ability to fend off either budget cutters or defence policy reformers. The military's response did not include naval helicopters, submarines, fighter jets, or main battle tanks. Its civilian, non-military character hardly contradicts the notion that in the post-Cold War period military establishments need not train for the worst possible contingency—war, for instance—but merely for that which is most likely, such as humanitarian emergencies both at home and abroad. The fact that Canada has been criticized repeatedly by many defence analysts for failing to face down the illogic of a military stance that rewards short-term gains over long-term preparedness will probably not be a deciding factor in the coming defence debate. Likewise, the fact that little or no evidence currently exists to justify the 1994 White Paper's impending rejection will be, unfortunately, irrelevant.

NOTES

1. To take just the latter, for example, the question of whether or not the CF's crimes in Somalia were the result of 'a few bad apples' or widespread institutional and cultural malaise has bedevilled both subsequent official inquiries and unofficial debate and public commentary. There is no easy or immutable answer to the question and, hence, no clear path to redress. The government's decision to curtail the public inquiry in early 1997 was accompanied by statements from the Defence Minister, Doug Young, that the 'culprits' had already been identified; many of the official reports produced under contract by the commission itself told a remarkably different tale (e.g., Winslow, 1997). As our collective interpretation of responsibility therefore evolves, Somalia's effect on the CF is likely to evolve as well.

2. Now the Organization for Security and Co-operation in Europe (OSCE).

3. Media response to the joint committee's report had been relatively positive, however. Both the *Toronto Star* and the *Globe and Mail* were supportive. See editorials 'A defence strategy for troubled times', *Toronto Star*, 2 Nov. 1994; 'Opening the door on defence policy', *Globe and Mail*, 2 Nov. 1994.

4. On the process of the defence review, see Stairs, 1995.

5. Confidential source.

6. For recent examples, see Gordon Legge, 'Navy dismisses captain from ship's command', *Ottawa Citizen*, 20 Oct. 1997; David Pugliese, 'Videotape, Photo show missile streaking towards warship', *Ottawa Citizen*, 31 Oct. 1997.

7. For recent statements of Axworthy's views on security policy, see 'Canada and human security: The need for leadership', and 'Between globalization and multipolarity: the case for a global, humane Canadian foreign policy', both on the DFAIT Web site at http://www.dfait-maeci.gc.ca/english/foreignp and dated December 1996.

REFERENCES

Axworthy, Lloyd. 1992a. 'Canadian Foreign Policy: A Liberal Party Perspective', *Canadian Foreign Policy* 1, 1 (Winter 1992–3).

———. 1992b. 'Forging the forces into peace police', *Globe and Mail*, 27 July.

Canada 21 Council. 1994. *Canada and Common Security in the Twenty-First Century*. Montreal: Masse Communications.

Canada, House of Commons and Senate. 1994. *Security in a Changing World: Report of the Special Joint Committee on Canada's Defence Policy*. Ottawa: Publications Service, Parliamentary Publications Directorate.

Department of National Defence (DND). 1994. *1994 Defence White Paper*. Ottawa: Minister of Supply and Services Canada.

Granatstein, J.L., and Robert Bothwell. 1990. *Pirouette: Pierre Trudeau and Canadian Foreign Policy*. Toronto: University of Toronto Press.

Lawson, Robert J. 1995. 'Construction of Consensus: The 1994 Canadian Defence Review', in Maxwell A. Cameron and Maureen Appel Molot, eds, *Canada Among Nations 1995: Democracy and Foreign Policy*. Ottawa: Carleton University Press.

Lenarcic, David A. 1998. *Knight-Errant? Canada and the Crusade to Ban Anti-Personnel Land Mines*. Toronto: Irwin.

Marteinson, John. 1994. Editorial. *Canadian Defence Quarterly* 24, 2 (Dec.).

———. 1995. Editorial. *Canadian Defence Quarterly* 24, 3 (Mar.).

Morton, Desmond. 1994. 'Shaping defence the Liberals' way means attacking the deficit first', *Toronto Star*, 20 Dec.

Nastro, Louis, and Kim Richard Nossal. 1997. 'The Commitment-Capability Gap: Implications for Canadian Foreign Policy in the Post-Cold War Era', *Canadian Defence Quarterly* 27, 1 (Autumn).

Pugliese, David. 1997. 'The Military and the Media: Time for Openness', *Canadian Defence Quarterly* 27, 1 (Autumn).

Rempel, Roy. 1996. *Counterweights: The Failure of Canada's German and European Policy, 1955–1995*. Montreal and Kingston: McGill-Queen's University Press.

Shadwick, Martin. 1996. 'Comment: Interesting Times', *Canadian Defence Quarterly* 26, 2 (Dec.).

Stairs, Denis. 1995. 'The Public Politics of the Canadian Defence and Foreign Policy Reviews', *Canadian Foreign Policy* 3, 1 (Spring 1995).

Winslow, Donna. 1997. *The Canadian Airborne Regiment in Somalia: A Socio-cultural Inquiry*. Ottawa: Minister of Public Works and Government Services Canada.

Young, M. Douglas. 1997. *Report to the Prime Minister: The Future of the Canadian Armed Forces: Opinions from the Defence Community* (by Tom Dimoff). Ottawa: Department of National Defence.

7

Providing Leadership for the Trade Regime

ROBERT WOLFE AND JOHN M. CURTIS

Globalization of economic activity may seem to be a vast and impersonal phenomenon, but unlike the weather, governments can and must do something about it. The world economy is being integrated by the accelerating reduction in the costs of transportation and communications, but such economic and technological integration must be matched by appropriate structures for governance. If markets were to become fully global, but political authority only local, then the resulting mismatch could again lead to political instability, financial collapse, and war. Providing such governance is not a simple task, however, nor is it a task to be accomplished once and for all by brilliant legal draughtsmen. The structure of governance is built day by day through hundreds of meetings. It takes consultation between people, firms, and governments; and it takes consultation and negotiation among states. The World Trade Organization (WTO) is an essential part of this system of governance, but some of its members worry that it is not yet strong enough to play a central role. In this chapter, we discuss how the WTO can provide stronger leadership for the trade regime, how members can provide leadership for the WTO, and, within that context, the role Canada plays as a leader within the trading system.

These three aspects of leadership in the era of globalization come together in the May 1998 anniversary meetings of the WTO.[1] The multilateral trading system formally began when the General Agreement on Tariffs and Trade (GATT) entered into force on 1 January 1948 as part of the construction of a postwar international architecture that included the World Bank and the International Monetary Fund (IMF). The proposal to celebrate this anniversary was first made in December 1996 by Canada's then Minister for International Trade, Art Eggleton, at the WTO's first biennial ministerial conference. He argued then that 'A 50th anniversary celebration would let us discuss whether this new institution has all the right machinery or whether we need to provide some further political guidance' (Eggleton, 1996). After intensive informal consultations, the Canadian delegation in Geneva proposed that the celebration take the form of a ministerial meeting (Canada, 1997). The central theme for the anniversary meeting will not be the past accomplishments of the GATT but a consideration of whether the WTO has the necessary internal characteristics to ensure that the organization can play a self-generating role in global governance. The challenge for ministers will be finding a way to move the trading system forward while helping to alleviate public disquiet about the extent and impact of globalization. Yet, while some officials may think the organization not strong enough, some environmental groups and social activists, as well as politicians, will argue that the dispute settlement system is already too strong or too remote to allow democratic accountability for its actions. A focus on this ministerial meeting, therefore, allows us to explore how abstract questions about leadership and dialogue become concrete in the actions of individuals and organizations.

We start from the assumption that global governance is essential because already vast markets are getting bigger, yet markets are not self-regulating. International regimes are the political response by states—they are the globalization of regulation. Regimes are the collective attempt to provide governance within particular domains of international life. The question for this chapter is: how can Canada provide leadership to other countries, all of whom collectively provide leadership for the WTO, so that the regime can play its role in global governance? The chapter is organized in four parts. In the first, we discuss the abstract problem facing the trading system—the need for global governance; we then show the concrete problem of unifying the WTO agenda and creating endogenous momentum. In the second part, we discuss the general problem of providing leadership to the trading system and why Canada should take the lead, rather than others such as the EU or US. In the third part, we outline the renovation that we think the institution needs. Finally, we conclude with a consideration of the prospects for the May 1998 ministerial meeting.

THE STATE OF THE TRADING SYSTEM

Two themes affect the current evolution of international trade agreements. One theme, the subject of a recent speech by the WTO director-general, Renato Ruggiero (1997), is the movement towards what he calls a borderless world, a world of 'deep integration'. The forces at work are seen in increased transaction flows of investment and services (especially telecommunications and financial services). The sources of the rules affecting these trade flows go beyond any one country. Trade is influenced not only by governments as regulators but also by the practices of multinational enterprises, big international law firms, and consumers in distant markets. Policy is shaped by interaction with international organizations and constrained by the views of global investors. The global flows of goods, services, and capital that pass through any country can be facilitated or impeded, but they are not caused by governments, and some traditional levers of economic policy have become disconnected.

The Canadian proposal for the 1998 ministerial meeting suggested that in addition to looking back at the trading system's remarkable accomplishments in underpinning global prosperity and stability after two world wars in the first half of this century, the commemoration should most importantly look forward to the challenges before members of the WTO, including the increased interdependence between the multilateral trading system and domestic economic policies. While tariffs remain high in some developing countries and countries in the process of joining the WTO, the future challenges for the trading system are primarily in the domain of domestic regulation rather than of border measures. The analytic challenge lies in understanding the effects on trade of things like rules on business practices, investment regulation, intellectual property rights, the environment, and labour standards. Citizens in many countries doubt the supposed benefits or inevitability of globalization and fear some of its apparent consequences for workers and the environment. The political challenge for the WTO will be finding ways to move forward on matters such as opening markets further or expanding and updating trade rules while providing reassurance that the trading system is not out of control or necessarily inimical to environmental or social objectives. The system has never been on auto pilot, since the WTO has no autonomous or supranational power. It must have political direction, however, and it must be seen to have political direction.

The second theme, therefore, which is just as important, is the continuing, even strengthening, role of the state. The state may be threatened on all sides, but it remains the locus of identity for most people, the basis of a sense of community. The global political order, in short, is a multi-state order (Zacher, 1997). The global economy has a powerful influence on this political order, but the global economy exists within the political space created by this system of states. States provide for the regulation of the global economy directly, since they are the only locus of authority, and they do it indirectly through the network of international regimes they have created. These international regimes in the narrowest sense solve the co-ordination problems that arise when states try to pursue their differing domestic objectives. The GATT, and its successor, the WTO, was from the beginning a functional approach to accommodating an open trading system to the welfare state. It was and remains remarkably successful.

The changing needs of international regulation need not result in complex new rules governing ever-widening areas of state authority, but the world economy must still be organized if it is to be stable. Our claim is that institutions matter a great deal for the conduct of trade. Government policy affects all sorts of costs of doing business, and does so differentially, from country to country. Almost all domestic policy can now be claimed to be an international economic policy, making policy harmonization impossible in the absence of a single world government. Nevertheless, the pattern of international institutionalization can affect domestic policy formation. What is needed are efforts to ensure that states talk to each other, co-ordinate their actions, and provide each other with lots of information. States must be left to make their own decisions, to strike their own distributive bargains, but to do so within an internationally under-stood compromise between state autonomy and international open-ness—the continuing paradox of living in a world of states.

States created the WTO to help them resolve this central paradox of global governance, but doubts persist about its effectiveness either to promote openness or to protect sovereignty. A common, if unstated, misconception about the GATT and now the WTO sees it as a forum of primarily cyclical relevance, as though it delivered all its benefits at the successful conclusion of a round of trade negotiations and then went into hibernation. It is important to think of at least three different time horizons for the WTO in its leadership role in the gover-nance of the global trading system.

The first task, the *immediate agenda*, is to provide a framework for the implementation of the results of multilateral trade negotia-tions. The successful efforts to finish leftover negotiations on trade in financial services and basic telecommunications services, and to implement recent negotiations on market access for information tech-nology products, also come under this category of making the sys-tem work. Members use the apparatus of the various WTO commit-tees, such as the Committee on Agriculture, to notify each other of their efforts to implement their commitments under WTO agreements, such as the Agreement on Agriculture. The trade policies of mem-bers are then subject to review in these committees and in the Trade Policy Review Mechanism, the WTO body charged with surveillance of the ensemble of members' trade policies. When members cannot agree on whether they are keeping their commitments, they can make use of the WTO procedures for consultation and dispute set-tlement. The other item on the immediate agenda is developing and maintaining coherence in the open, liberal, and multilateral system of trade and payments. The WTO must develop and strengthen its co-operation with the IMF and the World Bank, the other major organi-zations engaged in the governance of the world economy, and it must ensure that regional agreements neither act as a drag on mul-tilateralism nor fragment the trading system.

The second task of the WTO is to provide the forum for negotia-tions among members concerning their multilateral trade relations. The WTO has a *medium-term agenda*, which could be seen as a pro-longation of the GATT Uruguay Round, but which also includes acces-sion negotiations with nearly 30 countries. Successful completion of those accessions, especially of the negotiations with China, bringing a vast market under WTO disciplines, could have an effect on world trade comparable to that of an earlier round in the 1960s or 1970s. In effect, WTO members are committed to using scarce negotiating resources to make the trading system wider. If the process succeeds, accessions will not divert attention when the next full negotiating round is launched. It remains important not to fudge the terms of accession for these formerly centrally planned economies, however, because insistence on domestic regulatory transparency has major implications for the vital non-discrimination norms of most-favoured nation (MFN) and national treatment.

The medium-term agenda also includes a number of important negotiations already agreed to or in prospect for 1999 or 2000. The WTO agreements and the understandings at the Marrakech minister-ial meeting concluding the Uruguay Round in 1994 created a bewil-dering menu for further work. The WTO's first biennial ministerial meeting, held in Singapore in December 1996, performed a valuable function by allowing a consolidation of all of these things into the so-called 'Built-in Agenda'.[2] Members had agreed at Marrakech that negotiations on agriculture were to begin in 1999, and on services in 2000. They had also agreed to have reviews and other new work on institutional issues, notably the dispute settlement understanding, and on such trade rules as anti-dumping, subsidies, customs valuation, and rules of origin. Market access for manufactured goods does not feature on the Built-in Agenda, except for a review of progress in implementing the agreements on textiles and clothing.

The third time horizon affecting the WTO looks to the future. Prior to Singapore, many developing countries had been resistant to adding new issues to the WTO *longer-term agenda*. They favoured consolidation of the WTO and implementation of the Uruguay Round agreements rather than expansion of the WTO into new areas, given how stretched their limited bureaucratic capacity had been in im-plementing what had already been agreed upon. They had also been concerned with the slow pace of implementation under the Agreement on Textiles and highly resistant to pressure from some Organization for Economic Co-operation and Development (OECD) countries to include labour rights in the WTO. In the end, the agenda for Singapore evolved in a balanced way between an assessment of the implementation of commitments under the WTO agreements and decisions, including a review of the ongoing negotiations and the WTO Work Program; and a discussion of how to address the chal-lenges of an evolving world economy. With the reasonably strong language in the Singapore Declaration with respect to textiles and acceptance that the International Labour Organization was the proper forum for discussion of Core Labour Standards, developing countries agreed to the creation of:

- a working group on trade and investment;[3]
- a working group on transparency in government procurement;
- a working group to study issues relating to the interaction between trade and competition policy in order to identify any areas that may merit further consideration in the WTO framework (WTO, 1996b).

Even if these working groups find ways to make their new issues negotiable in the WTO, they do not exhaust the longer-term agenda. The WTO is not a negative list in which everything not explicitly excluded is covered. It is instead a positive list, since it applies to only those tradeable items covered by the rules and mentioned explicitly in the schedules of market access commitments submitted by members. The WTO must keep adding to this positive list as the world economy changes and expands: if something is not listed in a member's schedule or covered by a rule, then it is effectively outside the system. With respect to trade in goods, for example, newer products, such as those produced by biotechnology, are poorly covered. On trade in services, coverage of most sectors is still thin.

With such a complicated agenda, debate continues about when to start laying the basis for a *new round*, the ninth such set of negotiations since the creation of the GATT, or indeed whether a new set of comprehensive negotiations as such is needed to keep the system moving forward. The ongoing work in WTO committees is analogous to some of the conceptual work usually done in the beginning stages of any negotiating round. Recalling previous rounds that seemed interminable, many negotiators still hope that further comprehensive and time-consuming rounds will not be needed and that the biennial ministerial meetings will serve to force the agenda on negotiations conducted by the subsidiary bodies without the need for a round. By bundling issues ready for decision together they could be what Jeffrey Schott calls 'round-ups' instead of rounds. US officials see no value at present in a large, complex round if it is possible to reach agreements sector by sector and issue by issue. In this perception they perhaps misunderstand why the recent sectoral agreements were possible. In the current jargon, the agreements on financial and telecommunications services and on information technology products had a critical mass, a sufficient number of the right countries participating.[4] Some negotiators are now musing that an alternative to rounds is the cluster approach, in which like issues could be linked either vertically (e.g., grouping subsidies wherever the issue arises into one negotiation) or horizontally (e.g., considering all aspects of agriculture at once.)

Experience so far with the difficult issues, notably trade in maritime transport services, left over from the Uruguay Round and the Built-in Agenda suggests that a comprehensive set of negotiations will be needed, whatever they are named. Given the diverse elements and divergent time horizons of the three agendas, it is hard to imagine how the process can be managed without such negotiations, probably starting in 1999 or 2000, for exactly the same reason that the Uruguay Round proved to be so big and took so long. The 'single undertaking'[5] makes the WTO fully multilateral, and using so-called clusters would be a step back. In the discussions at Singapore, for example, agricultural exporters had been keen to launch analytical work in preparation for the 1999 negotiations, and some countries had wanted a discussion of whether all of these reviews and negotiations should be rolled into a new round. However, ministers were only able to agree to carry on with the WTO Work Program as previously agreed, without prejudging what the next steps might be.

Similarly, on trade and the environment, ministers agreed that 'The breadth and complexity of the issues covered by the Committee shows that further work needs to be undertaken on all items of its agenda' (WTO, 1996b). When issues were taken in isolation, movement was impossible. Clusters are unlikely to include enough issues to allow differing interests to be accommodated, either between countries or within them. It is in the nature of multilateralism that the trade-offs between issues and domains will be diffuse and in some respects non-commensurable. A round is a proven technique for aggregating issues and players into balanced compromises, once issues are well understood. It is true that the WTO sometimes moves at a frustratingly slow speed, but problems are not solved if the tough nuts are simply excised to allow progress to be made on easy issues. When the trading system is a single undertaking, packages have to have something for everyone. Given the divergent interests at play on investment and agriculture, for example, or maritime transport services and textiles, it seems particularly hard to envisage progress without a wider set of negotiations to allow countries to win in one area what they will believe themselves to have lost in another. No mechanism other than a comprehensive set of negotiations exists to ensure an appropriate aggregation of issues and participants, with a forcing mechanism to ensure that at some point countries large and small accept the best deal on offer.

In sum, the WTO does not lack for things to do. What it lacks is the ability to bring its medium-term and longer-term agendas into a coherent whole. How can the WTO develop sufficient self-sustaining forward momentum so that it can be seen to be the focal point for governance of the trading system? Can the WTO be a policy leader, as well as a policy forum, the place for settling policy and trade disputes?

LEADERSHIP IN THE TRADING SYSTEM

The argument so far is that continued international economic integration requires corresponding political management in international regimes. Some scholars have argued that the necessary systemic stability can be an artefact of hegemony, or leadership exercised through the structural preponderance of a dominant power. Since we do not see any likely candidates for such a role at the moment, we think that global governance is provided through regimes. The aspect of regimes of particular interest in this paper is leadership. Why leadership? Because we still live in a system of states. As long as states remain a useful way to think of world order, it is equally useful to think of the WTO attempting to lead the trade regime.

The central question in this context, then, is: what is required to guide the WTO to enable it to provide leadership? The launch of the WTO was a great success, and over its first three years the organization has been gathering momentum. A first ministerial conference has been held, and reasonable progress has been made in implementing the results of the Uruguay Round, although at Singapore ministers thought that some parts of the process had been slow.[6] Accession negotiations for new members have been so active that universal membership in the trading system is now in prospect, which is not to deny the difficulty of issues to be resolved before the larger applicants, China and Russia, are at last able to join. The integrated dispute settlement system has been busier and more successful than the GATT system it replaced, with over 100 cases launched in just three years. During 1997, major negotiations were concluded under the

WTO, without a 'round', on trade in basic telecommunications services and financial services and on information technology products. The appearance of gathering momentum is deceptive, however. All of these developments were mandated by the Marrakech ministerial conference, where the WTO agreements were signed. Speed has been gained on the downward slope of the roller-coaster, and the trough is approaching. As now constituted, the WTO lacks the endogenous capacity to maintain momentum on its own. Our discussion is in two parts: in this section, we discuss the leadership necessary for renovation, and why Canada should provide it. In the next section, we discuss the institutional renovation that will be necessary for the WTO to exercise leadership.

The literature on international co-operation has not reached a consensus on how international organizations can change. The relevant themes in the literature include the structural power of the major economies, the influence of so-called middle powers, the roles of non-state actors (business and NGOs), and the way leadership takes non-material forms—technical, intellectual, and entrepreneurial leadership, for example (Cooper et al., 1993: 24–5). The power of new ideas has been shown to be significant when the issue is rules; but ideas alone count for less when the problem is reciprocal bargains, as is the case for most market access negotiations. Large countries, it is said, often get their way—or at least can block what they dislike— while smaller countries must band together if they wish to influence the evolution of an organization. In the WTO, every member in effect has a veto, with the US and the EU having the strongest, but a veto is not worth much. A veto is a tool for blocking unwanted outcomes, but a veto cannot achieve a positive one (Bayne, 1997: 371). On balance, these factors point to the importance of leadership in the current conjuncture by a country such as Canada, when ideas matter more than structural power.

If structural power were all that mattered, then the prospects for the WTO would be gloomy at a time when the United States appears to be turning inward and the EU seems preoccupied by deepening its monetary integration and expanding to the east. Many claimed a leadership role for the US early in the Clinton administration with ratification of NAFTA and the Uruguay Round, but since then we have seen little direction. The administration attempted to reclaim the trade initiative in the fall of 1997, but the lack of congressional support for fast-track negotiating authority undermined the credibility of US leadership. A President weakened by divergent domestic challenges and facing political uncertainty in the Middle East and economic difficulties in Asia may well choose not to add the trading system to his list of troubles, especially if it means taking on his key domestic constituencies of workers, producers, and environmentalists who think that their country is harmed by increased trade. As political hostility to broad trade liberalization grows, US officials have focused on portraying the reciprocal benefits of negotiated deals and being tough on enforcement. In the 1997 trade agenda of the office of the United States Trade Representative or the debate over fast-track authority, we saw no discussion of institution-building. The policy stance is not so much unilateral as instrumental, but without fast-track authority the US will be less able to lead. This supposed weakness may not matter much for the WTO in the short term, but it will have a negative impact on the long-run stability and evolution of the system.

It is no accident that the idea leading to the creation of the WTO itself was the result of an initiative launched by Canada's then Trade Minister, John Crosbie, in 1990. Canada is well situated to exercise certain kinds of leadership. Nicholas Bayne, who had long experience serving the British government at the OECD and in the G-7 process, says that governments get what they want in international economic institutions through (1) singleness of purpose; (2) coalition-building; (3) manoeuvring for the middle ground; and (4) exploiting the machinery (1997: 371–3). All of these factors come more easily to countries like Canada than they do to the other Quad members.[7] When the US administration shows leadership in trade, it is sometimes accused at home of being a Boy Scout and abroad of being a bully. Japan often finds the process of domestic consultation and internal consensus-building difficult. Although responsibility for trade policy is shared in Canada, notably among the Ministers for International Trade, Finance, and Industry as well as the relevant sectoral departments, developing an interdepartmentally agreed position in Ottawa is less public and much easier than getting agreement among EU member states in Brussels or building a consensus on anything in Washington.[8] Canada belongs to many coalitions in the WTO because large and small countries alike feel safe in making common cause with us on a variety of issues. Our 4 per cent share in world trade makes us the largest of the small and the smallest of the big. These coalitions are easier to build because Canadian policy does occupy a middle ground between American free traders and French interventionists. We are a remarkably open resource-intensive economy with major interests in traded services. We are therefore welcome members of coalitions of some of the world's most advanced economies and of coalitions of resource exporters. We are members of the Quad yet fully involve ourselves in the Commonwealth and la Francophonie, dominated as they are by developing countries. Canada's relative wealth and currently robust growth are also leadership assets, lending credibility to arguments about openness. Finally, as committed institution-builders and multilateralists who have been been members since the creation of the GATT, Canadians start with natural advantages, which are accentuated by our ability to work in English and French. We are also comfortable working in an environment where legal decisions are based on precedent, as in common law.

The dissenting voice notes that countries that pursue a small number of national interests at any one time can be or can seem to be more effective; for example, Canada and Australia pursued different strategies within the Cairns Group of agricultural exporters during the Uruguay Round, with Canada's freedom of action being more constrained by membership in other coalitions and by a more diverse domestic farm community. Moreover, market size and willingness to use it aggressively become more decisive when reciprocal bargains are to be struck. Nevertheless, Canada has played a disproportionately important role involving itself in, and providing leadership for, the broader trade system. The public has supported this activity over the years, with the exception of defining events such as the elections of 1911 and 1988, because of the recognition, however imperfect, of the role of trade and of international markets in providing Canadians improved standards of living and of the need to deal on as predictable a basis as possible with our overwhelmingly important trade and investment partner, the United States.

Specific negotiating objectives within this broadly favourable Canadian policy environment have been developed within governments, primarily at the federal level, but increasingly—as domestic regulations become more important in trade matters—at the provincial level. Trade policy is the subject of frequent meetings of officials, occasional meetings of ministers responsible for trade, and, from time to time, of first ministers in both the economic policy and the constitutional contexts. Active consultations, based on both economic and political analyses and a perception of sectoral or other specific interests as well as on experience in specific markets, are undertaken with private-sector groups, particularly since the establishment in 1985 of formal advisory groups to the Minister of International Trade. Mechanisms for consulting the public are less well developed, although parliamentary committees have been used to air major policy initiatives.[9] The Prime Minister uses his Team Canada trade missions with provincial leaders and business representatives to dramatize the benefits of open markets. As well, ministers make frequent speeches to Canadian audiences about the impact of openness on jobs and growth in Canada.

In sum, Canada has certain advantages not available to other Quad members in providing leadership for the WTO. How should we use them? Canadian officials have been active both on a day-to-day basis in Geneva and in organizing meetings of the various informal groupings to which we belong. In the fall of 1997, for example, the 'invisibles group' met under Canadian chairmanship to discuss a Canadian background paper that outlined a set of ideas for managing the agenda for the May ministerial meeting. One of the most important things that Canada can do in the Quad is to encourage others to work within the system. It may be thought that since Canada has no choice but to be multilateral, we are free-riding by encouraging the US to work multilaterally. Rather, what worries us is that if the US begins to pursue a unilateral strategy, other large or regionally significant countries will see no reason not to do the same thing. A world in which Europe, China, India, Japan, Brazil, and Russia all acted unilaterally would not be in Canada's interests. Or that of the United States. The small size, for Canada, of most other markets combined with the sophistication of our engagement with world commerce means that multilateralism is the best use of scarce Canadian bureaucratic and political resources. Our participation in trade negotiations of any sort should aim at ensuring open arteries for commerce based on national treatment and MFN status, the key principles of the trade regime and ones especially important for small countries. While our dependence on the US market increases the value of other fora for us as a way to gain allies, multilateralism is also important because our firms are often part of production networks involving or centred on US firms; these networks, and their Canadian participants, benefit from US participation in the WTO. Engaging the US in multilateralism is a vital Canadian objective (Keating, 1993).

Canada has frequently exercised leadership in the past within the trade regime. Foreign policy initiatives, such as the promotion of the land-mines treaty during 1997, are better known because trade initiatives take place within an established institutional setting where the need is not to create something new but to move the system forward. Canada has long been a leader in this domain, beginning with the prominent role played by Dana Wilgress in the postwar negotiations that created the multilateral trading system.[10] More recently, Allan MacEachen as Secretary of State for External Affairs chaired the 1982 GATT ministerial conference, and, as noted above, in 1990 John Crosbie as Trade Minister proposed the creation of the WTO itself. Canada's current Trade Minister, Sergio Marchi, believes that Canada must continue to play a leadership role in liberalizing trade in various markets around the globe. Open markets have been good for Canada, but attracting investment and promoting trade depend on a transparent rules-based system that ensures the opportunity of equal treatment with larger trading partners. 'Rules are the equalizer', Marchi has said, and therefore 'Canada must help write the rules'. He had in mind not just the WTO, but also Canadian leadership in encouraging a trade-strengthening process such as hosting the 1997 APEC summit, pushing for the 1996 Action Plan with the European Union, championing the Free Trade Area of the Americas, and seeking a closer relationship with MERCOSUR, the South American regional trade grouping (Marchi, 1997). Canada's role in thinking of and building consensus for a forward-looking celebration of the first 50 years of the multilateral trading system is of a piece, therefore, with its general participation in the system.

WHAT RENOVATION IS NEEDED?

Why, after only three years of operation, might Canada think that the WTO as an institution needs renovation? The WTO has the *explicit* institutional structure that the GATT lacked. Ultimate authority rests with ministers, but in the intervals between the biennial meetings of the Ministerial Conference, its decision-making functions for both the GATT 1994 and the General Agreement on Trade in Services (GATS) are carried out by the General Council, made up of ambassadors resident in Geneva. The General Council also discharges the responsibilities of the Dispute Settlement Body and the Trade Policy Review Body. The Uruguay Round agreements also provide for a variety of subsidiary committees under these bodies. Officials attending meetings of these bodies come from permanent delegations in Geneva, supplemented by the participation of experts from capitals. All 132 members of the WTO can attend meetings of all WTO bodies. Unlike the World Bank and IMF, however, no power is delegated to a smaller executive group, and the WTO secretariat has no influence over individual countries' policies (although some analytical comments are made in the regular trade policy reviews).

With so many members, none of these bodies could function if all discussions involved all members all of the time in attempts to reach consensus in public. The WTO continues the GATT's tradition of making decisions on rules not by voting but by consensus.[11] Where consensus is not possible, the WTO agreement allows for voting, but that is rare. A new consensus-building process is emerging, along GATT lines, but it is slow and ad hoc. Informal meetings of heads of delegation play an important consultative role, but major decisions usually emerge from a series of smaller meetings of ministers and officials, such as the ironically prominent invisibles group.[12] The technique of holding smaller meetings was common in the GATT, as it no doubt is in most other international organizations. One former official called it the 'expanding-and-shrinking-concentric-circle-approach', in which issues may be broached in a plenary, but smaller groups meeting in private do most of the work, sometimes over a period of months (Patterson, 1986: 186). This traditional technique may have reached its limits now that the WTO has over 130 members; for example, ministers from many smaller countries were unhappy with how little they had to do during the Singapore ministerial conference, yet the number of formal and informal meetings strains the resources of even the largest delegations.

These structural difficulties are compounded by the unwillingness of member countries to allow a strong leadership role for the director-general, the most senior executive of the WTO. He does not control any agenda, and he has no formal table that he can convene, yet he is supposed to provide leadership to his organization and to the trading system—the reason that many members wanted a former trade minister, like Renato Ruggiero, to be the organization's first leader. The WTO lacks resources to apply the existing rules, let alone to undertake the analysis and discussion needed to develop endogenous momentum, and member countries frequently lack the necessary resources, especially in their national capitals, to play their part in the system. The dispute settlement system has no economic analytic capacity; it can consider legal issues as placed before a panel by the parties, but it cannot move the system forward.

The challenges facing the WTO after its first three years come in two forms—the need for political or strategic leadership; and the need for effective management. How can the world trading community ensure that WTO bodies both implement the agreements and look forward? Reconciling the equality of states with effective management is a problem that besets all international organizations; the UN Security Council, for example, is one solution to this puzzle, though changes in the world have led to demands that it, too, change (von Riekhoff, 1996). The state is not terribly useful as the only basis for membership and decision-making in international organizations because of enormous disparities of population and/or wealth, and when the relevant issue is the global economy this is especially the case. Nevertheless, states still remain the only legitimate form of authority in global governance, particularly when the matters to be regulated involve only the actions of states.

The leadership problem has been acute in both the IMF and the World Bank, the other major economic organizations. A comparative look at their structures helps in understanding the challenge facing the WTO. Formal decision-making in both organizations is vested in a Board of Governors; the Minister of Finance is usually the governor for Canada, but both organizations also have smaller Executive Boards. Smaller bodies have value, especially in ensuring that *formal decisions* will be translated into *actions* by the most powerful members, but the representative basis of such bodies is always delicate. The circle is squared in the IMF by the elaborate constituency system, whereby smaller countries that do not have a seat on the Executive Board as a matter of right must create voluntary constituencies of supporters large enough to ensure a seat (Lister, 1984). The creation of a smaller group of officials solved the decision-making problem for the organizations, but the Boards of Governors remained too large for effective ministerial discussion of complex policy issues. The solution to this problem came only when the Interim Committee of the IMF and the similar Development Committee of the World Bank were created in 1974 in the anxious climate that followed the apparent collapse of the Bretton Woods system in 1971, although the idea of such a body was proposed by J.M. Keynes and others at the original Bretton Woods conference in 1944. The composition of the Interim Committee mirrors that of the Executive Board, but where the members of the Executive Board are senior officials resident in Washington, members of the Interim Committee are the ministers who hold positions as governors of the IMF. Where the Executive Board is responsible for management and operation of the Fund, the terms of reference for the Interim Committee require it to advise the Board of Governors with respect to its supervising the management of the international monetary system. The Interim Committee has had considerable success in addressing political issues, leaving technical matters and implementation to executive directors (de Vries, 1985: vol. 2, 967, vol. 3, 213–14, 576–7).

The leadership question did arise during planning for the postwar trading system when delegates to the United Nations Conference on Trade and Employment held in Havana in 1948 debated whether the proposed International Trade Organization (ITO) should have an executive board (Hart, 1995: 49). Everyone accepted the need for such a body and that it might have a good deal of functional responsibility for management of the ITO. The conflicts were over whether the ITO should have weighted voting and who should be on the board. The eventual compromise, in which Canada, acting in its own interest, played a major role, was to give every member of the ITO an equal vote, but one of the criteria for the composition of the executive board was representation of the members of chief economic importance based on shares of international trade, a provision that would have made Canada a de facto permanent member of the board (see Article 78 of the charter, reproduced in Hart, 1995).

The ITO was never ratified, leaving the GATT as the only trade body. While the ITO would have had an elaborate institutional structure, the GATT, in contrast, was thought to be temporary, and the negotiators gave it almost no institutional structure. The GATT suffered from this structural weakness for decades. Article XXV of GATT 1947 deals with joint action by the Contracting Parties, as the members were known. It provides only that they shall meet from time to time, and that when they act jointly they should do so as the Contracting Parties.[13] The GATT as such could not act, and the executive secretary of the Contracting Parties had little authority. The dispute settlement system and other aspects of the GATT apparatus simply evolved over time. One of the most important institutional achievements of the Uruguay Round, therefore, was simply codification of more than four decades of constitutional innovation and evolution in the GATT.

The creation of the WTO, while a major achievement of the Uruguay Round, has resulted in an architecture that is not complete. In the 1980s, the group of experts who provided some of the ideas that informed the preparations for the Uruguay Round recommended the creation of a ministerial body whose limited membership would be based on a constituency system (GATT, 1985: 48). A similar body was also envisaged in the 1955 draft Organization for Trade Co-operation, an unsuccessful attempt to remedy the GATT's constitutional defects (Jackson, 1990: 16). A senior officials group was created, however, in 1975 during the Tokyo Round as the Consultative Group of Eighteen, known as CG-18. The CG-18 mandate was to facilitate the achievement of broad GATT objectives, particularly by following international trade developments. It was charged with forestalling sudden disturbances that could represent a threat to the multilateral trading system and with monitoring the international adjustment process, including co-ordination between the GATT and the IMF. The group appears to have had a special interest in the problems of development, the relation between trade and financial issues, agriculture, new trade issues, and the management of the trading system, notably in preparing for the 1982 GATT ministerial conference.[14] The CG-18 was a fertile source of new trade policy ideas in the Tokyo Round, but during the 1980s it gradually fell into disuse, although its members from developing countries had apparently wished it to meet more frequently.

Preparations during 1996 for the first biennial ministerial conference at Singapore exposed the continuing institutional weakness of the WTO. The routine sorts of preparation of operational issues proceeded smoothly within the new committee structure, though it was arduous and time-consuming, but the agenda itself had to be discussed in a series of ad hoc informal meetings, especially in the invisibles group. Ministers, having no forum in Geneva, held a series of ad hoc meetings of various groupings in Vancouver (November 1995), Lausanne (July 1996), and Christchurch (July 1996). Quad ministers met more than once, and there were many other meetings, conferences, and seminars, notably in Brisbane (February 1996) and Singapore (April 1996), all aimed at attempts to set the agenda and influence the direction of the meeting. And yet the agenda took shape slowly and seemed to be unambitious.

The WTO has inherited a double-edged characteristic of the GATT: it remains essentially a member-driven contractually based organization. The WTO, like the GATT, has no autonomous power, and the secretariat is kept on a tight leash—in contrast to the OECD, for example, which has a much larger secretariat able to take some policy initiative on its own. The WTO as such has no authority over anything: it does not regulate trade flows, and changes in the trade policy of members must be implemented at home. The initiative, therefore, remains with states. The possibility of replacing the CG-18 was discussed during the Uruguay Round. Some negotiators thought a group of 22 (as it was by 1987) too large to be effective or too small to be representative. The plethora of meetings outside the GATT were seen by some smaller countries as a problem, because the meetings had no clear mandate and the guest list was often ad hoc, but others were not concerned by meetings to which they were not invited since such meetings could safely be ignored. Developing countries wary of the Security Council syndrome resisted proposals to create a successor group to the CG-18, whether of officials or of ministers. The American proposal of a management board, made before the WTO idea emerged in 1990, was seen as especially hegemonic by some developing countries (Croome, 1995: 156, 274).[15]

Nevertheless, the future of the trading system should be on the table in the WTO, not just in ad hoc meetings of ministers. If it is in the WTO, it should have the benefit of a secretariat analysis of the state of the trading system, based on consultations with the World Bank and the IMF. (Such an analysis could also strengthen the quality, analysis, and profile of the WTO *Annual Report*.) Member-driven organizations are responsive, but they are also prone to drift; in the WTO, members are deeply suspicious of the organization having any autonomous capacity to move the system. Such leadership can only come from ministers, but they currently only meet biennially. As Ruggiero has argued, political issues do not arise only every two years. Moreover (a) every country has to feel itself involved in negotiations and management, but (b) the system has to be streamlined.

CONCLUSION

The May 1998 ministerial conference must begin the process of equipping the WTO to develop more independent momentum. After its first three years of operation, it is clear that the institutionalization of the governance of the trading system in the WTO is a great improvement over arrangements under the GATT, but the institution is still weaker than necessary. Initiative, along with authority, will and probably should remain with member states, but they can provide themselves with better machinery. The anniversary ministerial meeting was conceived as an important step in the process of institutional renovation.

The first significant element in the May 1998 meeting was the date, which was chosen to coincide with the Birmingham G-7 summit, providing major political figures the opportunity to attend the anniversary celebrations since they would be in Europe anyway.[16] The meeting was also timed to come six months earlier than required, as will be the subsequent biennial conference. The result will be that the third ministerial meeting, normally due in 2000, an American election year, will instead be held in 1999. With this schedule, the third biennial meeting will be held three years rather than four years after the first, but the trading system needs this impetus just now, and it needs to ensure that this vital decision-making body does not meet during American election years.

This emphasis on the US electoral cycle does not mean that we think the trading system depends on American leadership. We do agree, however, that no comprehensive set of negotiations could possibly succeed without active US participation, which is often not possible amidst the distractions of an election year. The American role, however, is more important for market access negotiations and more essential in the later stages of the process, when market size matters more than building a consensus for new ideas. The trade regime is not dependent on the presence of a hegemon. Observers who think the US role central believe that it is essential to set global free trade as a political objective to ensure that the WTO maintains its momentum (Bergsten, 1996). We are sceptical. The WTO already has a broad and continuing commitment to further liberalization. What it needs is the leadership to bring the various elements of its Work Program into a package of new negotiations, allowing the WTO to continue the process of including new domains and areas of the world economy within a single multilateral governance structure. We have long thought that that momentum can best be imparted from ministers meeting twice a year as an executive committee (Wolfe, 1996), although such ideas have more detractors than supporters at present.

The WTO is now engaged in what are effectively the preparatory stages for a new comprehensive set of negotiations. The anniversary ministerial meeting should give broad direction for the future. Absent the distractions of the US political cycle, the 1999 meeting should be the occasion for decisions on the various reviews on the Built-in Agenda and for the new negotiations mandated for services and agriculture. Since those two sectors are not self-balancing, even in combination, by 2000 something like a round, whatever it is called, should be under way so that the WTO, not regional arrangements, is the focus of attention and activity, with enough on the table to engage the leading developing countries. The United States will need fast-track authority by then, but although such authority may be desirable earlier for other reasons, it is not essential in this context to have it sooner. In the meantime, other countries, like Canada, can provide the leadership to proceed with the continuing institutional renovation of the system.

International regimes are essential because the nature of international order is not given by some force of nature: it is a political construction that responds to change in markets and societies. The relative balance between these two organizing principles determines the nature of collective organization for individual states and for sets of states. The paradox is that an increasing role for global markets will call for an increasing role for states and their global institutions, not least in the trading system (Wolfe, 1997). World markets are vastly larger, and more open, than when the GATT was created 50 years ago, but the WTO is a much larger and more sophisticated institution of governance than the GATT. Canada is not alone in wanting to retain the ability to regulate in the national interest, to allow the process of domestic dialogue to have a determining influence on policy. Canada will only have such scope in the domain of trade, however, if the WTO is able to keep pace with globalization. Small countries cannot provide global governance on their own, but Canada is rich enough, experienced enough, and multilateralist enough to see the value of the institution and the process, not just the market access outcome, and to have the credibility with other states necessary to provide institutional leadership. Canadian politicians have worked hard to convince the Canadian public and Canadian business of the benefits of openness to trade, ensuring that international leadership is supported at home. Canadian leadership is most important in the realm of ideas about the rules and principles of the trading system, and our strengths can be used to bring other members of the WTO together. Those skills were used to build support for the idea of a ministerial celebration of the first 50 years of the GATT; they were then used to ensure that ministerial meetings made a contribution to strengthening the WTO for the future.

NOTES

The views expressed in this essay are those of the author and do not represent the policy of the government of Canada.

1. We are vague about the details of the meetings since members had yet to take final decisions, including on whether leaders would attend, when this chapter was completed.
2. For a full description and discussion of the issues on this agenda, see the appendix to Ostry (1997). See also WTO (1996a).
3. One early issue for consideration in the new working party was how to make use of the OECD work on investment. (See the discussion by Elizabeth Smythe of the Multilateral Agreement on Investment in Chapter 12.) Periodic reports of the work of WTO bodies, including these new working parties, will be found in *WTO Focus*.
4. Critical mass differs by issue. It does not matter how many participants are engaged as long as they are the right participants; this depends on a mix of intellectual leadership and market weight, since MFN status and the single undertaking ensure that any agreement can be multilateralized to the full membership. In many sectors it is possible to reach over 90 per cent of the relevant global markets with under 50 members engaged.
5. Throughout the Uruguay Round, participants acted in the light of the General Principle in the Punta del Este Declaration, that 'The launching, the conduct and the implementation of the outcome of the negotiations shall be treated as parts of a single undertaking.' With some minor exceptions, all parts of the WTO system are covered by the WTO agreement, which members must accept in its entirety. This new regime principle is called the single undertaking.
6. On implementation, see WTO activities, in WTO (1996a).
7. The four largest trading entities, the EU, US, Japan, and Canada, meet frequently among officials and ministers.
8. One might add that the habits of consultation developed in a federal system serve us well abroad. See Stairs (1982).
9. Canadian consultative mechanisms are placed in an international context in Bellmann and Gerster (1990).
10. Wilgress was a talented multilateral negotiator who chaired key committees in the negotiation of the GATT and the ITO, then was chairman of the annual meeting of the GATT contracting parties for the first five years (Hart, 1995: 4).
11. Consensus works well for normative decisions on rules, but the WTO uses *de facto* weighted voting for the reciprocal exchanges inherent in market access negotiations. Bargaining in any domain is dominated by the countries with the largest markets; the results are extended to everyone else through the MFN role.
12. Participants include the Quad, as well as Argentina, Australia, Brazil, India, Korea, Morocco, New Zealand, Norway, Poland, Singapore, and Switzerland. The WTO director-general is also invited to attend.
13. The capital letters designate the collective entity, such as it was, since the GATT was an agreement, not an organization.

14. The CG-18 was established 11 July 1975 (GATT, *Basic Instruments and Selected Documents* (*BISD* 22S/15); made permanent 22 Nov. 1979 (*BISD* 26S/289); and has been in suspense since 1988 (*BISD* 35S/293). The last meeting was held 21–2 Sept. 1987.
15. See the chapter on the 'Negotiating Group on the Functioning of the GATT System' in Stewart (1993).
16. Ironically, the summit itself may not discuss the WTO at all, because Boris Yeltsin would attend that part of the meeting in the new G-8 format, but the Russian Federation is not yet a member of the WTO.

REFERENCES

Bayne, N. 1997. 'What Governments Want from International Economic Institutions and How They Get It', *Government and Opposition* 32, 3: 361–77.

Bellmann, C., and R. Gerster. 1996. 'Accountability in the World Trade Organization', *Journal of World Trade* 30, 6: 31–74.

Bergsten, C.F. 1996. 'Globalizing Free Trade', *Foreign Affairs* 75, 3: 105–20.

Canada. 1997. 'Commemoration of the Fiftieth Anniversary of the Multilateral Trading System: Statement By Canada', Geneva, 11 Feb. (WTO: WT/GC/8).

Cooper, A.F., R.A. Higgott, and K.R. Nossal. 1993. *Relocating Middle Powers: Australia and Canada in a Changing World Order*. Vancouver: University of British Columbia Press.

Croome, J. 1995. *Reshaping the World Trading System: A History of the Uruguay Round*. Geneva: World Trade Organization.

de Vries, M.G. 1985. *International Monetary Fund 1972–1978: Cooperation On Trial*, 3 vols. Washington: International Monetary Fund.

Eggleton, A.C. 1996. 'Statement by the Honourable Arthur C. Eggleton, Minister for International Trade of Canada, to the WTO Ministerial Conference', Singapore, 9 Dec. (WTO: WT/MIN(96)/ST/1).

GATT. 1985. *Trade Policies for a Better Future*. Geneva: General Agreement on Tariffs and Trade.

Hart, M., ed. 1995. *Also Present at the Creation: Dana Wilgress and the United Nations Conference on Trade and Employment at Havana*. Ottawa: Centre for Trade Policy and Law.

Jackson, J.H. 1990. *Restructuring the GATT System*. New York: Council on Foreign Relations Press for the Royal Institute of International Affairs.

Keating, T. 1993. *Canada and World Order: The Multilateralist Tradition in Canadian Foreign Policy*. Toronto: McClelland & Stewart.

Lister, F.K. 1984. *Decision-Making Strategies in International Organizations: The IMF Model*. Denver: University of Denver Press.

Marchi, S. 1997. 'Notes for an Address by the Honourable Sergio Marchi, Minister for International Trade, on the Occasion of the Debate on the Speech from the Throne', Ottawa, 25 Sept. Department of Foreign Affairs and International Trade: 97/35.

Ostry, S. 1997. *The Postwar International Trading System: Who's on First?* Chicago: University of Chicago Press.

Patterson, G. 1986. 'The GATT and the Negotiation of International Trade Rules', in Alan K. Hendrikson, ed., *Negotiating World Order: The Artisanship and Architecture of Global Diplomacy* (Wilmington, Del.: Scholarly Resources), 181–97.

Ruggiero, R. 1997. 'Charting the Trade Routes of the Future: Towards a Borderless Economy', Sept. (WTO: http://www.wto.org/new/press77.htm).

Stairs, D. 1982. 'The Political Culture of Canadian Foreign Policy', *Canadian Journal of Political Science* 15, 4: 667–90.

Stewart, T.P. 1993. *The GATT Uruguay Round: A Negotiating History (1986–1992)*, 3 vols. Deventer and Boston: Kluwer Law and Taxation Publishers.

Von Riekhoff, H. 1996. 'The Security Council: Trial and Error in Moving to a Post-Westphalian International System', in Fen Osler Hampson and Maureen Appel Molot, eds, *Big Enough to be Heard: Canada Among Nations 1996* (Ottawa: Carleton University Press), 175–99.

Wolfe, R. 1996. 'Global trade as a Single Undertaking: the role of ministers in the WTO', *International Journal* 51, 4: 690–709.

———. 1997. 'Embedded Liberalism as a Transformation Curve: Comment', in Thomas J. Courchene, ed., *The Nation State in a Global/Information Era: Policy Challenges* (Kingston: John Deutsch Institute for the Study of Economic Policy), 83–95.

WTO. 1996a. *Annual Report 1996*, vol. 1. Geneva: World Trade Organization.

———. 1996b. 'Singapore Ministerial Declaration', Singapore, 18 Dec. (WTO: WT/MIN(96)/DEC).

Zacher, M.W. 1997. 'The Global Economy and the International Political Order: Some Diverse and Paradoxical Relationships', in Thomas J. Courchene ed., *The Nation State in a Global/Information Era: Policy Challenges* (Kingston: John Deutsch Institute for the Study of Economic Policy), 67–82.

8

Is There a Future for Canadian Aid in the Twenty-First Century?

TIM DRAIMIN AND BRIAN TOMLINSON

Declining quantities of aid in the post-Cold War 1990s have accentuated a long-standing debate as to the purpose, relevance, and effectiveness of development assistance. Both domestic social welfare programs and foreign aid have been sustained by a strong postwar consensus on social values and the responsibilities of the state to its citizens. The implementation in the 1990s of neo-liberal economic policies in Canada and abroad has fractured this consensus. As a consequence, government treasuries, academics and research centres, and some from the business and non-governmental organization (NGO) communities have been asking whether the rationale and goals for donor programs are still relevant in the face of increasing globalization? Is a 30-year-old model appropriate to both the more diverse (and unequal) sets of economic and social circumstances evolving in developing countries and the increasingly acute global environmental challenges?

For some years aid reformers have said that change is long over-due. But now diverse (and uneven) reform initiatives, at the United Nations Development Program (UNDP), the World Bank, and the UK's Department for International Development (DFID) indicate institutional and programmatic overhaul is beginning internationally.

In Canada, it was hoped that the 1994 Foreign Policy Review and the government's response in 1995 (DFAIT, 1995) would offer a stimulus for reform. Instead, these initiatives merely tinkered with the status quo. Deprived of a reform mandate, the Canadian International Development Agency (CIDA) has updated its policy base and modernized its procedures and management systems. But taken together, these measures do not represent a reform agenda. In fact, the era of fiscal restraint has coincided with an absence of senior government leadership on the 'big picture'/frame-setting aid issues. This chapter reviews the Canadian debate on aid reform by analysing four key issues: (1) the quantity of aid; (2) the quality and focus of aid; (3) foreign policy coherence and aid; and (4) leadership. It concludes by identifying the core elements of a reform agenda and by examining the potential for foreign policy leadership to undertake aid reform in Canada.

DECLINING AID BUDGETS

As recently as June 1997 at a special session of the United Nations, donors repeated their commitment to the long-standing target of allocating 0.7 per cent of their gross national product (GNP) to Official Development Assistance (ODA) for development co-operation. Despite these pious statements, few countries have exercised the leadership required to achieve the target. When confronted by other pressing domestic choices, aid volumes have declined significantly in the 1990s.

Between 1992 and 1996, total aid from Organization of Economic Co-operation and Development (OECD) countries fell by 17 per cent, reaching a low of 0.25 per cent of donor GNP, down from 0.33 per cent in 1992. Non-governmental organizations monitoring aid spending reported in *Reality of Aid 1997/98* that there is little indication this decline will be reversed in 1997 or 1998 (Randel and German, 1997: 247). Canadian trends have been more sharply defined relative to other donors. By 1998–9 Canadian ODA will have declined by 38 per cent since 1991–92 (removing the effect of inflation). The

Figure 8.1

**Canadian ODA Performance: ODA to GNP Ratio
1991–92 to 1998–99**

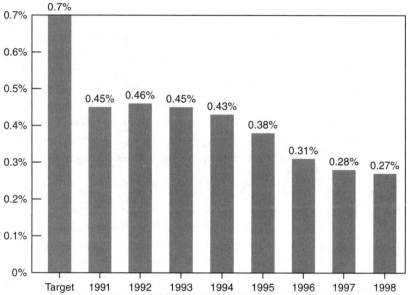

Source: OECD, Development Assistance Committee, Report on Development
Cooperation (1996); Government of Canada, CIDA Estimates Part III (Feb. 1997).

Development Assistance Committee (DAC) of the OECD, in reporting
the latest figures for 1996, reveals Canada's worst performance in 30
years with Canadian ODA of $2.4 billion for 1996 falling to 0.31 per
cent as a proportion of our GNP, from a high 0.46 per cent in 1992.

The February 1997 Canadian federal budget brought no respite,
although it appears that Canada may have turned the corner on further ODA cuts. Through an addition of $90 million to ODA for 1997–8
to prepay 1998 commitments to international organizations, $90 mil-
lion has been freed in the 1998–9 CIDA budget to partially offset the
impact of the previously announced cut to ODA of $150 million in this
year. A further $50 million has been added to the 1998–9 International
Assistance Envelope (IAE)[1] to meet additional payments to international financial institutions. Deep cuts in federal spending and
favourable economic circumstances eliminated the federal deficit two
years ahead of target, and in the lead-up to the 1998–9 budget, aid
proponents launched a strong campaign to rescind the cut for 1998–9

and to restore Canadian aid to at least 0.35 per cent of ODA over the next seven years. Without significant reinvestment, there is little doubt that Canadian aid will continue to fall as a percentage of GNP, reaching its lowest level since the mid-1960s—0.27 per cent by 1998–9.[2]

Are Private Capital Flows Making Up the Difference?

Are there alternatives for providing the finances needed for the elimination of extreme poverty and for investments in sustainable human development? Pro-market critics of aid suggest that aid can and should be replaced by expanding private flows to developing countries that now surpass aid flows by a ratio of 4 to 1 (a reversal of the experience of the 1980s and early 1990s). Has the private investment trend 'consigned aid to the margins of global development' (Stackhouse, 1997)?

A new development paradigm is emerging, according to this view, that is being driven by an expanding private sector, government deregulation and privatization, and a global trade and investment regime that protects and promotes the rights of private capital and expands market economies. These reforms, it is suggested, will eventually expand opportunities for all who participate in this global economy. Private net capital flows to developing countries have been growing rapidly, with $243.8 billion for 1996, up 30 per cent over 1995, a fivefold increase since 1990. But of this total only $110 billion was foreign direct investment (FDI), with the remaining flows being highly volatile speculative investments in stocks and bonds. Almost half of the FDI went to China in 1996.[3] Taken as a whole in 1996 a mere 12 'developing countries' received 73 per cent of the private flows (and these countries included Russia, Turkey, and Hungary) (Smilie, 1997).

While few countries are benefiting from these flows of capital (sub-Saharan Africa received less than 3 per cent in 1996 and much of that was directed to South Africa), poverty and inequality persist in countries receiving large amounts of direct foreign investment. Inequalities between and within countries are growing at an alarming rate. The 1997 UNDP *Human Development Report* highlights a widening gap in income between the richest 20 per cent of the world's population and the poorest 20 per cent. For every dollar of income received by the poorest 20 per cent, the richest 20 per cent have seen their share more than double from $30 in 1960 to $78 in 1994. What is even more alarming is that this share has grown by 28 per cent in a mere three years, during a time of increased globalization and unprecedented investment in open economies (UNDP, 1997: 110).

Considerable evidence indicates that private investments flow to the most profitable sectors where opportunities for the poorest people are limited at best. The OECD has pointed out in its *1996 Development Cooperation Report* that 'private resources generally do not flow directly to some key sectors of priority need, such as health and education' (Randel and German, 1997: 14). While many in the middle classes may be willing to pay for modern private health care, education, and urban services, people living in poverty will never have the resources to pay for their children's education or health care, both of which are so essential to escape the cycle of poverty.

The Asian financial meltdown that began in 1997 demonstrates that even dramatically expanding economies reach the limit of their capacity to absorb capital and invest it wisely, with adverse affects on global capital markets. But like the situation of Mexico a few years earlier, stabilizing these economies and bailing out financial institutions will have dramatic impact on the poor and will sharply reduce opportunities for the middle class, and these factors may ultimately lead to political crises in many of the affected countries (Unny, 1997).

Private capital is no substitute for targeted aid programs. But at the same time, aid alone is not sufficient. Different from conditions of poverty in developed countries, those living in poverty in developing countries are not a minority requiring special attention to their needs. People living in poverty form a growing majority of the world's population—with 1.3 billion people still living on less than $1 dollar a day and an astounding 3 billion people, two-thirds of the developing world's population, living on less than $2 a day (Elliott, 1997). Only concerted policy reform on the part of government, social organizations, and entrepreneurs will create the conditions for economic growth and social and political change for the benefit of the poor. Significant resources are required to meet these challenges. The UNDP estimates that a targeted investment of $40 billion per year over a decade would provide basic services for all and an additional $40 billion per year could eliminate absolute poverty (UNDP, 1997: 111).

Both the United Nations Children's Fund (UNICEF) and the UNDP have argued that aid, if properly targeted and managed, can and has made substantial progress. Since 1960, child death rates in developing countries have fallen by one-half, malnutrition rates have declined by almost a third, and the proportion of children not attending primary school has fallen by more than a third[4] (UNICEF, 1997; UNDP, 1997: 2). Much more can be accomplished with concerted planning and enhanced and sustained resource levels. If these are not forthcoming, we face the worrying signals that many of the poorest developing countries are in danger of losing the gains already made. Social indicators have worsened in the 1990s, with reappearing incidences among the poor of infectious diseases that were thought to be wiped out years ago, with expanding environmental crises that impact on human health and livelihoods, and with mounting attention needed to respond to humanitarian crises and to increases in violence and crime at all levels of society.

Can Declining Aid Flows Be Reversed?

Having achieved remarkable success in eliminating the federal deficit, the Canadian government now has an opportunity to examine again the adequacy of Canada's allocation of resources to development co-operation. This implies not only a reversal of cuts (a cut of $150 million is expected in 1998–9 despite the government's fiscal achievements), but also a clear indication on the part of the government that Canada will contribute its equitable share of resources to meet commitments made repeatedly during the 1990s at various fora of the United Nations. Regaining lost ground in Canadian ODA commitments will require a long-term plan for increasing the International Assistance Envelope each year. The Canadian Council for International Co-operation (CCIC) has calculated that reaching a target for ODA of 0.35 per cent of GNP by 2005–6 will require an average increase of 8 per cent in the IAE from 1999–2000 onward. When combined with a program to write off the debt of the highly indebted poorest countries, a total of $1.3 billion additional cash resources is needed. However, this amount is less than 5 per cent of the expected new revenue that will be available for reinvestments in federal programs from the fiscal dividend that will arise as a result of a balanced federal budget (including an allocation of half this dividend to tax cuts and paying down the federal debt).

Allocating the fiscal dividend is not the only source for meeting our international obligations for development assistance. Canadians have seen little of the 'peace dividend' from lower military expenditures. Canadian defence spending in the 1990s has defied global trends. By 1995 worldwide military spending (after accounting for inflation) was down by 23 per cent over 1980, while 'non-aligned' world military spending was 47 per cent lower. By contrast, Canada's defence expenditures for 1997–8 of $10.3 billion remain 11 per cent higher than the 1980–1 inflation-adjusted military budget of $9.3 billion. Even after the cuts planned for 1998–9, total expenditures will remain above those of the Cold War era (Robinson and Epp, 1997: 3). During the 1994 parliamentary review of Canadian defence policy, NGOs and the Canada 21 Council called for a fundamental reassessment of the mandate and requirements for Canadian defence forces. A more integrated international strategy was called for, one that would tackle the root causes of poverty and address global issues of demilitarization and peacekeeping, environment, health, refugees, and the spread of drugs. An assessment by Project Ploughshares suggests that a more specialized Canadian military, focusing on peacekeeping, domestic security, and coastal patrol would cost approximately $7.5 to $8.0 billion—an annual saving of $2.5 billion that could be directed to a common security agenda where ODA has a strong role to play (Robinson and Epp, 1997: 3). Investing a significant portion of these savings into implementing strategies for eliminating poverty through development co-operation would go a long way to re-establishing Canada's reputation as a generous and progressive donor.

SEEKING A STRATEGIC FRAMEWORK FOR IMPROVING
THE QUALITY AND FOCUS OF CANADIAN ODA

While declining volumes of aid receive public attention, the debate on aid has become less focused on the amount and channels for aid *per se*. Rather, the challenge is to better understand how aid resources should and can be employed (the quality of aid) to eliminate extreme poverty and promote sustainable human development (SHD). Simply put in the words of the UNDP, sustainable human development is a development paradigm 'that puts people at the centre of development, regards economic growth as a means and not an end, protects life opportunities of future generations, and respects the natural systems on which all life depends' (UNDP, 1994: 4).[5]

Aid has a strategic role to play in bringing resources, technical expertise, and long-term engagement to bear on human development. But how effectively can it achieve results? Has the aid agenda become too crowded? Are long-standing domestic political pressures to use aid for commercial advantages compromising the effectiveness of development co-operation in its primary mission of eradicating poverty? Can aid do more with less, or are aid programs so overburdened with conflicting pressures that they are effectively being set up for a perception of failure? While serving multiple political and commercial masters, aid is expected to demonstrate results that lead to sustainable poverty reduction, to the construction of peace in countries emerging from civil conflict, to the empowerment of women and the encouragement of gender equity, to an improvement in systems of governance and citizen participation, and to the promotion of private-sector development, among other demonstrable goals. While these are all legitimate and important goals in themselves, results will be difficult to identify with aid programs acting in isolation.

Canada's Mixed Experience

The Liberal government's 1995 foreign policy statement, *Canada in the World*, identified CIDA's mandate to be 'sustainable development in developing countries, in order to reduce poverty and contribute to a more secure, equitable and prosperous world' (DFAIT, 1995: 42). The statement set out six priority areas for ODA: basic human needs; women in development; infrastructure services; human rights; democracy and good governance; private-sector development; and the environment. These priorities, with the exception of human rights and democracy and good governance, have long been important areas for Canadian ODA.

This 1995 policy framework disappointed many who had appeared before the Special Parliamentary Committee Reviewing Foreign Policy the previous year and who had been looking for policy reform and innovation. Key among these was a resolution of the conflicting aims (e.g., serving Canadian business interests as well as contributing to poverty reduction in developing countries) that have plagued the aid program over the years.[6] The quality of the aid program—a steadfast focus on sustainable change to create new opportunity for those living in poverty—lies at the heart of aid reform.

Since 1995 CIDA has clarified a range of development policies on poverty and the six priority areas (including country and regional strategies) and there is greater public access to summary information on the content of country and regional programs. Progress is also being made in identifying, coding, and reporting the intent of development projects against these broad policy goals. At multilateral fora there has been significant policy input into donor policy debates (at the DAC, the World Bank, and regional development banks). For the most part, these are substantial thematic policies that reflect the latest development thinking on a subject. But taken together they offer no overall strategic framework for CIDA's interventions, and individually they set out only the broadest plans for implementation. The inclusion of infrastructural services and support for the private sector among the six priority areas, having more to do with politically appeasing domestic commercial interests in aid contracts than meeting the mandate, further diffuses the possibility for strategic focus on sustainable human development. Without doubt, deep budget cuts have left little room for new or innovative programs, a situation compounded by the fact that CIDA has had to absorb discrete program expenditures in its budget that in previous years might have been covered by other departments.[7]

The policy directions have for the most part been endorsed by the wider development community, with particular attention to the June 1995 policy on poverty reduction. Here it is clearly stated that 'poverty reduction will be a central focus of Canada's development cooperation programme', a goal that has been long advocated by Canadian NGOs. It goes on to affirm that poverty reduction 'requires that the root causes and structural factors of poverty be addressed' and that 'poverty reduction focuses on improving the poor's access to, control of, and benefits from economic, social and natural resources and decision-making' (CIDA, 1995: 2). It directs all CIDA programs to develop integrated poverty reduction strategies. Yet there remains an air of unreality about its relevance to the day-to-day practice of the agency.

Like most other recent CIDA policy statements, implementation strategies for reducing poverty are vague. There appear to be little baseline data from which to measure progress. Initiatives to reduce poverty are complex, whether the work is directly with those living in poverty or at the meso level of capacity-building; however, few accessible CIDA studies assess impact on poverty reduction for various potential strategies, or even best practices, that could inform a discussion of current programming. Those interested in monitoring the implementation of the poverty reduction policy face a daunting challenge.

One measure of Canadian ODA focus on poverty reduction is the percentage of Canadian ODA targeted to meet the basic human needs (BHNs) of those living in poverty—primary health care, basic educa-

---

Box 8.1

Donor Commitments

Reducing the proportion of people living in extreme poverty by one-half by 2015;

Eliminating gender disparity in primary and secondary education by 2005;

Reducing by two-thirds the mortality rate for infants and children under age five by 2015;

Reducing by three-fourths the maternal mortality rate by 2015; and

Providing access through primary health care to reproductive health services for all individuals of appropriate ages as soon as possible and no later than 2015.

Source: Development Assistance Committee, *Shaping the 21st Century: The Contribution of Development Cooperation* (Paris: OECD, May 1996).

---

tion, family planning, nutrition, water, and sanitation. *Canada in the World* commits the government to 25 per cent of ODA for these vital areas, but also adds shelter, humanitarian assistance, and food aid directed to emergency relief to the internationally recognized list of BHNs. In the multilateral fora Canada played a strong role in elaborating the DAC's 1996 *Shaping the 21st Century: The Contribution of Development Cooperation,* where a number of targets for donors are also set out (see box). At the 1995 World Summit for Social Development, Canada committed itself to a 20:20 compact whereby recipient countries would devote 20 per cent of their public expenditures and donors 20 per cent of their aid to basic services. The multiplication of overlapping and very broad targets only serves to 'muddy the water' when measuring impact.

As an example, in 1997 CIDA elaborated its policy on basic human needs and reiterated the broad *Canada in the World* definition of basic needs. The 1997 policy recognizes a distinction between sustainably meeting the basic needs of those living in poverty and thereby contributing to their capacities to improve their lives and the provision of humanitarian assistance that addresses critical survival needs of refugees and others as a result of crises and conflicts.

Unfortunately, the policy does not draw out the implications of this distinction for measuring CIDA's contribution to sustained poverty reduction by meeting basic human needs. As Alison Van Rooy from the North-South Institute has commented, 'the need for food aid is . . . very much a measure of the failure of development' (1995: 51). To include humanitarian assistance in the measure of the agency's impact on sustained reduction in poverty is misleading.

Interestingly, CIDA's regional framework for Africa and the Middle East, where a growing majority of people live in extreme poverty on less than $1 a day, commits to a target of 30 per cent for BHN expenditures, not including humanitarian assistance and emergency food aid, but CIDA reports suggest that less than 10 per cent was allocated to these BHN programs in 1996–7. Regarding the broader target of 25 per cent for ODA, the evidence is not as clear. In 1997 CIDA started to report on the allocation of CIDA program funds (not ODA) to BHNs. The agency calculated that in 1996–7, $630.1 million or 38.4 per cent of its programs were devoted to meeting basic human needs. Even if figures were available for ODA as a whole (i.e., including the World Bank and the IMF contributions managed by the Department of Finance), it is apparent that CIDA considers the target of 25 per cent met and exceeded. But significantly, when humanitarian assistance and food aid are removed, only an estimated 19 per cent (rather than 38.4 per cent) of CIDA's programs were allocated to basic human needs in long-term potentially sustainable programs (CIDA, 1997: 1).

In the end, whether the target is met or not, these calculations say little about creating opportunities for critical development thinking and learning within the agency and with the wider development community to rethink the content and delivery of its programs against its poverty reduction policy. While an imperfect indicator, the manner in which cuts have been carried out by CIDA suggests little strategic reflection on concentrating the remaining resources on the overarching goal of poverty reduction. A few examples will suffice.

1. At each stage of the cuts, the three bilateral regions—Asia-Pacific, the Americas, and Africa and the Middle East—have received an equal percentage cut, sometimes slightly more than the cut to the agency as a whole. While this may have satisfied the balance of stakeholder interests in the agency, the result has been that aid to sub-Saharan Africa, a region characterized by growing and extreme conditions of poverty, has declined in nominal dollars by 30.4 per cent between 1992–3 and 1996–7, a rate greater than that for either

ODA as a whole (21.2 per cent) or bilateral aid (16.8 per cent). Sub-Saharan Africa received no special protection.

2. Relative to many other donors, CIDA has maintained, and in recent years increased, its concentration (55 per cent of ODA in 1996–7) on low-income developing countries (relative to middle-income countries). However, Canadian ODA to the 48 UN-designated least developed countries (LDCs) (33 of which are in sub-Saharan Africa) shows a different pattern. For this group of countries, Canadian aid declined sharply between 1992–3 and 1996–7 by 33.1 per cent, compared to ODA as a whole (21.2 per cent). In 1990 Canada, along with other donors, agreed to increase aid to these countries with a target of 0.15 per cent of GNP. From 1992–3 to 1996–7 the proportion of Canada's aid to the LDCs as a percentage of GNP dropped significantly, from 0.14 per cent to 0.08 per cent.

3. Canadian multilateral aid channelled through the World Bank and the regional banks' concessional funds, the IMF's Enhanced Structural Adjustment Facility, and various United Nations institutions has declined more sharply than bilateral assistance. In recent years commitments to the replenishment of concessional windows for the international financial institutions (IFIs) have been reduced by as much as 40 per cent; however, because approximately $1.9 billion of previous commitments were still to be paid as of December 1996, payments to the IFIs will remain high for some years to come. CIDA's *1997/98 Expenditure Plan* suggests that Canadian multilateral programs will give priority to those UN organizations with a strong poverty reduction focus such as UNICEF, the United Nations Fund for Population Activities (UNFPA), and the UNDP. While this may be the case for 1997–8 (no figures were provided), between 1992–3 and 1996–7 these three agencies have been cut by $26.2 million or 27 per cent. The UNDP alone has been cut from $65 million to $43.2 million, or 33.4 per cent.

4. *Canada in the World* and a 1996 CIDA policy framework on the role of the voluntary sector in Canadian ODA recognize the contribution of this sector in supporting human development, in shaping the management of the global commons, and in involving Canadians locally and internationally as global citizens (CIDA, 1996: 4–5). However, a recent report for CIDA's Performance Review Division on basic human needs programming lessons noted that despite NGOs' substantial and innovative work, '[i]n some bilateral programs, there is a tendency to underestimate, undervalue or ignore altogether the

record of the non-governmental sector' (Jackson, 1996: 31). Up until 1996–7 Canadian aid channelled through NGOs continued to decline at about the same rate as ODA as a whole.

5. Poverty reduction programming is more likely to emphasize the importance of appropriate and sustained community-based interventions along with the strengthening of local capacity in government and civil society to create real opportunities for those living in poverty. However, there has been little assessment of the impact on poverty reduction goals arising from the 'privatization' of the implementation of Canadian bilateral aid, much of it to Canadian commercial firms and some to large contracting NGOs. With 27 per cent of bilateral aid and 38 per cent of multilateral aid fully tied to Canadian purchases in 1994, Canadian tied aid provisions have remained unchanged since the mid-1980s, despite estimates by the DAC that tied aid results in up to 15 per cent overpricing of goods and services (Randel and German, 1997: 251).

CIDA's *1997/98 Expenditure Plan* estimates that 1995–6 ODA expenditures 'provided 36,000 new or ongoing [Canadian] jobs, and led to contracts for 2,000 businesses, 50 universities and 60 colleges in Canada' (Canada, 1997: 38).[8] In 1996 the minister responsible for CIDA announced expanded and more accessible opportunities for bidding on agency projects. Aid privatization tends to transform complex development processes that require long-term commitment and local knowledge into 'biddable commodities'. To accommodate donor contracting arrangements, however transparent and fair, improvements in human welfare, expanded opportunities, and empowerment of the excluded become measurable short-term 'results', yet the inclination of the contractor will be to manage 'development' in the interest of future contracts.

Canada in the World reaffirmed a strong role for the private sector in Canada's development program, rejecting suggestions by NGOs and others that Canadian commercial interests in developing countries be more clearly separated from the core resources for development co-operation and poverty reduction. The Industrial Co-operation Program (INC) of CIDA has received only minor cuts since 1992–3 despite concern over the development impact of its allocations to Canadian companies. Moreover, a study by the Steelworkers Humanities Fund revealed that 44 per cent of CIDA INC assistance in 1994–5 supported involvement in developing countries considered by the OECD to have serious restrictions on freedom of association

(Steelworkers Humanities Fund, 1997). Even if CIDA was to implement reform strategies to address these ODA quality and focus deficiencies, only part of the challenge would be addressed. In a joint policy statement, the North-South Institute and the CCIC noted that foreign assistance is a catalytic factor in the struggle against poverty and environmental degradation. But '[m]ore important is the collective and cumulative impact of all our other policies: political, financial, trade, defence, environmental, etc.' (Plewes and Culpeper, 1997).

AID AND FOREIGN POLICY COHERENCE

Since aid cannot work alone, influencing government policies to make them coherent with a long-term agenda of sustainable human development is the goal. Increasingly, aid analysts are asking how aid resources can work together strategically with government initiatives, domestically and internationally, and with other sectors (the voluntary sector and the private sector) to address global challenges posed by the continuing degradation of the biosphere, tensions arising from trade and investment liberalization, and the fallout from volatile financial markets. But the issue is not coherence for the sake of coherence. A government-imposed coherence that responds exclusively to short-term political imperatives (domestic fiscal policies) and commercial interest in strong promotion of trade and investment linkages may come at a substantial cost to human well-being and sustainable ecosystems in the longer term. In balancing policy choices, aid bureaucracies and non-governmental actors have a crucial role in strengthening the voice for SHD in foreign policy. They should be bringing to public policy deliberations reflections based on their unique mandate and the window they have on policy changes needed over the long term to reverse growing inequality, injustice, and the exclusion of major portions of the world's population.

Canada's Experience: Market-Led or People-Led Coherence?

In 1995, NGO policy analysts and some academics predicted that *Canada in the World* would result in a further marginalization of ODA in Canada's relations with developing countries and in CIDA's role in government to press for human development goals. These concerns were apparent in the way *Canada in the World* addressed the issue of coherence: 'Canada's ODA policies should . . . work together with other aspects of our broader foreign and domestic policies to forge a consistent approach to developing countries and to contribute to common goals' (DFAIT, 1995: 41). It was noted at the time that coherence with 'the broad scope of foreign policy objectives leaves the government free to orient ODA more closely to almost any particular mix of Canadian policy objectives' (CCIC, 1996; see also Pratt, 1996, 1997). Indeed, government policy towards developing countries since 1994 has focused almost exclusively on bilateral and multilateral trade and investment initiatives, meeting the primary foreign policy goal of *Canada in the World* of strengthening Canada's economic prosperity.

By way of contrast, a recent UK Labour government White Paper, entitled 'Eliminating World Poverty: The Challenge for the Twenty-first Century', provides a vision for British development co-operation and its contribution to sustainable development that clearly situates ODA:

> This is not just a White Paper about aid. It is a White Paper about sustainable development and a secure future for our planet and its people. The new Department for International Development (DFID) has the aim, reflecting the themes of this White Paper—of contributing to the elimination of poverty in poorer countries, not just through its bilateral and multilateral development programmes, but through working collaboratively with other government departments to promote consistency and coherence in policies affecting their development. (DFID, 1997: para.1.22)

Since mid-1996, under the leadership of Foreign Minister Lloyd Axworthy, Canada has taken some high-profile initiatives on landmines, on human rights and democracy in Burma and Nigeria, on peacekeeping and peacebuilding in Haiti and the Great Lakes region of Africa, on democratizing global flows of information, and on the rights of the child. Important as these are, the policy influence of Canadian trade and investment interests is ever present and commercial interests of the marketplace seem to prevail in cabinet when difficult choices are to be made. The consequent tensions in Canadian policy are rising to the surface. A January 1997 Team Canada trade and investment mission to Asia, led by the Prime Minister and provincial premiers, chose to ignore the evidence of the social and environmental costs of their narrow focus on market opportunities and 'jobs for Canadians'. They were confronted with national strikes in South Korea, protests by NGOs against the possible sale of CANDU reactors to Indonesia, and demonstrations in the

Philippines against the environmental destruction brought by Canadian mining activity (Pacer Dome) in that country. The November 1997 Asia Pacific Economic Co-operation (APEC) gathering in Vancouver brought these contradictions to a head as the Canadian agenda for free trade and business promotion in the Asia-Pacific region came unhinged in the wake of the regional financial meltdown and numerous public meetings and demonstrations that brought attention to the human and environmental costs of this economic model.

It should be apparent that Canadian trade strategies and investment linkages in developing countries will contribute little to long-term and sustained Canadian prosperity if human development is relegated to 'trickle down' treatment. In a broader agenda, legitimate trade and investment interests are reconciled with human rights initiatives, with concern for child labour, or with the social and environmental impacts on affected populations, rather than the reverse. China is a good example of the current approach. Despite a strong environmental component to CIDA's country policy framework for China, in the fall of 1996 the government rescinded by edict its legislated environmental assessment requirement in order to permit the sale of CANDU reactors to China. In the same months, the Export Development Corporation played a key role in China's decision to award an estimated US$160 million contract to General Electric Canada to supply turbines and generators for the highly controversial Three Gorges Dam project, which will have a profound and largely unknown environmental impact on millions of people living along the Yangtze River (Eggerton, 1997).

The 1990s have also been a time of increased expectations that Canada and the world community would provide leadership on commitments that were made year after year at various United Nations summits. World attention was directed to emerging global environmental issues (genetic resources, deforestation, control of greenhouse gases, and global warming), to increasing social and economic inequalities (a deepening crisis of debt and exclusion from the global economy for the poorest countries and people), and to a seemingly intractable growth in the numbers of people living in extreme poverty.

The challenge has been to deliver sustained progress on these core global goals. But hope for progress has been replaced by a widespread sense of deadlock. Frustrations erupted onto the international stage at the June 1997 Special UN General Assembly to review progress on the Earth Summit's Agenda 21. An important breakthrough at the Rio summit in 1992 had been 'common but differentiate responsibilities' between developed and developing countries for realizing sustainable human development. But five years later the world community appears to be backtracking on many key issues in Agenda 21, ranging from climate change to debt and trade and finance. While the divisions are more complex than a North/South divide on many of the substantive issues, for developing countries the lack of progress on equalizing the fundamental terms of economic power between North and South lies at the heart of their concerns (Sreenivasan and Mitchell, 1997). The developed countries are equally divided on many key issues, and Canada seems to have lost its leadership on major issues that it had taken at the UN earlier in the decade.

A typical example has been Canada's failure to achieve its targets on stabilizing emissions of greenhouse gases, as seen at the December 1997 Kyoto summit. Not only did Canada abandon its target of reducing emissions to 1990 levels by the year 2000, but the government also predicted that our emissions will be 13 per cent higher. It joined with the US to insist that developing nations who are in the early stages of industrialization—little different from those industries that characterized the Industrial Revolution for developed countries more than 100 years earlier—should bear the costs of transition to more environmentally friendly industrial technology.

Reversing the flow of financial resources, particularly for the poorest countries, is essential for the goals of sustainable human development. In 24 out of 30 highly indebted poor countries, many of which are in sub-Saharan Africa, debt repayments absorb more than 20 per cent of government revenue, and in many it exceeds government expenditures on education and health combined (OXFAM, 1997). The North-South Institute recently calculated that in 1995 Canadian banks, public agencies, private firms, and individual investors had outstanding loans and investments of $60 billion in developing countries. The profits, interest, and other income flowing back to Canada from these investments was about $4.8 billion, more than one and a half times Canada's ODA for that year (Culpeper, 1997).

Many of these investments are in middle-income developing countries such as Mexico, Chile, and Brazil, where Canadian resource extraction projects and assembly production in free trade zones must

be reconciled with impacts on communities, the health and livelihoods of workers, and the local environment.[9] For the poorest countries that receive little in foreign investment, little can be accomplished with ODA for basic health and education when these
countries are locked into servicing a debt treadmill with multilateral
agencies, bilateral donors, and private banks.

To the government's credit, by the mid-1990s Canada had forgiven
much of its ODA debt to the poorest countries. But an estimated
US$6.8 billion in Canadian official bilateral debt remains on the books
for developing countries in 1996, primarily owed to the Canadian
Wheat Board and the Export Development Corporation (EURODAD,
1996). Of this amount, $1.2 billion is owed by high-indebted devel-
oping countries. Substantial debt forgiveness is essential to their
capacity to meet basic human needs. With a US$2.2 trillion total debt,
each person in developing countries owes about US$300 to donor
countries, much more than a year's wage for many. African countries
now spend four times as much on debt repayments as they do on
health care (Canadian Ecumenical Jubilee Initiative, 1997).

Despite some early progress for Uganda, the IMF/World Bank-
sponsored Highly Indebted Poor Country (HIPC) Debt Initiative for
low-income countries is bogged down with Canada's G-7 partners,
the United States, Japan, and Germany, reportedly holding up
progress. At best only six out of 41 highly indebted countries will
benefit by the year 2000 (EURODAD, 1997). While not a large creditor, Canada can play an important mediating role within the World
Bank and the IMF to ameliorate the terms of HIPC debt relief consistent with CIDA's policy for sustained poverty reduction, particularly
in countries where there are significant Canadian aid resources (see
a summary of issues relating to HIPC in EURODAD, 1997).

EXERCISING LEADERSHIP

Finally, the question of leadership is crucial. In the words of UNDP
co-ordinator James Speth: 'Poverty is not to be suffered in silence by
the poor. Nor can it be tolerated by those with the power to change
it. The challenge now is to mobilize action—state by state, organization by organization, individual by individual' (UNDP, 1997: iv).

Concerted and innovative action on the part of political leaders,
including setting an agenda and encouraging public understanding
and deliberation on issues that will affect our common future, is

essential to creating the opportunities for change. The December 1997 signing of a treaty banning the production, sale, and use of anti-personnel land-mines demonstrates what can be accomplished in a very short time through provocative Canadian leadership and innovative government-NGO partnership. But the absence of foreign policy on the public agenda in Canada is more characteristic of the past few years and most of the current debates are taking place behind closed doors. At the same time, many Canadians and Canadian institutions with direct overseas experience and expertise are well positioned to act as 'global citizen' public policy advocates for those living in poverty.

Consistent opportunities are required for these new voices to be effective in public policy dialogue, which must involve participants from developing countries as well as Canadians, implying greater policy transparency and accountability. Has government's recent openness in setting Canadian foreign policy priorities and carrying out initiatives created sufficient public and political conditions for the voluntary sector, here and abroad, to move beyond consultations and build joint SHD initiatives with government? What new forms of parliamentary, interdepartmental arrangements in international policy dialogue could facilitate these initiatives?

The UK Labour government's White Paper on eliminating world poverty asserts that failure to date to achieve sustainable development lies not in the lack of internationally agreed upon policies and principles, but rather in 'the political will to address them in poorer and richer countries' (DFID, 1997: Introduction). The Labour government demonstrates its own political will with an ambitious package of reforms for the Department for International Development, including: proposals to accelerate debt forgiveness, meeting global targets, building partnerships, policy consistency, eventually increasing resources towards the 0.7 per cent GNP target, ending the 'Aid and Trade Provision', and vigorously educating the public.

The dynamism with which the UK is approaching the ODA reform agenda contrasts with the way in which the Canadian government has had a revolving door policy at CIDA, which has had four Ministers of International Co-operation in four years. The lack of consistent political leadership undermines the capacity of the aid program to be an advocate for sustainable human development within Canada's foreign policy. To his credit, Foreign Minister Axworthy sought to promote policy integration through regular meetings of the P-5—the five ministers (Foreign Affairs, International Trade, International Co-operation) and secretaries of state (Latin America and Africa, Asia) with international responsibilities. Unfortunately, policy and resource allocation issues (as noted by Denis Stairs in Chapter 2) have led to a deterioration of DFAIT-CIDA relations, undermining the ability of the two to build common cause with their cabinet colleagues. Indeed, it is striking that no cabinet level committee exists to link the P-5 to the other key ministries: Finance, Defence, Environment, Natural Resources, and Agriculture.

Interdepartmental co-ordination is possible. In fact, in its preparations for Rio 1992, a highly effective interdepartmental team, co-ordinated by a national secretariat, shaped Canada's agenda and participated in global negotiations. But immediately after Rio, the collaborative policy mechanism was dismantled. An interdepartmental team also co-ordinates Canadian policy at World Bank and IMF meetings, in which CIDA is an active participant. In the past few years, there has been some opening for this team to meet with NGOs seeking reform of these multilateral institutions. But even here, these consultations are random and feed into an agenda largely driven by the Department of Finance, the lead department for IMF/World Bank policy.

At the present moment International Trade is rethinking its past reliance on business-dominated advisory groups (ITACs and SAGITs) for the trade negotiation processes. Will they be replaced by mechanisms reflecting the need to integrate social and environmental concerns in the dominant multilateral rule-setting negotiations? Given the recent decision to establish 'Team Canada Inc.' with a blue ribbon business board (leavened by one trade union representative), other issues continue to be given short shrift. Nevertheless, the government is becoming more receptive to *informal* parallel discussions.

How might policy consultations capture both diverse cross-sectoral knowledge and advice and lay the groundwork for coherent policy development and collaboration in implementation? An ongoing Canadian dialogue on peacebuilding in Guatemala begun in 1997 may offer a useful way forward. The Guatemala initiative involved the Peacebuilding and Human Development Division of DFAIT's Global Issues Bureau, CIDA Americas Branch staff, the International Centre for Human Rights and Democratic Development (ICHRDD), and the NGO Americas Policy Group of the CCIC. Each participant came to the process with institutional experience, involvement of partners in

Guatemala, and a commitment to seek out innovative approaches to building peace in Guatemala. The process involved independent documentation of issues critical for the success of the Guatemalan Peace Accords and the nurturing of peace more generally, invitations for non-governmental participants from Guatemala, and a series of workshops and consultations that build understanding and common ground for actions linking government and NGO perspectives. By January 1998, a progression had been made from consultation to concrete action-oriented dialogue. Joint government-NGO programming priorities have been set and smaller working groups are developing a number of projects to strengthen the capacity of civil society organizations in Guatemala (representing indigenous and other excluded social groups) to engage and make proposals in the fora established by the Peace Accords. It is expected that this initiative will influence program decisions of the new Peacebuilding Fund at CIDA.

Depending on the issue, a range of institutional collaborations undoubtedly can facilitate cross-sectoral leadership for building coherent approaches to SHD. But these initiatives will matter little without a significant Canadian public constituency that understands foreign policy choices and their relation to seemingly more important domestic issues. The public's interest in the international policy implications of sustainable development has been in decline since Rio, when prior to the conference national and global media maintained constant public attention on global affairs from an environmental perspective. Lacking any current independent stimulus for public interest, beyond episodic coverage of world events, we need to have a reinvigorated government–non-government partnership aimed at engaging the public in an informative discussion of global issues that would lead towards consensus on key policy areas. Given the understandable current drift of public opinion and faltering confidence in traditional aid strategies, arousing serious public attention will require strong political leadership focusing on a new agenda to revitalize the ODA program within a more coherent international policy framework.

CONCLUSION

The future of Canadian aid in the twenty-first century depends on two interdependent factors: the effective implementation of an ODA reform agenda and political leadership promoting policy coherence structured around sustainable human development.

The Reform Agenda

Recognizing the shortcomings in Canadian ODA and the importance of a more coherent approach in Canadian relations with developing countries, we can identify five key strategies that should be considered for improving the quality of Canadian aid.

1. *At least 60 per cent of ODA should be devoted to programs that directly promote sustainable human development*, with a significant increase in resources dedicated to sustained poverty reduction. SHD encompasses a much broader range of development interventions directed at social and economic empowerment of those living in poverty than suggested by a target for provisioning of basic human needs (food, primary education, and primary health), where the government has an existing target. This proposal also implies a more geographically focused bilateral program, with special emphasis on the poorest countries of sub-Saharan Africa.

2. *Transparent development strategies must be led and developed in developing countries*, with participation and commitment from the three sectors: governments, business, and civil society. CIDA contracting arrangements should take into account the importance and quality of long-term collaboration, local knowledge, decision-making, and ownership in measuring results for effective development co-operation.

3. *ODA for commercial purposes should be reduced* with the phasing out of CIDA's Industrial Co-operation Program and other bilateral programs linked to Canadian commercial advantage where the direct relation to poverty reduction is secondary.

4. *Development practice must be based on sharing information, building knowledge, and capturing evaluation lessons* that are cross-sectoral, learning-oriented, and accessible. Canada has built unique knowledge-based networks and international collaborations through its policy institutions (International Development Research Centre [IDRC], the International Institute for Sustainable Development [IISD], the North-South Institute, and the ICHRDD) and programming partners (NGOs, consulting firms, and businesses), many of whom are becoming increasingly active in policy issues (Strong, 1996). A learning community of development actors is a prerequisite to managing the changing environment where cross-sectoral partnerships (government–private sector–civil society) become more common.

5. *Development co-operation is a long-term process requiring a long-term strategic planning framework.* This long-term outlook can

only be sustained with predictable resources over extended periods of time. Reversing the cuts to Canadian ODA and advancing towards the 0.7 per cent ODA to GNP ratio is crucial if Canada is going to take up an equitable share of global responsibility.

Shared Leadership Towards Coherence

If our world is to create a truly effective regime to manage our global commons and improve the living standards of the world's peoples, development co-operation has an indispensable role to play. But the role of aid must be measured as much by its ability to set the standards and values by which the *ensemble* of international policy is structured as by the efficacy of its year-to-year programs on the ground. In fact, over the long term the results of aid depend entirely on the coherence and quality of the international community's policies to create (or undo) an environment propitious for sustainable human development.

As the post-Cold War era has shown, there is a profound challenge in building multilateral frameworks and norms that can successfully harness global resources for sustainable and people-friendly development. Each international event, be it the Rio process (and its failed follow-up), the World Summit for Social Development (and its weak commitments), or the recent Land-Mines Convention (with its mega-power recalcitrants), exposes the fragility of multilateral initiatives. However, each process builds on the successes and weaknesses of its predecessor. What is becoming clearer is that there is no White Knight to provide the leadership necessary to galvanize the global community. But as the land-mines initiative proved, grassroots people power can and will be a determining factor in successful global management. As Denis Stairs has noted elsewhere in this volume, successful Canadian niche diplomacy can be built around mutually advantageous partnerships between NGOs and political leadership within the government.

Public interest in international co-operation is a 'canary in the mine shaft' when it comes to the broader agenda of global co-operation. A lack of public engagement and support on aid augurs badly for public interest in finding global solutions to the accumulating deficit of global problems. Reigniting public interest is a shared responsibility of all sectors of Canadian society. An important contributing factor for success will be government's leadership in being able to articulate a coherent ODA reform agenda that sets ODA in a privileged position in the framework of Canada's international policies.

NOTES

The authors are policy analysts associated with the Canadian Council for International Co-operation. They gratefully acknowledge commentary on earlier drafts of this paper by Rieky Stuart and Gauri Sreenivasan at CCIC, Cranford Pratt, the Canadian Foreign Policy 'Ginger Group' (an informal gathering of academic and non-governmental policy analysts monitoring Canadian international policy developments), and the authors' meeting associated with the 1998 edition of *Canada Among Nations*. The authors, of course, are responsible for the final product. The views expressed here are the authors' own and do not necessarily represent those of CCIC.

1. The International Assistance Envelope (IAE) is made up of cash expenditures from CIDA, DFAIT, and the Department of Finance on official development assistance and on assistance to the former Soviet Union and Eastern Europe. What is included in ODA has been agreed upon by all donors represented in the DAC of the OECD. For Canada, ODA includes all expenditures in the IAE for all countries recognized by the DAC (i.e., excluding most of the former Soviet Union and Eastern Europe), the imputed value of expenditures at Canadian educational institutions for students from developing countries studying in Canada, debt forgiveness not previously written off for developing countries, and (since 1994–5) an imputed value for expenditures on refugees residing in Canada for the first year. Canadian ODA therefore is significantly higher than cash contributions to development assistance as reflected in the IAE. Measuring the performance of Canadian ODA is also distorted by some of these add-ons. For example, after 1994–5, Canada added up to $150 million each year to ODA for first-year costs for refugees in Canada from developing countries. Removing this amount in order to compare with years prior to 1994–5 reduces our ODA to GNP ratio by up to 0.02 per cent.
2. For a more detailed analysis of budget cuts and projections, see CCIC (1997), and information available on CCIC's Web page: <www.web.net/ccic-ccci>. See also the Canada chapter in the various yearly editions of *The Reality of Aid*.
3. This amount is overstated. The World Bank calculated that in 1994, 37 per cent of FDI to China for that year involved domestic funds that were routed internationally to take advantage of tax incentives for these investments and a further 12 per cent was the result of overvaluation of capital equipment for tax purposes.
4. See also the substantive discussion of aid effectiveness in Cassen and associates (1994) and Schmitz (1996). A useful overview of aid effectiveness and policy coherence can be found in van der Berg and van Ojik (1996).
5. A Canadian NGO understanding of the implications of sustainable human development has been elaborated in Plewes et al. (1996).
6. The 1987 Winegard Report, *For Whose Benefit*, from the Standing Committee on External Affairs and International Trade, strongly recommended a more focused poverty-reducing aid mandate, separating commercial interests from the aid program. In 1994 a substantive review of CIDA by the Auditor-General suggested a legislative framework as a means of resisting conflicting pressures and mandates.

7. Examples from 1996–7 included $10 million for DFAIT's peacebuilding fund, funds to support the training of Haiti's policy force by the RCMP, $5 million to preserve Radio Canada International, and contributions towards de-mining activities in Cambodia and Mozambique carried out by Department of National Defence personnel.

8. The Estimates also suggest that 70 per cent of total ODA in 1995–6 was used to pay for Canadian goods and services. Because these figures include 100 per cent of grants to Canadian NGOs and institutions, it should be adjusted to account for the fact that about 75 per cent of these grants are allocated directly to counterparts in developing countries. Our calculation of an adjusted figure for 1995–6 is 64.5 per cent (up from about 50 per cent in 1991–2).

9. IDRC has an ongoing research working group on mining and community development and the Americas Working Group of CCIC has a policy development project looking at community decision-making processes that would enable the latter to negotiate effectively with mining companies.

REFERENCES

Canada. 1997. *1997/98 CIDA Expenditure Plan and Estimates, Part III*. Ottawa: Department of Supply and Services.

Canadian Council for International Co-operation (CCIC). 1995. 'Canada in the World: A Review and Analysis of the Government's Foreign Policy Statements', mimeo, available on CCIC's Web site at <www.web.net/ccic-ccci>.

———. 1997. '1997/98 Federal Budget and CIDA's 1997/98 Expenditure Plan Estimates', mimeo, available on CCIC's Web site at <www.web.net/ccic-ccci>.

Canadian Ecumenical Jubilee Initiative. 1997. 'A New Beginning: A Call to Jubilee', mimeo.

Canadian International Development Agency (CIDA). 1995. 'CIDA's Policy on Poverty Reduction'. Ottawa: Department of Supply and Services.

———. 1996. 'Canadian Voluntary Organizations and CIDA: Framework for a Renewed Relationship'. Ottawa: Department of Supply and Services.

———. 1997. 'How CIDA Spends ODA Program Funds—The 1996/97 Priority Coding Report'. Ottawa: CIDA, mimeo.

Cassen, Robert, and associates. 1994. *Does Aid Work?*, 2nd edn. Oxford: Oxford University Press.

Culpeper, Roy. 1997. 'Private Markets and Social Equity in a Post-Aid World', *Diplomat Magazine* (Mar.-Apr.).

Department for International Development (DFID). 1997. 'Eliminating World Poverty: A Challenge for the 21st Century', London, on the Internet at <www.oneworld. org/oda/whitepaper/>.

Department of Foreign Affairs and International Trade (DFAIT). 1995. *Canada in the World*. Ottawa: Department of Supplies and Services.

Eggerton, Laura. 1997. 'Ottawa Backs Chinese Dam', *Globe and Mail*, 1 Sept., B1.

Elliott, Larry. 1997. World Bank Warning of Poverty Time Bomb', *Guardian Weekly*, 5 Oct., 19.

European Network on Debt and Development (EURODAD). 1996. *World Creditor Tables*. Brussels: EURODAD.

————. 1997. 'The HIPC Initiative Put to the Test: The Next Five Candidates'. EURO-
DAD Analysis, Sept., available at EURODAD's Web site, <http://www.oneworld.
org/eurodad/>.

Jackson, Edward T., et al. 1996. 'Learning for Results: Issues, Trends and Lessons
Learned in Basic Human Needs', Performance Review Division, CIDA, mimeo.

OXFAM. 1997. 'Poor Country Debt Relief: False Dawn or New Opportunity for Poverty
Reduction?', OXFAM Policy Paper, mimeo.

Plewes, Betty, Gauri Sreenivasan, and Tim Draimin. 1996. 'Sustainable Human
Development as a Global Framework', *International Journal* 51, 2 (Spring).

Plewes, Betty, and Roy Culpeper. 1997. 'Letter to Ministers Axworthy and Boudria',
17 Apr., mimeo.

Pratt, Cranford. 1996. 'Humane Internationalism and Canadian Development
Assistance Policies', in Pratt, ed., *Canadian International Development Assis-
tance Policies: An Appraisal*. Montreal and Kingston: McGill-Queen's University
Press.

————. 1997. 'The Coherence of Policies Towards the Developing Countries: The
Case of Canada', paper presented at the International Conference on Policy
Coherence in Development Co-operation, Geneva, 22–24 Apr.

Randel, Judith, and Tony German, eds. 1997. *The Reality of Aid: An Independent
Review of Development Cooperation, 1997/98*. London: Earthscan Publications.

Robinson, Bill, and Ken Epps. 1997. 'Swords into Ploughshares: Agenda for the Next
Parliament', *The Ploughshares Monitor* 18, 2 (June).

Schmitz, Gerald. 1996. 'The Verdict on Aid Effectiveness: Why the Jury Stays Out',
International Journal 51, 2 (Spring).

Smilie, Ian. 1997. Unpublished letter in response to the John Stackhouse 18 Oct. article in *Globe and Mail*, mimeo.

Sreenivasan, Gauri, and Anne Mitchell. 1997. 'Report to NGOs on June 1997 UN Special
Session, Earth Summit + 5', Canadian Council for International Co-operation,
mimeo.

Stackhouse, John. 1997. 'When Less Aid is More', *Globe and Mail*, 18 Oct., C1.

Steelworkers Humanity Fund. 1997. 'Labour Rights Assessments of Foreign Aid,
Trade and Investment Assistance Programs/Discussion Notes', mimeo.

Strong, Maurice, chairman. 1997. *Connecting with the World: Priorities for Canadian
Internationalism in the 21st Century (A Report by the International
Development Research and Policy Taskforce*. Ottawa: International Develop-
ment Research Centre.

United Nations Development Program (UNDP). 1994. *Human Development Report
(1994)*. Oxford: Oxford University Press.

————. 1997. *Human Development Report (1997)*. London: Oxford University Press.

Unny, Suresh. 1997. 'The Next Battle', *Far Eastern Economic Review* 20 (Nov.).

van der Berg, Max, and Bram van Ojik. 1996. *Rarer than Rubies: Reflections on
Development Cooperation*. The Hague: Novib.

Van Rooy, Alison. 1995. *A Partial Promise? Canadian Support to Social Development
in the South*. Ottawa: North-South Institute.

Winegard Report. 1987. *For Whose Benefit*. Ottawa: Standing Committee on External
Affairs and International Trade.

World Bank. 1997. *Global Development Finance, 1997*, vol. 2. Washington: World
Bank.

9

NATO Enlargement: The Way Ahead

ALAIN PELLERIN

At the North Atlantic Treaty Organization's (NATO) historic July 1997 summit in Madrid, the alliance leaders invited three former Warsaw Pact members—the Czech Republic, Hungary, and Poland—to start accession talks. Canada supported a wider enlargement to include these three countries, as well as Slovenia, Romania, and Slovakia, with a view to developing a broad transatlantic community. Provided all 16 NATO parliaments approve, the alliance intends to admit these three countries at the April 1999 Washington summit—the fiftieth anniversary of the alliance.

NATO enlargement, primarily a German-US project, is a process, not a single event. The Madrid invitation is the first phase to that process—some would say the easiest phase. Nine other countries have applied and some of these are likely to be invited at the 1999 summit. Indeed, NATO leaders confirmed that the alliance remains open for any European country that meets NATO's standards for democracy and peaceful relations with its neighbours (Madrid Declaration, 1997).

Canada, the fourth largest trading entity in the world, after the European Union (EU), the US, and Japan, is a global medium power, with real, concrete interests at stake in Europe. Because of these interests, Canada favours a stable European security environment, for we know that future instability in Europe will affect us as it has in the past. Whether NATO enlargement will provide that stable European security environment remains a subject of intense debate. As well, NATO enlargement is consequential, as it involves extending to the new members the nuclear and conventional security guarantees provided under Article V of the Washington Treaty. Notwithstanding the high stakes for Canada's broad security interests associated with the expansion of the alliance, the Canadian government has not played an active role in communicating the reasons behind and the security implications of NATO enlargement to Canadians. In fact, Canada became the first NATO country, on 2 February 1998, to ratify the enlargement of the alliance without any public debate or parliamentary discussion.

Grasping the immensity of events in Europe in recent years is difficult. The European security environment was dramatically transformed by the fall of the Berlin Wall and the reunification of Germany, the dissolution of the Soviet Union and the Warsaw Pact, the collapse of the Communist order in Central and Eastern Europe, and the emergence of 20 new sovereign states in the Organization for Security and Co-operation in Europe (OSCE). Security institutions such as NATO, the EU, and the OSCE have been under considerable stress as they have attempted to adapt to the kinds of challenges faced by post-Cold War Europe.

Of all these historical events, the fall of the Berlin Wall in November 1989 was probably the most dramatic and will be remembered as the turning point in post-Cold War East-West relations. The collapse of the Warsaw Pact and, later, the dissolution of the Soviet Union, however, are likely of even greater historical importance. This judgement is warranted given the tremendous impact these events have had, and will continue to have, on the three main players in the alliance enlargement debate: NATO, the fledgling democracies of Central and Eastern Europe, and Russia.

NATO enlargement is not an end in itself but a means to build security and stability within the wider Europe. This vision of a stable and secure Europe, where NATO has a vital role to play, must also include Russia. North America and Russia cannot be dissociated from Europe; they are both extensions of Europe. US President Bill Clinton, at his 18 December 1997 press conference on Bosnia, reminded Americans of the importance of the European continent: 'America', he stated, 'learned the hard way in this century that European stability and US security are joined.' How to get from where we are today to a Europe 'whole and free' for the twenty-first century is the primary policy challenge facing NATO.

In order to understand NATO enlargement and the 'way ahead' we need to understand where we came from. Firstly, I intend to review the security concerns of Central and Eastern European (CEE) states. This historical background helps explain the quest for a return to Europe by many countries from the region, the geopolitical central-ity of Russia and Germany in any vision of a new Europe, and the reasons for them wanting to join NATO (see Pellerin, 1997).

What is so attractive about NATO to the states from Central and Eastern Europe? In attempting to answer that question, I will review NATO's role in Euro-Atlantic security, the reasons for its survival to date, with particular emphasis on the extra- and intra-alliance func-tions, the transatlantic link, and the adaptation of the alliance. In the final part of this chapter, I will address the outstanding issues that current and new members will have to deal with post-Madrid. Successful resolutions of these issues, in the months and years ahead, will be key to determining whether the enlargement of NATO will enhance the stability and security of the Euro-Atlantic area.

CENTRAL AND EASTERN EUROPEAN SECURITY CONCERNS

In analysing the security concerns of the Central and Eastern Europeans it is important to point out that the notion of 'national security' has a different meaning for Western Europeans and North Americans, on the one hand, and Central and Eastern Europeans, on the other. In the West, the term generally refers to state security inter-ests. In Central and Eastern Europe, the term involves more funda-mental values, and the fears it addresses are far more stark, since it concerns the very existence of the nation itself. Unlike the Western nations, the people in the region have frequently been the subject of policies of forced assimilation. As a consequence, guaranteeing the survival of the nation is a vital concern.

History has had a heavy impact throughout the region (Pellerin, 1996). The memory of previous attempts by neighbours to subjugate them continues to exert a powerful influence on contemporary security assessments. Poland is perhaps the best example, having experienced three partitions in the late eighteenth century. It disappeared from the map of Europe for 130 years. It was again partitioned between the Soviet Union and Germany in 1939—the two neighbours who historically have inflicted the greatest injuries on the country and its people. After 1945 it became a vassal state of the Soviet Union until 1990. Poland is not the only such case in the region. The Czech state was destroyed in 1621 and did not reappear until 1918. Hungary was conquered by the Turks in 1526 and had to wait until 1866 for political autonomy under Austrian rule, and until 1918 for its political independence.

For North Americans, it is sometimes difficult to understand how these distant events and dates still have a great influence on the relations between European nations. Canada's first Prime Minister, Sir John A. Macdonald, lamented that Canada had 'too much geography and not enough history'. European policy-makers, on the other hand, are either blessed or cursed with too much history and not enough geography. In this vein, the current security concerns of Central and Eastern European countries can only be adequately understood by reviewing briefly the impact on national psyches of Versailles (1919) and Yalta (1945).

The peacemakers at Versailles created a group of independent states in the region, but left them, on the whole, unorganized and unsupported by any outside powers (except France) and, sometimes, with large ethnic minorities. As a result, in the late 1930s and early 1940s, Germany, itself resentful of the punitive consequences of the Versailles Treaty, and the Soviet Union carved up the region. The failure of the victors of World War I to fashion an effective security structure for CEE sowed the seeds of World War II.

In February 1945, a quarter of a century after Versailles, the political settlement of Central and Eastern Europe dominated the discussions between the United States, the United Kingdom, and the USSR at Yalta.

There are several different interpretations of the agreements reached by Roosevelt, Churchill, and Stalin. In the Western view, Yalta more or less established a new international equilibrium, with the apportionment of 'spheres of influence' between the victors, giving too much to the Russians but obtaining stability in return. Central and Eastern Europeans, on the other hand, view Yalta as a stab in the back, a view especially held in Poland, whose army and air force made a major contribution to the victory of the Western Allies. The West, in the view of these countries, bartered their enslavement for its own tranquillity. Notwithstanding the provisions of the Yalta Agreement of 'free and unfettered elections', these 'liberated' people never had the option of choosing their own democratic destiny.

For Cental and Eastern European states, the main impact of Yalta was their forced exclusion from the West by Soviet regional hegemony. Czech President Vaclav Havel described it as 'values and principles that communism denied us' (Ruggie, 1997: 112). As a result, their societies were traumatized by decades of totalitarian rule and extremely inefficient economies. The psychological impact of a 45-year-long occupation of these countries by Soviet forces does not die easily.

Central and Eastern Europeans now realize that the danger of a military attack from Russia has disappeared. Given the harsh facts of their history, however, it is understandable that anxiety about Russia remains and makes NATO membership attractive, as it combines US power and interests with those of all but one (Russia) of the principal European powers and the security guarantees this core relationship embodies. Poles, for instance, have been dominated and oppressed for most of the last two centuries. It is hardly surprising that they should want some insurance against the revival of Russian imperial behaviour.

For these historical reasons the new NATO members will insist on hard security guarantees from the alliance, implicit in Article V of the Washington Treaty. As well, they will monitor very closely the emerging NATO-Russia strategic relationship.

The end of the Cold War produced a situation that, in its fundamentals, is not unlike what emerged following this century's two world wars. Each postwar situation resulted in the defeat of a power or alliance of powers (Imperial Germany and Austria-Hungary, Nazi Germany, Italy, and Japan) that had sought Eurasian hegemony. Each postwar situation witnessed the temporary emergence of a 'security vacuum' in Central and Eastern Europe, presenting the victorious powers with a clear opportunity to fill that vacuum.

In the two previous occasions, at Versailles and Yalta, the failure of the victorious powers to settle adequately the Central and Eastern European question set the stage for the next confrontation among the great powers. A failure, in the present post-Cold War period, to address satisfactorily the current perceived security vacuum in Central and Eastern Europe could very well create a cancer for the security of Europe. Whether the planned enlargement of NATO, to include, in the first phase, three countries of that region, is the most appropriate remedy remains a subject of intense debate.

In the current NATO enlargement debate, some commentators are concerned that enlarging the alliance to the East will result in the creation of new dividing lines—in essence a 'new Yalta'—rather than in a Europe 'whole and free'. Those terms and phrases are a form of shorthand for a new division of Europe between Russia and the West, if not into armed camps, then into 'spheres of influences'.

At the end of the twentieth century, the CEE nations may face some of the same problems they faced in the post-Versailles and post-Yalta periods. Nevertheless, there are two fundamental geostrategic differences arising from the demise of the Soviet Union and from the active engagement of North America, particularly the US, in Euro-Atlantic security.

The collapse of the Soviet Union makes the current security environment in CEE very different from that of 1945. Russia's European border is now east of Ukraine, its armed forces are in a profound state of disarray, and Russia has withdrawn politically and militarily from CEE. Consequently, Russia no longer plays the role of hegemon in the region. Coinciding with the collapse of the Soviet Communist regime is the slow transformation of Russia itself into a democratic country with a popularly elected leader and Duma.

The second difference is the active engagement of North America, particularly the United States, in the Euro-Atlantic security architecture, as well as the existence of many effective multilateral security organizations created after World War II, including NATO, its outreach program, the Partnership for Peace (PfP), the EU, and the OSCE. These organizations are reinforced by a variety of arms control regimes, especially the Conventional Armed Forces in Europe (CFE) Treaty—a cornerstone of Euro-Atlantic security. These are important elements that should have been and still need to be factored into the discussions on how best to meet the security concerns of CEE countries.

NATO'S PERSISTENCE

With the end of the Cold War, the collapse of the Soviet Union, and the disappearance of the 'clear and present military danger', many analysts predicted that NATO, having lost its *raison d'être*, would wither away. NATO enlargement was, in fact, put forward in some circles as an answer to the question: 'How can a withering NATO be saved?' (Zelikow, 1997: 84).

Historically, nations have formed military alliances to respond to a common external threat. Alliances normally disintegrate when the threat that was the reason for their creation disappears, the best and most recent example being the World War II alliance of the Soviet Union, the United States, the United Kingdom, and Canada. That alliance was formed with the single purpose of defeating Nazi Germany (Walt, 1997).

The ink was not even dry on the Yalta Agreement before the alliance was obviously terminally ill, and, in fact, the alliance did not survive the end of World War II. 'An Alliance against the common enemy is something clear and understandable,' wrote Winston Churchill, 'far more complicated is an alliance after the war for securing lasting peace and the fruits of victory' (Churchill, 1953). When the Cold War ended, many observers predicted that NATO might follow. Contrary to this logic, NATO has not only survived but has become the most important Euro-Atlantic security institution for members as well as non-members. What explains its persistence? Put differently, why have alliance members found it in their interest to preserve NATO? Three important factors may help to explain the Alliance's enduring relevance:

- the importance of extra- as well as intra-alliance functions;
- the centrality of the transatlantic link to Euro-Atlantic security;
- NATO's capacity for adaptation to the new Euro-Atlantic security environment.

The Extra-Alliance Functions

The threat of a massive Soviet attack against Western Europe has now disappeared. It is a welcome development. However, the situation in Russia, a nuclear superpower with an army in disarray, is likely to remain very unsettled for the foreseeable future. European uneasiness about Russian intentions is therefore understandable. Russia is too big for Europe; it has been, and will continue to be, a problem in the European balance. Under these circumstances, a downsized alliance is seen as a 'strategic balance' or an insurance guarantee against a possible revival of Russian power.

While collective defence remains the core function of the alliance, a second post-Cold War task has assumed greater prominence for

NATO. This is the alliance's response to an array of emerging risks on the periphery of the alliance, such as: the proliferation of missiles and weapons of mass destruction (WMD); ethnic fragmentation, instability, and internal conflicts (as seen in the former Yugoslavia); mass migrations resulting from these ethnic conflicts and from instability; and dwindling energy resources, in particular oil and water. A cursory examination reveals that most of these risks emanate from the southern tier of NATO.

The Intra-Alliance Functions

Preventing an attack on the territory of the Allies (Article V of the Washington Treaty) was the defining role of NATO until the end of the Cold War. Lord Ismay, the first Secretary-General of NATO, recognized the alliance's responsibility of keeping the 'Russians Out', but also highlighted the intra-alliance function of 'keeping the Germans down, and the Americans in'.

The German function, early in the history of the alliance, was changed into keeping the Germans integrated. The most important intra-alliance function during the last 45 years has been one of reassurance. The transparency created by consultations, the integrated military structure, and the defence planning process assures its members that they have nothing to fear from one another. With the exception of the Greek-Turkish relationship, the possibility of conflict among the Western European countries has all but disappeared since the creation of NATO. Although this may seem to be a statement of the obvious in 1998, it was not always the case: witness the three bitter wars fought by Germany and France between 1870 and 1945.

NATO makes German power controllable and thus acceptable to allies and to political adversaries alike. The other European countries want to ensure that Germany remains tightly anchored in NATO and that the Germans understand full well that a US-led NATO reassures everybody else by shortening the shadow of German power. This intra-alliance benefit is even more evident with respect to a powerful unified Germany back in the heart of Europe (Duffield, 1994–5: 95).

Another reassuring dimension of NATO is the integration of national security policies within an alliance context. A collective approach to defence planning within NATO not only promotes transparency and trust between allies but also discourages the risky renationalization of defence, as well as being less expensive.

The Centrality of the Transatlantic Link

With the disappearance of the Soviet military threat some analysts predicted that the North Americans, particularly the United States, would inevitably withdraw their military forces from Europe and then, by extension, their nuclear and conventional guarantees to European security. These analysts believed this would result in a renationalization of European security policy coupled with a return to an unstable continent.

This did not happen. The US military presence in Europe remains at a credible level of some 100,000 troops, from a high of some 350,000 during the Cold War. Canada, although it withdrew its NATO contribution in Germany, has contributed significantly to European security with substantial participation in UNPROFOR and subsequently in IFOR/SFOR. Pessimists forget that the North American commitment to European security after World War II was meant to address more than just the Soviet military threat against Western Europe.

Despite the disappearance of the Soviet military threat, a continued US and, to a lesser extent, Canadian commitment to the security and stability of Europe remains important to both countries. The original US and Canadian commitments were not only about countering a Soviet threat. Had that been the case, NATO would, in fact, have lost its *raison d'être*. Economic links to a stable Europe were and still are critically important to North American commercial interests.

There is no doubt that Canadian and US trade with Asia has grown substantially over the last 20 years and, as a consequence, the relative importance of Europe as a trading partner has declined. Nevertheless, in 1995, 10 per cent of Canada's imports and 6.4 per cent of its exports of goods were with EU countries. This is not a negligible amount, considering that Canadian trade with the US is very high, at 70 per cent of our imports and 80 per cent of our exports. Bilateral investment, in Canada and the EU, is the most dynamic element of our economic relations, totalling, in 1995, some $32 billion in both directions. The EU is the second largest source of foreign investment in Canada and as host for Canadian investment abroad. The flows of investments are both larger and growing more quickly than Canada's comparable flows with Asia (Standing Committee on Foreign Affairs, 1996: 22).

The notion that Canada and the United States must make a choice between Asia and Europe should be dispelled. Both regions are vital to North America's economic health. In fact, the prosperity of both nations has never been more dependent on the world economy as a whole. Even so, the tremendous economic benefits that the United States and, to a lesser extent, Canada receive from their co-operative relationship with a stable and prosperous Europe are too easily ignored by some critics in Washington and Ottawa. Inside the zone of stability of Western Europe, the allies on both sides of the Atlantic have developed strong economic ties and shared values that have been, and continue to remain, of great mutual benefit (see David Long's Chapter 10).

NATO has developed into something much more than a classical military alliance. Today, it is a community of shared values between two continents, North America and Europe. Although it represents only 6 per cent of the world population, the economic power of the Euro-Atlantic area, which includes three of the four largest world trading entities, adds up to 40 per cent of the world GNP.

The transatlantic link thus remains essential to North American and European allies. Nevertheless, to reconcile the current process of European integration with a transatlantic security framework, and to achieve a new sharing of responsibilities between Europe and North American allies, 'may well become one of the most crucial challenges in the next decade', warns NATO Secretary-General Javier Solana (Solana, 1997a: 3).

THE ADAPTATION OF NATO

In its quest to remain relevant in a rapidly evolving situation, since the July 1990 London summit, NATO has gone through a major internal and external transformation. The approval of the new Alliance Strategic Concept at the November 1991 Rome summit, which emphasizes dialogue and co-operation as well as collective defence, signalled a shift to a more politically active and non-threatening alliance. An essential component of this transformation has been the establishment of close security links with states of Central and Eastern Europe and those of the former Soviet Union.

In 1992, the alliance agreed to support the Conference on Security and Co-operation in Europe (CSCE) and UN peacekeeping operations, thereby expanding the core function of collective defence to include peacekeeping and crisis management. At the January 1994 Brussels summit, NATO broadened its links with the rest of Europe by establishing the very successful Partnership for Peace (PfP), which now includes 28 non-NATO countries from CEE, as well as Central Asia and the Caucasus, and also took the decision to enlarge.

The year 1997 was most extraordinary for this new NATO. Within a few months, NATO invited three new members to begin accession negotiations, established new strategic relationships with Russia and Ukraine, created the NATO-Russia Permanent Joint Council (PJC) and a new Euro-Atlantic Co-operation Council (EAPC) with 44 partners, enhanced the PfP, gave higher profile to the Mediterranean dialogue, and undertook to review the strategic concept of the organization. In a sense, the alliance changed more during the 45 days from the signing of the NATO-Russian Founding Act in May to the Madrid summit in July than it had changed in the previous 45 years. These initiatives hardly suggest an alliance in decline.

New members will thus enter a NATO that is already adapting to the challenges of the post-Cold War in a variety of ways. Despite the extent of NATO's transformation, collective defence as well as the enduring transatlantic link remain the cornerstones of alliance solidarity, yet collective defence will not be the principal focus of NATO's activities in the foreseeable future. NATO's day-to-day activities are shifting from collective defence (Article V missions) to those involving crisis management and peacekeeping (non-Article V missions). In essence, NATO is evolving into a provider of 'co-operative security'. The best example of this new NATO is the 1995 decision to send 60,000 troops to Bosnia in support of the Dayton peace agreement. The current NATO-led force, known as SFOR, of some 35,000 includes 16 allies and 20 non-NATO countries, including Russia.

Notwithstanding its successful internal and external adaptation, the future character and identity of the new NATO will likely be one of the key issues in the forthcoming enlargement debate in the months and years ahead. If, for instance, collective defence against an emerging military threat, such as a resurgent Russia, is NATO's main purpose then it is obvious that the very act of taking in former Soviet bloc countries, particularly the Baltic states and Ukraine, will exclude and alienate Russia. If, on the other hand, the goal is to promote stability and security among NATO members, then there is no reason not to include Russia eventually in the alliance.

NATO ENLARGEMENT: THE DEBATE

Despite the radical changes introduced by NATO since the 1991 Rome summit, enlargement is the most symbolic of this new NATO and also the most problematic. If all goes well, the Czech Republic, Hungary, and Poland will likely join NATO in April 1999. The reality, however, is that the enlargement debate will not end on the day these new members enter the alliance. Indeed, the real debate may only be starting. What happens after NATO enlargement will be decisive for Europe's stability and security. After this initial enlargement, the alliance will face a series of difficult questions. Should it:

- stop the enlargement process after the current wave or after a relatively non-controversial second wave that could include Slovenia, Romania, and Austria;
- expand to Russia's border to include the Baltic states and possibly Ukraine; or
- pursue a broad enlargement that would include Russia?

None of these options is very attractive. The last one, notwithstanding all its drawbacks, may come to be seen as the least unattractive. The main advantage of this option is that Russia would not be excluded and hence alienated. As well, it would avoid the creation of dividing lines in Europe. On the other hand, with Russia as a member, the alliance would be a very different shell of its former self. This option, however, would make China very uncomfortable, as NATO's security guarantees would stretch all the way to the Pacific.

NATO enlargement has generated a great deal of debate, largely, thus far, among academics and former diplomats. Some argue that the enlargement issue is a low-cost, low-risk initiative that will reduce tensions, promote stability, and improve the security environment throughout Europe. Others assert that the initiative is ill-conceived, ill-timed, and, above all, ill-suited to the realities of the post-Cold War and that it will end up creating new dividing lines across Europe and alienate Russia. The Rand Corporation pro-enlargement study also issued a similar warning: 'Depending how it is handled, expansion could stabilize a new European security order, or contribute to either unraveling of the Alliance or a new Cold War with Russia' (Atkinson, 1996: 34). George Kennan, the noted American scholar, has argued that enlargement 'would be the most fateful error of American policy in the whole post-Cold War era.'

The reasoning on both sides of the enlargement issue is familiar, and it is not my intention to 'reopen' the debate at this late stage in the process. Nevertheless, some of these arguments are likely to surface during the ratification process. It is, therefore, important to review the respective positions of the proponents and opponents of NATO enlargement (see Haglund, 1996; Gordon, 1997; Legault and Sens, 1996).

Those who favour NATO enlargement for the three invited countries make the following arguments:

- History demonstrates that CEE has been traditionally unstable. Without secure membership in NATO, this region may grow unstable and become a source of contention between Germany and Russia.
- Yalta treated these countries unfairly: they suffered for more than 45 years under Soviet domination and now wish to rejoin the West, and the West, therefore, has a moral obligation to them.
- NATO needs to enlarge in order to survive. 'Not to enlarge is the do-nothing option, achieve-nothing option', in the view of Secretary-General Javier Solana. 'It is the option that the Alliance long ago rejected' (Solana, 1997b).
- Expansion of the EU, to integrate these nations fully, will take at least 10 years, and this is considered too long.
- For the US, European security organization enlargement must begin with NATO, where the United States is the leading member.
- NATO enlargement would cement the US security commitment to Europe for decades to come.
- The alliance should take advantage of a temporary Russian weakness and establish now a hedge against the possibility of a renewed Russian threat.

On the other hand, opponents assert that:

- The three invited countries are young, stable liberal democracies with market economies doing relatively well. Historical analogies regarding their future are misleading. Their situation is totally different from the 1930s or 1945.
- If the main objective of NATO enlargement was to enhance stability by reinforcing nascent democratization and economic reform, highest priority should presumably have been given to bringing Russia and Ukraine into NATO.
- The centrality of the US domination of NATO creates a problem for Russia: expanding the EU first would have been a less

provocative move and would have forced the Europeans to address what is seen, by some, as a European problem.

- The PfP offered the possibility of doing everything that formal membership would accomplish, short of Article V guarantees, but would do it without creating new dividing lines in Europe and without creating an open challenge to Russia, possibly replicating the Cold War division of Europe.

THE OUTSTANDING ISSUES

The first enlargement wave may have been the single most critical decision taken at the Madrid summit, but it must not become the single issue of the future Euro-Atlantic security debate. Successful resolution of the following issues in the months and years ahead will be the key in determining whether the enlargement of NATO will enhance the security and stability of the Euro-Atlantic area:

- the role of Russia in the evolving Euro-Atlantic security architecture;
- the need to reconcile the aspirations of new members to the new NATO;
- the need to reassure the non-invited countries, particularly Ukraine and the Baltic states;
- the security in the Mediterranean area;
- the unanimous ratification by the parliaments of all member states.

Russia

Russia has been suffering from what can be described as the 'Versailles Syndrome', which affected defeated Germany after World War I. Moscow thinks it is the victim, with NATO taking advantage of its temporary difficulties. It feels isolated and humiliated, and has had great difficulty in adjusting from its past superpower status to its post-Cold War situation. Moscow's humiliation stems mainly from the major defeat sustained when it lost its two empires: the inner Soviet empire, contiguous to the Russian heartland, which had taken centuries to build; and the outer empire, acquired after 1945, consisting of the CEE satellites. Russia is in a state of 'post-imperial collapse'.

In the spring of 1989, the political boundaries of the Soviet sphere extended to the Elbe River, in the heart of Germany. Before the end of 1991, these boundaries had changed to a greater extent than in the disastrous summer of 1941, following the Nazi invasion. Of Russia's major historical boundaries, only that in Siberia remains where it has been for the past several centuries. In the south, in the Caucasus, Russia's formal borders are today as they were at the beginning of the nineteenth Century. In Central Asia, Russia's borders are now roughly the same as those before the rapid imperial expansion that began in the region in the middle of the nineteenth century. More important still are those borders that reflect the country's standing as a European great power. Russia's western state borders are now those of more than three centuries ago. The rapid disintegration of the Soviet empire means that some 25 million ethnic Russians now live outside Russia in the so-called 'near abroad'. From the foregoing, it is obvious that Russia has undergone traumatic changes in recent years. These changes must be factored into the current NATO enlargement debate.

For Russia, the goal now is to avoid being isolated from the West. NATO's primary goal in expanding the alliance, on the other hand, is to 'enhance stability and security' in the whole Euro-Atlantic area. The two goals are not mutually exclusive. To achieve its goal, NATO, and the US in particular, must treat Russia as a valued and respected partner. The allies should be guided by the principles that guided their predecessors in their dealings with vanquished Germany and Japan at the end of World War II: treat former enemies magnanimously.

A stable, open, and prosperous Russia is in the long-term interests of the alliance and Euro-Atlantic security. This is particularly so when, as is the case in Bosnia, Russian co-operation is essential to the successful management of non-Article V security issues in Europe, in reaching agreements in the ongoing conventional and nuclear arms control negotiations, and in countering the proliferation of weapons of mass destruction (WMD)—a serious risk to global security.

NATO enlargement continues to be opposed across the entire Russian political spectrum. If not handled properly, it risks poisoning the relationship between Russia and the West for a long time. Russians will likely remember that the West exploited their country's temporary weakness to establish hegemony throughout CEE. NATO enlargement, therefore, could become the 1990s equivalent of the Treaty of Versailles, which sowed the seeds of revenge and an enormously destructive war. Some key negative consequences could be: an aggressive rebirth of Russia's sphere of influence among the now independent states of the former Soviet Union, with a particularly negative impact on Ukraine and the Baltic states; a strengthening of the non-democratic opposition, which would undercut those who favour reforms and co-operation with the West; an unwelcome nationalistic influence on internal Russian politics; an intensification of the relationship between Russia and China, to avoid mutual isolation; the annulment of the NATO-Russia Founding Act; encouragement of a new militarism in Russia; and a resistance in the Duma to various arms control agreements.

None of these issues is trivial. The arms control file, for instance, requires close attention. During the Cold War, the USSR and the US negotiated and implemented many arms control agreements, as it was felt to be in their mutual interest. Recently, with the polarized atmosphere surrounding the enlargement issue, the Russian Duma delayed the ratification of the Chemical Weapons Convention (CWC) and has not yet ratified the START-2 Treaty.

NATO was slow to realize that its enlargement to the east would not be successful without the active participation of Russia in the development of a Euro-Atlantic security architecture. The NATO-Russia Founding Act, signed in Paris on 27 May 1997, marks the beginning of a better understanding of Russia's legitimate security concerns.[1] The agreement establishes clear principles and arrangements for a NATO-Russia Permanent Joint Council (PJC) for regular consultation on issues of common interests, such as conflict prevention, joint action in peacekeeping, nuclear and conventional military doctrines, nuclear safety, theatre ballistic missile defence (TMD), and the proliferation of WMD. The signing of the Founding Act should, hopefully, form the basis of an enduring NATO-Russia partnership. This does not mean, however, that a difference of policy and outlook between NATO and Russia will automatically disappear, particularly on the future enlargement of NATO.

A broader strategy towards Russia—separate from the NATO enlargement issue and reflecting political and economic issues—is also being pursued. The second facet of that partnership reflects political and economic initiatives to draw Russia into institutions such as the G-7, the Organization for Economic Co-operation and Development (OECD), and the World Trade Organization (WTO). The overall goal is to persuade Russia that the West is not intent on threatening or isolating it, but in welcoming it into a broader democratic and prosperous Europe.

If the aim of NATO enlargement is the enhancement of Europe's security and stability, Russia's legitimate security concerns need to be addressed satisfactorily. Given that the integration of Russia into the Euro-Atlantic security architecture is one of the most pressing problems facing NATO security planners in the aftermath of the Cold War, an enlargement that infringes further on the Russian sense of insecurity and isolation carries enormous risks.

The main task of Euro-Atlantic security planners, as we approach the twenty-first century, is to find a place for Russia as was done for Germany in the post-World War II period. The unprecedented policies pursued by the Allies after World War II, including the Marshall Plan, brought the speedy recovery of the former enemy economies— Germany and Japan—and with them 50 years of impressive economic expansion and prosperity for the victors as well. These policies came into existence because the Allied leaders remembered the catastrophic consequences of the punitive Versailles peace after World War I and followed Winston Churchill's maxim: 'In victory: magnanimity. In peace: goodwill.' Alliance members need to show greater magnanimity and goodwill by enmeshing Russia in a series of economic, political, and security relationships to eliminate future threats.

New Members

New members will be joining a different alliance from the one that existed during the Cold War. They will be joining a new NATO adapted to the twenty-first century. While this new NATO retains its core collective defence obligations and capabilities, it has also embraced new missions, moving away, on a day-to-day basis, from collective defence and resistance to armed attack to co-operative security missions of crisis management and peacekeeping. An important facet to this 'softer' NATO approach to Euro-Atlantic security involves a deepened NATO-Russia co-operation, as seen from the recently agreed NATO-Russia Founding Act. Many of the countries wishing to join, however, are looking at NATO in terms of what it has been in the twentieth century. They wish to join NATO for the 'hard' security guarantees, which in their view best meet their historical security concerns *vis-à-vis* their Russian neighbour.

Enlargement under this scenario may be one of the alliance's most serious challenges in the years ahead. These differing views could undercut its political and military cohesion and saddle NATO with a group of new members who could be out of step with current NATO thinking on Euro-Atlantic security, particularly on the need for the alliance to have a closer co-operative relationship with Russia. Managing an alliance that includes one set of difficult partners (Greece and Turkey, without the focus of the Cold War, are again quarrelling publicly over Cyprus) is difficult enough, but if the new CEE members cannot overcome their historical anxiety towards Russia, the development of a consensus within the alliance—traditionally its strength—may not be possible. Reconciling the aspirations of the new members to a transformed NATO (which involves a strategic NATO-Russia relationship that in itself rekindles memories of Yalta) may be one of the alliance's most serious long-term challenges.

Non-Invited Countries

The NATO enlargement debate has primarily focused on the countries to be offered membership in the first wave and on the type of strategic relationship that needs to be developed with Russia to make enlargement more palatable. Equally important is how the alliance deals with countries left out of the first wave of enlargement.

Despite NATO's commitment to an open-door policy concerning further accessions, the enlargement of NATO—unless Russia is eventually invited to join—will likely create new dividing lines in Europe. At a minimum, these will be institutional dividing lines. On the West side will be NATO members, current and new, who, under Article V of the Washington Treaty, receive nuclear and conventional security guarantees. On the other side of that institutional line will be those European nations not invited to join the alliance. This dividing line issue is probably one of the strongest arguments against enlargement.

Just as important in avoiding a division of Europe into a western 'we' and a Russian-centred 'they' will be finding ways to reassure the countries in between, particularly Ukraine and the Baltic states. As the enlargement process moves forward, NATO must dispel any fear that the nightmare of Yalta will be revisited. Ukraine's future security orientation will have a critical impact on NATO enlargement. Although Ukraine has not yet shown an interest in joining NATO, it does not wish to become a forgotten grey zone between Russia and a new western bloc. Ukraine is in a position of weakness, being heavily reliant on the West for economic assistance. As well, Russia has three powerful levers: the close ties between Russian and Ukrainian industries, Ukraine's dependence on Russian resources, such as oil and gas, and the presence of some 12 million native Russians (more than 20 per cent of the population) within the borders of Ukraine. If Russia considers itself isolated from the Euro-Atlantic community, it may feel the need to strengthen its historical sphere of influence.

The same situation also applies to the Baltic states. The three Baltic states—Lithuania, Latvia, and Estonia—which arguably still have the most to fear of Russia, are also the ones that NATO is the least likely to invite in the foreseeable future. The question of their membership poses enormous problems for which there are no obvious solutions. Inviting the Baltic states would exacerbate tensions with Russia. The Russians have made it clear that while they may have accepted, grudgingly, the addition of three Central European countries to NATO, they would respond sharply if NATO were extended all the way to their borders, as would be the case if the Baltic states joined NATO. On the other hand, not inviting the Baltic states and Ukraine (should it wish to join) would send the signal to Moscow that these countries are isolated and subject to its influence.

Russia, therefore, will likely attempt to prevent future waves of enlargement, particularly if the Baltic states were being seriously considered. Thus, both the non-invited countries and Moscow will try, in their different ways, to force NATO's hand and win the assurances they seek. Baltic states leaders have publicly stated, after the Madrid summit, that their NATO membership is not a question of 'whether' but rather of 'when'. The alliance, therefore, will have to walk a fine line between keeping open the possibility of further enlargements— which the Baltic states and Ukraine wish, lest they become permanent buffer zones between an enlarged NATO and Russia—and addressing legitimate Russian security concerns.

The newly created Euro-Atlantic Partnership Council (EAPC), the Distinctive NATO-Ukraine Partnership, a closer security relationship between the US and the Baltic states as exemplified by the recently signed Charter of Partnership, a deepened Partnership for Peace, the development of an effective three-way dialogue between NATO, Russia, and the Eastern European non-invited countries, closer association and eventual membership in the EU for these countries, and increased economic assistance from industrialized nations like Canada—all are essential components in reassuring these countries that the West has not abandoned them. Notwithstanding the importance of these initiatives, in the eyes of most non-invited countries these are not alternatives to eventual full membership in NATO.

If NATO is to achieve its post-Cold War goals of stability and security in the Euro-Atlantic area, it must formulate a clear strategy towards these countries, many of which are unstable democracies with struggling market economies, such as Bulgaria, Albania, Ukraine, and the Baltic states. Developing a long-term strategy towards the non-invited countries is far from a side issue in the NATO enlargement debate; it is front and centre. Over the next few years there will be no more visible barometer of the alliance's priorities and leadership.

Mediterranean Security

As the alliance prepares to take in three countries from Central and Northern Europe, defence planners say the gravest risks of future conflict spring from myriad forces of instability along NATO's southern flank. For that reason the enlargement of NATO to Central and Northern Europe for countries like Spain, France, Italy, Turkey, and Greece is not as high on their agenda as it is for Germany, for instance. At the Madrid summit a large number of NATO countries promoted a 'southern enlargement' to balance a 'central enlargement' by taking in Romania and Slovenia. This French-led group argued that NATO should worry about the Mediterranean and the Balkans as well as Central Europe.

In the new post-Cold War strategic landscape, the Mediterranean and the Balkans have been transformed from a backwater of Euro-Atlantic security into an area of strategic importance to the alliance. Any conflict in the region, whether triggered by strategic resources, such as oil or water, political revolutions, or ethnic, historical, and religious rivalries, would have serious consequences for the alliance.

As well, within a decade, if not sooner, it is likely that every capital in Southern Europe will be within range of ballistic missiles based in North Africa and the Middle East. The spread of long-range missiles armed with weapons of mass destruction is of vital concern to the Euro-Atlantic community architecture. NATO must, therefore, develop a focused and relevant Mediterranean policy, not only because security and stability in the region are closely linked to security in the whole of Europe, but also because issues such as the current Greece-Turkey imbroglio over Cyprus and Turkey's non-admission to the EU may derail NATO enlargement.

Ratification

At the Madrid summit, NATO leaders invited three countries to begin accession negotiations. NATO's glue remains the commitment of its members to treat any attack on one as an attack on all. By extending the Article V nuclear and conventional security guarantees to these newly independent nations, NATO expands its sphere of influence and commits its members to 'take such action as it deems necessary, including the use of armed force, to restore and maintain the security' and integrity of these new members.

Will the electorate in NATO nations, particularly in the US, be willing to make security commitments to the three new members (possibly more in the future) and, if so, at what price? The protocols of accession, resulting from the consultations with the new members, were signed by NATO foreign ministers on 16 December 1997. The process of formally enlarging the alliance is not, however, a foregone conclusion. The ratification of these protocols, in 1998, could take up to one year in some NATO countries. The ratification process is likely to be easier in countries with parliamentary systems, such as Canada, where ratification involves the issuance of an Order in Council authorizing the Minister of Foreign Affairs to sign an instrument of acceptance of the protocols of accession. Support for the ratification may, on the other hand, be hard to mobilize in some NATO countries, such as France and Turkey, but particularly in the United States.

Adding new members to NATO will, in the United States, require ratification of the protocols of accession by a two-thirds vote from the Senate and approval by the House of Representatives. The advice and consent of the Senate will take the form of a resolution of ratification. To this resolution will be appended a set of conditions, reservations, and declarations by which the US Senate will establish the legal and political basis for American participation in the amended treaty regime. This resolution is binding only on the US executive branch. But given the US role in the alliance, the Senate's decisions will guide the formation of US policy to NATO for years to come. Its views on the ultimate political and territorial extent of the alliance and on the relationship with Russia, for reasons already discussed in this paper, will be of particular interest (Cambone, 1997).

In this view, many key questions are likely to be raised by inquisitive US senators and representatives during the ratification process. These are likely to include: What will be the cost and will current and new members be ready to pay their share? Why are we still in Europe and what are we getting for it? Will enlargement really produce greater stability and security in the Euro-Atlantic area or will it create new political dividing lines? And by extension, why should the United States provide nuclear and conventional guarantees when there is no clear and present Russian military threat to these countries? What will be the size and timing of further enlargements? And have we conceded too much to Russia?

The US Senate is taking up the enlargement issue in the spring of 1998, at about the same time the US Congress is considering whether to support President Clinton's decision to keep US troops in Bosnia beyond the self-imposed 30 June deadline. The two issues are separate and distinct, theoretically, but as a practical matter they are intertwined. European allies and Canada have indicated that if the United States withdrew its forces from Bosnia, they would also withdraw their own forces. If the US Congress does not support President Clinton's decision and the Bosnian peace effort seems in danger of unravelling, this coincidence in timing could prove very unfortunate for the ratification process in the United States. The spectacle of a European retrenchment on Bosnia, coming at the moment of NATO enlargement, would strike the US congressmen as a burden-sharing cop-out.

Given the importance of NATO enlargement, the Canadian government should submit the issue to Parliament for debate before signing the instruments of ratification. The Standing Committees of the Senate and House of Commons on Foreign Affairs and International Trade should also hold further hearings. The involvement of Parliament and of these two committees should have been essential components in promoting informed debate in Canada. A communication strategy should also be developed in all NATO nations, but particularly in the United States, to sensitize the public, the media, and legislatures. This strategy should clearly spell out the 'why' of enlargement and where it is headed, in particular how the membership aspirations of non-invited countries and Russia's legitimate security concerns will be reconciled, the consequences of the security guarantees provided by Article V to new members, and the costs and burdens involved and how these will be shared.

CONCLUSION

The Cold War has indeed melted away and taken with it NATO's primary mission to deter and defend against an attack on Western Europe. But the usefulness of the alliance has endured. Indeed, its members have found it to be in their mutual interest to maintain the alliance because it continues to perform several vital security functions, both external and internal, particularly the vital linkage of the United States and Canada to European security matters and the promotion of transparency and trust between allies. As well, the alliance's collective approach to defence discourages the risky and expensive renationalization of defence in Europe and provides an adequate residual insurance against a resurgent Russia.

NATO has also adjusted well to the new Euro-Atlantic security environment and by doing so has demonstrated its ability to remain relevant. It has undertaken a major internal and external transformation since the 1990 London summit. A key part of that adaptation process is the 1994 Brussels summit decision to welcome the enlargement of the alliance to Central and Eastern Europe.

NATO enlargement to three Central European countries may have been the most critical decision taken at the Madrid summit but it is only the beginning of the process. The major problem is how to manage any enlargement of NATO without risking a return to a confrontational and divided Europe. In this vein, successful resolution in the months and years ahead of the outstanding issues identified in this paper will be the key determinant of whether the enlargement of NATO achieves its stated goal of enhancing stability and security in the Euro-Atlantic area.

To ensure this, NATO now needs a vision of its role in the next century as farsighted as the Marshall Plan was 50 years ago. The alliance must design a long-term overarching strategic framework to bridge the gap between the likely admission of three new NATO members in 1999 and the distant goal of creating an undivided, democratic, and peaceful Europe in the twenty-first century. This vision, with NATO playing the leading role, must also include Russia.

NOTES

1. The full title of the agreement is the Founding Act on Mutual Relations, Co-operation and Security between the Russian Federation and the North Atlantic Treaty Organization.

REFERENCES

Atkinson, B. 1996. 'NATO Expansion', *Army* 46, 6 (June): 34.
Cambone, Stephen. 1997. 'Will the US Senate Endorse NATO Enlargement?', *NATO Review* 6 (Nov./Dec.): 12–16.
Churchill, Winston S. 1953. *The Second World War—Triumph and Tragedy*. London: Educational Book Company.

Duffield, John. 1994–5. 'NATO's Functions After the Cold War', *Political Science Quarterly* 109, 5.

Gordon, Paul. 1997. *NATO's Transformation: The Changing Shape of the Alliance.* London: Rowman and Littlefield.

Haglund, D. 1996. *Will NATO Go East? The Debate Over Enlarging the Atlantic Alliance.* Kingston: Queen's University Centre for International Affairs.

Legault, Albert, and Allen Sens. 1996. 'Canada and NATO Enlargement: Interests and Options', *Canadian Foreign Policy* 4, 2 (Fall): 88–93.

Madrid Declaration. 1997. Madrid Declaration on Euro-Atlantic Security and Co-operation, Issued by the Heads of State and Government, Madrid, 8 July.

Pellerin, Alain. 1996. 'Nations and Their Past: The Uses and Abuses of History', *The Economist*, 21 Dec.

———. 1997. 'NATO Enlargement—Where We Came From and Where It Leaves Us', Canadian Council for International Peace and Security, Aurora Paper #29 (30 May).

Ruggie, John G. 1997. 'NATO's European Pillar', *Washington Quarterly* 2, 1, (Winter).

Solana, Javier. 1997a. 'Building a New NATO for a New Europe', *NATO Review* 4, (July–Aug.).

———. 1997b. 'Speech to CSIF', Brussels, 21 Feb.

Standing Committee on Foreign Affairs. 1996. *European Integration: The Implications for Canada.* Ottawa: Queen's Printer.

Walt, Stephen. 1997. 'Why Alliances Endure and Collapse', *Survival* 39, 1 (Spring): 156–79.

Wolfe, Robert. 1997. *Transatlantic Identity? Canada, the United Kingdom and International Order.* Kingston: Queen's University School of Policy Studies.

Zelikow, Philip. 1997. 'The Masque of Institutions', in Philip Gordon, ed., *NATO's Transformation: The Changing Shape of the Atlantic Alliance.* Lanham: Rowman and Littlefield.

10

Canada-EU Relations in the 1990s

DAVID LONG

Hidden beneath the considerable media attention on the conclusion of the Conference on a Global Ban on Landmines, the Canada-European Union (EU) summit on 4 December 1997 in Ottawa hardly managed a blip on the media screen. This annual meeting, established under the 1990 Trans-Atlantic Declaration, was the occasion for the signing of agreements between the EU and Canada on customs co-operation and on humane trapping standards. This is hardly stirring stuff at the best of times, even were the signing not competing with other historical world events happening downtown. Even an event featuring the Canadian Prime Minister, Foreign Minister, Minister for International Trade, and Minister for Revenue, along with the president of the European Commission, the Prime Minister of Luxembourg (the country at the time holding the presidency of the European Union), and the vice-president of the European Commission, could not garner media moments. By contrast, the arrival of Commissioner Emma Bonino, the head of the European Community Humanitarian Office (ECHO), received considerably more attention, as she came bearing gifts in the shape of money from the EU for de-mining and victim assistance in support of the follow-up to the Ottawa Process. Commissioner Bonino's previous intervention into Canadian politics—a harsh and uncompromising reaction to Canada's seizure of a Spanish trawler in international waters during the turbot dispute in 1995—was quietly forgotten.

There are sound media and publicity reasons for the contrast in public attention. Certainly, considerable scepticism has been expressed about the lasting value of the treaty to ban land-mines. However, the apparent apathy regarding the Canada-European Union relationship might also signal continental drift across the Atlantic. After all, Canadians' attention was not simply distracted by the land-mines conference. Canada had just hosted an APEC meeting, although circumstances being what they were in international financial mar-kets, Foreign Affairs officials were no doubt cursing their luck. In January 1998 the Prime Minister and the premiers—the ice storm in central Canada notwithstanding—were off on another Team Canada trade mission, this time to Latin America.

By comparison, relations with Europe seem to be dull and life-less, despite certain government-led efforts to create a different impression. When there has been excitement, this has recently been over differences between Canada and the EU. The high points of media attention in Canada and Europe have arisen with conflicts, most recently over turbot, but before that over fur.

Judging an issue by media attention is superficial and not entirely fair, of course. The friendly relations of Canada and Europe are wide-ranging and highly institutionalized. They range from Canada's mem-bership in the North Atlantic Treaty Organization (NATO) and the Organization for Security and Co-operation in Europe (OSCE) to Canadian and European participation in a variety of global multi-lateral organizations, such as the OECD and the World Trade Organization (WTO). As one aspect of the relationship between Canada and Europe, Canada and the EU have a long-standing, friendly, and mutually profitable relationship. Indeed, the EU has increased in importance in Canadian foreign policy as it has grown in stature internationally and as the Canadian commitment to NATO has waned in its centrality for Canadian foreign policy (Halstead,

1996: 7–10). Thus, it would seem Canada-EU relations are a significant part of an important economic and security relationship across
the Atlantic.

Yet, concerns about the state of Canada-EU relations abound,
notably in the public pronouncements of both Canadian and EU officials as they announce initiatives to rejuvenate the relationship.
Canadian contributions to European security have been in decline for
some time. Canada's trade with the EU has of late been stable (stag-
nant, if your glass is half-empty). But the apparently constant bick-
ering over trade irritants and especially the fallout of what in Canada
has been dubbed the Turbot War have coloured the relationship
even more. While the tone of the political relationship is nowadays
set by the economic relationship, it would be easy to exaggerate the
significance of differences between Canada and Europe. A broader
context for understanding the relationship suggests we should not
expect Canada-EU relations to be either exciting or consistently rosy.

What is the character of the Canada-EU relationship, and how
important is the relationship to both parties? This paper answers
these questions in four stages. It first examines the aggregate record
on EU-Canada commercial trade and investment flows. Secondly, it
considers the significance of trade irritants between Canada and the
EU and the ways in which they are dealt with. As part of this discussion, the chapter briefly considers the implications of the Turbot
War for Canada-EU relations. Thirdly, it sets out the agenda for
Canada-EU relations as it is envisaged in the Joint Action Plan, but
notes in the fourth section that the future of the relationship is more
likely to revolve around salient issues in European integration, that
is, monetary union and enlargement, and their implications for
Canada. The chapter concludes that though trade disputes have
tended to preoccupy official relations between the two sides, these
are surely to be expected in the administration of a complex relationship. In general and in the long run, Canada and the EU and its
member states share interests in multilateralism, democratic principles and the rule of law, and an open trading system.

THE CANADA-EU TRADE AND INVESTMENT RELATIONSHIP

The EU is still Canada's second largest trading partner after the United
States.[1] But this statistic hides so much that though it is a mantra of
engaged parties on either side of the Atlantic, it is almost meaning-

Table 10.1

Canadian Merchandise Exports and Imports, 1980 and 1996
(figures rounded to the last digit)

	1980 $billions	%	1996 $billions	%
Canadian Exports to				
US	48	63	223	81
EU	10	13	16	6
Japan	4	6	11	4
World	76	100	276	100
Canadian Imports from				
US	48	69	158	68
EU	6	9	23	10
Japan	3	4	10	5
World	69	100	233	100

Source: Derived from Peter Hall, Dan Lemaire, Chris Roth, and Pierre Vanasse, *Strengthening Canada-European Union Business Relations* (Ottawa: Conference Board of Canada, 1997), Table 1.

less. Trade with the US dominates Canadian foreign trade. Canada's trade with Japan is almost as large as with the EU and trade with APEC countries (excluding the US) is larger than with the EU (Table 10.1). Canada's trade is mainly with the Big Four: the United Kingdom, Germany, France, and Italy. The proportions of imports to Canada from each have been relatively stable over the last decade, but there has been a marked shift of Canadian exports away from a concentration in the UK towards more trade with France and Germany in particular.

One significant trend has been the growing trade deficit with the EU. In 1980 Canada had a trade surplus of $4 billion with the EU; in 1996 it had a deficit of over $7 billion. This growing deficit has mirrored the growing surplus with the US (see Figure 10.2). This deficit is a result of decline in the proportion of Canadian exports going to the EU, while the value of imports from EU countries has been stable or steadily rising in proportion to Canadian imports in general. Perhaps the most disconcerting of the trends in Canada-EU trade is that Canada's share of the EU market has been falling, from a little

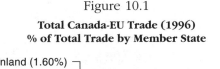

Figure 10.1

Total Canada-EU Trade (1996)
% of Total Trade by Member State

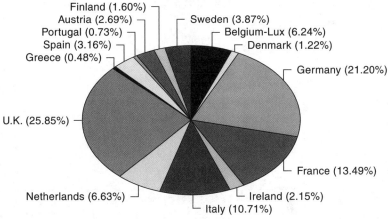

Finland (1.60%)
Austria (2.69%)
Portugal (0.73%)
Spain (3.16%)
Greece (0.48%)

Sweden (3.87%)
Belgium-Lux (6.24%)
Denmark (1.22%)

Germany (21.20%)

U.K. (25.85%)

France (13.49%)

Netherlands (6.63%)

Ireland (2.15%)

Italy (10.71%)

above 2 per cent to 1.7 per cent in 1994. Furthermore, trade with Canada now constitutes a small fraction of the EU's external trade. Canada ranks thirteenth behind Poland and Switzerland among EU trading partners.

By contrast to the relationship with the growing markets in the Asia-Pacific region and Latin America, the mature markets of Western Europe appear to offer only limited prospects for Canadian business. The prospects for trade would appear good because a small percentage growth in trade to the EU constitutes in absolute terms the creation of another Taiwan each year as a result of the sheer size of the EU market.[2] However, Canada is one of the few countries in the world that faces the full effect of the EU's common tariff. Many other countries have preferential status because of the Lomé Agreements or through a mix of trade, co-operation, and association agreements. In addition to this, there are significant non-tariff barriers to trade at the regional, i.e., EU, and national levels in the form of product standards or technical regulations (Brittan, 1998: 8). Formal barriers are only part of the story, however. The EU is only formally a single market; in reality it is considerably fractured by a mix of languages and different standards and regulations. For example, there is no standardization for something as elemental as electrical plugs. And, compare the eleven languages currently used in the EU to the Spanish domi-

Figure 10.2

**Canadian Trade Balances
Can-US and Can-Eur-12**

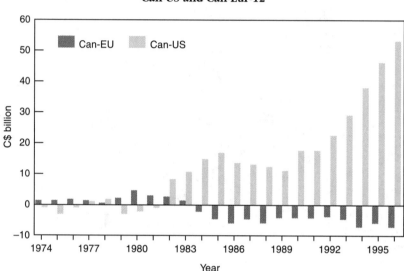

nance of Latin America and the size of the Chinese- and Japanese-speaking markets in Asia.

The picture on investment is rather healthier. In 1995, the EU came second in Canadian direct investment abroad (around 20 per cent of the total) and was the second largest investor in Canada (also around 20 per cent). Both figures are large and have been rising in percentage as well as absolute terms. While investment flows have not followed a trend, there was certainly a surge of European firms investing in Canada in the period after 1985, perhaps associated with the response of European multinationals to the Canada-US Free Trade Agreement (Crowley, 1997: 35). A large proportion of investment flows is accounted for by a few large multinationals on the Canadian side, for instance, Alcan, Bombardier, Hiram Walker, Hollinger, Nortel, and the Royal Bank, among others. And approximately 50 per cent of Canadian investment continues to be in the UK and about the same proportion of investment in Canada is from the UK (Senate of Canada, 1996: 30).

All of this can be put into perspective if one notes the similarities of the American and European markets. In 1995 EU GDP was US$8.4

Figure 10.3

Canada-European Community Direct Investment

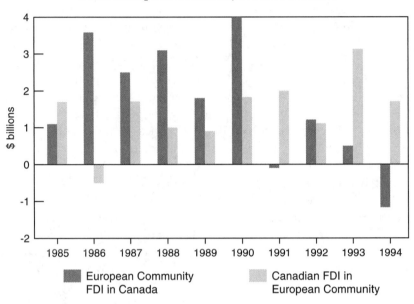

Source: OECD, *International Direct Investment Statistics Yearbook* (Paris: OECD, 1996).

billion compared to US$7 billion in the United States. The same year the population of the EU was 375 million compared to the American population of 271 million. Canadian trade with the US is, as the figures above indicate, 8–10 times the size of that with the EU. This suggests on the face of it the likelihood of missed opportunities for trade and investment.

CANADA-EU TRADE DISPUTES

Economic aggregates only tell a part of the story. Indeed, regarding the political relationship of the EU and Canada, they play a small role. Instead, Canada-EU trade irritants have come to preoccupy official relations between the two sides. There is a prevalent attitude that the Canada-EU relationship is mired in a variety of niggling disputes over minor trade issues. In fact, an overemphasis on this aspect of the relationship has led to considerable pessimism regarding future prospects for Canada-EU relations.

Nevertheless, these are the 'sexy' topics in EU-Canada relations, if there are any such things. The list of subjects of dispute between Canada and the EU is as esoteric as it is long. Fur and animal welfare have recently been the subject of an agreement, but in recent years differences have also surfaced over the treatment of lumber, growth hormones in beef, genetically modified organisms (GMOs) in oilseeds, and the appelation of wines. These trade disputes have recently been complemented by the Turbot War, a dispute over resources. Many of these disputes are multilateral, involving not only Canada and the EU but also third (and fourth, fifth . . .) parties—for example, fur, in which the Russians and the Americans were also entangled, and GMOs, in which the US is implicated.[3]

Such issues occupy the time and minds of many officials on both sides of the Atlantic. They tend to dominate the political and economic aspects of the Canada-EU relationship, making for a marginalization of the more purely political aspects of Canada's relations with the EU, regarding for instance political co-operation and Canada's place and reaction to the EU's Common Foreign and Security Policy framework.

Against this conflictual view, one might note that Canada and the EU have joined forces on a number of issues where there has been conflict with the US, most notably of late with respect to the extraterritorial application of the Helms-Burton legislation. In a different arena, Canada has co-operated with a number of European countries in advancing the campaign to ban anti-personnel land-mines, with support from the European Commission in terms of finance for de-mining.

In any event, we should recognize that no relationship is ever conflict-free (Bayne, 1997: 16). Furthermore, the differences over trade have in some cases been serious, though more often they have been less so. In almost all cases, there is an adequate and agreed upon framework for dealing with disputes, that is, the WTO. This leads to dull and arcane solutions or continuing negotiations. On most issues of concern, Canada and the EU settle their differences through the creation of a panel that makes rulings, through consultations, by recourse to arbitration, or simply by continuing to disagree.

Thankfully, Canada and the EU usually follow these agreed upon rules with very little public controversy. They pop up in statements by, for instance, the vice-president of the European Commission, Sir Leon Brittan, who addressed the concerns over beef imports into the

European Union subsequent to the mad cow disease crisis in the UK during his visit to Canada in December 1997.

There are a couple of exceptions to the rule where the dispute has escalated. In one case, regarding the fur trade and humane trapping, a low-level if publicly controversial dispute was successfully resolved; in the other, the Turbot War, the difference threatened to upset Canada-EU relations as a whole. In both cases, the usually banal passage of the dispute from the various affected interests to the bureaucrats in national ministries to the relevant international dispute mechanism was interrupted by the appearance of the issue on television screens. In the case of fur, the controversy involved the inhumane treatment of animals, especially the use of leghold traps, as well as the wider issue of the morality of wearing fur. These are not simple issues and are complicated further because the disputes or their settlement can implicate the rights and livelihood of Canada's indigenous peoples. In December 1997 Canada and the EU signed the Agreement on International Humane Trapping Standards. Apparently, though animal welfare continues to be a hot topic in a number of member states (for instance, the attempts to end fox hunting in the UK), the Canada-EU dimension has been resolved for the time being.

The conflict over turbot in early 1995 took on an entirely different character. Numerous contextual factors account for the sometimes vehement exchanges between Canada and Spain and for the negotiated settlement (Barry, 1997). Several features deserve to be highlighted. First of all, because the dispute was about resources rather than trade one might argue that it had a more intimate basis in Canadian (and indeed, Spanish) society, especially in Newfoundland, than do other trade issues. The salmon dispute between Canada and the United States has been similarly acrimonious. Resources that straddle or flow across national boundaries have been a cause of international friction in part because such disputes take on the character of a zero-sum game (i.e., 'these fish are ours, not yours') in a way that it is hard to portray trade issues.

The EU's Common Fisheries Policy occupies an anomalous status in the roster of common European policies under the jurisdiction of the European Commission. Fisheries became a common policy of the European Community in 1983, whereby a system was established regarding total allowable catches, conservation measures, and the like, of all which are supposed to be policed by the member states. However, such national implementation of these regulations is even more difficult in the case of fish than in other sectors (Nugent, 1994: 108). In any case, fisheries have long been contentious within the European Union, especially with the accession of Spain and Portugal (Dinan, 1994: 134). Two Norwegian referenda have failed to garner public support sufficient to join the EU, in large part because of the emotional significance of fisheries there. A cynical observer might suggest that the European Commission and EU member states exported their own conflicts over fishing within the territorial waters of the EU by turning a blind eye to infractions of international regimes on fisheries by Spanish trawlers. Whether this is a justifiable claim, it is nevertheless clear that a common EU front failed to materialize because the Union was riven with dissent, except at the basic level that Canada had broken international law in its extraterritorial application of its Coastal Fisheries Protection Act to the nose and tail of the Grand Banks beyond Canada's 200-mile limit and when it had seized the Spanish trawler, the *Estai*.

The European Commission had a couple of other difficulties. Emma Bonino was given a portfolio she was ill-prepared to deal with. Responsibility for fisheries was supposed to go to Norway before the failed referendum blocked its accession. In addition, the commission delegation in Ottawa faced an uphill struggle trying to co-ordinate and inform the various EU member missions in Canada while keeping the Canadian media informed.

Finally, the mechanism for dealing with the disagreement over catch quotas as well as compliance and verification mechanisms for the fisheries did not work well. The Northwest Atlantic Fisheries Organization (NAFO) is a weak regional organization and in the end the dispute was settled bilaterally between Canada and the EU in April 1997. Canada was willing to accept and in the end received a considerably lower catch quota than it had initially claimed, but it wanted a more intrusive verification regime than the self-monitoring that had been the norm in NAFO. Prime Minister Chrétien remarked of the agreement that it was 'a major breakthrough on conservation and enforcement—our primary objective' (cited in Barry, 1997: 24). The dispute was a result of Canada's desire for a change in regime rules. This is a stark contrast to the acceptance of the rules of the game that marks disputes dealt with in the WTO.

Whatever the dynamics and underlying causes of the conflict over turbot, the consequence was serious damage to the Canada-EU relationship, manifested most obviously in the delay in the conclusion of the Joint Canada-EU Action Plan (*European Union Newsletter,* Apr. 1997: 1).

THE JOINT CANADA-EU ACTION PLAN

The formal relationship between Canada and the European Union has been based on the 1976 Framework Agreement and the 1990 Transatlantic Declaration. In December 1996, the Joint Canada-EU Action Plan (henceforth, the Action Plan) and the Joint Political Declaration on Canada-EU Relations, which accompanied and introduced it, added another layer to the formal relationship. Its agenda for Canada-EU relations gives priority to consolidation of the trade relationship and the building of more active and substantial political and cultural links between Canada and the EU. However, in the near future, Canada-EU relations are more likely to revolve around the salient issues in European integration, in other words, monetary union and enlargement and their implications for Canada, than the formalities of the Action Plan.

The Action Plan was signed more than a year after the parallel EU-United States agreement because of the delay caused by the turbot dispute (for a discussion of the negotiations leading to the Action Plan, see Senate of Canada, 1996: 120–6). It calls for Canada and the EU to co-operate on enhancing the mechanisms of the global economic system, generally within the context of the WTO. Besides seeking to improve the context for the bilateral economic relationship, a series of measures were approved, including the ubiquitous trade study. The fisheries issue is discussed but it is noted in the Joint Political Declaration that the conciliatory words will not prevent Spain's case against Canada in the International Court of Justice from going forward. Transnational issues include the by now familiar shopping list of co-operative areas such as migration, drugs, terrorism, and so on. Finally, under fostering links, the Action Plan suggests increased contacts between academics, for instance, in joint conferences and the like. The Program for Co-operation in Higher Education and Training involving a number of consortia of Canadian and EU universities, an initiative envisaged in the 1990 Transatlantic Declaration, contributes to academic co-operation, as do the activities of the European Community Studies Association of Canada. The Action Plan also emphasizes the importance of trilateralizing the transatlantic business dialogue to include Canadian business in what has been a successful United States-EU initiative. And it highlights the need to foster people-to-people links, especially involving young people (Action Plan: 19–20; *European Union Newsletter*, July 1997: 1–2).

There is certainly a determination in the EU division of DFAIT and in the commission delegation in Ottawa to make the Action Plan work and this has resulted in a number of concrete initiatives. However, even should these succeed, it is hard to see the Action Plan as the most important feature of Canada-EU relations in the next several years. The Action Plan, after all, for the most part formalizes and repackages activities that were taking place already, such as co-operation on a variety of issues in the WTO. As Sir Leon Brittan put it, the Action Plan 'was an important step to enshrine . . . common interests in a formal, structured relationship' (Brittan, 1998: 4). The Action Plan does not so much add something new as it formally structures the Canada-EU relationship. In any case, that relationship is too multidimensional and dense to be capable of redirection by a few government-led initiatives. Finally, but most importantly, there are larger issues on the European horizon.

EMU, EU ENLARGEMENT, AND CANADA

The marginal relevance of the Action Plan is only partly accounted for by the embeddedness of Canada-EU relations in the dense network of bilateral and multilateral relations between Canada and Europe. In the next decade significant changes will take place in Europe and the European Union, many of which will have major implications for Canada. The most significant development will be Economic and Monetary Union (EMU). The timetable for EMU was agreed to at Maastricht in 1991, but in the years that immediately followed, currency turmoil and the *de facto* collapse of the exchange rate mechanism led many to believe that EMU had been irretrievably derailed. Since the mid-1990s, the prospects for EMU have improved considerably. EU members have striven to keep their currencies within or as close as possible to the criteria for membership in EMU, with only a few exceptions. In addition, the political will to go through with the project has been convincingly advanced, even in face of the prospective technical violation of entry criteria by a number of countries as well as extremely creative accounting and once-only transactions by governments to allow them formally to achieve the conversion criteria (for the problems that Italy is already encountering, see *The Guardian Weekly,* Jan. 1998:1). At the time of writing, the EMU is expected to be wider than many had thought five years ago and will essentially include all those countries that wish to join. Those that have chosen, for a variety of reasons to do with national sovereignty and economic cycles, not to join EMU in the first round, that is, the UK, Denmark, Sweden, and Greece, are being described in EU parlance as 'pre-ins' (European Commission, 1996; *The Economist,* 1997).

The collapse of a number of Asian currencies in the latter half of 1997 has a number of contradictory lessons for the move to EMU. On the one hand, it might mean that EMU should be speeded up and commitments firmed up in the face of the sorts of problems encountered in Asia. It might also be argued that the European economies are not vulnerable to the sorts of financial difficulties that have afflicted the Asian tigers. However, the currency crisis in Asia is expected to reverberate around the world for some time to come and European banks and companies, despite claims to the contrary, are exposed in terms of investment and trade relations with Asia. This suggests that 1999 might be an inauspicious moment to begin EMU. Furthermore, it may be that the markets will turn back to Europe in 1999, having moved from Europe in 1992–3 to the Americas (i.e., Mexico) and to Asia in 1997. Indeed, the period from 1999, when it is begun, to the year 2002, when EMU is formally completed, arguably makes the participating European currencies sitting ducks for the global financial markets.

As if EMU were not enough for the EU agenda, in December 1997 the EU's Council of Ministers confirmed the list of candidate countries with which the EU will begin negotiations for accession that were set out in the commission's *Agenda 2000.* These are the '5+1' countries: Poland, the Czech Republic, Hungary, Slovenia, and Estonia, plus Cyprus, which had already been promised the opening of negotiations subsequent to the 1996 EU intergovernmental conference. There was controversy over including some applicants in a first round of enlargement and not including others. The Council of Ministers tried to defuse the controversy by making enlargement negotiations a rolling process and announcing a conference of all the applicant countries to take place in 1998, thus including Bulgaria, Romania, Slovakia, Latvia, Lithuania, and, most controversially, Turkey.

While Estonia's inclusion in the 5+1 list was a surprise to many observers and there are plenty of problems associated with the accession of Cyprus, the most heated exchanges were over Turkey. The Turkish government angrily dismissed the EU conference as a fob that was no substitute for real negotiations towards Turkish accession. Although Turkish anger is certainly genuine, it had already been told that it was not ready for accession to the EU. In any event, the issue is more complicated than the suggestion that the EU is excluding a Muslim country. Turkey is a large, populous, relatively poor state engaged in counter-insurgency in the east. Such a characterization, which makes no reference to religion or culture, effectively rules out Turkish membership in the EU in the near future simply because the European states cannot afford it.[4]

Dealing with an agenda this full will be extremely demanding and might well lead to an inward-looking EU, despite protestations to the contrary. Relations with middle powers such as Canada are unlikely to be a priority in the near future. However, developments in the EU might have significant implications for Canada. If succcessful, EMU will convert international monetary relations into a tripolar system of the American dollar, the Japanese yen, and the Euro. Although there are trade and investment implications for Canada in the transition to monetary union, the theory and evidence suggest that EMU itself is unlikely to have the commercial impact that the 1992 Single Market program did (Hannah, 1997: 24–5; Duruflé, 1990). By contrast, an EMU that fails might introduce turbulence in international economic relations not only in Europe but more widely.

Enlargement of the European Community has affected Canada in the past, particularly when the UK joined. The next enlargement is unlikely to have the same sort of impact as the first EU enlargement or even of the most recent enlargement to include several EFTA countries. Compensation for the trade effects that sideswipe Canada has in the past been very difficult and time-consuming. It is likely to be so again. Insofar as, for example, Polish accession to the EU reduces trade barriers between the EU and Poland to the possible detriment of Canadian trade with either, Canada should address these concerns to the EU (Senate of Canada, 1996: 80–7).

THE 'REDISCOVERY' OF CANADA-EU RELATIONS

Official and academic discussions of the Canada-EU relationship are routinely opened with a nod to the participation of Canadians in the two world wars and the patterns of immigration that have made

Canada in a very real sense a European country. The Cabot celebrations in 1997 suggested the historical depth of the relationship of Canada and Europe. On the signing of the Canada-EU Action Plan, Foreign Minister, Lloyd Axworthy, and International Trade Minister, Art Eggleton, called for a rediscovery of Canada by Europe and vice versa as part of the strengthening and modernizing of the relationship.

Of late, there has been a questioning of the value of the transatlantic relationship in some quarters. While the proximate reasons might be related to trade disputes and incidents like the Turbot War, the more fundamental reason is that the relationship is not terribly interesting. It is hard for publics, academics, or even officials to get excited about the transatlantic relationship in general and the Canada-EU relationship in particular. Certainly, it is an important part of international trade relations and a significant element of the so-called zone of peace. But there are precious few historic victories to be won and at the same time lots of minor differences to settle.

The difficulties in the Canada-EU relationship entail the administration and management of a friendly and close relationship that is valuable but dull, warm but occasionally irritating. What is needed is a continuation of quiet conversation on both sides. Indeed, hoping for an exciting relationship is to hope for the wrong thing. We may not be, as Fukuyama has melodramatically suggested, at the end of history, but in Canada-EU relations it feels like it! A manifestation of this is the bizarre fact that world leaders meet and talk about fish or the appelation of wines. This may be cause for celebration, however: if world leaders are talking fish that is perhaps because there are no more major issues of conflict. Reinvigorating (or rediscovering) the Canada-EU relationship is akin to staying awake in the face of post-historical ennui.

This would be of little consequence were it not to enter the public mind. Yet, the lingering bitterness of the dispute over turbot has contributed to a cooling of the transatlantic relationship. Whatever one says about the continuing strong levels of trade and investment, the perception in the Canadian public at least seems to be of increasing distance from Europe. This is as disturbing as it is unsurprising. Canada has a great number of trade disputes with the United States. Yet, Canadians have been told to keep the conflict over west coast salmon in perspective on the perfectly sound basis that Canada and the US have more in common than they have differences. Such does not appear to be the case in Canada's relations with the EU.

It follows that dramatic gestures are not what is required to rein-vigorate the relationship. Team Canada trips to the EU are not the route to improved Canada-EU economic relations.[5] A renewed empha-sis on cultural and educational exchange among young people and business people is important, as is, among other things, the creation in 1995 of the European Community Studies Association of Canada, an academic association devoted to the study of the EU. In this regard, the Joint Canada-EU Action Plan contains practical steps in the right direction of reducing barriers to international trade and investment. As is recognized in the Action Plan, Canada and the EU have a shared interest in securing wider global acceptance of a more liberal trading system. But grand regional (or pan-regional) initiatives, such as the once-mooted Transatlantic Free Trade Area, are poten-tially problematic not only because they might politicize or exacer-bate already existing disputes among Canada, the EU, and the US, but also because they might offer few benefits to the global trading sys-tem. Insofar as a regional initiative creates special rules for the par-ties, of course, it contradicts the goal of global multilateralism.

Canada's relations with Europe are far from exhausted by the Canada-EU relationship. An exemplar of the shared values across the Atlantic was Canada's co-operation with a number of EU mem-ber states (as well as other European states) in the so-called core group that pushed for the total ban on anti-personnel land-mines. This was an important initiative that was led for much of the early period by the Europeans, including Austria, Belgium, and Norway. Canada's role was critical, however. The initiative to sign a total ban treaty by December 1997, the so-called Ottawa Process, and the integration of NGO representatives and views into the Canadian government's delegations were innovative steps in arms control negotiations.

Canada's unique status among the middle powers leading the ban campaign made it the natural leader of the group. As a G-8 country with administrative resources and international connections, Canada was able to move and co-ordinate the campaign in ways that the smaller European countries could admire but not match. In addition, as the land-mines ban was a foreign and security policy issue, the European Commission's role was limited to co-operation with the member states and to facilitation and representation of the common positions the EU could agree on.[6] Belgium, Ireland, and Austria, among others, were also constrained by the requirement for consensus on the land-mines issue within the EU, where there were and continue to be divergent views.

The land-mines issue was unusual in Canada's relations with Europe, and not only for the drama. Canada's dialogue with certain European states on a shared goal led to its leadership of the Ottawa Process. In the general run of Canada-EU relations, by contrast, the dialogue is likely to be less thrilling and less Canadian-led. Canada-EU relations are unlikely to be the stuff of grand narratives, but the quiet contribution to global security and prosperity is real nevertheless.

NOTES

My thanks to Jennifer Fellows for research assistance.

1. For overviews of the Canada-EU trade and investment relationship, see Crowley (1997); Senate of Canada (1996: ch. 3).
2. According to David Williamson, former Secretary-General of the European Union, 'New Money, New Treaty, New Members', presentation in the Carleton University Centre for European Politics and Society Seminar Series, Dec. 1997.
3. For a discussion of the nature of disputes over substantially the same issues between the US and the EU, see Vogel (1997).
4. For a discussion of the suitability of candidates for accession, see Long (1997); and compare the reaction in Mehmet (1998).
5. A Team Canada visit to Central and Eastern Europe might well be beneficial, however.
6. With Ottawa Process 2, the European Commission now has a prominent role in humanitarian de-mining and in mine victim assistance.

REFERENCES

Barry, Donald. 1997. 'The Canada-European Union Turbot War: International Politics and Transatlantic Diplomacy', paper presented at the European Community Studies Association meeting, St John's, Nfld, 6–8 June.

Bayne, Nicholas. 1997. 'The Nature of the Transatlantic Relationship', in Robert Wolfe, ed., *Transatlantic Identity? Canada, the United Kingdom and International Order*. Kingston: Queen's University School of Policy Studies.

Brittan, Leon. 1995. 'Relations Between the European Union and Canada in a Transatlantic Context', *Canadian Foreign Policy* 3, 3, (Winter).

———. 1998. 'The EU and Canada: A Transatlantic Partnership', Address to the International Seminar on Europe Towards the Millennium: The Relevance to Canada, Ottawa, Jan.

Department of Foreign Affairs and International Trade (DFAIT). 1996. Joint Political Declaration on Canada-EU Relations and Joint Canada-EU Action Plan.

————. 1997. 'The Canada-European Joint Political Declaration and Action Plan: Commemorating the First Anniversary', Dec.

Dinan, Desmond. 1994. *Ever Closer Union? An Introduction to the European Community.* Boulder, CO: Lynne Rienner.

Duruflé, Gilles, with Carl Sonnen and Lyne Raymond. 1990. '1992 Implications of a Single European Market'. Ottawa: External Affairs and International Trade Canada.

The Economist. 1997. 'European Union Survey', May: 5–8.

European Commission. 1996. *When Will the 'Euro' Be In Our Pockets.* Brussels: Office for Official Publications of the European Communities.

European Union Newsletter, various numbers, Delegation of the European Commission in Canada.

The Guardian Weekly. 1998. Vol. 158, No. 1, 4 Jan., 1.

Hall, Peter, Dan Lemaire, Chris Roth, and Pierre Vanasse. 1997. *Strengthening Canada-European Union Business Relations.* Ottawa: Conference Board of Canada.

Halstead, John G.H. 1997. 'European Security: What's In It for Canada?'. Kingston: Queen's University Centre for International Relations, Occasional Paper 54, Dec.

Hannah, Robert. 1997. 'European Monetary Union and Its Implications for Canada'. Ottawa: DFAIT Trade and Economic Policy Paper.

Long, David. 1994. 'Europe After Maastricht', in Maureen Appel Molot and Harald von Riekhoff, eds, *Canada Among Nations 1994: A Part of the Peace.* Ottawa: Carleton University Press, 131–53.

————. 1997. 'The Why and How of EU Enlargement'. Vancouver: University of British Columbia Institute of International Relations, Working Paper Number 16.

Mehmet, Ozay. 1998. 'Barring the gate against the Terrible Turk', *Globe and Mail,* 2 Jan.

Nugent, Neill. 1994. *The Government and Politics of the European Union,* 3rd edn. London: Macmillan.

Pentland, Charles. 1991. 'Europe 1992 and the Canadian Response', in Fen Osler Hampson and Christopher J. Maule, eds, *Canada Among Nations 1990–91: After the Cold War.* Ottawa: Carleton University Press, 125–44.

Senate of Canada. 1996. *European Integration: Implications for Canada.* Report of the Standing Senate Committee on Foreign Affairs. Ottawa, July.

Vogel, David. 1997. *Barriers or Benefits? Regulation in Transatlantic Trade.* Washington: Brookings Institution.

11

Canada and Hemispheric Governance: The New Challenges

JEAN DAUDELIN AND EDGAR J. DOSMAN

As a first step in what needs to be a revamped Latin American strategy, a consortium of institutions has proposed the establishment of a Canada-based working group on Canada and hemispheric governance (Daudelin, Dosman, and Hampson, 1997). That group, pulling together policy experts from the key countries of the hemisphere, would be charged with assessing the current challenges confronting the states of the hemisphere and the situation of hemispheric governance, with particular emphasis on the Organization of American States (OAS); developing an agenda for reform of the current system that could gain the support of the key middle powers of the region; and identifying the key tenets of a long-term strategic Latin American option for Canada. Through the organization of workshops and conferences, the working group process would help deepen the dialogue within Canada and with the rest of the region. Such a working group, were it set up soon enough, could report on time for Canada to propose a program of reform at the year 2000 general assembly of the OAS, which is to be held in Ottawa.

Ten years ago Foreign Affairs Minister Joe Clark announced a Latin American Strategy (see Dosman, 1992) designed to end a decade of neglect and begin a new era of Canadian engagement in the Americas. The conceptual shift was from the Americas as geographic 'house' to the continent as a community and as a 'home'. Approved a few months before the North American Free Trade Agreement (NAFTA) was conceived, the strategy centred on government leadership, particularly in joining and energizing the OAS as the principal vehicle for realizing this new frontier in Canadian foreign policy.

A decade later the 'new frontier' is so well established that DFAIT's *Strategy Update for Latin America and the Caribbean* (1996) is written in triumphalist tones rarely sounded in the sombre Pearson Building. From NAFTA to the Free Trade Area of the Americas (FTAA), from the OAS to the 1994 Miami summit, from trade to human rights, security, and sustainable development, it argues that Foreign Affairs has been leading the inter-American pack in strengthening regionalism. Epitomizing this attitude, the document argues that the Miami Summit Action Plan was largely consistent with Canadian objectives not by coincidence, since Canada was instrumental in forming the agenda and managing the outcome (DFAIT, 1996). A related claim of policy coherence and a bold assertiveness are also present in many of the key policy papers dealing with Latin America that were produced by the department in the last two years (Christie, 1995; Choudhri and Sharma, 1996).

This self-drawn image of a proactive, well-controlled, and effective regional policy requires a critical look even for the first glory years after 1990, but particularly since the 1994 Miami summit when the moorings of the inter-American system have shifted. Canada's insertion in the hemisphere remains centred on the United States, hopes for relatively swift progress on regional integration have been dashed, and the emergence of effective hemispheric governance centred on the OAS is proving slower and more difficult than many would hope.

This chapter briefly assesses Canada's hemispheric policy to date, reviews the challenges posed by the construction of regional governance in the Americas, and explores the key challenges that must be met for the hemispheric option to become feasible and advantageous to Canada. We contend that a Latin American option still makes sense for Canada. The hemisphere remains the only regional arena where Canada can be a major player on most significant issues. The region's economies offer plenty of potential as trade partners, and the outlook of its governments and civil society appear eminently compatible with those of Canadians. Opportunities for leadership exist, but very few, if any, of them offer Canada an easy sail or a guaranteed arrival at destination. To play a leading role will require more sensitivity to the peculiarities of multilateralism and integration in the Americas, a recognition of our continuing dependency on the United States, and more sensitivity to domestic fragilities and the vulnerabilities of our Latin American and Caribbean partners. Above all, the option calls for staying power and a government commitment to sustain the consolidation of a wider constituency and domestic capacity for the region. From these standpoints, it is appropriate that these reflections be found in a book whose theme is leadership and dialogue, for without the latter, Canada can only dream of the former.

CANADA AND THE AMERICAS AFTER
TEN YEARS OF COMMITMENT

An Enthusiastic Newcomer

At the turn of the decade, Canada literally jumped on the regional bandwagon. Joining the OAS was the first step, but NAFTA was the real detonator, opening quite suddenly a whole new avenue for an aggressive regional foreign policy. At the Miami summit, that policy was given a clear goal and schedule with the launching of a hemispheric trade liberalization process (the FTAA project), as well as a much broader agenda with a *Plan of Action* covering issues ranging from trade to human rights, education, and poverty reduction. The OAS, moreover, was to be the co-ordinating agency for this whole program. Canada became a key supporter of the process, perhaps the keenest among the countries of the region.

Canada made a definitive option for the Americas in 1990, but NAFTA provided the energy for Ottawa's first enthusiasm. What makes that year a turning point is not Canada's adhesion to the OAS, but instead its joining a negotiation table—already set, and with the US and Mexico already seated—where the economic integration of North America, and especially its structure, was at stake. With Canada already linked to the US by the Free Trade Agreement (FTA), Canadian policy-makers saw a bilateral free trade agreement between the US and Mexico as the omen of a huge hub-and-spoke trade structure threatening to divert regional investment flows towards the US, which would thereby become the only location guaranteeing free access to all three markets (Wonnacott and Wonnacott, 1995). A tripartite agreement lessened that risk and was favoured by Canada. The negotiations prospered and the result was NAFTA, formally launched on 1 January 1994.

In the meantime, however, Canada's policy towards the Americas had developed a momentum linking trade policy with export promotion. NAFTA, or more precisely NAFTA expansion, became absorbed by the old outlook of Canadian foreign and trade policy-makers, and was quickly reconceptualized, from a defensive manoeuvre to a strategic means to diversify trade and counterbalance Canadian dependence on the US market, as well as to contain the ever-rising phoenix of US unilateralism.

Canada's policy towards the region thus looked not only remarkably coherent, but also perfectly in keeping with the traditional thrust of its global outlook: NAFTA, and NAFTA extension into South America, would reinforce the international liberal economic framework of the World Trade Organization. The OAS for its part would serve as the primary political apparatus for an effective regional multilateralism consistent with Canadian policy in the UN and other international bodies. Dynamic and highly respected César Gaviria, former President of Colombia, was elected Secretary-General with Canada's energetic support. His persona gave greater credibility to the OAS reform process under way in earnest since 1990 and reinforced Canada's impression that a new era in the Americas had begun.

The office of Canada's permanent representative at the OAS, with its comparatively small staff (relative to Mexico or Brazil, for example), has been busy and visible, and has made significant achievements. DFAIT officials in Ottawa and Canadians in the secretariat have also brought energy and much needed idealism to the embattled organization, even if there was an initial over-optimism about the role of the OAS and its capacity for speedy renewal. Canada can be counted on to pay its bills on time. Moreover, the economic and political changes in the region coinciding with the termination of the Cold War made Latin America appear, quite suddenly, remarkably appealing to Canada. As the continent approached the December 1994 Summit of the Americas in Miami, all the economies of the region were liberalizing, and a host of dictatorships had given way to elected governments. Canadian activism in hitherto neglected areas of inter-American relations such as security, human rights and democratic development, and indigenous issues multiplied after 1990. Achievements vary according to agenda area: trade, security, human rights and democratic development, social policy, sustainable development, and indigenous affairs (McKenna, 1995).

Although DFAIT has tended to exaggerate Canadian influence and underestimate the damage caused by evident political appointments and micromanagement, Canada's influence was considerable during its first years of membership. Canada's multilateral vocation also often surprised Latin Americans—and not just its interventionism in hot areas such as human rights and democratic development. For example, Ottawa used the OAS as a building block for norm-generation at the regional level to project issues globally at the UN and other forums: deep-sea fishing; Helms-Burton; confidence- and security-building measures, such as the anti-personnel mine initiative. These were uses of the OAS not at all in keeping with typical Latin American and Caribbean concepts of the institution.

All in all, by the Miami summit, the Americas looked in truth like a welcoming family for a Canadian polity searching for new roles after the Cold War, while Latin America for its part was, at the same time, looking for chaperones to protect it from a sometimes stifling US embrace, but finding declining interest in old Europe or in busy Asia.

A Rough Ride

Straying far from the caution advocated in the 1989 Latin American strategy, Canada's policy from 1990 until the Miami summit was driven by enthusiasm, and the journey became somewhat intoxicating. Little heed was given to the many signs that the optimism underlying Canada's policy was proving unfounded; a few days after the summit the inter-American landscape abruptly changed. Mexico's peso crisis soon undermined the promises of security and stability that the NAFTA seal of approval had supposedly ensured. Symbolically, if not economically, NAFTA suffered a more severe blow than Mexico: whereas the latter was back to strong growth and was already welcoming heavy flows of foreign investment by 1996, the lineup to join NAFTA had evaporated as Latin American leaders absorbed the implications of NAFTA disciplines for national economic stability. After the crisis, the prospect that hemispheric economic integration—if it were to happen—would develop along NAFTA expansion quickly dimmed and then just disappeared.

Perhaps even more shocking, the other assumptions of the post-1990 policy also appeared to be crumbling: Canadian trade did not diversify following the establishment of NAFTA, and the rules-based regime of NAFTA did not appear to be enough to contain US unilateralism; the FTAA process had a hard time generating support among key players, especially the United States and Brazil; the OAS proved to be much harder than expected to nudge towards change; and the region as a whole, in spite of the huge progress realized in the last decade, still needed to confront a significant number of fundamental problems before any guarantee of economic and political stability could be given.

A potential disjuncture has opened between Canada's political and economic relations in the Western hemisphere beyond North

Figure 11.1

**Investments in South and Central America
(change in book value, % of world total)**

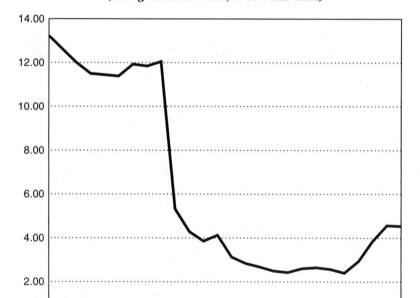

Source: Statistics Canada, CANSIM Series D65221 and D66107, 28 Dec. 1997.

Figure 11.2

**Canadian Direct Investment in Brazil and Mexico
(change in book value, millions of $, 1970–1995)**

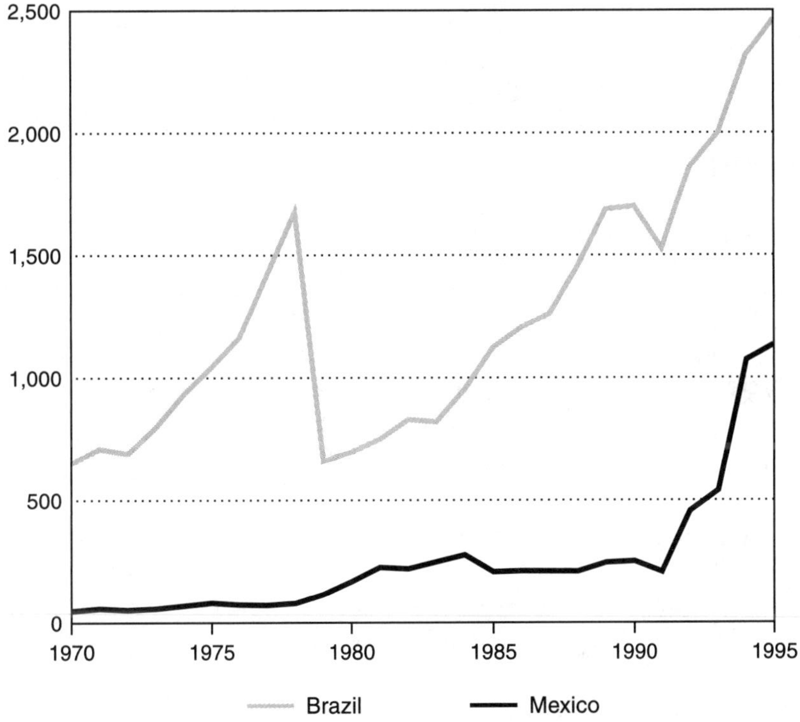

Source: Statistics Canada, CANSIM Series D66108 and D66105, 28 Dec. 1997.

America. The Latin American strategy can be credited with success in political terms; Canada has never been as much part of the hemispheric family as it is today. Diplomatic activity, high-level visits, large business delegations, involvement in the OAS, dialogues on security issues, educational linkages, and so on are well established compared with the 1980s. Yet all these activities appear to be floating in thin air, as an economic basis has yet to develop to ground this flurry of political activism into tangible mutual material interests. In spite of much efforts and rhetoric, Latin America and the Caribbean, beyond Mexico and Chile, have not yet become significant economic partners (Saéz, 1997). In relative terms compared with 1980s, both exports and investment in Latin America have fallen

Figure 11.3

**Canadian Direct Investment in the World and in South and Central America
(change in book value, millions of $)**

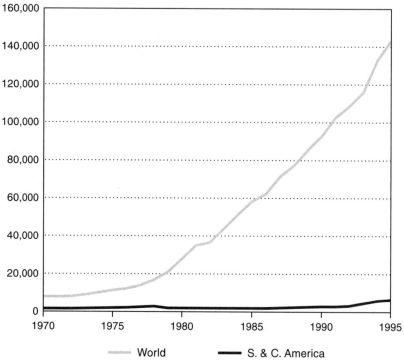

Source: Statistics Canada, CANSIM Series D65221 and D66107, 28 Dec. 1997.

sharply. In fact, never before has Canada's economy been so closely integrated into a strictly North American productive structure whose axis is the United States. The raw fact is that Canada's export dependence on the US has grown steadily, reaching over 80 per cent of total trade.

The figures presented here could not be clearer. By 1995, investments in South and Central America had barely recovered their 1982 level, itself well below what it had been in the 1970s (Figure 11.1). Investments in the region have been growing, but did not keep pace with Canadian investments in the rest of the world (Figures 11.2 and 11.3). The trade picture is no different. While both exports and imports to the region have been growing steadily between 1990 and 1996 (Figures 11.4 and 11.5), they barely kept pace with the tremen-

Figure 11.4

Canadian Exports to the Americas, 1990–1996
(millions of $)

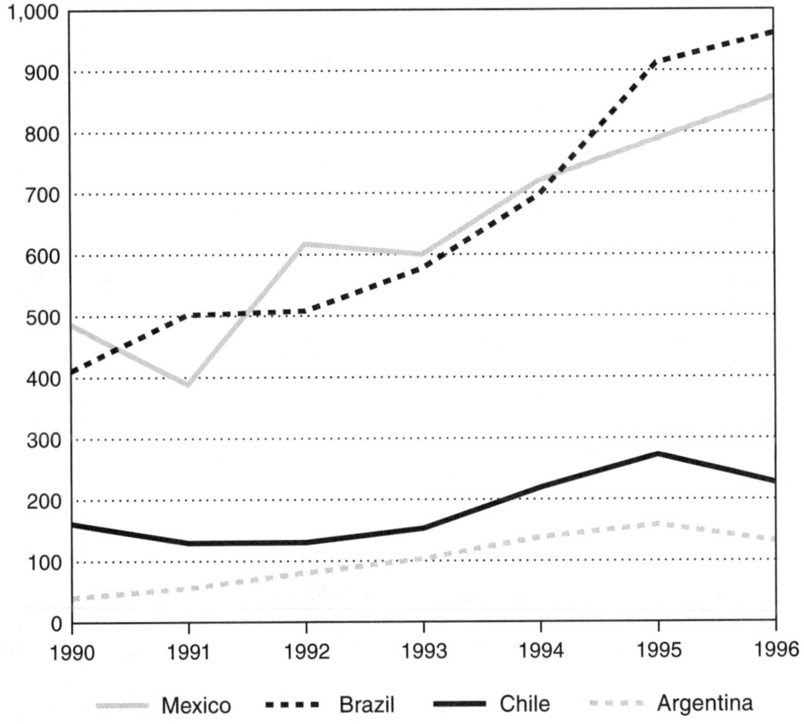

Source: International Monetary Fund, *Direction of Trade Statistics 1990–1996* (Washington: IMF, 1997).

dous growth of global Canadian trade (Figures 11.6 and 11.7), with imports from the Western hemisphere (minus the US) increasing from 3 per cent to about 4 per cent of Canada's total imports and exports remaining at about 2 per cent.

This situation is made worse by the fact that Canada now has a trade deficit with most of the world and a large (if falling) trade surplus with the United States. Prospects, moreover, are not good with the Canadian dollar weakening in relation to the US dollar, while strengthening in relation to the currency of most of its other trading partners, provoking a growing trade deficit with Latin America. Between 1990 and 1996, Canada has seen its trade surplus with the United States grow from $20 billion to about $50 billion, while its

Figure 11.5

Canadian Exports from the Americas, 1990–1996
(millions of $)

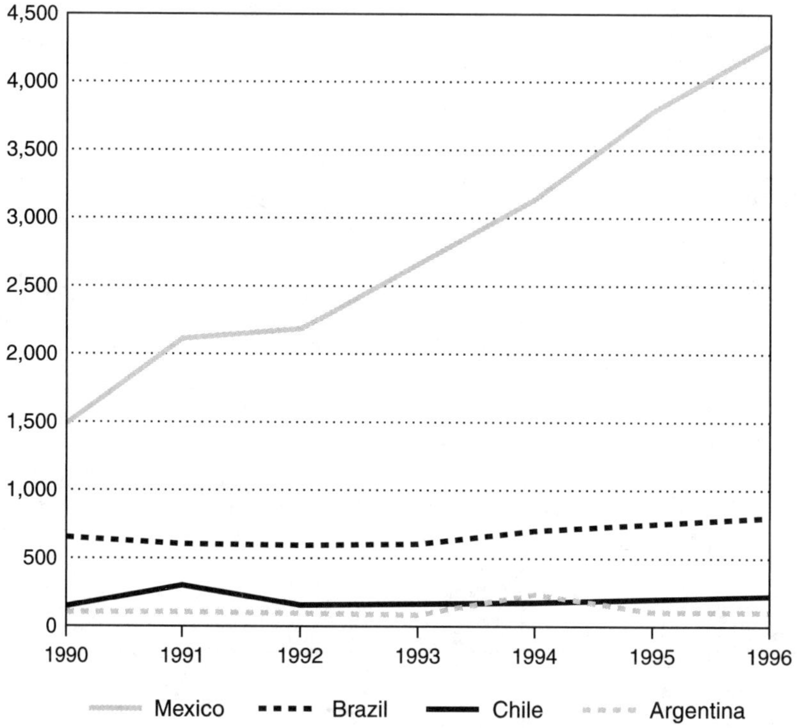

Source: International Monetary Fund, *Direction of Trade Statistics 1990–1996*
(Washington: IMF, 1997).

trade deficit with Latin America went from $1.7 billion to $3.7 billion during the same period (IMF, 1997).

To the extent that an opening to the region was meant to weaken Canada's trade dependence, either directly, through simple trade diversification, or indirectly, by enabling Canada to use the secure market base of NAFTA as a spring board towards world markets, strategic regionalism (Deblock and Brunelle, forthcoming) has proved to be a major disappointment. Admittedly, the enormous role of the automotive sector in this dynamic somewhat exaggerates the importance of integrated production processes at the North American level (Molot, 1997: 173–8). Yet, given that this sector is the core of Canada's manufacturing base, its consolidation as the spine of a North

Figure 11.6

Canadian Exports to Selected Regions, 1990–1996
(millions of $)

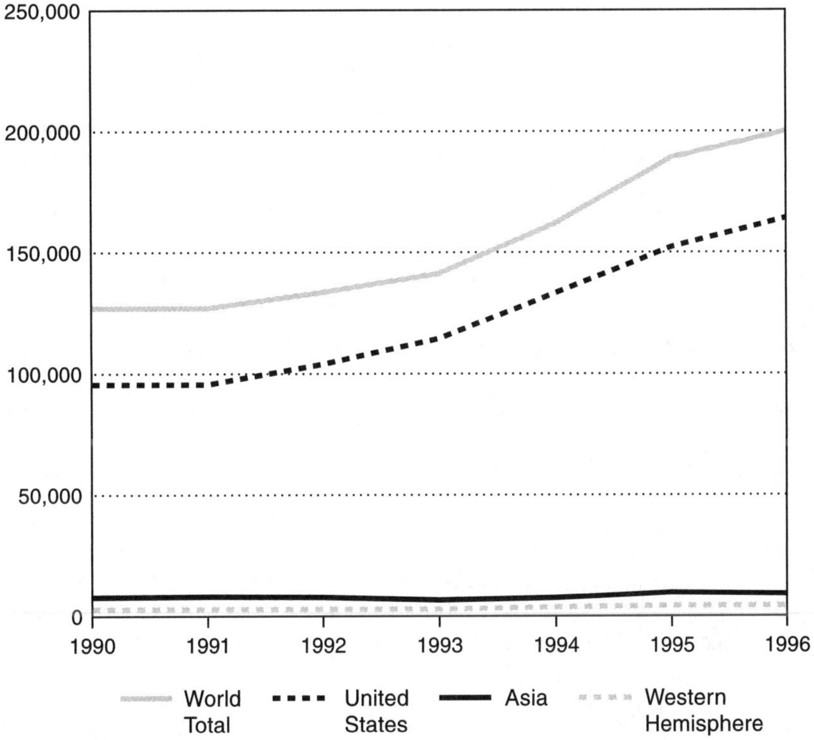

Source: International Monetary Fund, *Direction of Trade Statistics 1990–1996*
(Washington: IMF, 1997).

American economy including Mexico must certainly be considered a major post-Cold War development. However, Canada's export promotion to Latin America (including Mexico) compares unfavourably with its ability to penetrate the US market, where exports grew from $95 billion to $164 billion between 1990 and 1996 (IMF, 1997).

The commercial basis for Canada's integration into the whole hemisphere in fact appears to be shrinking. One could perhaps argue that political and cultural relations do not necessarily need such a basis to flourish, but one would have a hard time justifying them given the policy framework outlined in the 1995 government statement on foreign policy (DFAIT, 1995), which gives the promotion

Figure 11.7

Canadian Exports from Selected Regions, 1990–1996
(millions of $)

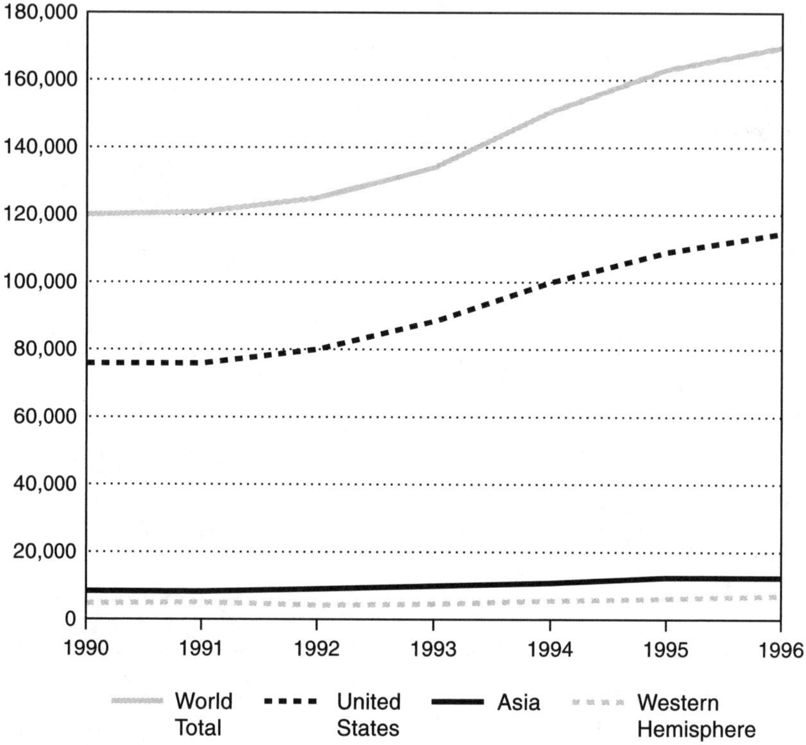

Source: International Monetary Fund, *Direction of Trade Statistics 1990–1996*
(Washington: IMF, 1997).

of economic prosperity and employment the first place in the list of priorities.

The government has spared no effort to change that situation. At the Miami summit, Canada openly promoted Chile as the next country to join NAFTA, and when the US Congress refused to give the Clinton administration the fast-track authority that would have enabled the deal Canada moved on and signed a quasi-NAFTA-level bilateral trade agreement with Chile. Similarly, important trade missions to the region were organized in 1995 and 1998, in the face of significant political, economic, and even commercial tensions and uncertainties. The first of these took a large delegation to Mexico a few months after the peso crisis and in the midst of serious political disturbances following the assassination of the governing party's candidate for the presidency. Similarly, another large mission visited Mexico, Brazil, Argentina, and Chile in January 1998, right during a financial crisis in Asia that was threatening economic stability. Most significantly, Canada was perhaps the keenest supporter of the FTAA process, contributing more than its share to the OAS trade unit and doing its best to keep some momentum in the initiative.

These efforts have met with growing obstacles. As mentioned, investments and trade between Canada and the region are *not* growing in relative terms, with the latest trade mission to the region producing disappointing results and some disenchantment among the hundreds of business people who joined in (at $15,000 a seat). A timetable for negotiation of an FTAA was discussed during the April 1998 Santiago Summit of the Americas. Yet, even such a momentous development is likely to have little relevance: the Clinton administration, unable in October 1997 to secure fast-track negotiation of such an agreement, is now even less likely to deliver, as it grows weaker by the day and is increasingly centred on domestic issues and foreign adventures in the Middle East.

Side initiatives could not possibly compensate for such a central tenet of Canada's hemispheric agenda as the FTAA, but they could sustain a certain momentum. Even these, however, have been plagued with difficulties. Negotiations with Chile became tense when Canada insisted that Chilean controls over capital movements, celebrated through much of the hemisphere as Chile's saviour during the peso crisis, be eliminated. Canada's insistence, and Chile's determination, led to a showdown and to President Frei's last-minute cancellation of the visit during which the treaty was to be signed. Canada, the foremost advocate of NAFTA expansion and of the FTAA, was forced to back down: Chile kept its capital controls, Frei's visit was rescheduled, and the treaty was signed. Much damage was done in the region's chanceries, however, to Canada's image of openness, flexibility, and understanding towards partners that were—or felt—more vulnerable to the vagaries of international capital flows.

While the agreement with Chile had an essentially symbolic value, the announcement in 1997 that Canada had started discussions about a potential association with Mercado Comun del Sur (MERCOSUR) was a truly significant development—although the planned agreement did little more than institutionalize contacts that have been taking place regularly in recent years, i.e., it does not contemplate Canada's joining MERCOSUR or even establishing an association similar to that between MERCOSUR and Chile. The Chilean economy is about the size of Montreal's, but Brazil's GDP is equivalent to that of Canada, and the total GDP of MERCOSUR, the customs union made up of Brazil, Argentina, Paraguay, and Uruguay, is much bigger, representing about two-thirds of South America's economic output and over 50 per cent of Latin America's. Progress, however, has been slow, in spite of visits by President Cardoso and Prime Minister Chrétien. The difficulties are many: the distance to be bridged, in terms of tariffs, is significantly larger than with Chile, and MERCOSUR is by no means a tight unit, with tensions surfacing periodically between its two key partners, Brazil and Argentina. Perhaps of most significance in the short term, progress is made difficult because of a major dispute between Canada's Bombardier and Brazil's Embraer, both linchpins of their countries' high-tech industries and, for distinct reasons, deeply embedded in their respective political universes. At the time of this writing, in sum, an association of Canada with MERCOSUR, and involving significant liberalization of trade and investments in the short or medium term, looks unlikely.

If the trade picture does not quite conform to Canada's hopes, the international, political, and social outlook that made the hemispheric option so natural after the region's return to democracy seems to hold fast, but barely. Democratically elected governments are still in power in all countries but Cuba and a few more peaceful transfers of power have taken place. Yet, there is a sense in the region that the democratization process has stopped in its tracks and that it threatens to regress as political institutions remain feeble and vulnerable (Dominguez, 1997), while corruption, social problems, and violence are increasing. Trade liberalization has not produced the kind of growth expected (except in Chile) (Edwards, 1977), and the benefits of what growth there was have been highly concentrated (Berry, 1997). As corruption scandals have rocked countries from Argentina to Mexico, political institutions have been weakened. Economies that are central to the stability of the region, Brazil and Argentina, in particular, remain vulnerable to external shocks. Military tensions have exploded into an all-out war between Ecuador and Peru (Klepak, 1998). There are now signs of a budding arms race among Chile, Peru, and Argentina, and major multidimensional crises are in the offing in Cuba, Haiti, and, most ominously, Colombia.

The hemisphere has changed since Canada made its bid for closer integration. As will be made clear later in this essay, we feel that these changes should not lead to a reassessment of that option. What is needed instead is a closer look at the region, and a clearer view of Canada's place and role in it. Before discussing this, however, an assessment of the state of regional governance is required, for Canada's long-term integration in the region depends, beyond trade, on its active involvement in the collective attempts at solving the problems that confront it. This was clearly seen in the modest perspective of the 1989 Latin American strategy, and to its credit, the government has stood by that view ever since.

REGIONAL GOVERNANCE AND THE OAS

Hemispheric convergence in the Americas feeds on converging political and economic outlooks, a shared agenda on key issues, such as human rights, long-term prosperity, and sustainable development, and a community of interests deriving from the transnational character and potential spillover effects—through migration, for instance—of problems such as political instability, economic collapse, and drug trafficking. Although these factors do not produce an overwhelming pressure to integrate on a hemispheric basis, they do create the opportunity, and they generate significant incentives for the countries of the region to work together. A number of problems, however, hamper the smooth emergence of effective regional governance in the region, as well as the consolidation of the logical focus of such governance, the OAS.

Obstacles to Regional Governance in the Americas
Asymmetrical Power Relationships
The asymmetrical power relationship between the US and Latin American partners remains the defining feature of the inter-American political landscape. The US penchant for unilateralism (or regional neglect) has led to Latin America's search for legal/institutional and subregional counterweights to US hegemony. The creation of the OAS (and its cumbersome structures) in 1948 embodied this tension, and despite the post-Cold War convergence of values regarding democracy, open economies, and trade liberalization, the legacy of its creation and subsequent failures continue to haunt the OAS.

The key problem is that the United States is unlikely to be constrained by even the strongest of regional institutions. As was clearly seen in the discussion of the World Trade Organization (WTO) in the US Congress, a significant number of US politicians do not recognize the binding character of international treaties when they clash with the views of nationally elected officials. As Canada saw in the softwood lumber case, NAFTA does not qualify as a constraint for Congress or even for the executive. This means that a consolidation of regional multilateralism will further limit the autonomy of small and middle powers, for whom it will be exceedingly costly to challenge the autonomy and sovereignty of the only superpower in the region even within a multilateral institutional framework. For countries such as Brazil and Mexico, this is enough to justify resisting the consolidation of the OAS or of any binding regional government arrangements.

The Complexities of Summitry Fever
The post-Miami period gave rise to additional complexities in hemispheric diplomacy. Three new multilateral activities arose from the Miami summit that are not within OAS jurisdiction. The so-called Summit Process, initiated under US leadership in Miami, has been followed in April 1998 by another in Chile, involving a series of working groups co-ordinated by the US (SIRG—Summit Implementation Review Group). In addition, the Williamsburg Process initiated by US Defence Secretary Perry after Miami involves regular meetings of defence ministers throughout the Western hemisphere. Notwithstanding the existence of its new Permanent Committee on Security, the OAS remains in the shadow of this exercise. The final element in this multitrack confusion is the Trade Ministerial Process, which began in Denver (1995), continued in Cartagena the next year, and then in Belo Horizonte Brazil (1997), with the next summit occurring in mid-March 1998, in San José, Costa Rica. While the OAS trade unit is performing essential preparatory work for the trade ministerial conference in collaboration with the Inter-American Development Bank and the Economic Commission for Latin America and the Caribbean, the OAS again is a marginal player in the FTAA agenda. Although all three efforts are potentially beneficial, the issues of overall co-ordination and the OAS role must be addressed.

The summit frenzy that appears to have engulfed the hemisphere after Miami introduces a modicum of uncertainty in regional governance. Under-institutionalized by definition, proliferating summits are open to raw power politics and thus give clear opportunities to the stronger player(s). At the same time, the summit process narrows the material basis of institutionalized multilateralism by absorbing significant amounts of human and financial resources. The outcome is certainly negative for the OAS, yet not necessarily advantageous for the United States, which predominates in the current arrangements. Countries such as Brazil, with a clear view of hemispheric politics, a coherent strategy, and a compact foreign policy establishment, might well benefit the most from such a *décloisonnement* of hemispheric political dynamics. Still, given the challenges confronting the region, it is hard to see much benefit in weaker institutional mechanisms. For if one accepts with Adam Przeworski (1988) that democracy requires the submission of all interests to uncertainty, it is only established when that universal uncertainty is institutionalized.

Competing Visions of Open Regionalism
The stakes in developing a stronger regional, multilateral order continue to grow for all countries in the Americas. All 35 of them recognize that they confront transnational issue-areas such as trade, sustainable development, and security that require co-operation. Every state is enmeshed in quite different ways within the multilateral networks at the global, regional, and subregional levels.

In trade policy, for example, the months following the Miami summit saw the end of general enthusiasm for NAFTA accession as the preferred model of hemispheric trade integration, while MERCOSUR emerged as an alternative mechanism for South America. The reasons for this mutation are complex, as are the long-term implications for multilateralism in the Americas. Fundamental questions are raised by the reality of the US and Brazil as anchor-states of NAFTA and MERCOSUR, respectively. Are the driving forces of regionalization creating not one but two economic regions in the Western hemisphere? Is MERCOSUR more appropriately viewed from a global perspective as a major trade integration bloc in its own right (as is NAFTA), or primarily as a subregional building block towards an FTAA? Is the Rio Group emerging as a counterpoint to the OAS? Is the vision of Bolivar disputing the Monroe Doctrine? Whatever the answers to each of those questions, the post-Miami summit era is clearly characterized by an increasing tendency towards decentralization in the Western hemisphere.

Each country, moreover, and particularly the major ones, has a different approach to multilateralism. While the United Nations system appears best equipped to handle some agendas, regional insti-tutional arrangements, such as the OAS, could have a comparative advantage in others. This challenge of subsidiarity requires careful attention: Mexico is pleased with the 'Puebla process' (on migration) precisely because it is not in the OAS. Ad hoc subregional initiatives have in fact been more successful than formal region-wide machin-ery in dealing with the accelerating rate of interstate co-operation in the Americas since 1990. Moreover, the integration process comprises a broad, complex, and multidimensional community-building process that goes beyond trade and involves growing civil society interaction.

An Overview of the OAS

The OAS, created in 1948 but evolved from a long pan-American tra-dition, remains the central focus of regional governance despite its inadequacies. Comprising all the governments except Cuba—which remains suspended—the OAS is unique in its representative function: the one regional political forum to include Latin America, the US, the Commonwealth Caribbean, and now also Canada. Whatever the strength, or continuing vitality, of regional consciousness associated with the century-long inter-American system, the OAS would have to be created if it did not exist: there is a strong consensus among all countries from the Southern Cone to the Arctic Circle, including Washington, on the need for something like the OAS. The problem facing the organization as the 1990s draw to a close is the continuing lack of consensus among the 34 governments on its appropriate role, structure, and authority in a period of increasing interdependence. That the OAS faces a historic debate is not in doubt. According to the most recent report reviewing the future of inter-American governance, the OAS is the logical and principal mechanism through which gov-ernments can collaboratively engage each other—and civil society—in the management of hemisphere affairs, and it should therefore constitute the central hub of the hemisphere's multilateral network (InterAmerican Dialogue, 1997: 3). But the emergence of the OAS from the sidelines, where it remains, to the centre of the political inte-gration of the Americas depends on the 34 national governments.

The OAS is now accepted as an essential part of the regional archi-tecture in the Western hemisphere. Although, during the 1980s, its very existence seemed in doubt, this is no longer the case. In the early 1990s significant achievements such as Resolution 1080 (Santiago Commitment, General Assembly, 1991) breathed new life into the battered institution, fuelling hopes that at last the OAS would emerge as the dynamic core of inter-American governance. (That resolution, inserted in the OAS Charter in 1992, created an automatic mechanism for the OAS to react to military coups and the overthrow of elected governments in member countries.) The advent of a new Secretary-General in 1994—César Gaviria, former President of Colombia—speaking the language of democratic liberalization and co-operative security also augured well for OAS renewal. The overall inter-American mood was upbeat when the 34 heads of government assembled in Miami in December 1994 for the first Summit of the Americas since 1967.

From one perspective, the OAS has come a long way since 1990. In several key agenda areas—such as the promotion of democracy and co-operative security—major advances have been achieved, crowned with the establishment of the Unit for the Promotion of Democracy (UPD) and a Permanent Committee on Hemispheric Security. Resolution 1080 has been invoked four times. Electoral observation remains an important OAS activity, most recently and successfully in Nicaragua. The new Inter-American Council on Integral Development (ICDI) offers the possibility of tidying up the small OAS technical assistance program and, more importantly, of providing an instrument for more effective inter-American leadership on socio-economic and sustainable development issues. The new trade unit has been a runaway success. The Secretary-General's Office maintains a heady production of 'vision' documents on all subjects. Nevertheless, despite every effort of the Secretary-General, this incipient OAS strengthening process has already largely stalled in the aftermath of the Miami summit. Since then the OAS (and the overall inter-American mood) has encountered unexpected turbulence, blunting the reform process undertaken by Secretary-General Gaviria, raising doubts, and lowering expectations of its role. There has been a recent drought of creative initiatives like the Santiago Commitment (Resolution 1080) and a sense of drift in the Permanent Council. Collectively and individually, the advances since 1990 have confirmed the presence and potential of the OAS, but these advances have not decisively shored up its legitimacy. The US, Brazil, and other governments are in arrears on funding commitments, lowering further the morale of the secretariat. Difficult to revive, easy to deflate, the cash-strapped OAS stands in the towering shadow of the Inter-American Development Bank, which has become the primary regional institution in the Americas.

Given these constraints, if the OAS is to become the central hub of hemispheric governance, it must perform two essential roles. Firstly, it must become a central deliberative forum through which governments and civil society shape a regional consensus on the principal issue-areas confronting them and develop the norms and guidelines for dispute settlement and inter-American co-operation. Secondly, the OAS must shake off the dust from previous decades and revitalize its capacity to perform the central secretariat/clearing-house role required by members for effective interaction in hemispheric community-building. Such an evolution of the OAS into an effective instrument of political integration would shift its organizing concept away from project execution to an overall, proactive forum, forging co-operation among member states, inducing agreements and commitments from governments, generating policy norms and principles as well as strategies, and co-ordinating co-operative ventures and activities of action bodies (InterAmerican Dialogue, 1997: 14–15), but *not* toward regulation and constraining regime-building.

THE LEADERSHIP CHALLENGE FOR CANADA

Functionalism and Leadership

There are clear advantages to Canada in having a sound and long-term hemispheric partnership, the first of which is the possibility of balancing, however partially, the economic and political weight of the United States. But there are other advantages relating to core Canadian values such as peacebuilding and human security. A key condition of such a development is the progressive establishment of compatible norms and rules-based regimes with Latin American, Caribbean, and American partners to manage interdependence more effectively. Hemispheric governance, or the strengthening of an institutionalized and organized system of co-operation and constraint, is therefore an essential condition of community-building in the Americas. Effective governance makes the hemispheric option both feasible and advantageous; since 1990 Canadian governments have invested heavily in regional institutions, starting with the OAS. The point is that a regional 'home' is most useful to have in the globalized world, and if Canada is ever to have one, that home will have to be the Americas (Klepak, 1994). Nowhere else can Canada find a group of countries willing to consider it as part of a first circle of allies and partners, in both political and economic terms.

This commitment to the Americas, and the effective integration and participation of Canada in hemispheric governance, will not be achieved through an automatic process driven by the emergence of common needs in the face of common challenges. There is no functional necessity to Canada's option for the Americas. In fact, one could argue in a classical functionalist manner that structural forces push in the same direction as commercial trends: towards absorption within a US-centred North American universe. Despite increasing interactions with Latin Americans at the bilateral and multilateral levels, in other words, effective and full membership in the Western hemisphere remains far from assured.

Without overwhelming functional pressures to drive the hemispheric orientation, only a decisive and long-term policy option can sustain it. The benefits of such a regional option must be much more widely understood within Canada to nurture an adequate political base to sustain it. To be of interest to an open economy and a modern, developed, and democratic polity such as Canada, a regional partnership must offer tools and avenues of co-operation that support and enhance bilateral and global coalition-building. Voluntarism and long-term strategic vision must fill the vacuum of functional pressure. Effective Canadian integration in the Americas requires government leadership; a cold look at the situation and prospects of our partners, offset by sensitivity to their difficulties and outlook; effective coalition-building at home; and investment in capacity-building on the region in Canada.

Leadership and Dialogue in the Hemisphere
Canada's capacity to take the lead on inter-American trade policy before 1994 resulted not so much from solid coalition-building based on sound convergence of Canadian and Latin American interests, but instead from the incapacity of the United States to move decisively and from the unwillingness of the Latin Americans to jeopardize the whole process. The prize of hemispheric trade liberalization was and remains access to the United States market, and this is what drives the process for the biggest players in Latin America. Yet, these countries, Brazil in particular, are not interested in moving too quickly into a demanding—and thus potentially costly and destabilizing—trade regime (Botafogo Gonçalves, forthcoming). For the United States, the energy that fed the hemispheric initiative, from 1989 on, was the prospect of economic fortresses emerging in Europe and Asia on what looked like

the ruins of the Uruguay Round. With the establishment of the WTO, that energy has dissipated (Hart, 1995). There are, moreover, few other positive US policy initiatives towards the region, now that USAID's budgets for the region are evaporating and US security policy is less coherent today than during the first Clinton administration.

The dependent nature of Canada's trade policy appears most vividly in the debate about fast-track and the recent developments on that question. In the wake of the Clinton administration's defeat in mid-October, it appears that fast-tracking could only come about if significant concessions are made to the Gephart-led protectionist lobby. These concessions would have a lot to do with Canada's trade surplus with the United States. As a result, Canada finds itself in the awkward situation of having to pay a potentially significant price for a hemispheric integration process over which it will have little control once the United States moves decisively forward. If no compromise is reached in the United States, then the Santiago summit will have a strangely hollow agenda, and while Canada could keep the initiative and even some control over what would remain of the integration process, it would be riding a pretty sick animal.

These issues must be taken into account immediately. Canada's enthusiasm for integration and trade liberalization, while crucial to maintaining the momentum of the FTAA process, now threatens to isolate it from the very countries it wants to get closer to. This is especially true on trade and investment. Whatever the theoretical case for or against capital controls, the rigidity shown in the negotiation with Chile damaged our long-term strategy in the region. To push for quick trade liberalization through an ambitious FTAA similarly goes against the political momentum in the region. Likewise, pushing too hard for the adoption of labour and environmental standards risks alienating Latin American countries, always wary of US tactics to introduce non-tariff barriers.

On all those issues, the key risks are for Canada to find itself alone in front or, perhaps more damaging politically, alone with the US against the rest of the hemisphere—as happened in Costa Rica last fall on the issue of a US proposal to set up working groups on labour and environmental standards. In the face of strong opposition from Chile and the MERCOSUR countries, who want those issues discussed in the International Labour Organization (ILO) fora, Canada was the only country to support the US. The fact is, in the short and medium terms, Canada has little to gain or lose from progress in any of these areas. This offers lots of leeway, but also limited legitimacy for pushing too hard.

The domestic politics of trade liberalization and capital control are complex in Latin America and the Caribbean. Whatever the personal views of the people in power, the whole program is not an easy sell with the public after a decade or more of painful adjustments. This is why the issue of the 'rhythm' of integration, as the Brazilians—fittingly—put it, is so crucial. As seen before, the prospect of a constraining trade and investment regime for the region generates lots of discomfort in countries accustomed to US unilateralism—something Canada should sympathize with. The paradoxical implication is that a strategy that endeavours to bring Canada closer to the region in the long term needs to promote less economic integration in the short and medium terms. Canada, in other words, should use the freedom that its still limited interest in the region offers to show understanding and sensitivity to the political, social and economic hurdles that confront free traders and integrationists in the region.

In the same perspective, and recognizing the peculiarities of hemispheric politics, Canada should promote a soft multilateralism and flexible regime-building in other areas, avoiding constraining regimes until universality of application (i.e., application to the US) can be guaranteed. This could, for instance, involve the development of a blueprint of a plan, likely to be supported by the key non-US players in the hemisphere, that would explore how hemispheric governance could be fashioned to avoid the pitfalls that currently befall it. Against an increasingly clear danger of isolation and ineffectiveness, in sum, Canada should better balance leadership and dialogue.

Coalition-Building and Dialogue in Canada

Beginning in the 1980s, global civil society—NGOs, business associations, and unions—has secured a strong presence in the global and hemispheric multilateral agenda. Parallel summits and fora have become standard fare at intergovernmental get-togethers, most spectacularly at the 1992 UN Conference on the Environment and Sustainable Development (UNCED) in Rio. Business associations, unions, and NGOs have shown a willingness to become increasingly closely involved in the larger politics of multilateral governance. Canadian civil society players have been very active on that front. Fast-growing networks of business associations, quickly expanding NGO coalitions, and increasingly tight North-South union linkages have developed into a social counterpart to the political enterprise of integration. This process has been to some extent welcomed by the Chrétien government. Under Foreign Affairs Ministers Ouellet and Axworthy, DFAIT has answered by widening the circle of consultees involved in the policy-making process. In addition to national fora on various dimensions of the country's foreign policy, the government has supported a national consultation in preparation for the Santa Cruz (Bolivia) summit on sustainable development, in 1996, and a series of regional consultations designed to feed into the preparation process for the Santiago Summit of the Americas.

The civil society basis for Canada's hemispheric enthusiasm is weak. It does not generally have strong converging interests or significant material investments. In a way, this should come as no surprise, given that, to a large extent, it is sustained and financed by the government. This, however, is only part of the problem, as government support could be seen as a kind of seed money. The rest lies instead in the lack of interest in the region, or in the inconsistencies of the commitment of those interested sectors.

The private sector, for one, has been betting on the South, but with utmost care. There is lots of talk about Canadian business interests in Latin America. Yet, while significant pockets of involvement do exist, such as the mining enclaves in Chile, the level of Canadian investment in Latin America, relative to total Canadian foreign investment, is not higher now than it was before the debt crisis. In some key sectors, banking in particular, the relative weight of Latin America is significantly less than at the beginning of the 1980s. In trade, when one compares the Team Canada harvest from visits in Asia and Latin America, the results from the latter look distinctly unimpressive. To use the latest two examples and accepting that number inflation is more or less proportional, the huge caravan of politicians and business people brought back $8 billion of contracts from its 1997 visit to Asia and barely $500 million for this January's foray in the biggest economies of Latin America.

Possibly more significant in the long term, the wider civil society linkages that have been established in recent years are led essentially by a coalition of NGOs and unions opposed to greater trade and investment liberalization. The NGO sector is probably the segment of Canadian society whose involvement in Latin America has been the most consistent over the last 20 years. In the 1980s, in fact, with government and business abandoning the region to its debt problems and political instability, NGOs provided the only significant link to Latin America. NGO pressures forced the government to take political stands in a region it was tempted to forget about. Involvement was concentrated in Central America, where the last gasps of the Cold War were being played out, to devastating effect. Canadian NGOs and unions, as well as a few committed academic supporters, took clear stands in favour of the Sandinista regime in Nicaragua and, to a lesser extent, guerrillas in El Salvador and Guatemala. Above all, they criticized US involvement in the region and governmental (in El Salvador, in particular) and opposition (the Nicaraguan Contras) elements that were supported by the Reagan and the Bush administrations.

The end of the 1980s was a major turning point for the region. Developments in Eastern Europe found echo in Central America, as the Sandinistas were defeated in the polls and the last all-out efforts of the Frente Farabundo Marti des Liberacion Nacional (FMLN) in El Salvador proved fruitless. Dreams of revolution and socialism vanished, and business people moved in. Quickly modernizing Mexico and Chile soon became international darlings, and the whole continent, suddenly governed by elected officials, embraced freer markets and trade liberalization. In Canada, the shock had come a year before, with the 1988 election, which became polarized around the Free Trade Agreement with the United States. Brian Mulroney's Conservatives won a majority of seats, but without a large political mandate. Yet, they ratified the treaty. This first move was soon to throw the country into NAFTA, which in turn determined the hemispheric option we have been living with since. The populist coalition of NGO and labour groups was opposed en bloc to the FTA— with Quebec perhaps less clearly divided. It then opposed NAFTA and now opposes the FTAA. At least since 1994, however, the hemispheric debate has taken trade liberalization and the basic parameters of liberal economics as givens. Moreover, with trade and economic issues becoming central to Canada's relationship with the region, the focus of interest has shifted from poor and small Central America to the much richer and bigger South American region. Refusing to accept the new parameters of economic policy in the hemisphere, NGOs and unions have none the less seen their weight in the policy debate diminish as business and government push for closer economic ties.

The long-term importance of the links established, especially through union networks, cannot be underestimated, however, if only because they are based on very real material interests. If there is one area where functional pressure is driving the political agenda, this is probably it. Obviously, there is an inherent contradiction in a hemispheric-wide coalition ultimately established to resist the drive towards integration. However, given that liberalization is unlikely to be stopped, this coalition may expand and diversify its membership. In the current context, moreover, its mobilization to force a reassessment of the speed and modalities of the liberalization drive puts it very much in the same camp as most countries of the region. Dialogue with these organizations and sensitivity to their concerns should fit quite neatly with the North-South government-level dialogue that is needed for a sounder longer-term rapprochement with the region.

Capacity-Building in Canada

In the wake of Team Canada's disappointing harvest in Latin America, the issue of overblown expectations has come to the fore. Indeed, the overview presented in this paper suggests that the region has been badly oversold. The temptation will be strong to put it back where it does *not* belong: on the sidelines of Canada's foreign policy and on the desk of the Canadian International Development Agency (CIDA). This should be avoided at all costs, and measures must be taken to avoid cycles of boom and bust in Canada's interest in the region. A key component of such a strategy has to be the deepening and widening of Canadian knowledge of and capacity on the region. The thinness of institutional memory regarding Latin America, both in government and outside, is striking. Similarly, expertise on the region, academic or otherwise, remains scarce: to point to a glaring gap, there are no first-rate specialists in Canada on the Brazilian economy, and only one published expert of its political system. Similar statements could be made, barely amended, on all other countries of South America. Mexico is the notable exception. But Canada will have to acquire expertise on Brazil, Argentina, Venezuela, Peru, Chile, and Colombia in the next decade if it is to forge a long-term relationship with the region.

Talks about the third pillar of Canada's foreign policy—culture and education—must be supported by significant investments in the development of domestic capacity and by the establishment and consolidation of academic networks throughout the hemisphere. Some CIDA programs have contributed to this, but the Canadian capacity-building side of these programs sits awkwardly with the mandate of an aid agency. The current Foreign Minister and his predecessor have indicated their desire to deepen Canada's domestic capacity, but talk has not been followed by requisite investments of resources.

CONCLUSION

The dream of an easy sail into the Americas is over, broken on the rocks of Latin America's lingering economic, social, and political problems and on the congenital limitations of multilateralism in James Monroe's hemisphere. An animal called hemispheric integration lives on, but it is hibernating now. The only success in recent years—a bilateral treaty with Chile—gave us access to a market that represented barely more than one-tenth of 1 per cent of Canada's exports in 1996.

The hemispheric option that Canada chose in 1989 and since then, however, still makes good sense. Canada has lots to gain and much to contribute in the consolidation of a regional community in the Americas. Significant progress was made at the beginning of the decade, but the somewhat lofty dreams of the early 1990s have to be abandoned. A number of challenges have emerged and opportunities for leadership abound, but they call for a more careful reading of the region's prospects, as well as more sensitivity to the preoccupations of the region's governments and peoples.

In Canada, exaggerated short-term expectations and a poor reading of the region's dynamics jeopardize the political basis of a hemispheric option. A long-term commitment to the region is required from the government. This commitment must be anchored in a strategic outlook that tackles the complexity of a dialogue with the region, engages civil society, and raises awareness and the level of Canadian knowledge about the region.

REFERENCES

Berry, Albert. 1997. 'The Income Distribution Threat in Latin America', *Latin American Research Review* 32, 3: 3–41.

Botafogo Gonçalves, José. Forthcoming. 'NAFTA, MERCOSUR, SAFTA: Competing Approaches to Hemispheric Economic Integration?', in Jean Daudelin and Edgar J. Dosman, eds, *Adjusting the Sights*. Ottawa: Carleton University Press.

Brunelle, Dorval, and Christian Deblock. Forthcoming. 'NAFTA and Strategic Regional Integration', in Jean Daudelin and Edgar J. Dosman, eds, *Adjusting the Sights*. Ottawa: Carleton University Press.

Christie, Keith. 1995. *The Four Amigos and Beyond*. Ottawa: Department of Foreign Affairs and International Trade.

Choudhri, Ehsan, and Prakash Sharma. 1996. *Capital Controls: Rationale and Implications for Canadian Trade and Investment*. Ottawa: Department of Foreign Affairs and International Trade.

Daudelin, Jean, Edgar Dosman, and Fen Osler Hampson. 1997. *Leading the OAS in the 21st Century: A Proposal*. Canadian Foundation for the Americas and The Norman Paterson School of International Affairs, Carleton University and York University.

Department of Foreign Affairs and International Trade (DFAIT). 1995. *Canada in the World, Government Statement*. Ottawa: Public Works and Government Services Canada.

————. 1996. *Strategy Update for Latin America and the Caribbean*. Ottawa: Department of Foreign Affairs and International Trade.

Dominguez, Jorge. 1997. 'Latin America's Crisis of Representation', *Foreign Affairs* 76, 1 (Jan.–Feb.): 100–13.

Dosman, Edgar J. 1992. 'Canada and Latin America: The New Look', *International Journal* 47, 3 (Summer) Toronto: 529–54.

Edwards, Sebastian. 1997. 'Latin America's Underperformance', *Foreign Affairs* 76, 2 (Mar.–Apr.): 93–103.

Hart, Michael. 1995. 'Whither NAFTA: To Expand or to Deepen?', in Joseph A. McKinney and Melissa A. Essary, eds, *Free Trade Area for the Americas: Issues in Economics, Trade Policy and Law*. Waco, Texas: Baylor University Press.

InterAmerican Dialogue. 1997. *Final Report: The InterAmerican Agenda and Multilateral Governance—The Organization of American States*. Washington: InterAmerican Dialogue, Mar.

International Monetary Fund (IMF). 1997. *Direction of Trade Statistics 1990–1996*. Washington: IMF.

Klepak, Hal. 1994. *What's In It For Us: Canada's Relationship with Latin America*. Ottawa: Canadian Foundation for the Americas.

————. 1998. *Confidence Building Side-Stepped: The Peru-Ecuador Conflict of 1995*. Ottawa: Carleton University Press.

McKenna, Peter. 1995. *Canada and the OAS: From Dilettante to Full Partner*. Ottawa: Carleton University Press.

Molot, Maureen Appel. 1997. 'The North-American Free Trade Agreement: Policy- or Investment-led?', in Richard G. Lipsey and Patricio Meller, eds, *Western Hemisphere Trade Integration: A Canadian-Latin American Dialogue*. London: Macmillan, 171–91.

Przeworski, Adam. 1988. 'Democracy as a contingent outcome of conflict', in J. Elster and Rune Slagstad, eds, *Constitutionalism and Democracy*. Cambridge: Cambridge University Press, 59–81.

Saéz, Raúl E. 1997. 'Trade and Investment between Canada and the LAIA Countries', in Richard G. Lipsey and Patricio Meller, eds, *Western Hemisphere Trade Integration: A Canadian-Latin American Dialogue*. London: Macmillan, 232–49.

Statistics Canada Online. 1997. CANSIM series.

Wonnacott, Ronald J., and Paul Wonnacott. 1995. 'El TLCAN y los acuerdos comerciales en las Américas', in *Las Américas: Integración Económica en Perspectiva*. Bogotá: Departamento Nacional de Planeación, Banco Interamericano de Desarrollo, 103–37.

12

The Multilateral Agreement on Investment: A Charter of Rights for Global Investors or Just Another Agreement?

ELIZABETH SMYTHE

The negotiation of the Multilateral Agreement on Investment (MAI) at the Organization for Economic Co-operation and Development (OECD) became an issue of some controversy in 1997–8, to the surprise and consternation of the Canadian government. In the process it raised, once again, many of the issues regarding Canadian sovereignty and the impact of deeper economic integration, echoing the previous debates over both the Canada-US Free Trade Agreement (FTA) and the North American Free Trade Agreement (NAFTA). The controversy over the MAI is all the more interesting because Canada was initially not very enthusiastic about negotiating investment rules at the OECD, although this country has been a keen supporter of investment rules in principle and has worked hard to try to get investment rules on the negotiating agenda of the World Trade Organization (WTO). Having become an active participant in the OECD process, however, the government then found itself under attack at home and at the OECD as the negotiations unfolded. Critics of the MAI claim it is a veritable charter of rights that will give foreign investors special rights and undermine Canadian sovereignty.[1] In contrast, the Minister of International Trade, Sergio Marchi, and those involved in negotiating the agreement claimed that it would merely extend the investment provisions of NAFTA to a wider group of countries and in no way constituted a further erosion of Canadian sovereignty (see Marchi, 1997). The government's slow move from a limited, selective dialogue with a few stakeholders to a broader, more inclusive process left it open, moreover, to charges of secretly acquiescing to an agreement that might have serious implications for Canada.

This chapter will analyse the negotiation of the MAI, the absence of leadership on this issue at the OECD, and, at least initially, the lack of much dialogue at home. In examining Canada's position on international investment rules this chapter will argue that a number of factors have shaped Canada's interest in such rules. These include how enhanced mobility of capital has altered the balance of power among states, capital, and labour, the reshaping of Canada's investment interests in the past two decades as a result of changed investment patterns, and the continued commitment of Canada to a rules-based global economy (Hart, 1997). These factors suggest that Canada would be a strong supporter of negotiations and perhaps play a leadership role in initiating and forging such an agreement. Yet Canada had concerns about the OECD as a venue for such negotiations from the start (Smythe, 1996). Moreover, the political sensitivity of investment issues in Canada was reflected in criticisms of the draft agreement. Questions were raised about who has influence over the writing of international rules on investment and whose interests these rules serve. The MAI thus provided an argument for opening up the process and having broader public consultations, both prior to negotiations and in the scrutiny and approval of the resulting agreements.

The chapter is divided into six parts. The first deals with the origins of the negotiations at the OECD and sheds some light on the reasons why Canada was not in the forefront of the efforts to launch negotiations in this forum. The second examines the OECD negotiation process, including the role of states, the OECD secretariat, and non-state actors. The third examines Canada's investment priorities and the factors that have shaped them, including: Canada's changing investment position, its history of reliance on US capital and the sensitivities that have remained, the desire to promote a rules-based international economy, and, finally, NAFTA. The fourth section discusses the relative absence of broad public consultations at the beginning of the negotiations and the subsequent pressure to expand the domestic dialogue. The fifth addresses questions related to the impact of the MAI should the draft agreement become a reality, and whether it would constitute limits on Canadian sovereignty that go beyond NAFTA. It also examines what the impact of not signing would be and whether this agreement is necessary to secure Canada's international investment interests. The final part discusses the MAI case and what it tells us about Canada's role in the creation of global investment rules. It argues that the power that globalization has given to mobile capital at the expense of states and domestic actors, such as labour, makes it necessary to define and develop global investment rules, but that this process must take place within a more meaningful dialogue with Canadians.

INVESTMENT RULES: THE OECD OR THE WTO

The ultimate source of the MAI negotiations lies in the changes in the magnitude and distribution of foreign direct investment (FDI) in the global economy and state policy responses to it after World War II. The rapid expansion of FDI early in the postwar period was followed, in the 1970s, by a wave of efforts to address the transnational issues arising from investment and host state efforts to control or manage it. The attempt to develop multilateral investment rules began at the United Nations with negotiations on a code for transnational corporations, which ultimately foundered as a result of host-home country, North-South, and East-West divisions.

In an effort to pre-empt UN action and create a strong consensus among Western industrialized countries, the United States pushed for rules to be negotiated at the OECD, which was seen to be a much friendlier environment to the interests of capital exporters. The non-binding Declaration on Multinational Enterprises, which included a national treatment commitment,[2] from which Canada exempted itself, and guidelines for multinational enterprises resulted in 1976. The US subsequently sought to further limit host-state discretion through a series of bilateral and multilateral initiatives, including bilateral investment agreements (BITs) to protect US investors. In 1983 the US was partially successful in a case it launched through the General Agreement on Tariffs and Trade (GATT) against Canada's Foreign Investment Review Act. This was followed by the inclusion of trade-related investment measures (TRIMs) on the agenda of the Uruguay Round of multilateral trade negotiations and in the negotiation of the 1987 FTA with Canada, which also dealt with the regulation of FDI. A wave of domestic liberalization of FDI regulations occurred in the 1980s, partly as a result of competitive pressures and the changing role of a number of economies from capital importers to both importers and exporters. Despite that trend a number of developing countries continued to resist the development of international rules that embodied principles of national treatment and severely restricted host-state policy discretion. This opposition was evident in the outcome of the TRIM negotiations at the Uruguay Round, resulting in limited restrictions on state policy regulation of FDI only where the impact could be tied closely to trade. Investment regulations were, however, also addressed in parts of the agreement dealing with services.

The ever-deepening integration of the global economy and the demands of multinational capital for enhanced access to, and security within, host economies have ensured, however, that the issue of global investment rules remains a part of the international economic rule-making agenda. Thus the decision of the United States to turn once again to the OECD to forge a consensus on multilateral investment rules was not surprising.

The United States had called on the OECD to initiate discussion on a wider investment instrument and, in 1991, OECD ministers agreed.[3] The US wanted a much tighter, more comprehensive and binding agreement than what was provided in the voluntary code and the national treatment instrument of the OECD and had been increasingly frustrated by the slow and incremental process of trying to strengthen them. Clearly, the slow, difficult process unfolding at the GATT in the Uruguay Round and the opposition that even the very limited trade-related investment measures had aroused there, as well as later experiences negotiating with similar opponents of investment rules within the Asia-Pacific Economic Co-operation forum (APEC), influenced the US decision to look to the OECD. In December 1991 the United States began a push to launch a full-scale negotiation at the OECD of a comprehensive, binding investment treaty with high standards of liberalization, protection of investors, and a dispute resolution process (United States, 1991: 1). Despite the strong consensus among OECD

members on the need for such a set of rules and the desire for investment liberalization, not all members, among them Canada, agreed
that the OECD was the preferred venue for such negotiations. Nor did
Canada see an urgent need to proceed quickly. Arguments for and
against the OECD as the venue for such negotiations over the next
three years centred on two aspects of the organization—its restricted
membership and the strengths and weaknesses of the organization
and its secretariat.

The OECD membership, until 1991, reflected its roots in postwar
co-operation among industrialized market economies. Since that time
Mexico, Poland, Hungary, and the Czech Republic have become
members, as has Korea. But their admission has not substantively
altered the organization, even though these four countries are primarily hosts to foreign capital. Admission came only after their adoption of sufficiently liberal economic policies, including adherence to
the various OECD investment and capital movement codes. For some
OECD countries the restricted nature of the membership of the organization was clearly seen to be an advantage in future negotiations.
The United States identified a large degree of consensus on many
aspects of the treatment of FDI, thus making ultimate agreement on
a strong treaty with high standards of liberalization, in its view, quite
likely. Other members, however, saw restricted membership differently. Any agreement negotiated by OECD members would not include
the very countries where investors had complained of discrimination.
When Canada and a number of other European countries canvassed
their own business communities they found few or no complaints
about the treatment of FDI within other OECD countries. All members
recognized that the ultimate targets for new discipline on the treatment of FDI were countries outside the OECD, including the dynamic
Asian economies that were attracting investment and countries such
as Brazil and India, which had led efforts to resist investment liberalization in organizations such as the GATT/WTO. From the US perspective, the advantage of the OECD was that agreement there would
both 'prevent backsliding within the OECD and promote the adoption of these standards outside the OECD' (United States, 1991: 3).
This reflected the view of the OECD as a forum for consensus among
the largest market economies and as a missionary for values of liberalization. In contrast, both Canada and the EU felt that efforts to
negotiate binding rules would ultimately be more fruitful, albeit
through a slower process, within the newly created WTO.

Concerns over the limits of the OECD as a negotiating venue are reflected in the report on the MAI that was finally adopted in May 1995. The ministers agreed to 'the immediate start of negotiations in the OECD aimed at reaching an MAI by the ministerial meeting of May 1997.' The agreement would:

> provide a broad multilateral framework for international investment with high standards for the liberalisation of investment regimes and investment protection and with effective dispute settlement procedures; be a free-standing international treaty open to all OECD Members and the European Communities, and to accession by non-OECD Member countries, which will be consulted as the negotiations progress. . . . (OECD, 1995)

The report on an MAI outlined the 'dramatic growth and transformation of Foreign Direct Investment which has been spurred by widespread liberalisation and increased competition for investment capital'. Foreign investors, according to the report, still encounter 'investment barriers, discriminatory treatment and uncertainty'. The MAI would set a high standard for the treatment of investors and provide 'clear, consistent rules on liberalisation, dispute settlement and investor protection'. Most importantly, it would create pressure on the non-OECD investment dissidents because 'The MAI would provide a benchmark against which potential investors would assess the openness and legal security offered by countries as investment locations. This would in turn act as a spur to further liberalisation' (OECD, 1995: 3).

Both the report and the communiqué make a commitment to consult with non-members, although the form and nature of consultations were left unclear. In actual fact the subsequent consultations have taken the form of workshops in various locations, such as Hong Kong and Brazil, where 'dynamic non-member economies' have been invited to discuss the MAI with sponsoring OECD members and officials of other organizations, such as the WTO and the United Nations Committee on Trade and Development (UNCTAD) and regional organizations (OECD, 1997e). In the fall of 1997 representatives of a number of these economies, such as Hong Kong, Argentina, and Brazil, were invited to the negotiating table as observers.

Even as negotiations were launched at the OECD, Canada continued to work, in co-operation with the European Commission, for the inclusion of investment rules in the WTO agenda. Canada, in co-operation with the EU and Brazil, sponsored two seminars[4] organized by UNCTAD designed to promote discussion and understanding of FDI with a view to moving the investment agenda forward at the Singapore ministerial meeting of the WTO in December 1996. The intent was to counter the opposition to investment rules on the part of a small group of countries (UNCTAD, 1996). US officials were uncomfortable with these efforts and questioned Canada's commitment to the OECD negotiations. In contrast, Canadian officials never saw the efforts at the WTO and the OECD as mutually exclusive and saw all of their work on investment, including that in regional organizations such as APEC, as contributing to the development of a set of rules that would ultimately have their place in the WTO.

NEGOTIATING AT THE OECD: NOTHING IS DECIDED UNTIL EVERYTHING IS DECIDED

To understand some of the concerns about negotiating at the OECD and the way the negotiations unfolded this section outlines the structure of the OECD and the way it operated in dealing with investment issues. The above heading is a quotation from the chair of the OECD investment negotiating group, which is drawn from the Uruguay Round multilateral trade negotiations. It refers to the idea of a single undertaking, a broad package agreement, relating all issues and providing, within it, numerous trade-offs for states bargaining across a set of interrelated issues. The reality, however, is that the structure and process of negotiations at the OECD are somewhat different from the GATT and the WTO and have had an impact on the progress of the negotiations, the kind of role Canada has been able to play, and the nature of the dialogue with non-state actors. As Wolfe and Curtis point out in Chapter 7 in this volume the WTO, and the GATT before it, is a minimalist international organization with a very small secretariat and a member-led process of periodic rounds of intensive negotiations. The OECD, in contrast, has a large secretariat of over 1,800 staff (about four times the size of the WTO) and a proliferation of over 200 committees and bodies whose ongoing work the secretariat supports through an elaborate and wide-ranging program of research. Moreover, the role of the OECD has been affected by global changes. The emergence of the WTO and its broader trade agenda, which now includes issues such as services and investment, along with a declining need to organize the co-operation of Western market economies with the end of the Cold War, has thrown the future of the OECD into question, something that the Secretary-General, Don Johnston (of Canada), has had to address. Moreover, unilateral reductions in US financial support totalling 20 per cent of its budgetary contribution resulted in a 10 per cent budget reduction over three years (Friedman, 1997) and added to the pressure to demonstrate the worth of the organization. It made the many divisions of the secretariat conscious of their need to compete for shrinking resources. As a consequence, both the Secretary-General and the Division on Financial, Fiscal and Enterprise Affairs (DAFFE) have embraced the negotiation of the MAI with enthusiasm.

Much of the OECD's work on investment issues has been undertaken by two committees, the Committee on Capital Movements and Invisibles Transactions (CMIT) and the Committee on Investment and Multinational Enterprises (CIME), which monitor and oversee the compliance of member countries with the OECD codes. Only the capital movements code, however, as part of the effort to free capital movements and promote currency convertibility, was binding on members. Member countries are represented equally on committees, which operate on the basis of consensus, as does the OECD as a whole.

In the case of the CIME and CMIT, representation has generally been the role of foreign ministries in some countries and economic departments or agencies in others. Thus the level of negotiating expertise and experience in matters such as services, intellectual property, and the process of creating binding enforceable investment rules varies widely among representatives. Moreover, the work of committees has tended to focus on research, consensus-building, and non-binding agreements. As a result, a number of member countries that championed the negotiations, like the US, were unwilling to use the existing CIME and CMIT committee structures to negotiate the MAI. Canada, as well as the European Union (EU), wanted a negotiating group and chair separate from the existing committee structure.

On the whole, the limited membership of the OECD and the major stake that the US, and more recently Japan and the largest European economies, have in capital exports has meant that the OECD's investment agenda and work program have tended to be dominated, for the past two decades, by their concerns. Key posts in the secretariat, up until the selection of a Canadian to the top post in 1995, reflected European and American domination. Not having a broader membership in which to forge alliances limited Canada's ability to manouevre on investment issues in the 1970s and 1980s.

The OECD has historically provided for the views of capital and labour to be heard on economic issues, including investment, through the Trade Union Advisory Committee (TUAC), which was founded in 1948, and the Business and Industry Advisory Committee (BIAC), founded in 1963. Both organizations include members from the 29 OECD countries and put the views of their members before the OECD on a regular basis through meetings with the various committees.

In the case of BIAC the organization is structured as a federation of business organizations of the member countries, headed by a smaller executive board, which is assisted by a small permanent staff in Paris. The United States Council for International Business is one of the most influential members of BIAC, staffed as it is by former members of the US Treasury and United States Trade Representative (USTR). In Canada, the Canadian Council on International Business, the BIAC affiliate, is closely linked to organizations like the Business Council on National Issues and the Canadian Chamber of Commerce. Internationally, BIAC works closely with the International Chamber of Commerce, also headquartered in Paris. Despite its small staff BIAC has access to major resources in its efforts to influence OECD decisions, especially via the corporate legal staff on which it can draw. Even on the part of BIAC, there has been a frustration with the limited access to negotiators and the limited flow of information about the negotiations. Its views, along with those of TUAC, have been communicated by meetings with the negotiating group or the chair (six in 1996) and often through letters to the chair (BIAC, 1997).

The Trade Union Advisory Committee is composed of union federations from the member countries and maintains links with the international umbrella labour organizations such as the International Confederation of Free Trade Unions. All of the affiliated organizations meet twice a year in plenary session to make key policy decisions, set priorities, and approve the budget and are assisted by a small permanent staff. For TUAC the strengthening of the implementation and follow-up to ensure that the Guidelines on Multinational Enterprises are being adhered to in member countries has been a priority.

Much of TUAC's work regarding the MAI has centred on building an acceptance of and a commitment to core labour standards within the member countries. They have asked the OECD for research studies and sponsored a conference (OECD, 1996) designed to demonstrate that adherence to labour standards will not deter investors. TUAC has sought to make adherence to core labour standards a central commitment shared by all OECD members and reflected in the MAI. These standards are defined as 'freedom of association, right to collective bargaining, freedom from forced or compulsory labour, freedom from child labour and freedom from discrimination in respect of employment and equal remuneration of men and women' (OECD, 1996: 13).

This issue has gained even greater salience with the recent admission of new members, especially Korea, the prospects of broadening OECD membership in the future, and the potential accession of non-OECD countries to the agreement. As capital mobility grows, increased state competition to attract FDI, without adherence to core labour standards, raises the possibility of states seeking to attract investment by suppressing labour rights, thus putting downward pressure on labour standards elsewhere. TUAC has cited a number of export-processing zones as evidence of this practice. From the start TUAC faced a challenge, since it is evident in the report to ministers in May 1995 that the central preoccupation of the negotiations was the liberalization of regulations and improving the treatment of foreign investors. Labour and environmental standards were scarcely mentioned in the initial report.

Negotiations began in September 1995 with the choice of a chair, Franz Engering, a well-respected Dutch official. A variety of groups discussing and drafting various portions of the agreement were established, and in some newer issue areas, such as intellectual property, substantial discussion was necessary prior to any text development. The European Commission negotiates along with the 29 members because of its competence in a number of investment areas related to trade. It endeavours to co-ordinate a common European position on issues at the OECD although members, such as the United Kingdom, jealously guard their autonomy.

By the beginning of 1997 general agreement on key principles of the MAI, including the protection of investors, the principle of national treatment, and a dispute resolution process, had been reached and differences on some key issues had emerged.[5] These included a number that divided the US and Canada from Europe, such as the question of whether the US and Canada would accept a clause for Regional Economic Integration Organization (REIO),[6] which the EU inserts in all international trade agreements to allow it to deviate from most-favoured nation commitments in pursuit of further intra-EU integration. The US and Canada have opposed such a clause as too open-ended, leaving the door open to discrimination. The issue of the Helms-Burton measures, which the United States uses to sanction foreign investors in Cuba, has also been divisive. The EU and Canada have proposed draft wording that would restrict 'secondary boycotts' and limit the extent to which 'conflicting requirements' can be imposed on investors.

Culture is an issue that has primarily divided France and Canada from the major negotiators. France has sought an undefined, general exemption of culture from the whole agreement,[7] which Canada has supported, along with a group of smaller European states including Belgium, Spain, Italy, Portugal, and Greece, as well as Australia. The United States has been opposed to this while other major European states have indicated their desire to keep general exemptions to an absolute minimum. In addition, Canada has had specific concerns over the list of prohibited performance requirements that go beyond the NAFTA list. Two additional restrictions would limit any host-state requirements that companies locate headquarter offices within host states and the requirement that the firms undertake commitments regarding their operations, such as achieving a given level of production, research and development, or employment. Canada has taken a reservation in the second of these two in reference to the undertakings that Investment Canada negotiates with foreign investors.

The extent of disagreement on issues was not apparent to outside observers until late in the process. This is, in part, a reflection of the way in which the secretariat and the chair of the negotiating group have sought to forge a consensus on the agreement. The secretariat, especially DAFFE, had a strong interest at the outset, along with the US, in a successful outcome and strongly promoted the MAI as an agreement that would be 'state of the art' and would lead to significant liberalization, raising the expectations of business. Creating a consolidated text as rapidly as possible became an important goal.

The draft text of early 1997 codified all of the major principles of the investment agreement, many of which were drawn from the language of BITs and NAFTA. These included a very broad a definition of investment, an obligation to provide foreign investors with national (i.e., non-discriminatory) treatment, and commitments to protect foreign investors from arbitrary actions and, in the event of expropriation, to provide prompt and adequate compensation to investors. A strong and broad dispute settlement mechanism that would be available to investors in disputes with states was also included. Objections of single countries to various provisions of the draft, whether major and substantive or fairly narrow and technical, were relegated to footnotes or commentaries to the text. By beginning with broad principles with which all could agree and leaving the issue of what sectors or countries these provisions would cover until later in the negotiations, the draft text created an impression that a sweeping agreement had been reached and a wholesale acceptance of the corporate agenda was a *fait accompli*. Combined with the rhetoric coming from zealous supporters of investment liberalization and the OECD as part of the effort to sell the agreement to non-OECD countries, an impression was left that all of the reservations and exemptions, yet to be negotiated, were simply minor details. The reality, however, was that there were much more diverse views on the scope and applicability of the agreement. These differences were apparent once countries began lodging their draft reservations with the chair in March 1997. While some countries listed over 80 non-conforming measures, others listed very few. Such disparities hardly provided a basis for negotiation. The NAFTA members drew heavily on the investment chapter of that agreement (Chapter 11), largely replicating the reservations listed in the annex. Delegates did not even have a shared meaning of what constituted a reservation, or how they were to be negotiated, resulting in a set of guidelines that had to be created to ensure some consistency in the process.

Differences also emerged among members on the applicability of the concepts of standstill and rollback, the chief mechanisms for liberalization, and their applicability to the exemptions and country-specific reservations. Standstill refers to the 'prohibition of new, more restrictive exceptions', in essence freezing existing policies that violate the agreement. According to the OECD, rollback is the 'liberalisation process by which the reduction and eventual elimination of non-conforming measures [are achieved]. It is a dynamic element linked with standstill which provides its starting point. Combined with standstill it would provide "a ratchet effect" where any new liberalisation measures would be "locked in" so they could not be rescinded or nullified over time' (OECD, 1997c: 152-4). The more exemptions and reservations that can be covered by standstill and rollback, the greater the future liberalization of investment regulations. By the spring of 1997, however, it was clear that most states were commit-

ted to little beyond standstill and that a number of areas, such as culture for Canada, might not even be subject to that obligation.
Standstill on most reservations, however, would provide at least a
measure of security and transparency to investors and set the stage
for further attempts to liberalize down the road.

At this point the process began to bog down and it became clear
that the negotiators would not meet the original deadline of May 1997.
Members agreed to finish the negotiations by the May 1998 ministerial meeting, whether or not agreement was reached (OECD, 1997d). The
leaking of the sweeping draft agreement, the exaggerated rhetoric of
liberalization, and the extension of the deadline provided momentum
to opponents of the agreement, who had been slow to mobilize both
within Canada and at the OECD. Both labour and capital had, of course,
sought to influence the negotiations from the start. TUAC demanded
that the MAI include stronger commitments to not lower labour and
environmental standards (White, 1997) in the preamble of the agreement and called for the annexation to the MAI of the Guidelines on
Multinational Enterprises, the non-binding principles that outline
socially acceptable corporate behaviour. BIAC strongly opposed
annexing the Guidelines, to the point of arguing against *any* linking
to the agreement, which, it claimed, would render the current voluntary guidelines obligatory and, therefore, depress investment flows
(BIAC, 1996). BIAC had more problems maintaining a unified opposition on labour standards, however, and faced the embarrassment of
the Belgian and French business associations publicly dissenting from
the BIAC official position of total opposition (BIAC, 1996).

Other groups were also being heard on the investment issue, both
in Canada and in Paris. A number of organizations, such as the World
Wildlife Fund and the Sierra Club, began actively disseminating critical information on the MAI, much of it via the Internet, in co-operation
with various other labour and social justice organizations. However,
the OECD, imbued with a long tradition of consulting labour and business, was slow to react and comprehend the level of concern. Even
earlier a number of groups had asked for an opportunity to be heard
and met with the chair of the negotiating group in November 1996 to
express their concerns regarding the potential erosion of environmental standards. But as an intergovernmental treaty-making process
with a separate negotiating group of state representatives, the negotiating group and the secretariat were reluctant to accord non-governmental organizations (NGOs) access to the negotiations or much infor-

mation about them. As a consequence, many of these groups focused simultaneously on key member countries, particularly those where they could find easier access to decision-makers and information.

The growing opposition to the MAI on the part of a number of NGOs has had an impact, as has a change in the British government. In September the British shift from total opposition to TUAC's demands to one of support was reflected at a meeting with representatives of non-OECD members, where the British delegate outlined the issues of stronger language on labour and environmental standards and the likelihood that the Guidelines on Multinational Enterprises would be attached to the agreement, although they will remain voluntary (Bridge, 1997). These moves met with a hostile reaction on the part of BIAC. It ultimately, and reluctantly, accepted the annexations of the Guidelines as long as their voluntary status was reaffirmed clearly in the agreement (Katz, 1997).

As criticism increased and after sustained lobbying by groups such as the Sierra Club, Friends of the Earth, and the World Wildlife Fund, the OECD negotiators finally scheduled a meeting with environmental and other NGO critics of the MAI on 27 October 1997. The meeting included the representatives of NGOs, several of them well-known critics in Canada of trade and investment policy who were followed to Paris by Canadian media. The extent of concern about the agreement came as a surprise to many delegates.[8] The groups demanded that the negotiations be suspended until a fuller review of the agreement's environmental and social impact could be assessed. They called for changes to the provisions on expropriation, elimination of the dispute settlement provisions, and more transparent and inclusive negotiations, with an extension of the deadline (Sierra Club, 1997). The negotiators refused, but undertook a review of the literature on FDI and the environment and released it quickly on the Internet (OECD, 1997b). Overall, however, the OECD has been rather unsure as how to deal with NGOs. Partly because they had been shut out of the earlier process in Paris, these groups have forged loose coalitions and focused on cultivating opposition to the MAI within member countries, including Canada.

Despite the importance of investment to Canada, it was not at the forefront of pushing for the MAI at the OECD. This has been more the role of the US and the OECD's secretariat. Canada's clear preference was to work in the longer term for rules at the WTO. The push to get a consolidated draft text early on in the negotiations, combined with the high expectations created by the rhetoric of some negotiators that the agreement would bring significant liberalization, backfired. When the negotiators moved to deal with reservations the extent of dis-agreement became evident, even as outside critics became alarmed at the seemingly sweeping nature of the draft agreement. Opponents became mobilized just at the point where the process was losing any momentum it might have had.

CANADA'S INVESTMENT PRIORITIES: NAFTA: NO MORE AND NO LESS

What has shaped Canada's investment priorities at the OECD? Clearly the experience of globalization has had an impact on Canada's view of the MAI. Increased integration of the American and Canadian mar-kets has resulted in a high level of dependence on the US market, which now takes in excess of 80 per cent of Canadian exports, and greater vulnerability of the Canadian economy to any threats to US market access. The negotiation of the 1987 FTA was a way to address that vulnerability. Secondly, globalization has meant that large Canadian firms (both Canadian- and US-owned) have become increasingly involved in investment abroad. Canadian outward flows and stocks of FDI have increased rapidly, especially since the late 1980s (Table 12.1) to reach levels comparable to that of the stock of inward investment, in excess of $170 billion by 1996 (Marchi, 1997). While most of this investment has gone into the United States, sig-nificant growth has also occurred in FDI going to Latin America and Asia. As part of one of the larger market economies, Canadian firms have a significant and growing stake of assets invested abroad. At the same time, sectors of the Canadian economy continue to be domi-nated by foreign-based firms.

As national investment rules have become more liberal, the grow-ing mobility of capital has contributed to a broad shift in ideas and attitudes among Canadian decision-makers since 1982. This shift has remained fairly consistent despite changes in governments. These attitudes are reflected in recent statements regarding the MAI and can be summarized as follows:

1. Increased direct investment, whether foreign or domestically based, both inward and outward, is the key to ensuring com-petitive Canadian firms and a competitive economy.

Table 12.1

**Canada's International Investment Position, Selected Years
(millions of dollars)**

	FDI in Canada	Canadian FDI Abroad
1950	4,098	990
1955	8,010	1,742
1960	13,583	2,468
1965	17,864	3,469
1970	27,374	6,188
1975	38,728	10,526
1980	64,708	26,967
1982	72,814	35,558
1984	85,984	50,092
1986	96,054	61,497
1988	114,480	76,169
1990	131,131	91,462
1992	138,696	107,451
1994	152,784	131,394
1995	168,077	142,347

Source: Statistics Canada, *Canada's International Investment Position 1995* (May 1996).

2. Due to changes in technology there are ever-greater needs for capital, and the global competition for such investment among states is intense.

3. Canada's attractiveness as a destination for new investment has declined in the eyes of foreign investors, as reflected in Canada's declining relative share of international FDI flows since the 1970s.

As Minister of International Trade Sergio Marchi's November 1997 statement on the MAI noted:

Canada is heavily reliant on foreign direct investment for capital. This foreign investment also plays a critical role in the Canadian economy. In 1996, foreign investment in Canada amounted to $180 billion-a twofold increase in 10 years. . . . $1 billion of new foreign direct investment creates 45,000 jobs over five years. However, we cannot rest on our laurels. A recent report by KPMG [Kleinveld, Peat, Marwick, Goederler] showed that Canada is one of the most competitive places in the world to invest and do business. Yet, at

the same time, the United Nations notes that our share of global investment
has slipped from 8.7 per cent in 1985 to 4.3 per cent in 1995. Joining the
right kind of MAI would reinforce Canada's attractiveness as a first class destination for foreign investment. (Marchi, 1997: 3)

Policy has been guided by this view that Canada can no longer
afford, nor should it seek, to bargain with investors over access to
the Canadian market. According to this view state policy instruments
should be used both to attract FDI inflows through promotional activities and policies that are attractive to international investors and to
facilitate outflows through efforts to attain investor access to other
markets and ensure the security of those investments, once made
(Smythe, 1996). Many of Canada's changing views on FDI were also
reflected at the global level in a heightened awareness of the role of
foreign investment within the globalized system of production and
its relationship to trade. Trade and investment were seen increasingly
by academic analysts and national policy-makers as complementary
and requiring more integrated treatment as policy issues, ideas that
organizations like the OECD reinforced.

These broad principles, however, have not meant that investment
as a policy issue has disappeared from the Canadian political agenda.
It remains a sensitive issue because of the high level of foreign ownership (mainly American) coupled with the influence of the US on
Canada and the periodic but fairly regular eruptions of bilateral trade
disputes. These remind Canadians of their vulnerability and the challenges to sovereignty that are often linked to this aspect of the
Canadian economy. As a result, even with the policy of liberalizing
Canadian regulation of FDI embodied in the 1985 Investment Canada
Act, the 1987 FTA, and NAFTA, selective sectoral restrictions remain,
especially in the case of cultural industries. But the Liberal government and its officials have embraced the view that liberalization of
investment regulation is good, as reflected in the decision to support
the launch of the MAI negotiations.

The Department of Foreign Affairs and International Trade (DFAIT)
has taken on the lead role in recent years in promoting both inward
and outward investment, in close co-operation with the business
community, as well as by negotiating rules on investment at the WTO
and the OECD. Industry Canada participates in the process, along with
the Department of Finance, but has seen its role shrink at the domestic level to one of enforcement of a limited set of sectoral regulations
on FDI. The Heritage Department has been consulted but has not

been a regular participant in the negotiations. At the political level the Liberals, as past opponents of the FTA and NAFTA and supporters of a positive role for the state and the need to preserve Canadian culture, are sensitive to any appearance that they are ceding additional Canadian sovereignty to protect the interests of investors.

NAFTA, which superseded the FTA and has more extensive investment provisions, has served to define Canada's negotiating position and the way in which both the Liberal government and DFAIT have dealt with public consultations on the agreement. NAFTA (Canada, 1992) added significantly to the FTA and created a fairly complete set of rules on the treatment of foreign investors. Chapter 11 of the agreement defines investment very broadly, commits governments to national treatment of investors (Article 1102), both new investors and those already established. It places limits on the types of performance requirements (Article 1106) that can be imposed on investors. It permits governments to continue to offer investment incentives, but limits the imposition of trade-distorting conditions in return for such benefits. The agreement commits governments to compensate investors in the event that expropriation occurs, either directly or indirectly, or as a result of acts that are 'tantamount to nationalization' (Article 1110). NAFTA also provides access to dispute settlement procedures for investors in disputes with states (section B).

Regulations that did not conform to the agreement were the subject of a series of negotiated exemptions and reservations. Culture is exempted from the obligations of the agreement, while specific reservations are listed in the Annex for each country. Canada exempted Investment Canada from the national treatment and dispute resolution obligations. Most of the reservations to the national treatment obligation were claimed for existing regulations in the transport, service, and resource industries. Indeed, the bulk of the NAFTA text is the list of each country's various reservations that exempt certain regulations. As a result, a number of existing investment regulations were left intact. At the same time, those investment regulations that did remain and the cultural exemption were clearly going to be the target of future US efforts to remove them in negotiations, as the annual report of the USTR on trade and investment barriers has repeatedly indicated (USTR, 1997).

Because of Liberal Party history of opposition to NAFTA, until its faults were supposedly repaired by the side agreements on the environment and labour, and the extensive coverage NAFTA already provided investors, its investment provisions were regarded by the Liberal government and the Canadian negotiators as the bottom line for Canada at the OECD. NAFTA was often referred to by Canadian negotiators as 'state of the art' and frequently provided the basis of proposed Canadian wording on various aspects of the MAI during the negotiations. Other members' proposals were similarly evaluated in terms of how close they were to NAFTA investment provisions.

The view of the MAI as a replication of NAFTA also shaped attitudes about the process of domestic consultation and how the government portrayed the MAI. In one CBC radio interview the Minister of International Trade dismissed concerns over a loss of sovereignty by pointing out that Canada was merely seeking to multilateralize these investment rules. The MAI was, in fact, 'NAFTA, no more, no less'. This implied there was no need for concern because the MAI would not go beyond NAFTA, and NAFTA itself had proved to be a satisfactory agreement. Not all of the critics of the MAI agreed with either of these propositions.

Thus Canada focused on replicating NAFTA obligations, exemptions, and reservations in an OECD agreement, including the protection of culture. Environmental and labour standards did not appear among Canada's top priorities, partly because these issues raised questions of provincial jurisdiction (House of Commons, 1997a). The goal of replicating NAFTA was tempered, however, by the desire to be supportive of a process of global rule-making that would liberalize investment regulations and capitalize on any potential to open other markets to and provide better protection for Canadian investors abroad. As a consequence, Canada was an enthusiastic supporter of the program to convince non-OECD members to accede to the agreement.

EXPANDING THE DOMESTIC DIALOGUE

The media and NGOs paid little attention either to the decision to negotiate the MAI or to the start of actual negotiations, although both business and labour were well aware of them as a result of their roles in BIAC and TUAC. The views of the sectoral advisory groups, established as part of earlier trade negotiations, were solicited by the minister.[9] Provinces were consulted prior to and briefed after each of the monthly negotiating sessions at the OECD, as had been the practice for earlier trade negotiations. Business was broadly supportive of Canada's involvement in the negotiations as well as of the efforts to build support for investment rules at the WTO (Chamber of Commerce, 1996). Beyond these initiatives, the government did little to provide information on the negotiations to others.

This limited and structured process of consultation is one that had, in the past, characterized trade negotiations, but it was not particularly accessible to other groups with concerns about trade and investment issues that have enjoyed increased access to decision-makers in other policy areas, as Stairs and other authors in this volume have noted. As a consequence, frustrated nationalist, environmental, cultural, and labour organizations, including the Sierra Club, the Canadian Conference for the Arts, and the Council of Canadians formed a loose coalition that mounted opposition to the MAI using the media, the Internet, and local town hall meetings. Groups took out a full-page advertisement in the *Globe and Mail* attacking the MAI two weeks before the June 1997 federal election. Liberal MPs and ministers were caught flat-footed by concerns and questions about the agreement. While the business press was largely dismissive of NGO concerns, continued criticism on the part of these NGOs and the appointment of a new Trade Minister, Sergio Marchi, led to a shift in the government's approach to the question of consultation. Concerned about the charges of a secretive process, a hidden negotiating agenda, and the lack of information flowing to the Liberal caucus, the minister ensured that DFAIT began providing information and briefings to opponents as well as to members of Parliament. Copies of the draft agreement and Canada's preliminary list of reservations were made available to those wanting copies. In September 1997 the minister referred the MAI to the House of Commons Standing Committee on Foreign Affairs and International Trade for study and input prior to a final round of meetings at the OECD, set to start in January 1998. Despite the short amount of time provided to the Subcommittee on International Trade, Trade Disputes, and Investment, its hearings over a three-week period in November 1997 provided opponents with additional opportunities to criticize the agreement. The numerous submissions reflected a level of public concern that impressed committee members.[10]

Opponents raised concerns about the sweeping nature of the agreement and scepticism as to how committed the government is to walking away from the deal, should it be unable to achieve the reservations on existing regulations that it is claiming. Questions were raised about environmental issues and the experience of NAFTA and the WTO. In the view of environmental NGOs, experience has shown how ineffective environmental provisions of existing agreements are proving to be when subjected to interpretation by panels dealing with dispute resolution (Environmental Law Association, 1997). Dispute resolution processes were criticized by these groups for their lack of transparency and the inability of affected third parties to be heard.

A number of lawyers raised concerns about the wording in the section of the MAI dealing with investor protection, which requires compensation for expropriation of assets or 'any measure having equivalent effect' (OECD, 1997b: 50) and is similar to the wording of the NAFTA section on expropriation. Since US court decisions have enlarged the definition of what constitutes expropriation, environmental organizations, in particular, fear that government changes to environmental regulations could become the basis for enormous compensatory claims on the part of foreign investors claiming that such regulations constitute expropriation. The case lodged by the Ethyl Corporation against the Canadian government under the investment chapter of NAFTA has been particularly alarming.[11]

Environmental groups fear that the Canadian government, which is already only weakly committed to strengthening environmental regulation, will find a convenient excuse not to legislate based on NAFTA and the MAI (Environmental Law Association, 1997). The commitments on both the environment and labour standards in the MAI have been criticized as too weak and lacking in any effective enforcement provisions, a concern in the event that non-OECD countries accede to the agreement. The Council of Canadians (Barlow and Clarke, 1997) and the Canadian Labour Congress (CLC, 1997), as they did in the NAFTA debate, have also raised, the broader concern about the potential of foreign investment in health care and other publicly funded and administered services in Canada and the inadequacy of reservations in this area. Finally, cultural organizations criticized the wording of the French cultural exemption, which Canada supports, as inadequate. Virtually all of the opponents of the agreement raised concerns about the process by which the agreement was negotiated and how Canada's negotiating mandate was developed, and called for broader consultations prior to concluding the agreement, a concern that several recommendations (3–5) in the final report of the subcommittee echoed (House of Commons, 1997b).

The hearings also raised questions about the extent to which provinces would be bound by the agreement and how effective provincial consultations had been. This concern was reinforced by the appearance of representatives of the government of British Columbia, who called for Canada's withdrawal from the negotiations. So far Canada has not indicated at the negotiations whether provincial measures would be covered. This is under discussion with the provinces and would also depend on the nature of the final deal (House of Commons, 1997a).

Thus, the government's answer to critics that the MAI would merely replicate NAFTA was of little comfort since they see NAFTA as flawed and are reluctant to see it extended to other countries. The assumption that this agreement could be dealt with as if it were merely a modest extension of NAFTA and that limited consultation with a few economic stakeholders would suffice also proved wrong. The government, in response, expanded the dialogue.

THE IMPACT OF THE MAI

At this stage it is not possible, for several reasons, to give a definitive answer as to what the impact of the MAI will ultimately be on Canada. Firstly, the final deal has not yet been concluded and the exemptions and reservations will be critical to defining the scope of the agreement and the extent to which it replicates or goes beyond NAFTA. Secondly, many of the arguments about impact are based on speculation about how various parts of the agreement will be interpreted in the event of disputes. The Canadian government has not always been able to predict what WTO panels will find regarding Canadian policies, as a number of disputes have shown.

However, we can speculate that if Canada does achieve the reservations it has lodged, along with the appropriate reservations to protect Canadian culture (since it is unlikely at this stage to see US acceptance of the general cultural exemption proposed by France), it would be hard to argue, barring future troublesome interpretations of the expropriation provisions, that it would significantly alter the current situation under NAFTA. Whether the MAI provides new and sufficient protection to Canadian firms abroad depends more on which non-OECD states accede to the agreement and under what conditions. Many of the host countries already receiving a lot of FDI have no need to accede to the agreement to attract more.[12] Clearly, the interest of some large Latin American countries in the agreement, such as Argentina and Brazil, may signal their willingness to accede. Chile, however, is already covered by a bilateral trade agreement with Canada that also includes investment.

On the other hand, if Canada failed to achieve its goals regarding reservations and were to accede to the agreement anyway, it would put sectoral investment regulations in a number of areas in jeopardy as a result of the national treatment obligation. Further limits would also be placed on the performance requirements that could be imposed on investors. Even with the exemptions Canada has requested, if exempted sectors were still covered by the commitments to standstill and rollback it might lead to the freezing of existing regulations so that only change in the direction of liberalization is permitted, or to progressive pressure to remove existing measures that contravene the agreement.

Despite the minister's statements that signing the MAI will increase investment in Canada, it is doubtful that the agreement will have a dramatic effect on investment flows, either inward or outward. Economic conditions, business opportunities, and a host of other factors shape these kinds of business decisions. What may be more critical for Canadian negotiators is how the outcome of the MAI will affect efforts to move investment forward on the future agenda for WTO negotiations. As this chapter and that of Wolfe and Curtis indicate, Canada views a stronger, more institutionalized WTO as playing the pivotal role in the development and enforcement of trade and investment rules. Building an effective WTO is a key policy objective. A successful MAI negotiation could both build momentum at the WTO and perhaps serve as a model agreement, or at least a basis, for a future agreement there. If Canada is able to once again secure a cultural exemption in the MAI, whether general or country-specific, it will have strengthened the claim that culture requires special measures outside the normal trade and investment disciplines of national treatment. On the other hand, should negotiations fail, it could set back the effort to move forward on investment at the WTO. A failure of the like-minded members of the OECD to agree would fuel the arguments of sceptics at the WTO who claim the time is not right to deal with investment. One could argue, however, that there is little real downside for Canada, in terms of investors, should the MAI fail. After all, over half of Canada's investment, both inward and outward, is covered by NAFTA. An agreement is already in place with Chile and bilateral foreign investment protection agreements have been signed with 23 countries, with many more in the negotiation stage.

CONCLUSION

While the MAI draft agreement may not be the Charter of Rights for multinational corporations that the critics claim, neither is it, as this case study indicates, just a routine extension of NAFTA investment rules to a few more countries. The agreement highlights the Canadian government view of investment rules as part of the commitment to multilateralism. Despite Canada's desire for global investment rules, however, it did not take a leadership role on this issue at the OECD, but rather at the WTO. While the US championed negotiations at the OECD to maximize the likelihood of liberalization, Canada and the EU continued to push for inclusion of investment on the WTO agenda. Having concurred with the initiation of negotiations at the OECD, Canada's position was largely defined by the path-breaking Chapter 11 of NAFTA and concerns about the political fallout should it fail to defend the limited regulations remaining in sensitive sectors such as culture.

Canadian business organizations have largely supported the MAI and the goals of multinational capital to obtain enhanced investor mobility through greater liberalization of investment regulation, greater protection of investments, and access to dispute resolution mechanisms (Chamber of Commerce, 1996). Yet the negotiations are still very much an interstate process and have proved slow and difficult, largely because of national policy differences. In Canada's case, the political sensitivity of investment issues, a result of the historical role of US capital in Canada, complicated matters. A growing public concern about the implications of capital mobility is also reflected in the opposition to the agreement, which provided an opportunity for those concerns to find a focus and allowed opponents to revisit many of the issues and express their dissatisfactions with NAFTA. Despite ongoing negotiations in various service sectors at the WTO and Canada's continued investment efforts there, NGOs seized upon the MAI as a vehicle to channel much of what has been labelled by the OECD Secretary-General and others as a 'globalization backlash'. Citizens have been asked to bear many of the costs of adjustment to a changing global economy even as state assistance to do so is cut back. At the same time, because citizens and workers are immobile, while capital is increasingly free to move, there are concerns about issues like the environment and labour standards as governments continue to compete to attract new, and retain existing, investment. As a consequence the MAI, much like NAFTA, has provided another opportunity for those concerned about the impact of globalization to raise these issues in a dramatic way, charging that the agreement will tie the hands of the Canadian state.

The MAI case has also raised new issues about the role of citizens in a democracy in a context of global economic rule-making and has pointed to the need to forge a more inclusive dialogue within Canada if those rules increasingly affect major areas of domestic policy. At the global level, within organizations such as the OECD and the WTO, a dialogue with a broader range of interests than just those of multinational capital will also be necessary if the investment rules that states write are to be balanced. Both processes are critical if Canadians are to remain supportive of their government playing a role in the process to build an effective set of rules for the global economy.

NOTES

1. The Council of Canadians and Tony Clarke of the Polaris Institute have described the MAI in these terms. See Barlow and Clarke (1997), especially Chapter Two. The view that this agreement confers rights on foreign investors that supersede those of citizens or domestic firms was also echoed in many of the submissions made to the House of Commons Subcommittee on International Trade, Trade Disputes, and Investment, such as that of the Sierra Club, 18 Nov. 1997.
2. National treatment refers to the obligation to treat foreign investors no less favourably than domestic investors, in other words, a commitment not to discriminate based on the nationality of ownership or control of a company. In the mid-1970s the operation of the Foreign Investment Review Agency, as well as numerous tax and other regulations, did not conform with such an obligation and Canada did not want the national treatment instrument to be a part of the Declaration on Multinational Enterprises. When OECD members decided that it would be, Canada exempted itself from that obligation.
3. This account of the origins of the MAI negotiations and Canada's views is based on a review of documents covering the 1991–5 period obtained under the Access to Information Act and on interviews with Canadian negotiators in June 1996.
4. The seminars were held in Divonne, a suburb of Geneva, in 1995 and the fall of 1996 and were organized by UNCTAD with the support of Canada, the EU, and Brazil. They involved the participation of various firms (such as IBM Canada) and organizations (such as the WTO).
5. The following analysis is based on interviews conducted in May 1996 and February-April 1997 with investment negotiators in the Canadian Departments of Foreign Affairs and International Trade and Industry Canada and on documents regarding the OECD negotiations obtained under the Canadian Access to Information Act in February 1997. Additional interviews with non-Canadian

negotiators and members of the OECD secretariat, BIAC, and TUAC were conducted in Paris in April 1997 and in London, November 1997.

6. Such a clause is inserted in trade agreements involving the EU and involves permitting members of a regional economic organization such as the EU to offer more favourable treatment to each other in order to further integrate or harmonize regulations. In essence it does permit some discrimination in favour of greater liberalization of economic rules within the region (OECD, 1997c: 161).

7. The clause is worded: 'Nothing in this agreement shall be construed to prevent any Contracting Party to take any measures to regulate investment of foreign companies and the conditions of activity of these companies, in the framework of policies designed to preserve and promote cultural and linguistic diversity' (OECD, 1997c: 168).

8. Based on interviews with British negotiators in November 1997.

9. As part of the consultations leading up to the Free Trade Agreement of 1987 an International Trade Advisory Committee and 15 Sectoral Advisory Groups on International Trade covering various industrial sectors, such as the auto and energy industries, were appointed after consultations with industry associations and provinces. The creation of these groups is described in Doern and Tomlin (1991: ch. 5).

10. Hearings were held 5–27 Nov. 1997 in Ottawa. Some 35 organizations and individuals appeared before the subcommittee; approximately 100 statements were submitted.

11. The case involves a $350 million claim against the government of Canada under the investment chapter of NAFTA because of changes to regulations regarding the importing and interprovincial shipment of MMT, a gasoline additive, and has been cited repeatedly by environmental critics of the MAI. The case raises concerns not only about the interpretation of wording in Chapter 11, but also about what these groups regard as the secretive and undemocratic process by which such disputes are addressed. See the Sierra Club of Canada's presentation to the Subcommittee on Trade, Trade Disputes, and Investment, 18 November 1997, especially page 9.

12. This observation was made by a member of DAFFE in the secretariat at the OECD during an interview in April 1997.

REFERENCES

Barlow, Maude, and Tony Clarke. 1997. *The MAI: The Multilateral Agreement on Investment and the Threat to Canadian Sovereignty*. Toronto: Stoddart.

BIAC. 1996. *The Multilateral Agreement on Investment and the OECD Guidelines: Environment, Labour and Consumer Matters*. Paris.

BIAC. 1997. 'Letter to Mr. Franz Engering', 24 Mar.

Bridge, Charles. 1997. 'The OECD Guidelines and the MAI', presented at MAI briefing for Non-OECD Countries, OECD: 17 Sept.

Business Council on National Issues. 1997. *Canada, Investment and the Multilateral Agreement on Investment*. Statement to the House of Commons Subcommittee on International Trade, Trade Disputes, and Investment, 25 Nov.

Canada. 1992. *North American Free Trade Agreement*. Ottawa: Supply and Services.

Canadian Chamber of Commerce. 1996. *A Multilateral Agreement on Investment: Views of the Canadian Chamber of Commerce.*

Doern, G. Bruce, and Brian W. Tomlin. 1991. *Faith and Fear: The Free Trade Story.* Toronto: Stoddart.

Environmental Law Association. 1997. *The Multilateral Agreement on Investment and the Environment: Context and Concerns.* Prepared for the House of Commons Subcommittee on International Trade, Trade Disputes, and Investment, 24 Nov.

Friedman, Alan. 1997. 'OECD Chief, Bedeviled by Budget Woes, Tries to Shift Focus', *International Herald Tribune,* 3 Apr.

Hart, Michael. 1997. 'Canada in the Global Economy: Where Do We Stand?, in Maureen A. Molot, Fen Osler Hampson and Martin Rudner, eds, *Canada Among Nations 1997: Asia-Pacific Face-Off.* Ottawa: Carleton University Press.

House of Commons. 1997a. Subcommittee on International Trade, Trade Disputes, and Investment. *Proceedings-Evidence,* Statement of Bill Dymond, Chief Negotiator of the MAI, DFAIT. Ottawa: Public Works and Government Services Canada, 5 Nov.

————. 1997b. *Canada and the MAI, First Report of the Subcommittee on International Trade, Trade Disputes and Investment of the Standing Committee on Foreign Affairs and International Trade.* Ottawa: Public Works and Government Services Canada, 11 Dec.

Katz, Abraham. 1997. 'Letter to the US Administration: USCIB Concerns with Environmental Provisions of the MAI', 11 July.

Marchi, Sergio. 1997. 'Notes for an Address by the Hon. Sergio Marchi, Minister of International Trade, to the Standing Committee on Foreign Affairs and International Trade "The Multilateral Agreement on Investment"', Ottawa, 4 Nov.

OECD. 1995. *Meeting of the OECD Council at Ministerial Level, 24 May,* and *A Multilateral Agreement on Investment Report by the Committee on International Investment and Multinational Enterprise and the Committee on Capital Movements and Invisibles Transactions.* Paris.

————. 1996. *Labour Standards in the Global Trade and Investment System.* Nov.

————. 1997a. *Canada: Revised Draft Reservations.* 18 Nov.

————. 1997b. *Foreign Direct Investment and the Environment: An Overview of the Literature.* Paris.

————. 1997c. MAI Draft Consolidated Text and Commentary, Oct.

————. 1997d. *Meeting of the Council at the Ministerial Level, Paris, 26–27 May, Communiqué.*

————. 1997e. 'Second Workshop on Multilateral Rules on Investment, Brasilia, Brazil, 4–5 February'. Paris: OECD Press Release, 3 Feb.

Office of the United States Trade Representative. 1997. *National Trade Estimates Report on Foreign Trade Barriers, 1997.* Washington, Mar.

Sierra Club of Canada. 1997. *Presentation to the Standing Committee on Foreign Affairs and International Trade, Subcommittee on Trade, Trade Disputes, and Investment,* 18 Nov., app.1, Joint Statement on the MAI.

Smythe, Elizabeth. 1995. 'Multilateralism or Bilateralism in the Negotiation of Trade-Related Investment Measures in the Uruguay Round', *Canadian-American Public Policy* (Dec).

————. 1996. 'Investment Policy', in G. Bruce Doern, Leslie Pal, and Brian W. Tomlin, eds, *Border Crossings: The Internationalization of Canadian Public Policy*. Toronto: Oxford University Press.

————. 1997. 'Your Place or Mine? States, International Organizations and the Negotiation of Investment Rules: The OECD versus the WTO', paper presented at the annual meeting of the International Studies Association, Toronto, Mar.

TUAC. 1997a. 'The Multilateral Agreement on Investment: The Treatment of Labour Issues', Briefing Notes for Affiliates, Feb.

————. 1997b. *Working Group on Global Trade and Investment: Up-date on Developments in the MAI*. 27 Mar.

UNCTAD. 1996. 'Report of the Second Seminar on "Foreign Direct Investment in the Globalizing World Economy"', Divonne, Switzerland, 12 Feb.

————. 1997. *World Investment Report 1996*. New York: UN.

United States. 1991. 'New OECD Investment Instrument', 6 Dec.

White, Robert. 1997. Letter to the Hon. Arthur C. Eggleton, 10 Apr.

13

Environment Policy: The Rio Summit Five Years Later

LINDA C. REIF

International initiatives to protect the environment appeared to be gaining new momentum at the time of the 1992 United Nations Conference on Environment and Development held in Rio de Janeiro. In fact, there had been a steady increase in the number and scale of international commitments on the environment in the two to three decades prior to the Rio summit. Canada was a full participant in bilateral and multilateral fora, particularly in the years leading up to the Rio summit, and became a party to most of the major multilateral treaties relating to the environment. In the context of the Canada-US relationship, bilateral regimes covering boundary waters (including the Great Lakes water quality), air quality, movement of hazardous wastes, and some migratory species had been established by 1992.

The Canadian government placed considerable importance on the Rio summit and its outcome. Two treaties were signed—the

United Nations Framework Convention on Climate Change and the Convention on Biological Diversity.[1] Canada became a contracting party to each agreement. In addition, non-binding instruments were adopted, indicative of the consensus of the international community on the principles and guidelines contained therein. These were the Rio Declaration on Environment and Development, the massive Agenda 21 (a detailed plan of action for governments on methods of achieving sustainable development in all sectors of activity), and a Statement of Principles on Forests.[2] In addition, a Commission on Sustainable Development (CSD) was established as a subsidiary UN body to monitor and report on the implementation of the Rio summit agreements and the sustainable development initiatives of states.

Although sustainable development was a thread running throughout the Rio summit agreements, both the areas of concern and the mixed results reflected the increasing impact of the economic interests of state and civil society actors. For example, the development concerns of South countries and industrial interests (e.g., forestry, energy) played roles in shaping the outcome of the summit. The Rio summit also notified the international community of areas of the environment where more protection was needed, or where no international regulation existed at all.

Thus, the Rio summit produced a long action agenda for the participating states, both for the implementation of international commitments made at the conference and for the development of new policy and normative frameworks. The environmental policies of the government of Canada over the last five years have been influenced considerably by the Rio summit agenda, and 1997 was no exception in this respect. This chapter will examine developments in Canadian foreign policy on the environment during 1997. A review of these events suggests that, although Canada remains committed to the development and implementation of international norms on environmental protection, its commitments are being negatively affected by economic pressures originating either in the government itself or from civil society actors. This is due, in part, to the fact that environmental protection issues are becoming increasingly intertwined with socio-economic concerns—the protection of the habitat of wildlife species, fisheries concerns, and the control of greenhouse gases emitted by industry and vehicles are examples of these complex issue-areas. Further, increasing numbers of non-state actors and stakeholders are voicing their concerns and are trying to influence the policy formation and implementation processes. Thus, the formulation of foreign policy on the environment has become more complicated, and it must cover a large number of sectors. For all these reasons, the Canadian government is required to engage in dialogue with a broad range of players, both state and non-state entities, across an expanding spectrum of issue-areas relating to the environment. The leadership position of Canada has also been detrimentally affected by these, and other, factors.

Canadian foreign policy developments on the environment in selected sectors will be analysed: the five-year review of the Rio summit, the atmosphere and oceans, the Pacific Salmon Treaty dispute with the United States, protection of wild species and biological diversity, and the intersection of international trade and environmental protection. The chapter ends with some concluding thoughts on Canadian international environmental policy in 1997.

THE 1997 UN GENERAL ASSEMBLY REVIEW OF THE IMPLEMENTATION OF AGENDA 21

On 23–7 June 1997, a special session of the UN General Assembly was held to commemorate the fifth anniversary of the Rio summit and to review the implementation of the Rio summit Agenda 21 (called the 'Earth Summit + 5'). It was attended by 53 heads of state or government, ministers, and other delegates. Its objectives were to evaluate the progress of governments, international organizations, and civil society in implementing the commitments in the comprehensive Agenda 21 and to focus on redefined priority action areas. At the session, Prime Minister Chrétien presented the Canadian position and its priorities.[3] Sustainable forest management, proposals for a forest treaty, implementation of the Convention on Biological Diversity, international action on toxic chemicals, and improving the condition of the oceans were highlighted as some of the priority areas for Canada. However, in a defining moment, the Prime Minister recognized that a number of Rio initiatives had not been realized, admitted that Canada would not meet the Climate Change Convention targets for stabilizing greenhouse gas emissions, and said nothing on any specific greenhouse gas reduction commitments for Canada.

Admittedly, the nations participating in the 1992 summit had set out an ambitious, some would say unrealistic, agenda for action. In the interim period, a few multilateral treaties have been adopted, such as the 1994 Convention to Combat Desertification and the 1995 Agreement on Straddling Fish Stocks and Highly Migratory Fish Stocks.[4] International negotiations or consultations are also proceeding in a number of other areas. Further, various nations, including Canada, have been building domestic policy and legal frameworks to promote sustainable development.

The leaders were unable to agree on a declaration at the end of the session and could only reach consensus on a Statement of Commitment.[5] The 1997 General Assembly special session also resulted in a lengthy Program for the Further Implementation of Agenda 21. In the Statement of Commitment, the leaders reaffirmed all the principles in the Rio Declaration and the Statement of Principles on Forests. Agenda 21 was reaffirmed as 'the fundamental programme of action for achieving sustainable development'.[6] However, the leaders acknowledged that, despite some positive achievements, both the sustainable development movement and the state of the world environment had deteriorated since the 1992 Rio summit. At best, all the leaders could do was to commit to accelerating the implementation of Agenda 21.

The 1997 special session was a formality that confirmed what many commentators were already stating: in the five years following the Rio summit there have been a few additional legal developments, but all of these commitments have not had much apparent positive effect on the general state of the environment. Weaker political support for environmental protection and budgetary cutbacks appear to be the main causes of the lack of progress inside many states. The special session passed without much fanfare, symbolic of the lower profile given to the environment in foreign policy during the past few years, both in Canada and in other countries.

FROM THE ATMOSPHERE TO THE OCEANS

Industrial and human activity over the twentieth century has forced greater pressures on the oceans, the atmosphere surrounding the planet, the air spaces, and international watercourses. As pollutants and damaging activities often cross territorial borders or find their way into the oceans and atmosphere beyond the jurisdiction of states, international co-operation to protect these spaces has slowly developed.

Transboundary air pollution, including acid rain, has been a problem for geographically adjacent industrialized states for decades.

Because of its location and prevailing wind patterns, Canada has been the recipient of transboundary air pollution from industrial activities in the US. Regional co-operation has evolved in Europe and North America. In Europe, the United Nations Economic Commission for Europe (UNECE) sponsored the adoption of the Convention on Long-Range Transboundary Air Pollution (LRTAP Convention), followed by a series of protocols that have imposed emission reduction commitments on sulphur dioxide, nitrogen oxide, and volatile organic compounds. Canada has become a party to these European regional agreements; also, Canada and the US were able to reach a bilateral agreement on air quality in 1991.

Regulating toxic chemicals—found in the atmosphere and sea, or traded across state boundaries—has become a Canadian foreign policy priority. In particular, persistent organic pollutants (POPs), including polychlorinated biphenyls (PCBs), are seen as a particular problem even for Canada, which has a relatively strong domestic regulatory system. For example, some of the Arctic population are experiencing the bodily effects of PCBs, even though they have never been used in the North, because these chemicals are drifting into the Arctic from sources in other parts of the world through the atmosphere and water. Controlling the use of these chemicals is being discussed in various regional fora such as the Arctic Council, the North American Commission for Environmental Co-operation (created by the North American Free Trade Agreement's side agreement on environmental co-operation), and the UNECE. In 1997, negotiations were conducted under the auspices of the UNECE on a protocol to the LRTAP Convention to control POPs. Also, the Intergovernmental Forum on Chemical Safety (IFCS) met in Ottawa in February 1997 and agreed, *inter alia*, on the establishment of an Ad Hoc Working Group on POPs to work towards starting negotiations on a multilateral treaty to limit their harmful effects on human health and the environment.[7] At the same meeting, the Canadian government was elected president of the IFCS for a three-year period. In February 1997, the Governing Council of the United Nations Environment Program (UNEP) decided to convene an intergovernmental negotiating committee to draft a treaty controlling POPs, taking into account the conclusions and recommendations of the IFCS Working Group and the UNECE work.

At higher levels in the atmosphere, the deterioration of the stratospheric ozone layer has been observed since the 1970s. The 'dread factor' comprising the fear of skin cancer and other human health

problems, coupled with the relatively small size of the industries producing ozone-depleting substances, enabled an international consensus to coalesce in the late 1980s on a treaty regime. The Vienna
Convention and the Montreal Protocol on Substances that Deplete
the Ozone Layer have imposed production and consumption phase-
outs on a growing number of ozone-depleting chemicals.[8] Canada
was a leading player in the establishment of this treaty regime, and
starting on 9 September 1997, the tenth anniversary conference of the
Montreal Protocol was held in Montreal. Measures to accelerate the
phase-out of the production and consumption of methyl bromide
were agreed on, and measures to control smuggling of banned substances were addressed through the creation of a licensing system.
Consistent with its early leadership position on the regulation of
ozone-depleting substances, the Canadian government proposed an
acceleration of the phase-out of methyl bromide that was more stringent than the plan actually agreed on at the conference.[9] Compared
to the climate change sector, the proposal was of relatively low cost
to Canada in both industry and political terms.

In contrast, the regulation of greenhouse gases that are collecting
in the atmosphere, and potentially contributing to global warming,
has proved to be more problematic. The Rio summit produced the
Framework Convention on Climate Change, which contained provisions on reporting and research and directed developed nations to
reduce greenhouse gas emissions to 1990 levels by 2000. The major
greenhouse gas is carbon dioxide, which is emitted from vehicles,
industry (especially the energy industry), and other commercial activities. Huge sectors of business and civil society will be affected by
binding commitments, and many of these actors do not have the
same fear of the consequences of climate change as was the case
with deterioration of the ozone layer. Thus, there are strong economic pressures militating against further action, especially in Canada
and the US. The parties to the Climate Change Convention scheduled
a meeting in Kyoto in December 1997 and were successful in reaching agreement on developed nation commitments on greenhouse
gas emissions. Paul Halucha explores the dynamics of the climate
change convention process in Chapter 14 in this volume on the Kyoto
Protocol on Climate Change.

On general oceans issues, the Canadian foreign policy attitude in
1997 was one of caution, looking to the implementation of international agreements. The 1982 UN Convention on the Law of the Sea

finally entered into force in November 1994. Canada has signed the Convention, but still has not ratified it. The delay is essentially based on the desire of the Canadian government not to fall afoul of the international law in this area, specifically the Law of the Sea Convention and the Agreement on Straddling Fish Stocks and Highly Migratory Fish Stocks. The latter treaty is not yet in force because the required number of state ratifications has not been reached. The 1995 dispute between Canada and the European Union over the high-seas seizure of the Spanish vessel *Estai* while fishing Greenland halibut is tied in with the situation.[10] The Straddling Fish Stocks Agreement attempts to conserve and manage these fish species by creating a co-operative relationship between coastal states and those whose ships are fishing on the high seas. Accordingly, the Canadian government is gradually changing federal law to comply with both treaties. The new Oceans Act entered into force on 31 January 1997, establishing in law Canada's maritime boundaries, such as the 200-nautical-mile exclusive economic zone (EEZ), and providing for an oceans management strategy based on sustainable development and the precautionary approach, which are two principles also found in the Rio Declaration on Environment and Development.[11] In addition, new fisheries legislation to implement Canada's nascent legal obligations under the Straddling Fish Stocks Agreement was introduced in Parliament in late 1997. Thus, the year saw progress by Canada towards the realization of its policies and international commitments on law of the sea matters.

THE PACIFIC SALMON SAGA

The Pacific salmon dispute was ongoing between Canada and the US during 1997. The struggle to agree on bilateral quotas for the annual catch of Pacific salmon illustrates the contemporary tension between conserving natural resources and promoting economic interests. It also exemplifies the complexity of modern environmental issues that involve a variety of state and civil society actors. The dispute involves governments at the national and subnational levels—both federal governments, the British Columbia government, and the US state governments of Alaska, Washington, and Oregon—with the subnational units either at odds with each other or with the federal unit in which they are located. In addition, First Nations fishers and a variety of civil society actors, ranging from environmentalists to commercial and sport fishers, are implicated and have divergent interests.

The 1985 Pacific Salmon Treaty between Canada and the US stands at the heart of this dispute.[12] It is accompanied by a Memorandum of Understanding (MOU) between the two nations, an arrangement not considered to be legally binding under international law that provides further interpretation of one of the legal principles in the treaty. The treaty is supposed to act as the vehicle for the allocation of the salmon caught by each nation's fishers. Salmon start their life in the rivers of one country, swim to the ocean, and then years later return to the rivers to spawn and die; most of the fish are caught in the ocean with the result that US fishers sometimes catch Canadian-origin salmon and vice versa.

The Pacific salmon dispute between the two countries, which was in the headlines for so much of 1997, illustrates that the treaty is poorly drafted and has a weak mechanism for allocation-setting. The dispute centres on the interpretation of the rather vague legal principles in Article III, which contains the obligations of each nation. These are stated to be to (a) prevent overfishing and to provide for optimum production, and (b) provide for each nation to receive benefits equivalent to the production of salmon originating in its waters.[13] The non-binding MOU provides further details on this latter provision, stating that the principal goals of the treaty are 'to enable both countries, through better conservation and enhancement, to increase production of salmon and to ensure that the benefits resulting from each country's efforts accrue to that country', and it also looks to longer-term erasure of inequities if one country is obtaining substantially greater benefits than those provided from its rivers.[14] The Canadian government takes the position that the treaty should be interpreted as containing two principles: conservation and equity.[15] The US takes a markedly different position on the interpretation of the treaty's obligations, that the various 'treaty elements must be implemented together and that one does not take precedence over others'.[16]

The flawed treaty mechanism for management of the annual salmon catch led to a breakdown in co-operation in 1992, although the concept of equitable sharing had never been properly established and Canadian data indicate that US fishers have caught more salmon than Canadians from the outset.[17] In 1993, intergovernmental negotiations commenced to try to reach agreement on management of the catch. During 1995 and 1996, Canada and the US unsuccessfully attempted to use international mediation to resolve the dispute over the interpretation and implementation of the treaty. In the summer of 1996, the US state governors suggested a new procedure for settling the bilateral fisheries problem—asking the affected private stakeholders in both countries to come up with a method of determining the allocations.[18] In February 1997, the two federal governments agreed to use intergovernmental negotiations that included 'direct participation' by stakeholders from the affected regions who would make recommendations to the governments.[19] Although the stakeholder meetings progressed, they did not come to a final agreement. The Canadian and US government positions remained polarized, dialogue between the chief negotiators collapsed on 20 May 1997 when the US negotiators stated that they could not make any proposals on specific catch reductions, and bilateral negotiations terminated on 20 June 1997 without any resolution. On 23 June 1997, the Canadian government made a final proposal on implementation of the treaty, including conservation elements.[20] It was rejected by the US government, which did not want to move from its negotiating position. On 26 June 1997, the Canadian government attempted to lift the dispute out of the political arena by asking that the matter be resolved through international arbitration, which would result in a decision legally binding on both parties.[21] Again, the US government rejected the proposal, and the Canadian government gave up calling for arbitration in the face of US intransigence on this point.

On 23 July 1997, the two governments agreed to return to the stakeholder process, as detailed in a Canada-US Joint Statement on Pacific Salmon.[22] In addition, they turned to another diplomatic method of dispute settlement in appointing an ad hoc commission of two eminent persons, one Canadian and one American, to consult with all interested parties to give new life to the stakeholder process and to report and make recommendations to the two governments.[23]

Meanwhile, in the background, other affected actors began responding to the breakdowns in the negotiating process in ways that further irritated the tense situation. Alaskan fishers markedly increased their catch-rate of Canada-bound salmon, and Canadian fishers responded by upping their catches. The British Columbia government openly criticized the Canadian and US governments, and reacted in May 1997 by announcing it would cancel a US lease of a weapons testing ground and in September by bringing a lawsuit against the US government in the US federal courts. British Columbia fishers blockaded a US ferry in Prince Rupert harbour, the Alaska government responded with a lawsuit, and the federal government is suing the British Columbia government over its attempts to cancel the US lease.

In early 1998, the Pacific salmon saga continued. The ad hoc two-person commission issued its report in January 1998, concluding that the stakeholder process is unproductive and calling for the resumption of government-to-government negotiations. The difference of opinion over the implementation of the Pacific Salmon Treaty and the management of the annual salmon catch has been a bilateral foreign policy problem for Canada that has increased in severity over the past five years. Although the dispute focuses on the legal interpretation of the treaty and the weight to be given to the MOU, it is founded on the desire of the two countries to protect the economic positions of their respective fishing industries while attempting to manage the Pacific salmon stocks. Their divergent positions have hindered the dispute resolution process, and events during 1997 highlighted the point that diplomatic methods of conflict resolution are unlikely to meet with success when the disputants are polarized in their views and unwilling to move to compromise positions. The Canadian government was unsuccessful in persuading the US to accept an adjudicative method of conflict resolution, and it had to fall in with the US insistence on using political processes and giving greater influence to local interests. Although the report of the ad hoc commission rejects the stakeholder role for the larger issues, it still calls for retention of the political route for dispute settlement. In this respect, it is a return to the status quo, unless both states can soften their rigid positions, backed up by the political will to do so at the higher levels of government.

PROTECTION OF WILD SPECIES AND BIOLOGICAL DIVERSITY

Although the Pacific Salmon Treaty dispute dominated the news relating to species conservation in 1997, it was only one of a number of active files involving species conservation and broader issues of biological diversity. In 1997, the Canadian government also addressed other issues, including endangered species protection, animal trapping methods, and forestry protection.

One of the treaties signed at the Rio summit was the Convention on Biological Diversity. The Convention is an attempt to conserve biological diversity and ensure the sustainable use of its components through measures such as national strategies and *in situ* conservation. The Biological Diversity Convention is an attempt to preserve species, their habitat, and ecosystems. Canada is a contracting party to the treaty and has the duty to comply with its obligations. Canada's record during 1997 in passing federal endangered species legislation to support its earlier foreign policy initiative was not stellar. An endangered species legislative bill introduced in Parliament in 1996 died when Parliament was dissolved in early 1997, and it had not been reintroduced by the end of the year. In any event, the contents of the bill were soundly criticized by environmentalists, who argued that the proposed legislation did not go far enough in protecting a sufficient number of threatened species and the habitats upon which they depend. The federal-provincial division of powers has played a role in the delay, with the provinces wishing to limit the federal initiative as much as possible out of fear that federal legislation will impinge on provincial jurisdiction and interests.

From another perspective on the protection of wild species, the hunting of animals using leghold traps has been decried by animal welfare activists, especially those located in Europe. The practices of Canadian, Russian, and US trappers came under fire, and the European Union (EU) took up the cause in 1991 by passing a regulation that prohibited the use of jawed leghold traps inside the EU and banned the import of fur and fur products from animals caught by leghold traps not meeting humane standards. The import ban was not activated during intergovernmental negotiations between the EU and the affected states. In July 1997, an Agreement on International Humane Trapping Standards was finalized by Canada, the EU, and Russia. It was signed by Canada and the EU on 15 December 1997, and Russia is expected sign during 1998.[24] This agreement is mainly the result of economic pressure exerted on Canada and Russia. Canada was faced with the threat of trappers (including Aboriginal trappers) and the fur industry losing most of their export markets located in European nations. Domestic stakeholders in Canada have different viewpoints on the agreement. Animal welfare activists and environmentalists are supportive of the initiative, whereas opinions among the trappers and fur industry are mixed. Some trappers are unhappy about the governmental regulation of their activities, including indigenous trappers who see infringements of their Aboriginal rights. Other trappers and industry interests are more pragmatic, taking the position that the deal has helped to preserve the lucrative fur trade.[25]

The agreement covers 19 listed species and is designed to establish standards on humane trapping methods, prohibit the use of traps that are not certified, and maintain trade in fur and fur products between the parties without hindrance. In addition, Canada has agreed that it will prohibit the use of all jaw-type leghold traps for seven species when the treaty enters into force and that conventional steel-jawed leghold traps will be banned for the remaining Canadian listed species.

From an environmental perspective, forests are important sites of biological diversity, they are the habitat of numerous species, and they also act as 'sinks' by drawing carbon dioxide out of the atmosphere. Forests also are the homes of many indigenous peoples and a source of economic wealth for many countries. At Rio, these potentially conflicting uses could not be reconciled in a manner sufficient to produce anything more than the non-binding, and substantively incoherent, Statement of Principles on Forests and a chapter in Agenda 21. Clearly, the interests of states and civil society actors were divergent and further consultations were required, although there was some pessimism concerning the chances of building a consensus. Dialogue continued informally with Canada taking an active role, and in 1995 an Intergovernmental Panel on Forests (IPF) was created by the Commission on Sustainable Development. The IPF mandate was to obtain proposals for furthering the conservation and sustainable development of forests and to submit its final report to the commission in 1997.[26] The final report was submitted to the CSD in April 1997. It contained numerous recommendations for action, but the IPF could not reach agreement on some important points, including trade-related concerns and whether a forests treaty should be negotiated.

At its 1997 Special Session, the UN General Assembly decided to continue the intergovernmental communications on forests through the medium of an Intergovernmental Forum on Forests (IFF) under the auspices of the CSD.[27] Among its tasks, the IFF will facilitate the implementation of its own proposals and address the nature of international mechanisms, including the possibility of a treaty. The establishment of the IFF has been seen by some as the sole positive initiative arising out of the 1997 special session of the General Assembly.[28]

During 1997, the Canadian government made foreign policy statements that one of its objectives in the area of environmental policy is to support the negotiation of a forests treaty to promote sustainable forest management.[29] Again, Canada is faced with conflicting economic and environmental concerns. On the one hand, the Canadian forest products industry (lumber, pulp, paper) is an important element of Canada's export trade. On the other hand, environmentalists and First Nations wish to protect the forests for various reasons. In trying to forge an international consensus, Canada is promoting a policy position that tries to reconcile preservation of the forest environment with protection of industry. The developments at the international level indicate that the process is moving forward, albeit slowly, with Canada fully involved. The concept of a forests treaty, however, remains a contentious one, and it remains to be seen whether the Canadian position will meet with success in the period following 2000 when the IFF will submit its report.

INTERNATIONAL TRADE AND THE ENVIRONMENT

In 1997, the North American Free Trade Agreement (NAFTA) among Canada, the US, and Mexico, plus its companion North American Agreement on Environmental Co-operation (NAAEC), entered the fourth year of operation.[30] Although NAFTA is a free trade agreement, it does contain some provisions that permit government trade controls to be imposed for environmental protection objectives. In contrast, the NAAEC is not directed at government measures relating to international trade; rather, it is designed to improve the domestic environmental laws, and their enforcement, in each of the three states. The side agreements were demanded by President Clinton as a means to assuage the domestic pressures for better environmental and labour protection in order to obtain approval of NAFTA in Congress. The NAAEC comprises various methods for attaining its objectives, and the NAAEC secretariat (headquartered in Montreal) has been active in monitoring and reporting.

The NAAEC also includes provisions permitting non-governmental organizations (NGOs) and individuals to make submissions that a government is failing to enforce effectively its environmental law. The process is not a particularly strong weapon for civil society actors; at most, there may be the preparation of a factual report that can then be used to pressure the government to make changes to comply with the law. Between 1995 and 1997, 11 submissions that the member states have not been enforcing their environmental laws effectively were made by NGOs, with five of these initiated during 1997. Of these five, four submissions were made by Canadian NGOs—against the federal government in three cases, and the Quebec government in one.[31] However, it was only on 24 October 1997 that the first factual record was issued under the NAAEC—the Final Factual Record on the Cruise Ship Pier Project in Cozumel, Mexico, based on a submission made against the Mexican government by a Mexican NGO.[32] The NAAEC and its submission mechanism have marked a policy change among all three NAFTA states to attempt to strengthen environmental laws through transnational co-operation and to permit civil society actors to make claims of non-compliance.

In December 1994, during the Miami Summit of the Americas, the three NAFTA states invited Chile to begin negotiations to accede to the NAFTA. Negotiations commenced, but began to break down in late 1995 when the US President failed to get fast-track negotiating authority from Congress in order to protect the final agreement from congressional interference. By the time the NAFTA accession talks sputtered out, Canadian foreign policy orientation was changing to favour seeking regional trade ties in Latin America. In December 1995, Canada and Chile agreed to negotiate an interim free trade agreement with the idea that it would be eventually incorporated into NAFTA. The Canada-Chile Free Trade Agreement was signed on 5 December 1996 and entered into force on 5 July 1997.[33] It is modelled generally on NAFTA, but with some differences to conform to the Canada-Chile trade and investment relationship. There are also side agreements similar to those accompanying NAFTA, on environmental and labour protection.

The Canada-Chile FTA deals primarily with freeing trade and investment between the two countries by eliminating tariffs on goods and reducing other non-tariff barriers. Based on the NAFTA template, there are very similar provisions in the Canada-Chile FTA that attempt to protect legitimate government measures to protect the environment.

The Canada-Chile Agreement on Environmental Co-operation (CCAEC) was finalized on 6 February 1997 and also entered into force on 5 July 1997.[34] Like the NAAEC, the CCAEC attempts to protect the environment in Canada and Chile through the improvement of the substance and enforcement of their domestic environmental laws. As with the NAAEC, the general commitments of each state include ensuring that domestic laws provide for high levels of environmental protection, effectively enforcing environmental laws, and ensuring that persons have appropriate access to procedurally fair judicial or administrative remedies for the enforcement of these laws. Similarly, an individual or NGO can make a submission to the institutional mechanism, arguing that a state party is failing to enforce effectively its environmental law, and if deemed warranted a factual record will be prepared.

CONCLUDING THOUGHTS

A review of recent Canadian foreign policy on the environment indicates that Canada remains fully committed to participation in the international environmental norm-setting process and the institutional co-operation that this entails. Indeed, the Canadian government is engaged in international dialogue across the broad spectrum of environmental concerns that are currently the subject of intergovernmental consultation and negotiation. In a few specific sectors the Canadian government has attempted to take a leadership role in forging or strengthening international normative frameworks; protection of the ozone layer and forests are two examples. Yet, for the most part, Canada has not stood out as a leader in foreign policy formation on international environmental protection. The sheer number of sectors involved, the complexity of policy formation, the relatively low priority given to environmental matters by the government, and the increasing financial implications of further environmental regulation are some of the factors acting to keep Canada's leadership profile low in environmental foreign policy.

Further, as issues of environmental protection have become increasingly interconnected with economic and social interests, the processes of international dialogue, norm creation, and norm implementation are becoming more difficult and drawn out. This phenomenon can be seen both in the multilateral sphere, as evidenced by the results of the 1997 Special Session of the General Assembly, and specifically in relation to the Canadian foreign policy process.

The formation, content, and implementation of Canada's international commitments on environmental protection are, in the majority of sectors, being influenced by the economic interests of both government and civil society actors, the latter primarily in the commercial and industrial sectors. For example, the fear of loss of international markets in the fur industry, controls on greenhouse gas emissions with the resultant costs for business and industry, and regulation of land spaces to protect endangered species have influenced the formation of Canada's policy and legal responses. In contraposition, support for environmental protection has come from diverse government and civil society actors, either for altruistic environmental and protective reasons or because economic interests are indirectly supported, such as in the Pacific salmon dispute and the leghold trap agreement. The range of competing interests, found in both the international and domestic spheres, has complicated Canadian foreign policy formation and execution in both bilateral and multilateral fora. In addition, as the Pacific salmon dispute has illustrated, bilateral conflict surrounding conservation matters can be drawn out and complex, involving multiple issues and actors. The frequent breakdown of conflict resolution processes is indicative of the wide gulf between Canada and the US on the means of reconciling fisheries conservation and wealth allocation.

Yet, perhaps ironically, in the international trade sphere, an area of core policy concern to the Canadian government, environmental protection measures are fully supported by Canadian foreign policy and are appearing in the subregional and regional free trade agreement regimes that Canada has recently negotiated. Starting with NAFTA and its side agreement on the environment, the model was copied in the 1997 Canada-Chile Free Trade Agreement and its companion agreement on environmental protection. Thus, in part a consequence of the evolving trade integration of Canada with other nations in the Americas, transnational environmental protection regimes are being created by treaties that have also established institutional co-operation between Canada and the other partner states. The NAFTA relationship is becoming the site for intergovernmental and civil society dialogue and action on a range of environmental issues affecting the territories of the member states, and it stands as a precedent for the new Canada-Chile arrangement. While the bilateral Canada-US relationship will always remain the most important focus for regional Canadian foreign policy-making on the environment, the environmental institutionalism developing in the Americas, and involving Canada, parallels the growing economic links with Latin America.

NOTES

1. Framework Convention on Climate Change, reprinted in *International Legal Materials* 31 (1992): 851 (entered into force 21 Mar. 1994); Convention on Biological Diversity, reprinted in *International Legal Materials* 31 (1992): 822 (entered into force 29 Dec. 1993).

2. Rio Declaration on Environment and Development, reprinted in *International Legal Materials* 31 (1992): 876; Agenda 21, reprinted in Nicholas Robinson, ed., *Agenda 21 and the UNCED Proceedings* (New York: Oceana Publications, 1993); Non-Legally Binding Authoritative Statement of Principles for a Global Consensus on the Management, Conservation and Sustainable Development of All Types of Forests, reprinted in *International Legal Materials* 31 (1992): 822.

3. 'Notes for an Address by Prime Minister Jean Chrétien on the occasion of the United Nations Special Session on Sustainable Development', 24 June 1997. http://www.un.org/dpcsd/earthsummit/.

4. Canada is a contracting party to the Convention to Combat Desertification, reprinted in *International Legal Materials* 33 (1994): 1332, and has signed the Agreement on the Conservation and Management of Straddling Fish Stocks and Highly Migratory Fish Stocks, reprinted in *International Legal Materials* 34 (1995): 1547.

5. Statement of Commitment, in Programme for the Further Implementation of Agenda 21, A/RES/S-19/2, adopted by the General Assembly, 19 Sept. 1997.

6. Ibid.

7. 'Finding a Chemical Solution', *Global Agenda* 4, 4 (Mar. 1997): 6. The IFCS is working in co-operation with the United Nations Environment Program.

8. 1985 Vienna Convention for the Protection of the Ozone Layer and the 1987 Montreal Protocol on Substances that Deplete the Ozone Layer, as adjusted and amended, reprinted in Ozone Secretariat, United Nations Environment Program, *Handbook for the International Treaties for the Protection of the Ozone Layer*, 4th edn (Nairobi: UNEP, 1996). Ozone-depleting substances that have been controlled include chloro-fluorocarbons (CFCs), halons, carbon tetrachloride, and methyl chloroform.

9. Agreement was reached that developed countries must phase out methyl bromide by 2005, and developing countries must do so by 2015. Canada had proposed the dates of 2001 and 2011. See Anne McIlroy, 'Experts sound ozone warning', *Globe and Mail*, 9 Sept. 1997, A1; Karen Unland, 'Methyl bromide imperils ozone goal, activists say', *Globe and Mail*, 16 Sept. 1997, A5; Environment Canada, News Release, 17 Sept. 1997.

10. See Canada's Coastal Fisheries Protection Act, RSC 1985, c. C-33, as amended in 1994; followed by the Canada-European Community Agreed Minute on the Conservation and Management of Fish Stocks, 20 Apr. 1995, reprinted in *International Legal Materials* 34 (1995): 1262. The precautionary approach seems to be a developing principle of international law under which states are to take steps to protect the environment in areas where there is still not 100 per cent certainty that there will be environmental harm in that sector.

11. Oceans Act, SC 1996, c. 31.

12. Fisheries Treaty Between Canada and the United States (1985) Can. TS No. 7 (in force 18 Mar. 1995).

13. Ibid., Article III(1) (a) and (b).

14. Memorandum of Understanding Between Canada and the United States in Connection with the Pacific Salmon Treaty, A. 'Implementation of Article III, paragraph 1(b)'.

15. 'Speaking Notes for the Hon. David Anderson, Minister of Fisheries and Oceans', before the House of Commons Standing Committee on Fisheries and

Oceans, Ottawa, 18 Nov. 1997; Department of Foreign Affairs and International Trade, The Pacific Salmon Treaty (May 1996), 2.

16. James Pipkin, US Special Negotiator for Pacific Salmon, 'The stumbling block in the salmon dispute', *Globe and Mail*, 10 Nov. 1997.

17. The Pacific Salmon Treaty, 2–3. 'Bilaterally agreed data (which was not available in 1985) show that in 1985 the United States intercepted 2.4 million more salmon than Canada. Today [1996] the figure has more than doubled to 5.3 million more salmon'. Ibid.

18. Government of Canada, 'New Effort to Settle Salmon Dispute Announced', News Release No. 20, 5 Feb. 1997.

19. Ibid.

20. Government of Canada, 'Canada Calls for Binding Dispute Settlement Following U.S. Rejection of Final Offer', News Release No. 108, 26 June 1997.

21. Ibid.

22. Department of Foreign Affairs and International Trade, *Statement*, Canada-US Joint Statement on Pacific Salmon, Washington, 23 July 1997.

23. Ibid.

24. Agreement on International Humane Trapping Standards Between the European Community, Canada and the Russian Federation.

25. Susan Smith, 'Trapping accord ensures EU market for Canadian furs', *Globe and Mail*, 7 Jan. 1998, B12.

26. 'Recent Intergovernmental Forest-Related Decisions', *Earth Negotiations Bulletin* 10, 4 (24 Oct. 1997).

27. Programme for the Further Implementation of Agenda 21, para. 40.

28. 'United Nations Activities—19th Special Session', *Environmental Policy and Law* 27, 5 (Sept. 1997): 392.

29. For example, 'Notes for an Address by Prime Minister Chrétien'; 'United Nations Activities—19th Special Session', 390; 'Canada's Path to Sustainable Development', *Global Agenda* 4, 4 (Mar. 1997): 2.

30. North American Free Trade Agreement, reprinted in *International Legal Materials* 32 (1993): 289; North American Agreement on Environmental Co-operation, reprinted in *International Legal Materials* 32 (1993): 1480.

31. See Commission on Environmental Co-operation, http://www.cec.org. The submissions were made by the BC Aboriginal Fisheries Commission and Others, Centre québécois du droit de l'environnement (CQDE), the Canadian Environmental Defence Fund, and the Animal Alliance of Canada and Others.

32. Commission for Environmental Co-operation, *Final Factual Record of the Cruise Ship Pier Project in Cozumel, Quintana Roo* (1997). See also Noemi Gal-Or, 'Multilateral Trade and Supranational Environmental Protection: The Grace Period of the CEC, or a Well-Defined Role?', *Georgetown International Environmental Law Review* 9 (1996): 53–93.

33. Canada-Chile Free Trade Agreement, reprinted in *International Legal Materials* 36 (1997): 1079; Dan Daley, 'Introductory Note', ibid., 1067.

34. Canada-Chile Agreement on Environmental Co-operation, reprinted in *International Legal Materials* 36 (1997): 1193.

14

Climate Change Politics and the Pursuit of National Interests

PAUL HALUCHA

In December 1997 the more than 150 countries that are signatories to the 1992 Framework Convention on Climate Change (FCCC) met in Kyoto, Japan, and forged an international treaty that binds industrialized nations to reduce collective emissions by 5.2 per cent below 1990 levels by 2010.[1] Since the 1992 Rio summit (United Nations Conference on the Environment and Sustainable Development), climate change has matured into a critical foreign policy issue with serious economic, as well as environmental, implications. This has forced a divergence between the optimal international outcome from an environmental perspective and the national interests of several industrial powers, including the United States. The following chapter will sketch the evolution of international climate change politics and analyse the crucial factors that determined the negotiating positions of the major players and Canada as they headed towards Kyoto.

BACKGROUND

Climate change refers to the long-term change in the earth's climate brought about by alterations in the global atmosphere due to human activity. Approximately one-half of solar radiation entering the earth's atmosphere is absorbed by the earth's surface, where it evaporates water and heats the earth and air. How much of this heat eventually escapes back into space is a function of cloud cover and greenhouse gases such as water vapour, carbon dioxide, methane, and nitrous oxide. As greenhouse gases accumulate in the atmosphere, they prevent the natural re-radiation of heat into space and lead to warmer surface temperatures. Global warming is therefore the consequence of the elevation of atmospheric concentrations in greenhouse gases.

For purposes of policy analysis, it is useful to separate natural processes of warming from the human-induced or anthropogenic causes, even if this distinction is often complex to draw scientifically. Carbon dioxide (CO_2)—emitted through the combustion of fossil fuels—is by far the most significant greenhouse gas, accounting for 75 per cent of the global greenhouse gas effect and representing 82 per cent of Canadian greenhouse gas emissions in 1995. Any serious effort by Canada to reduce its contribution to the global greenhouse effect must achieve real reductions in CO_2 emissions. Canada is responsible for 2 per cent of global emissions of greenhouse gases and Canadian emissions of other greenhouse gases are growing quickly. Between 1990 and 1995, methane releases grew by 16 per cent while nitrous oxide (N_2O) emissions grew by 28 per cent (Jacques, Neitzert, and Boileau, 1997: xi, 5).

The Intergovernmental Panel on Climate Change (IPCC) reported in 1995 that given current emissions trends around the world, global average temperatures could increase between 1.5° and 3.5° Celsius by the year 2100. Globally, the effects of even a 1.5° warming, which is considered a very conservative estimate, will be extremely serious.[2]

Global predictions for climate change are so dire that even sober scientific forecasting cannot help at times but sound apocalyptic. Melting glaciers will cause elevations in sea levels, threatening coastal areas with flooding (118 million people are expected to be vulnerable by the end of the next century) and small island nations with disappearance. Climate change is also expected to deepen and extend current trends towards desertification, subjecting millions more to the threat of famine.

The IPCC expects increases in infections from all 10 major tropi-
cal vector-borne diseases in the developing countries for the next
century. Higher extreme temperatures in the Northern hemisphere
will allow the spread of vector-borne diseases and the speedy return
to the North of defeated diseases such as malaria (Shell, 1997).
American Vice-President Al Gore summarized the problem of infectious diseases as 'one of the most significant health and security challenges facing the global community' (quoted in Shell, 1997: 46).

Despite the IPCC's pronouncement that the Northern hemisphere
will be one of the regions most affected by climate change, government assessments of the potential impacts of climate change for
Canada yield decidedly weaker pronouncements. In contrast to
developing nations, Canada has the social capacity to reduce the
human costs of climate change.

In November 1997 the government of Canada released the eight-
volume Canada Country Study (CCS), which was launched in 1996 to
weigh the likely effects of climate change on Canada. Timed for
release shortly before the Kyoto conference, the report was clearly
designed to bolster domestic support for a likely multilateral agreement. However, the report also served to inform the Canadian negotiating position by providing a clearer picture of the possible extent
of the impact.

While the CCS predicts regional variation in the impact and severity of climate change, the hydrology cycle was identified as the key
national sensitivity. At the Canada Country Study conference in
Toronto (following the CCS release on 24 November) different speakers repeatedly emphasized that increased precipitation patterns characterized by a greater frequency of extreme events (storms) and separated by drought could lead to disruptions in agricultural yields and
less water for hydro-generation. Richard Robarts of the National
Hydrology Institute indicated that a 3° increase in temperature would
cause a 56 per cent loss in wetlands located in the parklands region
of the Prairies. Wetlands cover 14 per cent of Canada and are both
an important sink for carbon storage and a critical resource for habitat (over 290 vertebrate species in Alberta depend on wetlands for
survival). Canada has already lost 6 million actual wetlands (60 per
cent of its total) since 1963.

The more lengthy (six-year) Mackenzie Basin Impact Study (MBIS)
also issued its final report in August 1997. The guiding question of
the MBIS was 'how would an economy based on natural resources and

288 LEADERSHIP AND DIALOGUE

a northern culture cope with climate warming?' One of two key findings of the report is worth repeating: 'most participating stakeholders said the region can adapt if the changes occur slowly . . . but if
the area warms up quickly, adapting will be considerably more difficult' (Cohen, 1997: 1.1).

THE ROAD TO RIO

In analysing the historical maturation of global warming as a policy
issue during the 1980s, it is not possible to draw clean distinctions
between scientists and policy advisers. Consistent efforts were made
by the United Nations Environmental Program (UNEP) to link all new
evidence of global warming to the need for nations to take action. At
the first World Climate Conference in Geneva in 1979, scientists issued
a declaration appealing for nations to 'foresee and to prevent man-
made changes in climate that might be adverse to the well-being of
humanity' (quoted in Paterson, 1993: 30). At the 1985 Villach conference on the assessment of the role of greenhouse gases on climate
change scientists recommended that governments increase support for
the analysis of economic and policy options to mitigate greenhouse
gas emissions. By the summer of 1988 delegates to an international
conference on climate change hosted by the Canadian government
began to discuss quantitative targets for emissions reductions.

The language of conference declarations grew suddenly bolder
during the period after 1988 as extreme weather events in North
America seemed to suggest that climate change was upon us. The
Canadian prairies and American Middle West experienced the worst
drought since the 1930s as record temperatures were recorded in
both countries. More than $1.3 billion was paid out to grain farmers
and cattle producers in Manitoba and net farm income losses were
50 per cent in Manitoba and 78 per cent in Saskatchewan
(Environment Canada, 1997). The statement encapsulating the new
mood on global warming was delivered by James Hansen, a senior
climate scientist with NASA, before a US Senate hearing on energy
policy. Hansen stated unequivocally that 'it is time to stop waffling
so much. We should say that the evidence is pretty strong that the
greenhouse effect is here' (Paterson, 1996: 33).

At this time the federal Canadian policy community engaged in climate change was still limited to Environment Canada and more precisely to the department's Atmospheric Environment Service (AES).

However, broad senior policy interest in the climate change issue evolved rapidly in Canada following the Changing Atmosphere conference hosted by the Canadian government in Toronto in June of 1988. Senior representatives from more than a dozen federal departments attended, as did Prime Minister Brian Mulroney. The official conference statement endorsed, as an 'initial global goal', a 20 per cent reduction in CO_2 emissions from 1988 levels by 1992 (Atmospheric Environment Service, 1988). The conference is less memorable for what it proposed than for what it accomplished in the Ottawa policy community. Doern and Conway (1994: 143) have argued that it is a mistake 'to dismiss these major events and conferences as paradigm and agenda setters'. Indeed, the Toronto conference generated extensive domestic policy research—including the establishment of a task force of deputy ministers to review the Toronto targets (Parson et al., forthcoming: 8)—and raised the profile of those who wanted to subsume energy policy within climate policy.

As the climate issue gained momentum and international public opinion in favour of concerted action began to weigh on policy-makers, the question of scientific uncertainty came to the fore. From the beginning this issue was entangled with the results of early economic modelling exercises that revealed the costs of stabilizing CO_2 emissions to be very high. In fact, by the end of 1988 a policy of CO_2 stabilization was rejected by the deputy ministers' task force after early modelling analysis yielded a 'substantial projected cost' (Parson et al., forthcoming: 8) instead of the savings that environmentalists had predicted would accrue from energy conservation. While Canada was prepared to delay action on the basis of economic costs, senior officials in the US administration pointed to inconclusive scientific evidence, a posture they had well rehearsed during the bilateral debate with Canada over acid rain.

The IPCC was founded in 1988 by the UNEP and World Meteorological Organization (WMO) to deflect the brunt of claims of scientific uncertainty by the United States and build a compelling consensus around the impacts of climate change. Such a consensus, it was believed, would stimulate US agreement to the adoption of global targets. As the United States contributes 23 per cent of global CO_2 emissions and 31 per cent of global emissions of total greenhouse gases, its co-operation was recognized as vital to the achievement of an effective convention. The IPCC's *First Assessment Report* was adopted by the United Nations General Assembly in August of 1990, and four months later the UN established an Intergovernmental Negotiating Committee (INC) to prepare an 'effective framework convention on climate change' (United Nations Resolution A/RES/45/212) to be ready for signature at the Rio conference in 1992.

THE 1992 FRAMEWORK CONVENTION ON CLIMATE CHANGE

Formal negotiations of the Framework Convention on Climate Change spawned five sessions between February 1991 and February 1992, with the fifth (New York) session resuming in the spring to produce an acceptable text for signature in Rio. Any fair assessment of the FCCC must measure not only the success of the convention in mitigating climate change but also the contribution that the interstate negotiations made towards institutionalizing multilateral negotiations on climate change. It was naïve for observers of the Rio conference to anticipate either that international commitment for binding targets would come easily or that action to move the international economy away from its reliance on fossil fuels would occur quickly. Rather, the FCCC must be judged for its success in moving the United States to accept more than was anticipated, thus broadening the realm of possible policy outcomes for Kyoto.

Two formative fault-lines[3] conditioned the Rio negotiations: (1) a North-South divide that reflected the incongruity between the historic fact that global warming was a product of industrial activity in the North and the discourse from Rio that defined global warming as a global problem requiring an international response; (2) an intra-North fault that divided countries according to their differential dependence on fossil fuels.

The North-South fault is highly charged and based on each side offering self-serving interpretations of who should undertake action on climate change and when. Answers to these questions remain critical to the choice of policy instruments available in the North, particularly in the design of an international emissions trading system. There was general agreement during the Rio process that action by industrialized nations needed to happen first, both as an ethical reflection of the fact that 66 per cent of current annual emissions and 85 per cent or more of the CO_2 accumulated in the atmosphere since the Industrial Revolution can be sourced to the developed world (World Resources Institute, 1997; Timmerman, 1996: 237). Industrialized nations, however, emphasize the global effects of climate change, the weaker adaptation capacity of southern states, and the fact that based on current projections developing nations will account for 50 per cent of annual emissions by 2010—at which point the South will be half the problem. North-South divisions would become more pronounced during the Kyoto negotiations, as we shall see below.

None the less, intra-North divisions were apparent at Rio because while commitments by the South were not on the table, a bloc of northern countries was committed to the adoption of targets and timetables at Rio. This contingent revolved around the European Community (EC) and included countries with a strong sense of international responsibility, including Canada and Australia (Paterson and Grubb, 1993: 300–1). Opposed to the adoption of stabilization targets was the United States, which perceived mitigative action to be too costly and remained unconvinced that it could not more efficiently adapt to climate change. Influential American economists Alan Manne and Richard Richels reported research in 1990 indicating that reducing CO_2 emissions by 20 per cent would cost the US economy between $800 million and $3.6 trillion, figures cited in the 1990 Report of the President of the United States. In contrast, the unification of Germany and the prospect of EC expansion eastward would allow Western Europe to cushion its stabilization, first as a result of hugely reduced industrial activity in the East and again as the eastern infrastructure was rebuilt with a reduced reliance on fossil fuels and higher cross-sectoral energy efficiency standards.

Although the United States did not budge in its opposition to the adoption of quantitative targets in Rio, it did move significantly in allowing both the mention of 1990 as a target date for stabilization in the FCCC and the inclusion of text that singled out CO_2 as the major greenhouse gas (Paterson, 1996: 61–2). Moreover, Article 2 of the FCCC states that its 'ultimate objective' is to achieve 'stabilization of greenhouse gas concentrations in the atmosphere at a level that would prevent dangerous anthropogenic interference with the climate system'. This recognition focused international pressure for a greater commitment to emissions reductions and situated the issue of quantitative targets at the heart of subsequent negotiations.

PRE-KYOTO POSITIONING

The Berlin Mandate

The Ad Hoc Group on the Berlin Mandate (AGBM) was established during the first Conference of the Parties to the FCCC (COP-1) in the spring of 1995. The purpose of the AGBM was to build support for adoption of an international legal instrument that included both targets for emissions reductions and timelines for achieving and reporting progress. The Berlin Mandate established the parameters for the subsequent Kyoto round of negotiations. Most importantly, the inclusion of targets and timetables was settled at the outset. This guaranteed that the Kyoto agreement would be more substantial than what was achieved at Rio. This early commitment to action weakened the thrust of claims of scientific uncertainty by countries wishing to postpone commitments. Also, the Berlin Mandate excluded developing nations from having to undertake international commitments to mitigate emissions. The AGBM met seven times on the road to Kyoto, but its most significant achievement was this initial framing of the climate change negotiations.

In 1995 the IPCC issued its *Second Assessment Report on Climate Change*. The report was promptly adopted by the UN Secretary-General as the 'state of the knowledge' on climate change and was reflected in the Geneva (Ministerial) Declaration issued at COP-2 in July 1996. The IPCC summarized its findings by noting that the warming recorded over the past century (0.5°) is 'unlikely to be natural in origin . . . the balance of evidence suggests that there is a discernible human influence on global climate' (Watson, Zinyowera, and Moss, 1996: 10–11). The Geneva Declaration accepted outright the IPCC's findings and called for legally binding mid-term targets.

National Circumstances and National Interests

Despite early agenda-setting by the AGBM, the process of positioning by individual countries was protracted and the distance between the major blocs of countries on the key issues (targets and timelines) narrowed little, if at all, prior to the eleventh-hour negotiations in Kyoto. The lack of negotiating progress throughout the AGBM process is attributable to the strong tendency for countries to advance positions promoting their national interests and reflecting their national circumstances.

While the method for calculation of national interest differed from country to country, three primary components can be identified: (1) the expected costs-benefits of unmitigated climate change; (2) the expected economic costs of adjusting energy use to meet targets; (3) the anticipated economic opportunities of leading technological innovation based on renewable energy resources and efficiency gains. A short examination of each factor provides insight into the general dynamics of pre-Kyoto positioning.

1. *Differential costs of adaptation.* While there is much uncertainty in measures of the vulnerability of different populations, there is evidence that vulnerability decreases where the state has the capacity to respond to extreme weather events and individuals have access to the resources required for recovery (World Health Organization, 1996: 127–9). In comparative terms the most important division is between those countries that will measure costs in terms of financial loss and those that measure in terms of lives lost. As WHO has concluded, 'Many of the anticipated impacts would be greatest among the world's poor and disadvantaged populations' (World Health Organization, 1996: 127–9). Similarly, the IPCC has identified small island states and countries with large, poor coastal populations as highly vulnerable to climate change. Hence, the proposal from the Alliance of Small Island States during the AGBM process called for a 20 per cent cut in industrialized country emissions by 2005 (China, India, and Indonesia also supported swift emissions reductions).

2. *Differential costs of adjusting energy sources.* Both the availability of alternative low-carbon energy sources (natural gas, hydroelectricity, nuclear, solar, and wind-power) and the expected market costs relative to oil and gas are critical determinants of national interest. For instance, Australia has no nuclear reactors and very limited opportunities for hydro development. In contrast, 70 per cent of Sweden's energy and 75 per cent of France's energy are generated by nuclear reactors. Different 'energy endowments' were reflected in each country's determination of its negotiating position. Other related factors included the economic effect of higher domestic energy prices and reduced economic output (employment impact) to the coal and oil and gas sectors.

3. *National opportunities.* National opportunities arising from technological innovation are extraordinarily difficult to measure. In its survey of econometric models used to measure the predicted national impact (as measured in GDP) of different climate change policies, the World Resources Institute (WRI) identified the autonomous energy efficiency improvement (AEEI) variable as 'critical'. The institute noted that 'one model predicts that the present value of the cost of reducing emissions below 1990 levels drops from $1 trillion to a negligible level as AEEI rises from 0.5 per cent to 1.5 per cent' (Repetto and Austin, 1997: 19). Still, the expectation that climate policy would induce innovation through higher fossil fuel prices and the fear that competitors would discriminate against exports from

industrialized countries were vital. This was certainly true in the case of Canada, which anticipated that its primary trading partner, the United States, would reach agreement in Kyoto. In contrast, Australia conducts approximately 60 per cent of its trade with Asian countries—and its exports are energy-intensive, and Asian countries, except for Japan, were not required to make binding commitments in Kyoto.

Additional factors were the specific political considerations centred on the distribution of income loss across regions and sectors and the degree of mobilization that this precipitated among affected industries and substate actors, especially in federal systems. As a rule, domestic political cleavages followed the expected logic of national circumstances analysis.

The primary instruments for measuring the economic impact of adopting policies to mitigate climate change have been econometric models that apply scenario-based mathematical modelling techniques in an effort to derive a quantified forecast of the domestic impact of different policy measures. The attraction of econometric modelling is that it allows policy advisers to provide political decision-makers with numeric estimates of the costs of political action (and inaction) and the costs of specific policies. However, modelling exercises have two primary weaknesses. (1) As the case of the AEEI demonstrates, models above all depend on assumptions. The WRI has shown that in the case of 16 widely used models, over 80 per cent of the variation in predicted economic impacts was accounted for by small differences in only eight modelling assumptions (Repetto and Austin, 1997: 14). (2) Current modelling does not value either the environmental or economic benefits of averting climate change (which have proven difficult to quantify) and hence current models provide only a cost analysis and not an adequate accounting of national circumstances.

Still, the one undeniable contribution of economic modelling has been to confirm for governments the seriousness of Kyoto commitments. There would be economic costs involved with implementation, and failure to meet commitments would have both political and economic repercussions. This insight helps explain the stagnation of international negotiations (as well as the very cautious Canadian approach). The national interests of the United States and Europe were in opposition; this translated into a deepening of the inter-North fault.

The European Position

The European negotiating position was hailed by the environmental NGO community as a demonstration of the EU's recognition of the seriousness of climate change and its 'willingness to make progress in this round' (*ECO*, 1998: 1). Far from representing an altruistic acceptance of or instance of global consciousness, the EU position was soundly based on an assessment of what it could reasonably achieve and on an effort to press the United States to commit to more than it was prepared to. All three core elements of the EU position bear out this contention. Firstly, the European Union entered negotiations as a bubble—although the final Kyoto Protocol was signed by member nations—with a single-plan EU target and timetable. This allowed it to select a target and timetable that would not necessarily be reached by any one country. Furthermore, individual country targets would be decided after Kyoto. Although the European bubble allowed for subsequent differentiation of targets within the European Union according to the national circumstances of member states (thus allowing Spain and Portugal to increase their emissions), Europe objected to the principle of differentiation during the AGBM process and maintained that the same target and timetable had to be accepted by all countries.

Secondly, Europe's insistence on 1990 as the base year for all countries was founded on a calculation of national (or EU) interest. From 1980 to 1990 total global greenhouse emissions grew by 15 per cent mainly as a result of the growth of CO_2 emissions from developing nations. This trend was reversed from 1990 to 1995, when global emissions declined by 5 per cent due to global recession and the dramatic decline in industrial activity in the transitional economies of Eastern Europe and the former Soviet Union, whose emissions dropped by more than 20 per cent between 1989 and 1992 (enough to stabilize global emissions) (United States Department of Energy, 1997: 23). Europe recorded a 2 per cent emissions reduction during the same period partly as a consequence of the reunification of Germany in 1990. The European Environment Agency's self-assessment of its success in mitigating climate change since 1990 is instructive.

From 1990 to 1994 emissions of several countries (Germany, France, UK) decreased, resulting in an emission reduction of approximately 2 per cent, mainly due to *short term factors* like the temporary decrease of industrial and economic growth rates, the restructuring of industry in Germany, the closing of coal mines in the UK and the conversion of power plants to natural gas. (European Environment Agency, 1995: 21; emphasis added)

Adopting the 1990 baseline allowed the European Union to claim that its current policy of climate change mitigation was successful, as UK Prime Minister Tony Blair did at the Rio+5 conference in June 1997. In fact, European energy consumption had grown in all sectors (transportation, residential, and electrical) save for the industrial sector, where significant efficiency gains offset increased capacity (European Environment Agency, 1995: 21).

Finally, the European Union tabled an extremely ambitious proposal calling for a 7.5 per cent reduction in emissions below 1990 levels by 2005 and a 15 per cent reduction by 2010. As with the choice of baseline, the EU proposal reflected EU circumstances and was widely thought to be unrealistic and unachievable by other OECD countries, including the United States, Canada, Australia, and New Zealand. Simon Upton, New Zealand's Minister of the Environment, conveyed the collective frustration of other countries involved when he accused the EU of operating a double standard by 'insisting on uniform targets for other countries but differentiated targets within its own bubble' (Upton, 1997: 5).

The US Position

Although the United States did not announce its negotiating position for Kyoto until late October 1997, it gave a clear indication of the magnitude of its commitment and preferred instruments well in advance. All parties to the FCCC were required to table proposals to revise the convention by January 1997 during the AGBM process. The US proposal contained three elements: (1) a recommitment to binding targets; (2) an identification of 2010–20 as the period from which to draw a timeline; and (3) commitment to the principle of national flexibility in implementation. Significantly, the United States supported the Europeans in opposing country differentiation, contending that allowance for multiple targets and timelines would confuse reporting procedures.

Although Europe witnessed a decline in emissions for the period to 1995, CO_2 emissions from the US grew by 9 per cent between 1990 and 1996, with much of the increase occurring during the last year (emissions declined slightly from 1990 to 1991) (United States

Department of Energy, 1997: 25). The trend is largely explained by high levels of economic growth since 1992, a levelling off in the growth of nuclear power capacity, and a peaking of hydroelectric power in 1996 (due to record rainfall in 1996). Emissions have increased in every sector of the US economy since 1990 (transportation, industry, residential, and commercial) and coal production has grown (6.5 per cent in 1996 alone). Emissions from industrial sources, which had plummeted by approximately 17 per cent from 1980 to 1982 due to the onset of the world recession and the adoption of cleaner fuels, have now surpassed pre-1980 levels.

Because the US was already 9 per cent above 1990 levels by 1996, even a target of stabilization at 1990 levels would require a de facto 9 per cent reduction from current levels. Adoption of the European target would require the US to achieve a whopping 25 per cent reduction in emissions by 2010—and projections are that the US will be 13 per cent above 1990 levels by 2000 (Reifsnyder, 1997). Domestic opposition to the US proposal was swift and included powerful representatives from the coal, oil and gas, mining, steel, and automobile sectors. Political opposition also followed as the US Senate unanimously passed the Byrd Resolution (95–0, July 1997) signalling that it would not support the ratification of any treaty in Kyoto that did not meaningfully include developing countries. The North-South fault became a critical domestic issue for the White House and was the touchstone for the advertising campaign launched by US industry. The campaign stressed the comparative advantage afforded to developing nations, especially China, Mexico, and South Korea, which would benefit from lower international energy prices.

The US negotiating position was announced in late October 1997 and arose clearly from these national circumstances. The US would seek a target of stabilization at 1990 levels by the end of the budget period 2008–12 and support flexibility in the use of national and international instruments. The US extended national flexibility to include joint implementation (JI). Under JI, signatories to the Kyoto accord would receive credit for emissions reduction projects undertaken in non-signatory developing countries. Also, the US indicated it was prepared to participate in an international system of emissions trading. Both JI and emissions trading would allow emissions reductions to occur where costs were lowest. Finally, the US declared that meaningful participation of key developing countries would be required before the US would ratify a Kyoto agreement.

The Canadian Position

The Canadian negotiating position evolved from the interaction of two pressures, one rooted in the country's historic dependence on low-cost energy sources to offset the high energy costs of extracting, processing, and transporting raw materials, the other rooted in our growing trade dependence on the United States. The first pressure dictated that Canada be very cautious in its adoption of targets and timetables and placed it in opposition to Europe. The second pressure demanded that we closely harmonize our response with that adopted by the US. Ensuring that Canada's national interests were safeguarded at Kyoto required that the federal government strike a careful balance that reflected Canada's unique national circumstances.

Canada's experience since 1992 was similar to that of the United States. Political pressure on the federal government to stabilize emissions by 2000 did not extend significantly beyond the narrow population of environmental activists, and environmental issues did not even register during the federal elections of 1993 or 1997 (the last election was only six months before COP-3). The government's election commitment to job creation and deficit reduction weakened its willingness to oppose the interests (real or perceived) of Canadian industry. Hence, the federal government's response to the FCCC, the National Action Program on Climate Change (NAPCC), was developed in partnership with industry through consultations and not by regulatory fiat.

Although there are numerous components to the NAPCC, the flagship response was undoubtedly the Voluntary Challenge and Registry (VCR) Program. The VCR was established in December 1995. Despite being considered too weak by Canadian environmentalists, more than 600 companies accounting for more than 50 per cent of the greenhouse gas emissions in Canada have registered (Beaulieu, 1997).

The short duration of the VCR—it is only two years old—makes it exceedingly difficult to assess, especially since the registry is designed to influence mid-term and long-term planning decisions, for instance, capital stock investments that normally turn over at a rate of 1 per cent per year (Schwanen, 1997: 27). However, there is early indication that the VCR has merit. While economy-wide emissions grew by 9.2 per cent between 1990 and 1995, emissions from manufacturing increased by only 4.2 per cent, this despite a 9 per cent growth in output (Schwanen, 1997: 27). The federal government projects that by 2020 initiatives under the current NAPCC would be responsible for a 108-megatonne savings in greenhouse gas emissions or 35 per cent of the growth in emissions from 1990 that would otherwise have occurred (Canada, 1997: 49).

Still, the NAPCC does not reduce the growth of emissions or the widening of the gap from 1990 levels. Rather, the growth in Canadian emissions is inexorably upward. Emission trends in Canada are similar to those experienced by the United States. Emissions declined from 1980 to 1983, but then began an upward trend in 1984 that deviated only at the height of the world recession during 1990 and 1991. Higher than expected rates of economic growth in the recovery since 1993 have led Natural Resources Canada to unofficially adjust its year 2000 projection from 8.2 per cent to 13 per cent (Natural Resources Canada, 1997: 73). Significantly, the doubling of Canadian exports between 1990 and 1995 is the largest single cause of the emissions increase during the same period, accounting for 31 per cent of total emissions growth (Canada, 1997: 10). Designing a climate change policy that reverses the emissions trend but does not adversely affect the competitive position of Canadian exporters will be a challenge.

Regional variation in economic growth and domestic population movements are critical factors determining provincial emission trends. For instance, BC's emissions are now 21 per cent higher than in 1990 largely due to population growth; Ontario's emissions are 5 per cent lower as the province's traditional manufacturing sector has declined.[4] Alberta's emissions will be 18 per cent above 1990 levels by 2000 and the province's strong comparative advantage in fossil fuels has driven its economic growth in the 1990s.

Federal-provincial consultations took place at an early fall meeting of the Canadian Council of the Ministers of the Environment (CCME) and a Joint Energy and Environment Ministers Meeting (JMM) in mid-November. The CCME meeting was primarily directed towards building federal-provincial consensus for Canadian involvement in the Kyoto process. The JMM yielded two important results: (1) consensus on the need for action on climate change, and (2) agreement that 'it was reasonable to reduce aggregate greenhouse gas emission in Canada back to 1990 levels by 2010' (JMM, 1997: 1). Significantly, the JMM press release indicated that Canada would 'ensure that its commitments and actions are consistent with major trading partners' (JMM, 1997: 1). Taken together with the JMM's adoption of the US targets and timetable, it is logical to assume that there was federal acceptance and provincial awareness that Canada would need to harmonize its climate change policy with that of the United States.

The federal government delayed announcement of its formal nego-tiating position until the beginning of the Kyoto conference on 1 December. The delay was prompted by Prime Minister Chrétien's directive that the Canadian negotiating position should be stronger than the US proposal. The Prime Minister's injection on the issue was prompted by the serious criticism attached to the US proposal (adopted by JMM) and an unwillingness to allow Canada to seem to be less than a leader in progressive international politics (especially given Ottawa's success on land-mines). The consequence of delivering a directive without target specification was that cabinet became mired in technical discussions that delayed announcement. The Canadian negotiating position called on industrial countries to reduce emissions by 3 per cent below 1990 levels by 2010, with a further 5 per cent reduction by 2015. It also supported flexibility of domestic imple-mentation, including joint implementation and international emissions trading. Finally, Canada echoed the US in advocating the development of a mechanism to guarantee the 'ultimate participation' of develop-ing countries in the agreement (Environment Canada, 1997: 1).

THE KYOTO PROTOCOL

As an OECD official said, 'No one has come to Kyoto to sacrifice national economic interests' (Priddle, 1997: 1). The Kyoto Protocol obligates the industrialized nations of the world to reduce collective emissions of greenhouse gases by 5 per cent from 1990 levels (for the three most important gases: carbon dioxide, methane, and nitrous oxide) by 2010. Canada agreed to a target of 6 per cent; the US to a target of 7 per cent; Europe to a target of 8 per cent; and Australia will be allowed to increase emissions by 8 per cent. The year 2005 is identified as an interim target by which time signatories must show progress towards the 2010 target. The protocol will remain open for signature from March 1998 to 15 March 1999 and will enter into force when ratified by two-thirds of Annex 1 signatories representing 55 per cent of total CO_2 emissions in 1990. This double-trigger formula was intended to circumvent the possibility that failure to ratify by the US could damn the protocol.

The amount of unfinished business evident in the protocol makes it difficult to estimate definitively the economic impact of imple-mentation. Currently, the protocol is missing a compliance mecha-nism, there is no agreed upon methodology for estimating carbon sinks, and the machinery for an international emissions trading system remains to be negotiated. All of these elements are to be studied by the IPCC during 1998 and the agreement is to be amended accordingly at the First Meeting of the Parties to the Kyoto Protocol in November 1998 (MOP-1). Still, the acceptance of differentiated national targets in the protocol and broad acceptance of the principle of flexibility in national implementation offer assurances that the parties to the protocol have safeguarded national interests. Indeed, protection of national economic interests is broadly enshrined in Article 2 (section 2), which commits parties to 'strive to implement policies and measures . . . in such a way as to minimize adverse effects . . . [including] effects on international trade.' Specifically, two aspects of the protocol should reduce the structural impact of compliance: (1) the protocol's design of accounting procedures, and (2) its promotion of international market-based instruments.

The method for calculating national greenhouse gas emissions in the protocol is a net approach that allows the sequestration of carbon from the atmosphere by carbon sinks (i.e., forests, wetlands) to be subtracted from the total national emissions of gases covered in the protocol. Because the baseline for sinks is 1990 all industrial nations will now have the opportunity to recalculate national net emission trends. The IPCC has been charged with calculating the stock of sinks in 1990 and developing methodological guidelines for the identification of sinks and the amount of carbon being sequestered. Although environmental groups have characterized sinks as a 'disastrous loophole' due in large part to the difficulty of global monitoring, their inclusion in the protocol was important for Canada (Singer, 1997: 2). How important will become clearer over the next year.

The inclusion of international, market-based instruments in the protocol is clear evidence of the imperative for industrialized countries to reduce atmospheric emissions at the lowest global cost. The protocol facilitates least-cost solutions in two ways. Under joint implementation, companies can transfer credits for emission reductions achieved in any Annex 1 country to any other Annex 1 country on a project-by-project basis and as long as the exchange is approved by both nations involved in the transaction. The clean development mechanism (CDM) extends the concept of JI to developing countries. Especially in the case of the CDM the objective is to synchronize the protocol timeline and targets with the natural rates of capital stock depreciation so that new investments in infrastructure are environmentally sound, while existing fixed investments are more gradually replaced. The following benefits were enumerated by a senior Environment Canada official during a post-Kyoto debriefing: 'The atmosphere gets exactly the same positive impact. The developing country gets access to the new technology and the economics of it are a lot cheaper [than the early replacement of domestic capital stock]' (Canada, 1997). The same benefits accrue through emissions trading but without the need for project-by-project approval by national governments. In essence, market-based instruments will allow nations dependent on fossil fuels, such as Canada, to externalize some of the burden of adjustment; again, quantitative estimates are not known. Speaking on this point a senior Environment Canada official stated that 'there is no doubt that Canada will have to achieve most of its reductions domestically . . . there is no escaping that' (Canada, 1997).

CONCLUSIONS

The implementation of the Kyoto Protocol will be a significant challenge for Canada due to the complexities of horizontal management among federal departments, including Finance, Transport Canada, Natural Resources Canada, DFAIT, and Environment Canada, and the imperative of provincial co-operation. More substantive dialogue with the provinces will be necessary since provincial co-operation is a condition of national implementation.

As has been shown, the tenor of climate change negotiations in the period from 1992 to 1997 was set by the efforts of FCCC signatories to safeguard national interests. The signing of the protocol brings to an end the chapter of climate change politics that began with the politicization of the issue in the mid-1980s. Three variables will determine if and when a second chapter will commence.

Firstly, it is almost certain that no further commitments will be accepted by industrialized countries without the formal inclusion of key developing countries, especially China and India, in the protocol. Secondly, the pace of technological development and innovation will be a critical determinant of whether the world economy can be weaned from its carbon dependence and still maintain a rate of growth. Finally, the pace of climate change and the frequency and severity of extreme events in the industrialized world will dictate whether the costs of climate change become an issue. The interplay of these factors will go far in determining whether subsequent emission reductions are deemed to be in the national interest of signatory states.

NOTES

I would like to thank Dr Margaret Hill for her comments on an earlier draft of this chapter.

1. Industrialized countries are termed Annex 1 nations in the FCCC.
2. By comparison, the difference between an ice age and the intervening warming period is between 5° and 6°.
3. Note, that the number of fault-lines can be expanded to capture nuances in country alignments that do not concern us here.
4. Forecasts are based on projection to the year 2000. Emission in Ontario will likely be significantly higher due to Ontario Hydro's decision to temporarily close seven nuclear reactors.

REFERENCES

Atmospheric Environment Service. 1988. *The Changing Atmosphere. Report of a Conference.* Toronto: Atmospheric Environment Service, Environment Canada.

Beaulieu, Patricia. 1997. 'The VCR Doesn't Work', *Alternatives Journal* 23, 3 (Summer).

Canada. 1997. *Canada's Second National Report on Climate Change.* Ottawa: Environment Canada, May.

Cohen, Stewart J. 1997. *Mackenzie Basin Impact Study Final Report: Summary of Results.* Ottawa: Environment Canada, 1997.

Doern, G. Bruce, and Thomas Conway. 1994. *The Greening of Canada.* Toronto: University of Toronto Press.

ECO. 1997. 'AGBM Rolls Up Sleeves', *ECO* 96, 1 (1 Aug.): 1.

Environment Canada. 1997. *Canada Country Study: Volume III, Responding to Global Climate Change in the Prairies.* Ottawa: Environment Canada.

European Environment Agency. 1996. *Climate Change in the European Union.* Copenhagen: European Environment Agency.

Hambley, Ambassador Mark. 1997. 'The Heart of the US Proposal', *Global Issues* 2, 2 (Apr.): 13–15.

Jacques, A., F. Neitzert, and P. Boileau. 1997. *Trends in Canada's Greenhouse Gas Emissions: 1990–1995.* Ottawa: Air Pollution Prevention Directorate, Environment Canada, Apr.

Joint Energy and Environment Ministers Meeting (JMM). 1997. Press release. Nov.

Justus, John R., and Wayne A. Morrissey. 1997. *Global Climate Change.* Congressional Research Service Issue Brief, IB89005, updated 10 Jan.

Kyoto Debrief. 1997. Official transcripts of the Kyoto Debrief prepared by Media Qin, 12 Dec.

Natural Resources Canada, Energy Forecasting Division. 1997. *Canada's Energy Outlook: 1996–2020.* Ottawa: Minister of Supply and Services Canada, Apr.

Parson, Edward A., A.R. Dobell, Adam Fenech, Don Mutton, and Heather Smith. forthcoming. 'Leading While Keeping in Step: Management of Global Atmospheric Issues in Canada', in W.C. Clark, J. Jaeger, and J. van Eijndhoven, eds, *Social Learning in the Management of Global Environmental Risks.* Cambridge, Mass.: MIT Press.

Paterson, Matthew. 1996. *Global Warming and Global Politics.* London and New York: Routledge.

Paterson, Matthew W., and Michael Grubb. 1992. 'The International Politics of Climate Change'. *International Affairs* 68, 2: 293–310.

Priddle, Robert. 1997. Speech to the Third Session of the Conference of the Parties to the UN Framework Convention on Climate Change (COP-3), on behalf of the Organization for Economic Co-operation and Development (OECD) and the International Energy Agency (IEA), 8 Dec.

Reifsnyder, Dan. 1997. 'US Negotiating Position', presentation to the Canadian Energy Research Institute Climate Change Conference, 4–5 Sept.

Schwanen, Daniel. 1997. 'Confronting the Greenhouse Challenge: Matching Protection with Risk', C.D.Howe Institute Commentary.

Singer, Stephan. 1997. 'Sinks Destroy Natural Forest Systems', *ECO* 98, 5 (5 Dec.): 2.

Repetto, Robert, and Austin Dunan. 1997. *The Costs of Climate Protection: A Guide for the Perplexed.* Washington: World Resources Institute.

Shell, Ellen Ruppel. 1997. 'Resurgence of a Deadly Disease', *Atlantic Monthly* (Aug.): 45–60.

Timmerman, Peter. 1996. 'Breathing Room: Negotiations on Climate Change', *Earthly Goods: Environmental Change and Social Justice.* Ithaca, NY: Cornell University Press.

United Nations. 1992. Framework Convention on Climate Change (FCCC). New York: United Nations.

———. 1998. Kyoto Protocol to the United Nations Framework Convention on Climate Change. New York.

United Nations General Assembly. 1990. 'Protection of global climate for present and future generations of mankind'. Resolution 45/212, 21 Dec.

United States Department of Energy. 1997. *Emissions of Greenhouse Gases in the United States: 1996.* Washington: US Department of Energy, Oct.

Upton, Simon. 1997. 'New Zealand's Climate Change Policy Speech to Energy Federation Wellington', 31 Oct.

Watson, Robert T., Marufu C. Zinyowera, and Richard H. Moss, eds. 1996. *Climate Change 1995. Impacts, Adaptations and Mitigation of Climate Change: Scientific-Technical Analysis.* Contribution of Working Group II to the Second Assessment Report of the Intergovernmental Panel on Climate Change. Cambridge: Cambridge University Press.

World Health Organization. 1996. *Climate Change and Human Health*, A.J. McMichael, A. Haines, R. Slooff, and S. Kovats, eds. Geneva: WHO.

World Resources Institute. 1997. *World Resources: 1996–97: A Guide to the Global Environment.* Washington: World Resources Institute.